The European Union and Global Governance

This book explores and analyses the multidimensional influence that the EU exerts in the world, focusing on its contribution to regional and global governance.

Presenting a multidisciplinary approach with contributions by a panel of outstanding scholars from political science, economics, legal studies, philosophy and history, the book examines the EU as a global player and international power-in-the-making. The book is divided into three parts:

- Part I examines the influence of the EU on global governance, considering the euro, the common market, the modernisation policies for a knowledge society and the EU's global role as both a multinational and a regional democratic political system
- Part II focuses on the EU's external policies, including trade, humanitarian aid, the environment, climate change, migration, terrorism, crime and foreign policy
- Part III explores the EU as a global actor-in-the-making, looking at issues including enlargement and the EU's neighbourhood policy, and interregionalism, and critically addresses the weight of the historical legacies of Europe in the world and its cosmopolitan perspectives as well.

The European Union and Global Governance will be of vital interest to students and scholars of European Politics, International Relations, and European Studies.

Mario Telò is Professor of Political Science at the Université Libre de Bruxelles. He is also President of the Institute of European Studies, member of the Royal Academy of Belgium, and President of the GARNET International PhD School. He has served as advisor to the European Parliament, the European Commission and the European Council Presidency.

Routledge/GARNET series: Europe in the World

Edited by Mary Farrell and Karoline Postel-Vinay,
Centre for International Studies and Research (CERI), France

Editorial Board: Dr Mary Farrell, *Sciences Po*, Paris; Dr Karoline Postel-Vinay, *CERI*, France; Professor Richard Higgott, *University of Warwick*, UK; Dr Christian Lequesne, *CERI*, France and Professor Thomas Risse, *Free University Berlin*, Germany.

International Advisory Committee: D. Salma Bava, *Jawaharlal Nehru University*, New Delhi, India; Dr Knud Erik Jørgensen, *University of Aarhus*, Denmark; Professor Sunil Khilnani, *SAIS, Johns Hopkins University*, USA; Dr Anne-Marie Legloannec, *CERI*, France; Dr Xiaobo Lu, *SIPA, Columbia University*, USA; Professor James Mittelman, *University of Washington*, USA; Dr Karen Smith, *London School of Economics*, UK; Professor Elzbieta Stadtmuller, *University of Wroclaw*, Poland.

The Routledge GARNET series, *Europe in the World*, provides a forum for innovative research and current debates emanating from the research community within the GARNET Network of Excellence. GARNET is a Europe-wide network of forty-three research institutions and scholars working collectively on questions around the theme of Global Governance, Regionalisation and Regulation: The Role of the EU, and funded by the European Commission under the Sixth Framework Programme for Research.

The European Union and Global Governance

Edited by Mario Telò

Routledge
Taylor & Francis Group

LONDON AND NEW YORK

First published 2009
by Routledge
2 Park Square Milton Park Abingdon Oxon OX14 4RN

Simultaneously published in the USA and Canada
by Routledge
270 Madison Avenue, New York, NY 10016

Routledge is an imprint of the Taylor & Francis Group, an informa business

Transferred to Digital Printing 2009

Typeset in Garamond by Pindar NZ, Auckland, New Zealand

British Library Cataloguing in Publication Data
A catalogue record for this book is available from the British Library

Library of Congress Cataloging-in-Publication Data
The European Union and global governance / [compiled by] Mario Telò.
    p. cm. — (Routledge/Garnet series : Europe in the world ; 6)
    Includes bibliographical references and index.
    1. European Union. 2. European Union countries — Foreign relations.
3. European Union countries — Social policy. 4. European Union
countries — Economic policy. 5. World politics — 1989- I. Title.
    JN30. T45 2008
    341.242'2—dc22   2008030175

ISBN 10: 0-415-46506-0 (hbk)
ISBN10: 0-415-54950-7 (pbk)
ISBN 10: 0-203-88366-7 (ebk)

ISBN 13: 978-0-415-46506-9 (hbk)
ISBN13: 978-0-415-54950-9 (pbk)
ISBN 13: 978-0-203-88366-2 (ebk)

Contents

Illustrations

Figures

Tables

Contributors

Paola Conconi holds a BA in Political Science from the University of Bologna, an MA in International Relations from the School of Advanced International Studies of Johns Hopkins University, and an MSc and a PhD in Economics from the University of Warwick. She is an FNRS Research Associate, a Research Affiliate of the Centre for Economic Policy Research (CEPR) and a research fellow of the Centre for the Study of Globalisation and Regionalisation (CSGR) at the University of Warwick. Her main research interests are in the areas of international trade, regional integration, and political economy.

Philippe De Bruycker is Professor at the Institute for European Studies and the Law Faculty of the Université Libre de Bruxelles, where he teaches International European and Belgian Immigration and Asylum Law. He founded in 1999 the Academic Network for Legal Studies on Immigration and Asylum in Europe, with the financial support of the European Commission, which has organised an annual Summer School since 2001. From 2001 until 2003, he served as adviser to the European Commission in the General Directorate Justice and Home Affairs for the drafting of proposals for directives on immigration policy. He is advisor to the OECD, the International Center for Migration and Policy Development as well as several national governments. After having published extensively on issues of constitutional and administrative law, his publications focus on immigration and asylum law in a European and comparative perspective. His recent books include: *Immigration and Asylum Law of the EU: Current Debates* (Brussels: Bruylant, 2005), *The Emergence of a European Asylum Policy* (Brussels: Bruylant, 2004), *The Emergence of a European Immigration Policy* (Brussels: Bruylant, 2003) and *Regularisations of Illegal Immigrants in the European Union* (Brussels: Bruylant, 2000).

Barbara Delcourt is Junior Professor at the Institute of European Studies, Université Libre de Bruxelles, where she teaches Common Foreign and Security Policy and External Relations of the European Union. She is also Professor in International Relations at the Faculty of Social, Political and Economic Sciences and member of the Centre for International Law. Her main research focuses on security studies, international administration of territories and political uses of international legal norms. She has authored several books and articles about the role the EU in crisis management, in particular towards the Balkans. Her PhD dissertation has been published under the title *Droit et souverainetés. Analyse critique du discours européen sur la Yougoslavie* (Bruxelles, Bern, Berlin, Frankfurt-am-Main, New York, Oxford, Wien: PIE–Peter Lang, 2003). Other recent publications include: 'International norms in theories of interdependence: towards state-less law?', in Klaus-Gerd Giesen and Kees van der Pilj (eds), *Global Norms in the 21st Century* (Newcastle: Cambridge Scholars Press, 2006) and 'The doctrine of "responsibility to protect" and the EU stance: a critical appraisal', in Giovanna Bono (ed.), *The Impact of 9/11 on European Foreign and Security Policy* (Brussels: VUBPRESS, 2006).

Mathias Dewatripont holds a PhD in Economics from Harvard University, 1986. He is a part-time Visiting Professor of Economics at the Massachusetts Institute of Technology and a full-time Professor of Economics at the Université Libre de Bruxelles, where he was Co-Director of ECARES. He is the laureate of the 1998 Francqui Prize and of the 2003 Jahnsson Medal. He was President of the European Economic Association in 2005. He is the Research Director of the Centre for Economic Policy Research, a member of DG Competition's Economic Advisory Group on Competition Policy (EAGCP) and European Commission President Jose Manuel Barroso's Group of Economic Policy Analysis. In 2005, he became a Founding Member of the European Research Council. His general research area is the theory of incentives and contracts, with applications to the internal organisation of firms, industrial organisation and corporate finance, and the economics of higher education. Recent publications include: 'Moral hazard and capital structure dynamics' (with Steve Matthews and Patrick Legros, *Journal of the European Economic Association*, 2003), 'Modes of communication' (with Jean Tirole, *Journal of Political Economy*, 2005), *Contract Theory* (with Patrick Bolton, Massachusetts Institute of Technology Press, 2005), and '"Wasteful" public spending and state aid control' (with Paul Seabright, *Journal of the European Economic Association*, 2006).

Marianne Dony is Director of the Institute for European Studies of the University of Brussels. She holds the Chair of European Law at the University of Brussels, and also teaches *inter alia* the courses of State Aid and Subsidies to Public Undertakings, Law of External Relations of the European Union, and Introduction to Economic Law. Professor Dony has published extensively in European law. She is also the author or editor of many books relating to European law, including *La responsabilité des Etats membres en cas de violation du droit communautaire* (with G. Vandersanden, Brussels: Bruylant, 1997), *L'Union Européenne et le monde après Amsterdam* (Editions de l'Université de Bruxelles, 1999), *Relations extérieures* (with Jean-Victor Louis, Commentaire J. Mégret on the Law of the European Community, vol. 12, second edition, Brussels: Editions de l'Université de Bruxelles, 2005).

Jean-Marc Ferry is Professor of Philosophy and Political Science at the Université Libre de Bruxelles (ULB), Director of the Centre for Political Theory and President of the PhD School in European Studies of the ULB. He was Visiting Professor also at the Collège de Bruges and at the University of Louvain. Among his books are: *Habermas: l'éthique de la communication* (Paris, 1986), *La pensée politique* *contemporaine* (with J. Lacroix, Bruxelles: Bruylant, 2000), *La Question de l'Etat européen* (Paris: Gallimard, 2000), *Europe, la voie kantienne* (Paris: Cerf, 2005). The Institut de France has twice awarded his scientific work.

Pieter Lagrou studied history at the universities of Leuven, Yale and the European University Institute in Florence. Since 2003 he has held the Chair in Comparative History of States and Societies Since 1914 at the Université Libre de Bruxelles and heads the History section of the Institut d'Études Européennes. He was previously a researcher at the Institut d'Histoire du Temps Présent (CNRS, Paris, 1998–2003), of which he is still an affiliate member. Among his publications are: *The Legacy of Nazi Occupation: Patriotic Memory and National Recovery in Western Europe, 1945–1965* (Cambridge University Press, 2000), 'Between Europe and the nation: the inward turn of contemporary historical writing', in Konrad Jarausch and Thomas Lindenberger (eds), *Conflicted Memories: Europeanizing Contemporary Histories* (New York and Oxford: Berghahn Books, 2007) and 'La storia del tempo presente nell'Europa postbellica. Come si sviluppa un nuovo campo disciplinare', *Novecento. Per una storia del tempo presente*, vol. 11, July–December 2004.

Patrick Legros, PhD California Institute of Technology (1989), is Professor of Economics at the Université Libre de Bruxelles. He has taught at Cornell University, and was Visiting Professor at Tinbergen Institute, Université de Strasbourg, and at the Massachusetts Institute of Technology. He is co-editor of the *Journal of Industrial Economics* and was associate editor of *Economics Bulletin*. Most of his current research focuses on the general equilibrium aspects of organisations. Among his recent publications are: 'Monotone matching in perfect and imperfect worlds' (with A. Newman, *Review of Economic Studies*, 2002), 'Auditing and property rights' (with E. Iossa, *Rand Journal of Economics*, 2004), 'Pricing of scientific journals and market power' (with M. Dewatripont, *et al.*, *Journal of the European Economic Association*, 2006), 'Beauty is a beast, frog is a prince: assortative matching with nontransferabilities' (with A. Newman, *Econometrica*, 2007), 'Competing for ownership' (with A. Newman, *Journal of the European Economic Association*, forthcoming).

Jean-Victor Louis is Honorary Professor of the Université Libre de Bruxelles (ULB), Honorary General Counsel of the National Bank of Belgium, and former President of the Institute of European Studies of the ULB (1980–92). He has been a visiting scholar at the Woodrow Wilson Center for International Scholars, Washington DC, at Universities of Paris I (Panthéon-Sorbonne), at Columbia Law School, New York (2001–02), and at the European University Institute, Florence. He holds an Honorary Degree (*Docteur honoris causa*) from the University of Paris II. He is President of the Foundation Philippe Wiener-Maurice Anspach, responsible for relations with the universities of Oxford and Cambridge, and editor of the *Cahiers de Droit européen* (Brussels, Bruylant), Trans European Political Studies Association (TEPSA) board member, and member of the Committee of International Monetary Law of the International Law Association (ILA). Among his recent publications are: *Relations extérieures* (with Marianne Dony (ed.),

Commentaire J. Mégret on the Law of the European Community, vol. 12, second edition, Brussels: Editions de l'Université de Bruxelles, 2005) and *L'ordre juridique de l'Union européenne* (with Thierry Ronse, Dossiers de droit européen, No. 13, Basel, Brussels, Paris: Helbing & Lichtenhahn, Bruylant, LGDJ, 2005).

Paul Magnette is Professor of Political Sciences at the Université Libre de Bruxelles, and was Director of the Institute for European Studies (IEE) for five years. He has served as advisor to the European Commission and the European Council. In 2008 he became Minister for Energy and Environment of the Belgian Federal Government. Among his publications are: *Repenser l'Europe* (co-edited with Mario Telò, Editions de l'Université de Bruxelles, 1996), *Le nouveau modèle européen* (co-edited with Eric Remacle, Editions de Université de Bruxelles, 2000), *The Convention on the Future of Europe: Working Towards a Constitution* (with Jo Shaw, Lars Hoffmann and Anna Vergès Bausili, London: Federal Trust, 2003) and *What Is the European Union? Nature and Prospects* (London: Palgrave-Macmillan 2005), *Citizenship: The History of an Idea* (London: ECPR Book Series, 2005) and *Democraties en Europe* (co-edited with Jean-Michel De Waele, Paris, 2008).

Kalypso Nicolaïdis is a professor of International relations and Director of the European studies centre at the University of Oxford. She teaches in European integration, international relations, international political economy, negotiation and game theory and research methods as University Lecturer in the Department of Politics and International Relations. She holds a PhD in Political Economy and Government from Harvard University, a Master in Public Administration from the Kennedy School of Government, a Master in International Economics and a Diplôme Service Public from the Institut d'Etudes Politiques in Paris. She has published widely on EU institutional and constitutional debates, EU external relations including with Mediterranean countries and the USA, issues of identity, justice and cooperation in the international system, the sources of legitimacy in European and global governance, as well as preventive diplomacy and dispute resolution. She has published in numerous journals including *Foreign Affairs, Foreign Policy, The Journal of Common Market Studies, Journal of European Public Policy, International Organization* as well as in French in *Politique Etrangère, Politique Européenne* and *Raison Critique*. Her latest books include: *Whose Europe? National Models and the Constitution of the European Union* (Oxford University Press, 2003) and *The Federal Vision: Legitimacy and Levels of Governance in the US and the EU* (Oxford University Press, 2001).

Sebastian Oberthür has been Academic Director of the Institute for European Studies (IES) at the Flemish Free University of Brussels (VUB) since October 2005. He focuses on issues of international and European environmental and climate governance, with an emphasis on institutional issues and perspectives. Among his book publications are: *Institutional Interaction in Global Environmental Governance* (co-edited with Thomas Gehring, MIT Press, 2006) and *The Kyoto Protocol* (with Hermann E. Ott, Springer, 1999). The chapter in this volume has been written in cooperation with Claire Roche Kelly, research fellow specialising in international and European environmental policy at the IES at VUB. She obtained an MA in International Studies from the University of Limerick in Ireland.

Frederik Ponjaert holds a BA and an MA in Political Science from the Université Libre de Bruxelles (ULB), is a doctoral research fellow with the Belgian National Research Foundation and is attached both to the Institut d'Etudes Européennes at ULB and the Center for Japan Studies at the Katholieke Universiteit Leuven. His current research focuses on the opportunities and limits for regional cooperation provided by the forms of leadership delivered by non-military powers such as Germany and Japan. This research has included research stays at various international institutions, among which: the International Christian University (Tokyo), Warwick University (GARNET Mobility) and *Princeton University* (Fulbright Scholarship). He is also the ULB Junior Coordinator for the GARNET and NESCA Networks of Excellence.

Eric Remacle is Professor of Political Science at the Université Libre de Bruxelles (ULB) and Visiting Professor at the University of Pittsburgh. His main fields of research are the EU's external action and problems of peace and conflict. He is the Director of the Bernheim Chair for the Study of Peace and Citizenship at ULB and was awarded the Francqui Prize in 2000 (jointly with Paul Magnette) for an Institute for European Studies–ULB research project on The New European Model. His two most recent publications are: *The Security-Development Nexus and the Millennium Development Goals* (Peter Lang, 2008) and *L'état des citoyennetés en Europe et dans les Amériques* (co-edited with Jane Jenson and Berengère Marques-Pereira, Presses de l'Université de Montréal, Canada, 2007).

Maria João Rodrigues is Professor of European Economic Policies at the Institute for European Studies, Université Libre de Bruxelles, and at the Higher Institute of Social Sciences and Business Studies, Lisbon. She has been involved in the development of the Lisbon Agenda since the beginning and supported the European institutions in turning the Lisbon Strategy into an operational agenda of common objectives and measures in various policies such as research, innovation, education, employment and social inclusion. She was Minister of Employment in Portugal and was also President of the European Commission's Advisory Group for Social Sciences. She is currently Special Advisor to the European Commission on several issues. Her recent publications include: *The New Knowledge Economy in Europe* (London: Elgar, 2002) and *European Policies for a Knowledge Economy* (London: Elgar, 2003).

Sebastián Santander holds a PhD in Political Science from the Université Libre de Bruxelles and is a Professor at the Department of Political Science and Head of the International Relations Research Unit at the Université de Liège. His articles, mainly on regionalism and interregionalism, have appeared in such publications as *Journal of European Integration*, *European Foreign Affairs Review*, *Études internationales* (Québec), *Annuaire Français des Relations Internationales* (Paris), *Relazioni Internazionali* (Milan) and *Revista de Derecho Internacional y Mercosur*

(Buenos Aires). He has coordinated a special issue of *Europa & America Latina* on the EU interregional strategy towards Latin America (2, 2007) and of *Les Cahiers du GELA-IS* (3, 2004) on regionalism in the Americas. His most recent book is *Le régionalisme sud-américain, l'Union européenne et les États-Unis* (Editions de l'Université de Bruxelles, 2008).

Nico Schrijver holds the Chair of Public International Law at Leiden University and is the Academic Director of its Grotius Centre for International Legal Studies. He also serves as Visiting Professor of the European Union and Co-operation with Developing Countries at the Institute for European Studies, Université Libre de Bruxelles. Furthermore, he is the President of the Netherlands Society of International Law, a member of the UN High-level Task Force on the Right to Development and elected expert member of the UN Committee on Economic, Social and Cultural Rights. He is a member of the Royal Netherlands Academy of Arts and Sciences. Among his publications are: *Sovereignty over Natural Resources: Balancing Rights and Duties* (Cambridge University Press, 1997 and 2008), *The Evolution of Sustainable Development in International Law: Inception, Meaning and Status* (Leiden: Martinus Nijhoff/Hague Academy of International Law, 2008) and *The United Nations of the Future: Globalisation with a Human Face* (co-authored, Amsterdam: KIT Publishers, 2006).

Reimund Seidelmann is Professor for International Relations and Foreign Policy at the Institute of Political Science, Justus-Liebig-University Giessen, Germany, Professor for Political Science at the Institute for European Studies, Université Libre de Bruxelles, as well as Honorary Professor for International Politics, Renmin University Beijing, Honorary Professor Universitas Katolik Parahyangan Bandung, Indonesien, and European Chairman of the Academic Board EU–China European Studies Programme 2004–08, and coordinator of the EU–NESCA Research Dialogue project. He is Director of the research and cooperation project Germany, the EU and Central Asia (2007–09), funded by Volkswagen-Foundation, and Co-Director of a cooperation programme in Indonesia (2006–09), funded by the German Foreign Ministry. He works on international relations theory, European foreign and security policies, peace and conflict studies, and transformation studies. In addition, he has worked as consultant for political bodies and industries.

Mario Telò is Professor of International Relations and European Integration and currently holds Presidency of the Institute for European Studies, Université Libre de Bruxelles (ULB) (2005–09). As well, he is Director of the PhD School in EU Studies, holds the Jean Monnet Chair *ad honorem* and is a member of The Royal Academy of Sciences, Belgium. Furthermore, he is a senior ULB scholar of the Network of Excellence, GARNET (Europe and Globalization), financed by the Sixth Framework Programme of the Directorate General Research, EU Commission (2004–10). He has been Visiting Professor in many European, American and East Asian universities, has served as consultant for the EU Commission (2000–06), and held Presidency of the European Union Council

(2000) and the European Parliament (2007). Among his recent books are: *Europe: A Civilian Power? EU, Global Governance and World Order* (Palgrave, 2005), *Relations internationales: une perspective européenne* (Preface by R. O. Keohane, Editions de l'Université de Bruxelles, 2008) and *The European Union and New Regionalism* (Ashgate, 2007).

Anne Weyembergh is Professor at the Institute for European Studies of the Université Libre de Bruxelles and Assessor in the Belgian Council of State. Her main field of research is the establishment of a European penal area, involving police and judicial cooperation in criminal matters between member states of the EU. She coordinates the European Criminal Law Academic Network (ECLAN), which gathers together around a hundred specialised academics and researchers from the member states as well as some third states. She has published more than sixty articles or book chapters in French and in English and has directed ten collective books, most of them with Gilles de Kerchove, including *La confiance mutuelle au sein de l'espace pénal européen* (Editions de l'Université de Bruxelles, 2005). Additionally, she has authored a book on the harmonisation of penal legislations: *L'harmonisation des législations: condition de l'espace pénal européen et révélateur de ses tensions* (Editions de l'Université de Bruxelles, 2004).

Preface and acknowledgements

This book stems from virtuous synergies fostered between the Institute for European Studies (IEE) at the Université Libre de Bruxelles (ULB) and GARNET, a Network of Excellence on Globalization and Regulation Network: The Role of the European Union, financed by the European Commission through the Directorate General Research's Sixth Framework Programme. The IEE has already published two collective books, in 2000 and 2008, on the ongoing changes shaping the EU and its international influence since the end of the cold war.[1] This third collective volume on the EU and global governance has greatly benefited from the positive cooperation within the GARNET research community.

The contributors of this volume all share the idea that the *sui generis* features of both the EU's external presence and its actions undoubtedly need to be analysed by combining various disciplinary points of view. What is particularly innovative is that such a multidisciplinary approach allows for a new comprehensive understanding of the EU. Accordingly, the EU is simultaneously presented as: a relevant international entity; a multiple and multifaceted policy-maker; and an unprecedented kind of power-in-the-making. Consequently, the multidisciplinary approach is an identity-shaping factor of this textbook. Taking stock of the achievements of such multidisciplinary research agendas is the most consistent way to address the EU as a broad thematic area of studies, which includes political science and international relations as well as comparative politics and international political economy, history, law and political philosophy.

Moreover, the international group of contributors benefits from the accumulated skills of ongoing, parallel interdisciplinary/disciplinary research projects. The multidisciplinary approach and the openness to interdisciplinary research have been a shared distinctive feature of the IEE-ULB for several decades. A sizeable majority of the contributors play an active role within outstanding European and global networks – including, among others, ECLAN, Odysseus, ECARES, GARNET and NESCA – which further strengthens the volume's openness and internationalisation.[2] Additionally, the authors hail from a large array of nationalities and intellectual backgrounds. These various scientific perspectives converge on common lines of inquiry related to the EU as both a relevant multi-dimensional entity within global governance, and as a new kind of actor and power.

The process behind the elaboration of the book has been remarkably fruitful and smooth: a team of forty researchers met several times, discussing the draft chapters in a collegial, frank and constructive way. The IEE-ULB has the pleasure of thanking by name both the authors and discussants for their precious contributions: Nico Schrijver, Reimund Seidelmann, Paola Conconi, Paul Magnette, Kalypso Nicolaïdis, Jean-Marc Ferry, Anne Weyembergh, Philippe De Bruycker, Maria João Rodrigues, Pieter Lagrou, Patrick Legros, Mathias Dewatripont, Emmanuelle Bribosia, André Sapir, Mauro Zanardi, Laurent Scheeck, Philippe Vigneron, Eric Remacle, Barbara Delcourt, Marta Martinelli, Véronique Dimier, Myriam Bacquelaine, Janine Goetschy, Justine Lacroix, P. van Elsuwege, Pierre Vercauteren, Frederik Ponjaert, Sebastián Santander, François Foret, Denis Duez, Michel Walbroeck, Sebastian Oberthür, Marc Pallmaerts, Jean-Victor Louis, Giovanni Grevi, Marianne Dony and Dominique Servais. All of these contributors represent the four departments of the IEE as well as some partner universities and institutes, such as Oxford, Leiden, Lisbon, Giessen, Liège, Mons, the Flemish Free University of Brussels (VUB), FUSL, Ghent, and the Institute for Security Studies in Paris.

This complex yet stimulating manner of book-writing made it possible to fully take advantage of common backgrounds and shared criteria, thus enhancing the quality of contributions. Furthermore, the editor interacted for several months with the contributors' first and final drafts to strengthen the book's internal coherence and consistency.

Frederik Ponjaert (FRS-FNRS), assistant researcher at the IEE-ULB, made an invaluable contribution to the main stages of this complex editing process, while Ms L. R. Barr translated the chapter by J.-M. Ferry. As both a recognised specialist and native English speaker, our former colleague and a current Professor at the University of Greenwich, Mary Farrell, was kind enough to proofread the book with an eye to improving its overall form. This book also benefited greatly from the support of the Belgian FNRS (Fonds national de la recherche scientifique) and the research network GARNET. We very warmly thank all of them.

The authors and the IEE-ULB dedicate this book to our Masters and PhD students. These students, at the GARNET International PhD School and the many international research networks interacting with the research projects on Europe in the world, cultivate within us the clarity and all the other qualities needed when compiling a book aimed at a broad readership including both students and scholars.

Notes

1 See Paul Magnette and Eric Remacle (eds) (2000), *Le nouveau modèle européen*, Editions de l'Université de Bruxelles, and Paul Magnette and A. Weye,bergh (eds) *L'Union européene: la fin d'une crise?*, Editions de l'université de Bruxelles, 2008.
2 ECARES is a network of economists linked to the Centre for Economic Policy Research (CEPR), based in London; ECLAN and Odysseus are international networks based in Brussels IEE-ULB and focusing on the European space of security, liberty and justice; GARNET is a Network of Excellence involving forty universities and financed by the DG Research, EU Commission, which focuses on EU and global governance, and NESCA supports research cooperation between European and East Asian universities.

Abbreviations

ACP	Africa, Caribbean and the Pacific
AETR	Accord européen sur le transposrt routier (European agreement on road-transport)
AFSJ	Area of Freedom, Security and Justice
ASEAN	Association of South East Asian Nations
ASEM	Asia–Europe Meeting
BCBS	Basle Committee for Banking Supervision
BIS	Bank for International Settlements
BRIC	Brazil, Russia, India and China
BWs	Bretton Woods
CAN	Andean Community
CAP	common agricultural policy
CCP	common commercial policy
CDM	Clean Development Mechanism
CDSP	common defence and security policy
CET	Common External Tariff
CFI	Court of First Instance
CFSP	common foreign and security policy
CSCE	Conference on Security and Cooperation in Europe
DAC	Development Assistance Committee
DG Comp	Directorate General Competition
DG ECOFIN	Directorate General Economic and Financial Affairs (EU Commission)
DM	Deutsche Mark
DOJ	Department of Justice (USA)
EAEC	European Atomic Energy Community
EAGCP	Economic Advisory Group on Competition Policy
EB	Executive Board (IMF)
EBA	Everything But Arms
EBRD	European Bank for Development and Reconstruction
EC	European Community
ECB	European Central Bank
ECJ	European Court of Justice

ECOFIN	Economic and Financial Affairs Council
ECOSOC	Economic and Social Council
ECSC	European Coal and Steel Community
ECOWAS	Economic Community of Western African States
ED	Executive Director (IMF)
EDF	European Development Fund
EEC	European Economic Community (before the Treaty of Maastricht)
EFC	Economic and Financial Committee (EU)
EIB	European Investment Bank
EMU	Economic and Monetary Union
ENP	European neighbourhood policy
EPA	Economic Partnership Agreement
EPC	European Political Cooperation
ESCB	European System of Central Banks
ESDP	European security and defence policy
ETS	Emissions Trading Scheme
EU	European Union
FAO	Food and Agriculture Organisation (of the UN)
FRF	French franc
FTC	Federal Trade Commission (USA)
FSF	Financial Stability Forum
GAB	General Arrangements to Borrow
GATS	General Agreement on Trade in Services
GATT	General Agreement on Tariffs and Trade
GDP	Gross Domestic Product
GECAS	General Electric Commercial Aviation Services
GEF	Global Environment Facility
GHG	greenhouse gas
GNI	Gross National Income
GSP	Generalised System of Preferences
ICC	International Criminal Court
ICN	International Competition Network
IGC	intergovernmental conference
ILO	International Labour Organisation
IMF	International Monetary Fund
IMFC	International Monetary and Financial Committee
IPCC	Intergovernmental Panel on Climate Change
JHA	justice and home affairs (policy)
JI	Joint Implementation
LDCs	least developed countries
MERCOSUR	Mercado Común del Sur (trade area between Argentina, Brazil, Paraguay and Uruguay)
MFN	Most Favoured Nation
Mt	Mega tonne

NATO	North Atlantic Treaty Organization
NIEO	New International Economic Order
NTBs	non-tariff barriers
ODA	Official Development Assistance
OECD	Organization for Economic Co-operation and Development
OPEC	Organization of Petroleum Exporting Countries
OSCE	Organisation of Security and Cooperation in Europe
PTA	preferential trade agreement
QMV	qualified majority voting
R&D	Research and Development
R&D&I	Research, Development and Innovation
SAAP	State Aid Action Plan
SADC	South African Development Community
SDR	Special Drawing Rights
SEA	*Single European Act*
SGP	Stability and Growth Pact
SME	small and medium enterprises
SWF	Sovereign Wealth Funds
TBT	Technical Barriers to Trade (Agreement)
TEC	Treaty of the European Community
TEU	Treaty of the European Union
TFEU	Treaty on the Functioning of the European Union
TRIPs	(Agreement on) Trade Related Intellectual Property Rights
UK	United Kingdom
UN	United Nations
UNCTAD	United Nations Conference on Trade and Development
UNDP	United Nations Development Programme
UNEP	United Nations Environment Programme
UNFCCC	United Nations Framework Convention on Climate Change
UNIDO	United Nations Industrial Development Organization
USA/US	United States of America
USSR	Union of Soviet Socialist Republics (Soviet Union)
VERs	voluntary export restraints
WEU	Western European Union
WHO	World Health Organization
WTO	World Trade Organization

1 Introduction

The EU as a model, a global actor and an unprecedented power

Mario Telò

Summary

This introduction first presents the volume's contents and the questions addressed by each chapter. Second, it shows that the EU's influence on global governance is based simultaneously on its long-term achievements as a model of regional cooperation, a multiple actor and policy-maker, as well as on its incipient and unprecedented kind of power. By assessing the EU's current and future external impact, two kinds of variables are taken into account. On the one hand, external ones, linked to the evolving international post-cold war system, between unipolar, anarchical, multipolar and multilateral tendencies, where the EU action, interests and values look as underpinning a new multilateral order, albeit in a controversial and oscillating way. On the other hand, internal variables matter as well since the emerging EU co-leadership is concerned – that is, the material, strategic and institutional capacities of a two-level polity, including the states and the European common dimension.

The volume's distinctive approach to EU and global governance

This collective volume addresses the multiple influences, impacts and policies of the EU on its external environment, analyzed from multisciplinary approaches sharing a distinctive inside/outside perspective. This means that the book does not rest upon a narrow understanding of EU foreign policy, nor on mere external relations, but aims at a comprehensive presentation of the multidimensional influence the EU exerts on the surrounding world, focusing on a broader understanding of its diverse contribution to global governance and international relations.

Furthermore, this book's approach stresses an encompassing *longue durée* (long-term) presentation of the EU's contribution to regional and global governance. This means that more than a half-century after the Schuman Declaration of 1950, and twenty years after the end of cold war, the EU's international influence can be assessed by a certain distance towards the still relevant questions raised by any given single event, such as a conjunctural crisis or a controversial Treaty revision. The contributors share the conviction that the EU's weight in the world is rooted in its very existence, as a mature form of multilateral governance of national and local diversities towards increasing regional convergence at the European level. What matters is the consolidation at quasi-continental level of a highly sophisticated set of common institutions and intergovernmental/supranational regimes among the fifteen, twenty-five or twenty-seven (even more, if the long waiting list of applicants or pre-applicants is taken into consideration) member states, sharing several common interests, objectives, values and policies. That is why the most relevant external influence stems from the economic, social and political sides of the EU as an international reference, or, in a Weberian understanding (i.e., free of any value implications), as an "ideal-type" or a "model." This will then be combined with the analysis of various dimensions of the Union's explicit roles as a global and regional actor, its external relations and foreign policies.

This volume is a critical book. It is not only far from falling to any temptation of Eurocentric euphoria, but was conceived and implemented as a textbook rather than as a collection of essays. The panel of contributing authors is pluralist and rich in variation as to each author's national, theoretical and academic competence. Each chapter thereby investigates both successes and failures, the positive and negative influence of the EU, and how this influence is manifested, including some problematic, conflictual and unintended consequences.

The fifteen chapters provide a large array of information and empirical analyses on the EU's external influence. It is only on such a broad basis that a new conceptualization of the evolving nature of the EU as the second relevant global player is possible. The book's ambition includes showing the present state of the art regarding the controversial debate on the nature of the EU as an international actor, while underlining the unprecedented nature of both the EU's regional governance and its interconnections with the overall global governance systems. Taking stock of the diverging and common findings as well as the currently ongoing process of European construction, several chapters address a common question: what are the theoretical implications of the nature of the EU as both a regional, multi-level and multi-actor entity, as well as a global power-in-the-making?

The book consists of three parts. Part I focuses on the external impact of the EU's achievements and its sheer presence within the world; it examines how the EU's main external influence is shaped by its internal achievements and dynamics, including the famous *acquis communautaire*[1]. In Part II, the book deals with a large array of EU external policies and policy-making, and their legal framework. It approaches these issues from the most integrated to the most decentralized, from objectives to instruments, from rhetoric to action. Part III of the book addresses relevant horizontal and perspective issues: on the one hand, the EU's near and far abroad agendas; on the other, the challenges that the external dimension of the European construction poses to historical and theoretical research. This introductory chapter aims both to stress some guidelines behind the common inquiries underlying all chapters, and to set out the conceptual framework and the book's distinctive approach.

The influence of the EU on its external environment

Aside from its foreign policy, the EU in itself, as a coordinating institutionalized framework among national entities, exerts a bottom-up influence on its near and far external environment. This volume's Part I focuses on the relevant external implication of the EU's internal achievements and policies: ranging from its complex democratic polity to the competition policy, the euro and its modernization policies. The part's opening chapter, Chapter 2 by Paul Magnette and Kalypso Nicolaïdis, deals with two essential and distinctive dimensions of the EU's contribution to global governance: the EU internal/external influence as a value-free model of national and supranational democracy and its impact on international democratization. Since its creation in the 1950s, the European Community (EC) has played a key role in underpinning a framework for the democratic consolidation of some founding as well as certain non-founding member states, which had recently gone through their own specific experiences of fascist dictatorships (Mediterranean enlargements). These supranational and transnational pressures became more explicit after 1989, and helped set the tone behind the Central and Eastern enlargements to post-communist countries. Furthermore, the EU as a regional democratic political system-in-the-making is a reference for its near and far international environment.

When taking into consideration the EU's explicit policies, including enlargement and various external relations, the question arises to what extent the EU can, in comparative terms, be considered an effective international "democratizer" (at national, regional and global levels). Within that context, how for example does the internal conditionality (Articles 6–7 of the TEU and the Copenhagen Criteria) interplay with the EU's external policies and, beyond that, the EU's political democratic identity in the world? Finally, Magnette and Nicolaïdis underline that the EU is not only an intergovernmental association of democratic states but also a new kind of non-state supranational political system at the macro-regional level. Its emerging regional democratic polity as such is already offering a twofold international reference for near and far abroad:[2] for democracy within the state and for democracy between states.

The next two chapters address two further achievements of the EU which are non-controversial within international literature and entail salient international effects: the common currency, the euro; and the single market. In Chapter 3, Jean-Victor Louis investigates the euro's international dimension, and the maturing of the Eurozone's monetary policy. He evaluates the impact of monetary integration and the common currency on the global financial system; namely the influence it has had on, and interaction with, the International Monetary Fund (IMF). The euro is evaluated as an international anchor currency, a unit of account, a medium for exchange, and a store of value. Although the euro is the only case in modern history of a currency without a state, the drive towards a European currency has, since the early failed Werner Plan (1970–71) and the successful Delors committee (1988–89), endeavoured to enhance European international autonomy within an unstable financial system. Furthermore, given the limited role of the EU within the Bretton Woods institutions (where Europe is only represented through its member states), the role of the European Central Bank (ECB) and the euro are the only way for the EU as such to exert an albeit indirect role within global financial governance.

This third chapter illustrates how the euro's international role has suffered both from internal asymmetries between the monetary and economic dimensions of the European Monetary Union (EMU), as well as from divergences between policies and/or among member states. However, given the increasing international influence already wielded by this centralized and successful EU policy, it has helped to address or revalue the twin challenge of consolidating regional monetary stability and addressing the controversial leading role played by the relatively overrepresented European states within the IMF. The chapter is crucial when considering the evolving responsibility of the EU with regard to the perspective of a new global financial architecture preventing and managing the financial crises – a particular challenge given the radically changing international economic environment (in comparison with the first decades of the IMF's exitence). The current post-hegemonic world is characterized by both declining US financial leadership within the G7, and waning G7 leadership, within a critical and less legitimate global financial system. The chapter concludes by presenting four alternative scenarios for the future global multilateral monetary system and the place occupied by the regional Eurozone therein.

Chapter 4, by Mathias Dewatripont and Patrick Legros, deals with the external impact of the EU's competition policy, which is central to the world's largest market: the European single market. As one of the most efficient internal policies – legally based on the "Community method"[3] – the competition policy has a sizeable external impact. It influences not only internal, but also international private and public actors. Accordingly, this regulatory power engenders for the EU a sizeable external influence, and a distinct identity as a major global rule-setting actor. This rule-setting function is often exerted in competition/cooperation with the USA. The chapter examines how this regulatory approach is being developed within the wider global arena, notably with regard to other international economic actors, states and multinational companies. Moreover, a comparative analysis with the USA offers valuable insights. Two questions are especially pertinent to this analysis. To what extent has the "European competition and antitrust model" succeeded in setting global standards and suggesting rules abroad? And, under what conditions will EU policy continue to shape global policy further in the future?

The final chapter of the first part, Chapter 5 by Maria João Rodrigues, focuses on the socio-economic model (again, in a value-free sense) within the globalized economy. More precisely, the issue to be tackled is the external implications of the national socio-economic models and their European convergence, namely through coordination and supranational regulation. First, the chapter introduces readers to the objective international relevance of the European economies – among them, four members of the G7 – and the very appealing and rich common market, while not negating the problems it faces in adapting to global competition. Second, the chapter analyzes the achievements and the shortcomings of the so-called Lisbon Strategy. This modernization agenda, launched in 2000, aims at enhancing internal convergences within the EU towards a "European model of a knowledge economy" by combining international technological competitiveness and social cohesion.

This fifth chapter fulfils a bridging function between the volume's first two parts, as it addresses a crucial dimension of the existing model of policy coordination, thus hoping to enhance the EU external structural power. The EU's socio-economic model and the dynamics of the Lisbon Strategy already entail large external implications affecting both the Union's near abroad as broader global governance dynamics.

Of course, the EU cannot master globalization by acting as a credible leading player without successfully implementing necessary internal reforms, and addressing the open challenges of energy dependency, immigration and sustainable development.[4] However, compared with the 1990s, the internal impact of a rapidly changing international economic environment and increasing competition are fostering a pro-active evolution of the concept of external relations itself. This evolution leads us to a pressing question: under which conditions would the distinctive European combination of political regulation, social cohesion and market dynamics (between negative and positive integration) bring about the potential for a pro-active role in shaping the process of globalization?

The external policies of a multidimensional actor-in-the-making

The introductory chapter of Part II, Chapter 6 by Marianne Dony, focuses on the complex legal basis of the Union's external actions within a context where even the domestic aspects of government are "going global." The legal and institutional provisions – the clearest expressions of the competence distribution decided upon by the states – are gradually changing beyond the baroque "three pillars structure" established by the Maastricht Treaty (1992). This incremental evolution has been ongoing, ranging from the many Treaty revisions, established in Amsterdam (1997), and Nice (2000), to the Reform Treaty – or Lisbon Treaty – of 2007.[5] This chapter provides the non-specialized reader with a clear presentation of both the general legal framework of the Union's external policies, and the significant impact of the EU Court of Justice's jurisdiction in expanding the Union's implied competences. Furthermore, the Union's treaty-making power, its international agreements, its participation in international organizations and the issue of its legal personality are also addressed.

Among the evolving dynamics, the potential impact of the Lisbon Treaty's provisions is underlined, notably regarding the EU's international objectives, its legal personality, and the reform of its institutions. Notably, the first and foremost among these institutional reforms are the High Representative for Foreign Policy – combining the former Council and Commission roles in external relations – and the European External Action Service. However, given the structural importance of two-level policy-making within the EU (states and Union), the many brakes to Treaty reform, and the legacy of the three pillars structure, questions remain on the overall coherence and consistency of the EU's external policies as they result from various decision-making procedures and implementation mechanisms. Coherence and consistency remain the main open challenges for the second decade of the century.

In Chapter 7, Paola Conconi presents the EU commercial policy and its impact on regional/global trade regulation. The most centralized and consolidated external policy of the EU is examined from the perspective of both its achievements and its current controversial evolution, as far as global governance is concerned. The EU share of merchandise imports and exports is the largest in the world, and the intra-EU trade record (complementarities among the European economies) is the highest among regional groupings of states. Much data as well as many instruments and external audiences show complementarities between the EU and World Trade Organization (WTO). However, the question remains to what extent the EU could further encourage the WTO to become a stronger regulatory regime – one with teeth – without reforming relevant internal policies. And, to what extent are the specific conflicts between the WTO and the EU (e.g., the issues over bananas, hormone beef, genetically modified organisms, the airline industry) significant examples of an increasing contradiction between the two organizations, despite the EU's commitment to the "harmonious development of world trade"?[6]

A further relevant question turns on what the EU's distinctive balance should be between its commitment to global multilateralism and its orientation to foster limited Free Trade Agreements, bilateral, regional and interregional agreements. Is the strategy to multilateralize regionalism a step beyond the classical Bagwati-Summers controversy (regional versus global)?[7] Beyond the singular reference to Article XXIV of the WTO charter, what are the possible contradictions between regional rule-setting and the still absent global rules? On the one hand, the EU's internal modes of governance offer possible inspiration for improving the WTO trade regime as well as multilateral rule-making. On the other hand, the EC/EU in itself is a regional project and its internal integration process as such was given a top priority for many decades – a reality which might have resulted in conflicts with global regulation (explicitly, but in no way exclusively, the case of agriculture and the common agriculture policy comes to mind). An expanding EU is a significant part of the globalization process: yet tensions still remain. This point is confirmed by the growing demand for new norm-setting. This has emerged as a challenge to the EU's commitment to a multiple free-trade agenda (see the Doha Development Round (DDR) and the recent Transatlantic Economic Council arrangement on non-tariff barriers to exchanges and investments) with regard to internal pressing demands of reciprocity, mutual benefit, respect of property rights, the fight against trade dumping, social regulation and, last but not least, the uncertain consequences of the global DDR (see the Commission's communication of October 4, 2006 entitled *Global Europe*).

At the beginning of the twenty-first century, and from a quantitative perspective, the EU's cooperation policies *vis-à-vis* developing countries – which are addressed by Nico Schrijver in Chapter 8 – are, in relative terms, the most sizeable dimension. In spite of falling short of meeting the UN Millennium Goals so far, the EU's cooperation policy remains a noteworthy force within the world order. It is also the most sophisticated cooperation policy as far as its structure and conditionality mechanisms are concerned. After sketching the historical evolution of the EU's development cooperation from the 1960s up to the new millennium, this chapter introduces the reader to the objectives and results of the cooperation and humanitarian policies pursued by the EU, the world's first donor.

As well, Schrijver critically examines the main issues at stake in areas such as Africa, where the EU seeks to enhance its governance influence, in the presence of competitors, such as China or several other powers, characterized by differing approaches to development. The distinctive EU concept of conditionality is thus challenged and questioned on account of its controversial impact and complex implementation.

Furthermore, the chapter asseses to what extent the EU's waverings between aid and trade on the one hand, and between multilateral (e.g., the African, Caribbean and Pacific, or ACP) and bilateral approaches (e.g., Economic Partnership Agreements) on the other, are a long-term feature of its development policy. The EU's response to global governance emergencies (from poverty and underdevelopment, to the consequences of climate change and water/food shortage) is thus viewed in the light of the ambiguous impact of these fluctuations.

The EU's environment policy, its interaction with its energy policy and the Union's role in regulating global climate change are all issues addressed by Sebastian Oberthür in Chapter 9. This clearly represents a promising and rapidly emerging research field. The issues at stake are both of a pressing and a long-term nature. The core question is whether the EU presents as a credible leading actor when addressing what temperature levels will be acceptable within fifty years. The salience of the external challenges combined with the EU's competences in this policy field make this chapter a necessary pillar for any inside/outside examination of the EU's contribution to global governance. The EU acts through bilateral cooperation and multilateral regime-building (namely the Kyoto Protocol and its follow-up after 2012, the outlines of which were drawn up in the Bali Action Plan of 2007). Obviously, this chapter also takes into account some of the questions and challenges raised by the inevitable interplay between the environment policy and the emerging European energy policy. Energy has become a salient policy field as the current energy scarcities reflect in a shift in global power (involving all major emerging powers – Russia, India, China and Brazil).

Focusing on the credibility of the EU's internal environmental and energy policies may allow one to assess what leadership the EU could further exercise on the emerging regulatory arrangements – aimed at more sustainable forms of development – both at the level of global multilateral regime-setting and the level of partnerships with its near abroad. As a result, a pressing need emerges to assert with more consistency and coherence the goal of sustainable development as an EU priority among the Union's several internal policies.

The external policies framed by the second (common foreign and security policy) and third (justice and home affairs) "pillars" of the Treaty (since the Maastricht Treaty of 1992) reflect the will of member states to provide the EU with a more explicit, even if incipient, political dimension. The European area of freedom, security and justice, originally referred to as the "third pillar," has increasingly come to include several notable external implications. In Chapter 10, Philippe de Bruycker and Anne Weyembergh cover the external impact of internal European evolutions in these crucial policy fields. The EU cannot act alone when looking at an area of freedom, security and justice. Instead, the question is how to combine security concerns (which are increasingly prioritized within the domestic political agendas) with European values (and interest) dedicated to an ever more open global order.

The EU is making significant progress as cooperation in this essential policy field has evolved beyond the limits initially set out within the three pillars structure. The chapter's analytical object is twofold. On the one hand, it addresses the immigration and asylum policies which call for a comprehensive strategy: efficient decision-making, shared priorities, and working cooperation agreements with neighboring countries. On the other hand, the chapter also looks at the emerging European criminal policy and its fight against drugs and terrorism. The reform process, from the Treaty of Maastricht to Amsterdam and ultimately the Lisbon Treaty, is explained in detail. Changes are driven by a complex set of internal and external forces. This chapter seeks to identify the dynamics involved in such a sensitive policy field, and to assess the international impact on the Union's near abroad policies without overlooking the pending issues at stake. For example, two key controversies that are broached are the debates surrounding illegal migration and the evolving framework of the transatlantic cooperation.

In Chapter 11, Barbara Delcourt and Eric Remacle examine the EU's common foreign and security policy (CFSP), and its defense policy, as well as the interplay with the broader heterogeneous international system. The strengths and shortcomings of the CFSP are examined while taking into account both the limited European socialization of national state actors and the dynamics behind a certain soft institutionalization of a common EU dimension. The background is set by the transatlantic alliance on the one hand, and the European security identity on the other (from the Maastricht and Amsterdam treaties to the Lisbon Treaty of 2007). The central question being asked is whether the European multilateral and "cooperative power" – including its cooperative diplomacy, multiple agreements, and peace missions – is fit to cope with the current post-cold war transition as well as with the new global threats of the twenty-first century.

The CFSP and ESDP are also analyzed as relevant frameworks when facing the challenges of conflict resolution and prevention, both on the European continent and beyond. This beckons the question whether the call for a multilateral approach and the asserted conformity to the UN framework and values is always implemented in a consistent way. What of the burdens arising from the UN's efficiency deficit, the multiple natures of present threats, and mounting internal and transatlantic pressures? The chapter focuses on some relevant case studies (notably the Western Balkans), by presenting and evaluating several missions, showing convergence and divergence among member states, and detailing their various records.

The chapter finally examines what the literature commonly refers to as the new dimension of the EU's "second pillar", namely its incipient defense policy. Here, the chapter goes beyond the account of the aims, objectives and decision-making processes of EDSP, so as to assess its problems and challenges within the context of the changing international system. Are its shortcomings to be explained by capacity deficits, by an overly decentralized institutional decision-making process, by a lack of strategy, or any other factors? Among the open research issues, the chapter addresses the controversial literature on the impact on the evolving features of the EU and its overarching coherence of innovations, such as: a deepening ESDP, the European Armaments Agency, or the Lisbon Treaty's provision on internal "solidarity" in the advent of an external attack. The literature ponders whether we are witnessing a militarizing EU or the emergence of a more credible and less idealistic civilian power. The question remains whether the controversy surounding the follow-up of the European strategy and the acceptance and scope of humanitarian interventions will push the EU's defense and security policy beyond the original limits of the Petersberg Missions and the UN multilateral framework and values.

The EU's geographic agendas and horizontal issues

Part III examines Europe as a global actor in relation to horizontal issues. The first two of these are linked to distinctive geographical relations with the European macro-region (Continental plus Mediterranean) on the one hand, and interregional and intercontinental relations on the other. There is a specific dimension of the EU's external policies regarding its near abroad – the large macro-region of neighboring countries belonging to the so-called "arc of crisis" stretching from its shifting Eastern border to the explosive Mediterranean area. The widening EU has not yet struck a precise, effective and accepted policy framework with regard to this sensitive area still characterized by political conflicts, risks of civilizational clashes, legal and illegal migration flows, a growing energy dependence on the part of the EU, and uncertainties regarding the Union's final borders.

In Chapter 12, Reimund Seidelmann examines the fundamental realities and the growing complexities behind the EU's efforts to manage its changing role as a quasi-continental, multi-tiered and multi-layered governance model. Both the Barcelona Process and the EU's partnership with its Eastern neighbors have rather disappointing track records. This chapter will introduce the reader to the highly controversial interplay between the EU's ongoing enlargement policy and its external policies *vis-à-vis* its new neighborhood. Seidelmann explores whether the European neighborhood policy (ENP) – covering some sixteen countries – is a possible way out of such a blatant efficiency gap, or whether will it just make this issue even more confused and controversial. The ENP (divided into the Mediterranean and Eastern partnerships) and the still ongoing enlargement policy lack a comprehensive strategic design, which has resulted in some misunderstanding among partners. In 2007, the EU managed to contain and frame the worst scenarios of political fragmentation, both in the Western Balkans (the independency of Kosovo from Serbia) and in the Mediterranean (the French idea of an *Union pour la Méditerranée* was integrated within the multilateral Barcelona Process). However, a stable architecture for the whole region is still wanting. Furthemore, the weak legal basis and the lack of political coordination of the EU's immigration and energy policies hinder its effectiveness in this fundamental area.

The second horizontal geographic agenda concerns the interregional arrangements with partners overseas, notably – but not exclusively – with regional associations of states belonging to Africa, Asia and the Americas. For several decades the EU has provided a *de facto* distinctive contribution to global governance. The EU has already been recognized for setting up multiple agreements with its far abroad. Such interregional relations are becoming multidimensional and more political. In Chapter 13, Sebastián Santander and Frederik Ponjaert first analyze and compare these EU-led group-to-group relations by detailing the two most relevant case studies: the Rio de Janeiro Process started in 1999, and the Asia–Europe Meeting (ASEM) started in 1996. These two cases, along with the older ACP conventions (discussed in Schrijver's chapter) are identified within the literature as being distinct identity-building vectors, thus associating the EU – at least since the late 1990s – with a novel contribution to multilateral governance.

While detailing the variations in institutionalization and providing an assessment of their different impacts, the chapter highlights common features, aims and emerging problems within the EU's interregional arrangements. For example, to what extent is the "mirror effect" of interregionalism – as reflexively strengthening the EU's own regional common identity – undermined by the growing number of strategic partnerships with individual large countries (such as Brazil and China)? Are they an inevitable consequence of the maturation of the EU as a leading global actor? How do interregional relationships interplay with bilateralism and global governance? How are the multidimensional agendas, including political dialogue, about to evolve? Do they vary according to the various partners, according to a kind of "Zelig"[8] syndrome of accommodation?

Of course, a growing political actor is expected to establish special bilateral and comprehensive relationships with the biggest global and regional states. The EU has thus established strategic partnership with China, Japan, India, Brazil, Canada, Russia and the USA. Second, EU competition with the USA has in the past fostered bilateral free-trade agreements with Asian, Latin American, African and other ACP countries. Last, but not least, varying ways of effecting regional cooperation imply differences in the nature of the interregional relations with the EU. Accordingly, international institutionalization is bound to take various forms, as are the EU's external relations. However, the overall coherence of the EU's relations with its far abroad remains an open research question.

Opting for a long-term approach to the European role in the world implies the need for research cooperation with historians and political philosophers. From the Renaissance and the Enlightenment up to the contemporary era of a multilateral trade system, the European political tradition encompasses two approaches to the crucial issue of the relationship between Europe and the wider world. These correspond to two opposite visions of both the state and capitalism. The first is colonialism and imperialism, while the second is cosmopolitanism and universalism.

In Chapter 14, Pieter Lagrou focuses on the bearing of the historical legacies of national colonial policies on the EU's contribution to global governance and its relations with other continents and regions. To what extent and how does the somber legacy of national history still matter with regard to the role of EU in the world? Over the last five centuries, European states have profoundly shaped the world. On the one hand, through colonization, empire, exporting the model of nation-state; thus ensuring that mainly intra-European conflicts became the background of two tragic world wars. On the other hand, multilateral trade underpinned capitalist development and the spreading of culture, ideas and political philosophies, including democracy and human rights. The growing relationships between the EU and its abroad are still ambiguously affected both by Eurocentric tendencies reminiscent of past domination, as well as by novel features and distinctive aims, which underpin new partnerships at the bilateral and interregional levels. This poses the question of the existing balance between continuity and discontinuity. Lagrou's innovative hypothesis is that what matters when considering the nature of the EU's contribution to global governance is that within only fifteen years – from 1945 to the 1960s – almost all European states experienced the harsh realities of defeat, either as supporters of the losing side in World War Two or as colonial powers because of the decolonization process. During the same years, the European integration process started. To what extent do these convergent circumstances support the thesis of discontinuity and the lower international profile of the EC compared with the traditional European states power politics?

Finally, for centuries the global implication of European contribution towards peace has been addressed by a second tradition of political thought, from Immanuel Kant to Jürgen Habermas. In Chapter 15, Jean-Marc Ferry analyzes the modern cosmopolitan perspective in light of the European structural peace and democratic construction. Even for realist scholars, such as Christopher Hill, the EU is already a "regional form of international society"[9] and, for the comparative regionalist, it is a "regional polity" marked by reconciliation, recognition and deep cooperation among former enemies. This undisputed internal achievement is a pro-active message for the outside world, even for those far removed from European experiences and values. This is what the political philosopher Habermas alludes to when arguing that there is no risk of overestimating the international relevance of the Franco-German reconciliation, and the quasi-continental settlement it brought about.

Some idealist social scientists, such as Ulrich Beck, have professed the EU to be a "cosmopolitan Empire," a carefree island of sorts within a Westphalian[10] world. However, the EU should not be seriously considered a kind of happy post-modern, post-sovereign, post-Westphalian political entity. Its relationship with other actors is an essential part of the analysis, and its interplay with power politics as well. From his point of view, Ferry addresses the question of the extent to which and the way in which the EU's peaceful and democratic transnationalism is and could become a dynamic component of a more global and diffused cosmopolitan trend. This chapter addresses three possible combinations of the idea and practice of European integration with a global perspective, including: the traditional supranational avenue; the recent theory of a "Federation of States"[11] – supported by Jacques Delors among others; and the perspective of "Cosmopolitan Union" explicitly inspired by Kantian views and asserted by Ferry himself. This approach implies far-reaching consequences in terms of Europe's distinctive international identity, its external policy-making, and its innovative notions of power.

The book offers several considerations on the possible combination – or contradiction – between the particular unification process of 500 million Europeans and the universal dimension of 6.5 billion world citizens. The main challenges relate to the relationships with the 500 million neighbors studied by Seidelmann, the peoples from former colonies mentioned by Lagrou and Schrijver, and the far abroad studied by Santander and Ponjaert. Two centuries after Kant's enlightened universal cosmopolitan vision, the European region and its particular interests, distinctive historically rooted values and specific international identity can no longer be simply equated with the universal dimension of human development, human rights protection and human security.[12] All in all, defining the evolving balance between

European relativism and universalism, notably within a non-European world – the socially unbalanced, economically and politically unstable, culturally heterogeneous international post-Cold war system – is one of the main common research guidelines of this collective volume.

The EU's impact on global governance

This book also evaluates the EU's effective impact, through multiple forms, on global governance. All the contributors have taken up the concept of global governance[13] as a shared communication tool. Global governance[14] is a familiar concept in multidisciplinary literature, which this volume – avoiding the ideological euphoria of the 1990s – seeks to interpret beyond the trivial opposition between the emerging decentralized and informal forms of *governance* and the declining traditional institutionalized state-centric *government* of political and security issues. Understanding to what extent global governance could be driven by economic globalization and complex interdependence will be crucial in defining the EU's future status as either a leader or a marginalized international player.

As for the scope and efficiency of the EU's impact on global multilevel governance, is it about to increase or decline? In general, the contributors in the present volume share the hypothesis that since World War Two and in particular following 1989, the European role has been increasingly noteworthy. However, in spite of its recognized spontaneous bottom-up influence, the EU's actorness and its incipient contribution to a more stable continental and world order is still not convincing enough to answer such a question without qualifications.

A comparative evaluation should allow for a discriminate understanding. First, such understanding needs to be based on familiarity with the diverse relevant geographical and policy agendas, principal among which: the various priorities associated with the surrounding regions; the new strategic partnerships with Brazil, Russia, India and China (the BRICs) and other overseas regions; the transatlantic relation; and the future of the UN and Bretton Woods institutions. Second, bearing in mind the broad variety of concerned policy fields, it needs to be noted that variations are particularly wide: from economy to trade; from human welfare to defense; from environmental standard-setting to security issues. Even the mix, between spontaneous attraction and incentivized persuasion on the one hand; and coercion (through multiple clauses of conditionality, commercial sanctions, or peace-making measures) on the other, varies significantly in keeping with both geographical agenda and policy field.

Throughout this comparative impact evaluation, a twofold horizontal question emerges: which are the internal causes of success and failure? And what influence should be attributed to external variables, namely changes within the heterogeneous international system? The contributors offer tentative answers to these questions, each from their own disciplinary and thematic point of observation. We will in turn focus on the near abroad and the far abroad agendas, while distinguishing between the regional and global levels, as well as between civilian governance and political regulation.

Europe as an expanding regional polity? – challenges of the near abroad

More than twenty years after the end of the cold war, despite surprizing oscillations, serious failures, and still pending challenges to integration, the EC/EU is largely recognized as a stabilizing factor for peace, democracy and prosperity at a quasi-continental level. Enlargement, conditionality, the neighborhood policy, multilateral/bilateral association agreements and partnerships are the fundamental elements of this success story. The enlargement process cannot be considered merely as the most successful foreign policy, nevertheless it is indisputably in itself a significant and non-controversial contribution to global governance. It offers every continent an example of how to master both internal fragmentation and globalization at the regional level. This was in no way an easy challenge. The wars in the former Yugoslavia and in Georgia have sent warning signals of the risks that a return to the old phantoms of Europe's history would entail. However, in a long-term perspective, it is a matter of fact that Eastern enlargement, the "stability pact" and various partnership arrangements with Eastern neighbors (e.g., with Russia, Serbia, Ukraine and Turkey) have all been and still are crucial means in efficiently managing the potentially explosive consequences of the end of the bipolar order in Europe following the breakdown of the Soviet-led bloc in 1989–91. Peaceful reunification of the continent and the containment of border and minority conflicts have become the prevelant alternative to the potential chaos this massive changes could have wrought.

The famous Copenhagen Criteria of 1993 set the conditions for new memberships. These criteria brought about both a certain number of constitutional features associated with the Europeanization process affecting an applicant's internal economy and polity,[15] and a contribution to more stable continental governance. Furthermore, they represent a pro-active factor in the dissemination of the European notion of democracy, which includes the protection of human rights, the rule of law, the assimilation of the *acquis communautaire* (fundamental achievements of the Community) and a distinctive understanding of the public sphere. To what extent it will be efficient in the long run and for an even broader membership, despite shortcomings and open controversies, is one of the topics of this book.

There is no evidence that the enlargement policy from EU-15 to EU-27, and maybe up to thirty-five future member states (Western Balkans, Turkey and other potential members) on the one hand, and the European neighborhood policy started in 2002–04 on the other, have been two sides of a coherent strategic design. On the contrary, their vague features and schedules have provoked overlapping and reciprocal inconsistencies. This strategic deficit still matters and could matter in the future, as some examples have clearly shown. Several case studies, including the two very different examples of Kosovo and Turkey, have controversial records with regard to the efficiency of the prospect of enlargement as the main "carrot" or enticement functioning as the core lever favoring cooperation, conflict prevention and "Europeanization" of the applicants. In 2008, both the controversy surrounding Kosovo's independence and the troubled relationship with Turkey highlighted how complex the stabilization process still is. Stabilizing and developing these areas can take anywhere from five to over twenty years, depending on a host of internal and external variables. Furthermore, none of the sixteen partners is keen that ENP participation should become a permanent status. Obviously the EU cannot endlessly expand; however, there is evidence that the more the neighbors are removed from a prospective full membership, the less efficient EU policies of stabilization and democratization prove to be.

The ENP is facing first-class strategic stakes. On the one hand, when dealing with the Eastern side of the enlargement and neighborhood policies – namely with Ukraine and the Western Balkans – the EU is facing one of the major challenges of the twenty-first century: the role of Russia within the new global order. As a determining issue both within the transatlantic relations as well as for the EU's future political unity, the EU's stance on Russia will be pivotal. EU practice is twofold: first, pushing for a bilateral deal with Russia based on strategic partnership, deepening the respect of shared values and developing common interests, including the ones of energy customer and energy producer. Second, the EU is supporting an hypertrophic multilateral network of interlinked institutions framing and consolidating the stability area in Eastern Europe from north to south: the Stability Pact, the Arctic Council, the Barents Sea Euro-Arctic Council, the Council of Baltic States, the Black Sea Cooperation, and so on.

On the other hand, when dealing with Turkey and with the Mediterranean partnership, the challenges facing the EU are equally salient. Are the EU's member states able to remain united? Will they continue to stick to the wisely balanced double option of 2004 and 2005 for a multilateral partnership with the region and an "open-ended negotiation" with Turkey? And, is this twofold policy likely to succeed in Europeanizing the largest and poorest applicant countries (by supporting domestic modernization, democratization and a dialogue of civilization)? Furthermore, will these developments unfold without hampering the EU's development as a political actor within one of the world's most unstable regions? The Israeli–Palestine conflict and the political, economic and cultural relations with the Muslim world are central issues within the Mediterranean dialogue. Accordingly, they do carry considerable internal and international significance. All in all, facing both key challenges associated with the EU's near abroad requires the implementation of a high-profile European contribution. It needs to be a contribution not only within such politically relevant civilian policy fields as immigration and energy, but also with regard to two of the main strategic challenges of the twenty-first century's global order: the future relationship between the West and a new energy-powered Russia on the one hand, and rapport entertained by the West with the diverse components of the Muslim world.

Achievements and challenges of the EU's impact on regional and global governance

The political credibility of the EU's contribution to global governance within the international system is founded on the consolidation of the peaceful settlement of a region historically known for its extreme turbulence. Moreover, the EU's past policy successes, if further consolidated, not only in regional conflict prevention but also in framing new democratic polities within post-fascist and post-communist countries, would provide an additional source of international influence. This concept of a bottom-up contribution to global governance provided through good example is deeply rooted in European political thought, from Kant to Hegel, from Kojève to Duchêne. The growing realization that the EU is not a federal state-in-the-making – as hoped by some founding fathers – can paradoxically help the interaction with other regional entities. However, even if still necessary as solid background, this example-driven contribution of the EU to global governance looks inadequate when coping with a still asymmetrical world order: the "securitization" of the international agendas after 2001 (September 11) and 2002 (US New Security Strategy), and the shifts of global power towards the Pacific, following the emergence of new economic giants and a multipolar agenda.

Despite overarching dramatic changes within the global environment, the EU stands out as a remarkable source of peace. Through its sheer existence within the changing international system, the EU constitutes a factor of stability and exemplifies successful management of globalization, consolidation of democracies, and prevention of political conflicts. What makes the most significant difference is that the EU focuses the partner's attention away from the eternal truths of national sovereignty, and onto the changes affecting the conditions under which said sovereignity is exercised. This has clearly convinced a broad range of states not to surrender their aspirations under duress, but to pool their sovereignty, or at least to engage in and strengthen several forms of binding multilateral cooperation.

The most pressing question which has arisen since the end of the 1990s is to what extent such European regional models of cooperation offer innovative forms of actorness, and relevance in an economically, environmentally and politically changing world. Europe will undergo a demographic decline from 20 percent of the global population in 1900, to 11 percent in 2000 to 7 percent in 2025 and 4 percent by 2050.[16] Will the EU's present contribution be enough within the new context of the twenty-first century, or does it call for a new step forwards towards a more united political actor? In order to better summarize the input of this book, we break down the new challenges facing the EU into three sub-questions: Does the EU's experience offer a relevant model for regional governance elsewhere? Are the EU's policies relevant for international organizations and global governance mechanisms? Is the EU's emerging power pertinent to future evolutions of the interstate system?

A relevant model for regional governance?

The first sub-question already benefits from a large international and multidisciplinary comparative literature on regional cooperation. It has shown that in every continent there are diffused, internal and international factors, as well as endogenous and exogenous pressures, favoring a continent-wide dissemination and deepening and enlargement of regional groupings among neighboring states. Both emulation and competition matter. Calls for larger domestic markets emanating from the business community and calls from states striving to recover lost sovereignty will continue as such claimants hope to better compete with the EU as well as with other international entities, while facing the uncertainties associated with global trade negotiations and the unstable post-cold war world. All these factors foster regional cooperation worldwide. Regionalism is a structural and multidimensional feature of global governance, and thus international society has become increasingly regionalized. Research networks share the conviction that we will have more regional cooperation in the twenty-first century than in the twentieth.[17] One of the EU's contributions to global governance already consists of its directly and indirectly underpinning regional cooperation as a barrier to fragmentation and nationalism, by reducing the number of global players while promoting a bottom-up push towards better global governance. Such regionalization would notably entail a potential significant streamlining of global negotiations. Where this has already occurred, it has done so through spontaneous emulation of the EU by other regional groupings-in-the-making (rather than through the improbable export of an "EU model").

Regional cooperation abroad is evolving from the stage of fora to intergovernmental cooperation, to coordination of national policies towards enhanced and multi-dimensional convergence. The East Asians and the Latin Americans, the South Asians and the Africans are all clearly following their own paths to regional cooperation. However, even if as a *sui generis* experience, the EU is still a reference for them and not a counter-model of sorts. The EU offers the most advanced laboratory for institutionalized regional cooperation and integration to date. And if we take into account a broader concept of "institutionalization" (including not only organizations, with staff and postal address, but also single-issue regimes and arrangements), and go beyond Balassa's classical Eurocentric model,[18] then the comparative bridging with the current evolutions of various entities – such as ASEAN, MERCOSUR, the Andean Community, the African Union, ECOWAS and SADC – is much easier. Now, the EU appears much less isolated and exceptional than it used to be in the first decades after World War Two, and it is no longer perceived as a one-of-a-kind "case study."

Even if supranational law and strong institutions remain distinctive features of the European experience, other regional entities are evolving towards enhanced inter-governmental institutionalization. For example, we can point to the ASEAN Charter of 2007 (including democracy and human rights protection in its Articles 1.7 and 2.i, as well as provisions for sustainable development); the MERCOSUR parliament and regional fund; the creation of the larger Southern American political organization UNISUR in 2008; the various regional dispute settlement mechanisms; and the evolving agenda of the African Union, which has come to include a growing role in regional conflict prevention and security cooperation. All these trends, among others, clearly illustrate a diffused bottom-up politicization of regional cooperation, albeit by alternative ways and with varying levels of efficiency and respect for democratic standards.

Regional association of neighboring states do not necessarily imply democratic consolidation, even if the third wave of democratization has involved to a large extent those areas mentioned above, ranging from Latin America to South East Asia. In contrast to the EU's institutional set-up, which includes the provisions detailed in Articles 6 and 7 of the Treaty of European Union (see the chapter by

Magnette anad Nicolaïdis), other regional entities have so far stuck to the principle of non-interference in internal affairs. Although the highly sophisticated legal basis and the original combination of intergovernmental and supranational features remain unique to the EU, comparison between regional tendencies of increasingly binding cooperation are certainly possible.

As a global assessment, the record of regional entities is not a poor one. Notwithstanding the various degrees of institutionalization and democratic consolidation, regions have contributed both by fostering economic convergence and by framing policy cooperation as well as multicultural and multi-religious dialogue in times of supposed threat from "civilizational clashes" and ethnocentrism. The comparison between the EU and other regional entities makes more sense now than before the end of the cold war, since it is no longer like comparing a Ferrari formula-one car and a South East Asian *tuc-tuc* (tricycle).[19] Interaction with the EU has so far proven possible both at the economic and the political levels. The agendas of the EU's interregional relations with East Asia (ASEM), Latin America (the Rio Process) and Africa (ACP) include not only trade but also an increasingly rich and varied set of issues, such as: the fight against poverty; the need to improve access to water; sustainable development; fostering a knowledge society; new multilateralism; human rights; and broader political dialogue. Furthermore, even if loosely institutionalized, interregionalism (as a relationship between two regions belonging to different continents) is already intensifying mutual understanding at the cultural and political levels.

Through interregional bargaining and region-to-region cooperation, the EU should prove able to influence regionalism abroad in a more coherent and consistent way. The EU can thus strive to strengthen regional entities and their common positions against national fragmentation, while marginalizing protectionist "regional fortresses" tendencies. The EU could thus make several distinct contributions to global governance efforts. First, it could foster openness by underpinning global arrangements (along the Most Favored Nation clause included in the WTO's Article XXIV and beyond), instead of weakening them. Second, it could encourage regional groupings to converge on global challenges and underpin the necessary parallel reforms of the global framework. And finally, it could help to balance by means of a deep political dialogue both unipolar US tendencies and the multipolar Chinese and Russian agendas. Is this virtuous scenario idealistic? It depends upon, among other things, the further bottom-up politicization of several multidimensional regional entities within a pluri-regional world system.[20]

In conclusion, our first answer to the questioning above is a quite positive one indeed: at the global and regional levels, despite oscillations and new challenges, the EU is not only a relevant player in the ongoing efforts to underpin a multilevel type of multilateral governance but, if more coherent in its action, it may become a salient reference in the world in light of its successful internal features and strategies grounded in regional and interregional cooperation.

However, emphasizing the relevance of new regionalism does not imply supporting a mere regional solution to global challenges, or ignoring the millions of the world's citizens whose states are not part of regional associations of neighboring states.

Relevant policies for international application?

Whatever our forecast regarding the relevance of new regionalism, it is quite evident that the global governance and world order of the twenty-first century will not simply emerge out of a sum of regional entities, neither as far as security challenges are concerned nor as far as civilian issues are concerned. The regional entities are too varied, and still far from including all the major global players in a sufficiently binding way, to make overcoming and substituting the global level of regulation a plausible prospect. Several areas of the planet are still showing a negative record of bottom-up and multidimensional regional cooperation: e.g., the Middle East, the Maghreb, Central Asia, Central and Eastern Africa, and North East Asia. Focusing only on regionalism would make the EU hazardously reliant on other states' willingness. As well, it would increase the risk of a deficit of coherence emerging in global governance – something variously refered to as a "noodle bowl" effect or a new medieval scenario – because of the lack of any centripetal order, universal rule, shared procedures or common values at global level.

The huge and urgent issue at stake is that of combining multi-regionalism with a great reform process of the global institutions of governance, towards a kind of new Bretton Woods system and a revised UN system, which would produce a universal framework including all the major players. In this respect, the chapters in this book show clearly that the EU's role is very relevant, although laden with several astonishing paradoxes.

On the one hand, the EU is not only underpinning the traditional economic and political international organizations founded in the post-World War Two period, but it is also the main supporter of the new multilateral regime-building, started or revised after the end of the cold war and including the OSCE, WTO, ICC, Kyoto Protocol, multilateral environmental treaties and post-Kyoto process, UN global conferences from Monterrey to Johannesburg, and so on. More broadly speaking, the EU's support for international organizations includes the entire scope of their role and functions from cooperation/coordination (all the international organizations), to conflict management (UN, IMF, WTO), to political confrontation (UN Charter, chapter VII) in extreme cases. In several cases, as noted in the Louis chapter, EU achievements – namely, regional monetary stability – may work as both an example of and a driving force for global financial governance. Last but not least, the EU is acutely aware of the binding impact of stronger global institutions within the international state society and is relatively more favorably disposed towards a deeper dialogue with NGOs, transnational associations of citizens and representatives of public opinion and civil society. There is some evidence of a willingness by the EU to act as a counterweight to the declining US engagement with multilateral organizations, which explains the large literature on "cosmopolitan Europe" (see the chapter by Ferry).

On the other hand, the European states (rather than the EU as such) clearly share a large responsibility in the failure of the UN Security Council reform of 2005–06 and the shortcomings of the WTO Doha Development Round in 2006–08. Furthermore, the IMF micro-reform of 2008 cannot hide the still anachronistic asymmetrical representation of the IMF, where not only does the USA have a *de facto* veto power but, for example, Belgium's weight is heavier than that of India, and European countries with less than 10 percent of the world's population hold 60 percent of the voting rights. European states share huge responsibilities in the still poor results in the fight against poverty and underdevelopment. All in all, the European states have failed to address the legitimacy and efficiency gap within the present global network. According to many observers, contrary to its discourse, Europe's image is deteriorating because of its contradictory practices. At times, the EU appears as follows: similar to the USA, it operates through a kind of "hub and spokes" model rather than combining its particular regional interests with the universal ones in a more credible and acceptable fashion. Is the EU a relevant but particularist and egoistic player, acting in contradiction with global rules and its own universal values? Or is it, despite the oscillations of member states, a forerunner and even an early adopter agent of institutional innovation at the global level, striving towards enhanced efficiency and legitimacy?

The relevance of these legitimacy challenges is crystallized in the open criticism of public opinion and Third World countries, namely the clear emergence of the politics of protest against asymmetrical, non-transparent and unfair multilateral regulation. In some instances, as with the G8, informal global governance arrangements only express the overwhelming power of a few major states, which in this case includes four European states. In some situations, imbalances in the favor of Western countries are unacceptable according to our own values. Paradoxically, within the Triad (US, Europe, Japan), the EU has shown a potentially better understanding of the so-called "global governance dilemma", whereby the more global regulation is needed and implemented, the more demands are necessarily going to rise from the bottom up for democratic legitimacy and accountability of decision-makers. However, this particular EU realization still seems unable to overcome member states' resistances in the face of urgent necessary reforms within global governance.

The opinions on such contradictions and inconsistent actions vary a great deal. For instance, in the case of trade: on the one hand, the EU's multilateral and structural policies represent a reference, an anchor of stability and an objective contribution against global fragmentation, while balancing unipolarism and hard multipolarism. On the other hand, the fifty-year process leading from common market to single market has not only caused global trade deviation but established rules which have no equivalence at the global level. This cannot but provoke problems for universal global governance in trade matters. Inevitably frictions arise from these new rules, standards, regulations and procedures which are not always complementary with – or even related to – inexistent global rules. Consequently, the actions of the EU sometimes appear inconsistent with its asserted multilateralism. Whatever the intention and the discourse, the EU appears to J. Bagwati and other free-trade supporters as one of the main driving forces of a fragmented "noodle bowl" sort of global governance in trade.

Both schools of thought entail something true: the EU is a multilateral regime and a multi-dimensional actor, more credible than any other as development policy and environmental policy is concerned. However, it is hard for third states to distinguish the EU from the practices of its strongest member states. Furthermore, several

EC/EU policies – such as the common agriculture policy (CAP), staunchly defended by some member states – lead to controversial and unintended consequences.

Our provisional conclusion on the second question above is that the EU at the present level of integration is still an ambiguous actor and not yet consistent enough in supporting a more efficient and legitimate multilateral governance at the global level. This is, to a large extent, quite understandable, given the internal and external weight of the Westphalian logic. However, we will verify whether the evolving political will by major member states in favor of allowing an enhanced internal – vertical and horizontal – political coherence within the EU could eventually improve the current controversial state of affairs.[21] That would make the interplay with major politics issues unavoidable.

A pertinent power for future interstate systems?

Here we broach the third challenge: the EU's political impact on the alternative, competing, world orders.

The concept of global governance is challenged by the high international political stakes emerging within a still asymmetrical and heterogeneous system of world politics. The challenge is how to better grasp the post-cold war global system, notably by explaining the crisis of the multilateral network itself, which has previously been quite successful for decades. Furthermore, a historically important legacy, the multilateral system created after World War Two, is being tested both by the contemporary efficiency deficits and legitimacy gaps, as well as by an increasingly uneven and multifaceted process of globalization.

This international political uncertainty currently interplays with a multitude of civilian and economic agendas. First, the diffused "globalization malaise"[22], growing up to an international financial crisis in 2008, is interplaying with new national priorities and protectionist policies which might make shifts within geopolitical conflicts easier to occur. There is no guarantee at all that, in a foreseeable future, a more stable and just global governance will frame the current level of globalization, as far as its economic, trade, financial, direct foreign investment, cultural and environmental dimensions are concerned. On the contrary, the international crisis, which is more significant than it was in the 1990s, is strengthening demands for inward-looking defensive policies in Europe, the USA and Japan. Within many of the EU's member states, the influence of lobbyists and socio-political pushes supporting national barriers and/or "fortress Europe" approaches to global governance is increasing, both in scope and in intensity. Indians and the Chinese are asserting that the West does not welcome Asia's progress, and denounce an emerging Western protectionism.

Second, after 2001–02 the influence of the security agenda on civilian agendas spread and engendered uncertainties and new international hierarchies. The dominant global security agenda interfered with many regional civilian agendas. Moreover, the tendency towards peaceful, decentralized multilateral and multilevel global governance has come to face quite salient alternative tendencies currently shaping the heterogeneous and asymmetrical world system in opposite directions, wherein interconnectedness does not mean enhanced cooperation.

All in all, it is hard to imagine better global governance for the twenty-first century without coping with the challenges of building a stable world order. A better political order demands the territorial dimension to be taken into account. Even if neglected for decades by functionalist and neo-medievalist analysis of the eroding state, the territorial dimension still matters, both at the national and regional levels. Territorial demands to be framed and represented are still important. Additionally, notwithstanding overlapping jurisdictions and supranational agencies of regulation, hierarchies still matter within the current redistribution of political and economic world power, the centre of which is shifting globally towards the Pacific. And furthermore, a series of traditional and new security challenges, including informal terrorist networks, are at the centre of the international agenda. In contrast to its situation within and worldview shaped by the bipolar world, the EC/EU can no longer feel safe with its status of security consumer provided for by the US hegemony and its protective shield. The EU is for the first time facing a regional and global security agenda, even if within its own distinctive approach.

The current heterogeneous and asymmetric international system makes several alternative scenarios theoretically possible. First, great powers and mainstream media are asserting that against any attempt to strengthen international regulation and order, failing states, fragmentation of international power hierarchies and informal terrorism could prevail both at regional and global levels during the next decade. Second, even though the unilateral momentum between 2001 and 2005–06 clearly failed in its own objectives of regime change and democratic expansion through preventive strikes, unipolarity is far from disappearing. On the contrary, the hard power hierarchies after the break-up of the USSR and the long-term military, technological and – to a lesser extent – economic supremacy of the USA are increasingly unbalanced. Third, the shifts of global power provoked by the emergence of new actors, namely China and the other BRICs, in conjuncture with diffuse tendencies towards renationalization, trade protectionism and hard economic competitiveness, could also stop any of the EU's and other actors' attempts at improving multilateral regulation. The EU faces difficult dilemmas: it cannot succeed by asserting its interests and values within a vacuum. And it is not fit to accommodate to either a unipolar or a multipolar world: any long-term revival of Westphalian logic would be fatal to any emerging civilian power.

From global governance to world politics: EU leadership and power

Under which conditions could the EU mature from a pre-political and somewhat patchily formed actor of multilevel global governance towards a co-leadership role within a multilateral regional and global system, strong enough to frame the post-cold war world disorder? What are the main variables? This virtuous scenario, rooted in important existing multilateral tendencies, is a territory not yet clearly defined. It first depends on the readiness of states, including greater states, to cooperate in a more binding way, even in the absence of traditional hegemonic power clearly underpinning, financing and fostering cooperation. This volume's hypothesis is that it also relies to a certain extent upon the EU, its credibility, strategy and capacities.

The contributors to this volume agree that the EU cannot afford to retreat from the world, and that it cannot limit its responsibilities and role to a merely pre-political kind of regional governance. However, while a just and legitimate world government remains a more or less utopian perspective, this book is characterized by situating the EU international actorship within the real context of the vast evolving network of regional, national and global institutions, transnational agencies and actors, which are currently dealing with the complex regulation of the common affairs of humanity. An enhanced role for the EU in global governance and a new multilateralism will be analysed as two sides of the same coin. What about their interaction with the global power system? What about the EU's and the global institutions' current and potential impact on the many forms of the Westphalian interstate system?

Regarding the evolution of the interstate cooperation system itself, the existing multilateral governance institutions already demonstrate very diverse degrees of delegation of power and functions, including rule-setting at various levels of institutionalization – from simple, informal arrangements to international single-issue regimes (with common rules and procedures), up to reformed or newly established regimes and organizations. The legitimacy of the decision-making process, and the participation of citizens and stakeholders vary as well, according to the different institution and policy field.

While a degree of consensus exists that the colonial and imperial past prevents the EU from imperialist or hegemonic approaches, it is, however, not yet clear enough whether this rejection of classical power politics models implies a distinctive vision of international relations – not only a new global governance, but also a new multilateral order. What needs to be understood is the kind of evolution that is both desirable and possible beyond the two traditional forms of multilateral cooperation that have for several decades been framed by and dependent upon multipolarity or unipolarity, respectively under UK and US hegemony. To what extent and how is the EU able to actively contribute to redesign the whole world politics architecture by deepening its post-hegemonic approach? This is the core question.

Leadership varies very much, first of all according to its level. Regional leadership is the first step; the second is linkage with one's near abroad; the third involves interregional arrangements with one's far abroad; and finally comes the global leadership. Is the EU already a regional leader? The answer is positive if the EU is compared with other regional entities such as ASEAN and MERCOSUR, or historically with the EC during the cold war (a mainly economic organization limited to Western Europe). Even MERCOSUR and ASEAN are about to grow up as agenda-setting and catalyzing organizations for their respective regions. As seen above, the EU benefits from a network of pan-European complementary organizations, such as the Council of Europe or the OSCE. One must mention the EU's role as an economic leader and stability-provider in Eastern Europe (Caucasus, Ukraine), the Western Balkans (Macedonia and Kosovo) and the Mediterranean macroregion, in spite of the serious problems the EU has had to face when addressing these regions. Second, this book underlines the EU's role as noteworthy interregional actor, even with various records of success and external perceptions. Third, the EU is already recognized as a global player by overseas partners as well as by international organizations (as an observer or even as a participant), while not always as a leader willing to address global issues.

At times the answer to the question of whether the EU is a leadership provider remains no, or at least not yet. This is certainly the case when considering either the major security providers or the prevailing controversial security issues of the day, i.e. the Israeli–Palestinian conflict, Afghanistan, the Korean peninsula. Furthermore, the EU still seems unable to foster meaningful changes in behavior by the great powers. Among key civilian issues one might, for instance, consider the EU's limited impact on the USA's and China's exchange or their environment policies, or on Iran's nuclear policy. All in all, the EU's "structural foreign policy," involving the limiting of anarchy through cooperation and fostering favorable changes by the partner's environment, faces increasing difficulties when dealing with fragmentation, reconstruction of failing states, assertive renationalization of strong states, and the proliferation of weapons of mass destruction. This poses the question of whether it is even possible to distinguish the EU's destiny as a global co-leader from the future health of the multilateral network of peaceful cooperation.

Regarding the evolving nature, strength and limits of global leadership, one must obviously look at the benchmark provided by the USA, the sole established and comprehensive leader at global level.[23] The USA is, in the eyes of a majority of global actors, a legitimate world leader not only because of its economic and military supremacy, but also thanks to the combined historical legacy born from the successive conclusion of the cold war (1989–91), the victories at the end of both world wars, and the two centuries of Anglo-Saxon hegemony (since Waterloo, in 1815). The nature of leadership needs long-term efficiency and legitimacy, combining hard and soft power, and balancing oscillations in popularity and mistrust. However, the USA is challenged by the changes occurring in the twenty-first century, calling for smart power: an ability to accommodate new trends and effectively include more actors and demands.

According to some of the literature, US leadership is still strong enough to underpin unipolar predictions. There is no doubt that, for several decades, only the USA will dispose of a unique combination of soft and hard power – notably the power to move troops in a few days anywhere on the planet. That is precisely why many governments again commit themselves to the USA as the sole supplier of military security. US leadership goes beyond an "empire of military bases" of sorts dotted across every continent, which is nevertheless a unique feature in the world's history.

However, before the election of Obama, a large literature has provided evidence of the limits of US leadership, stressing internal and external causes moving the USA away from its past multilateralism and changing the existing mix of force and consent.[24]

- A mainly military leadership within the framework of the New Security Strategy (2002) not only provoked the worst crisis in transatlantic relations since 1945,[25] but has also proven its limits in terms of efficiency and capacity in achieving its aims and objectives (as shown by the results of the second Iraq War).
- The said shift towards hard power occurred just as external domination and arrogance were being less and less welcomed not only within advanced European

democracies, but also by many nations in Latin America, Asia and Africa, among which several American allies.

- Domestic politics within the national core (the USA) has clearly confirmed the decreasing support in the electorate for the costs associated with global military leadership.
- Alternative agendas are emerging within an instable and asymmetrical global system (competitors for a multipolar world).
- The influence continues of both old and new multilateral networks which remain essentially non-hierarchical and increasingly institutionalized.
- Legitimacy issues are emerging as a central issue of multilateral cooperation.

A concept of power which is increasingly military, material, based on coercion, and without bargaining, shared rules, procedures and institutions is no longer acceptable in the eyes of the global and national community. Even the most ground-breaking changes within the American political system and its presidential administration will hardly change the diffused perception of disappointment and missed opportunity increasingly associated with the "new liberal world order" promised after 1989–91.

All in all, talk surrounding the relative decline of US leadership compared with the post-World War Two era is legitimate, not only because of the end of the Bretton Woods monetary system in 1971, but because of the negative performances of the American project for regime change (towards democratization) and banning terrorism, launched in the early twenty-first century. The dramatic failures of the successive plans for a US-centred world order and the shortcomings afflicting the implementation of their own anti-terrorist agenda have dramatically confirmed the US's relative decline during the first decade of the new century. And this in spite of the breakdown of its main competitor, the USSR. Furthermore, multilevel multilateral cooperation has gone on even without the US as a main driving force.

Accepting the thesis of a long-term US decline does not mean at all that a comparable rival EU leadership is about to emerge, at least in the largely accepted theoretical understanding of "hegemony" as a distinctive combination of cultural influence and domination, of hard and soft power. A twofold and mutually counteracting international literature has followed the transatlantic rift of 2002–08: the first literature has focused on the EU's lack of power and leadership ("Europe as Venus" versus "the USA as Mars"); the second, on the emerging "EU military superpower" or "cosmopolitan empire" within global governance. Contrary to these opposite perceptions, the EU is about dealing with the challenge of providing its own comprehensive global security concept beyond the limits of the European continent: facing climate change, terrorism, financial imbalances and the fight against poverty. The concept and practice of comprehensive security favored by the EU is only a part of an emerging political culture which coexists and interplays with a still mainly Hobbesian or Westphalian world.

The USA's experience since 1944 demonstrates that values are essential in underpinning a new European contribution to global leadership. On the one hand, there is a legacy of transatlantic consensus around the shared values of democracy and the market economy; on the other hand, relevant long-term differences exist between the two main Western allies – i.e., regarding the understanding of law, including international law and the death penalty; the notion of internal and international regulation; the need to combine economic competitiveness with the welfare state (and welfare budget) and its effects on the defense budget; as well as the overarching vision of global governance and international relations. The challenge arising from the emergence of new Asian giants is also becoming one of the crucial and most controversial issues for Western actors.

The Western developed world currently shares the main responsibility for the international economic crisis (and related protectionist demands) and worries about its poor performances in Afghanistan, Iran, and in the fight against terrorism, which have all been so many ambiguous signals in the direction of leading Asian actors. The shift of the planet's centre of gravity from the Atlantic to the Pacific, and the burgeoning "Eastern century," are seen to be heralded in the rapidly increasing weight and role of China, India and the economies of the Pacific rim, which combine the free market with a new multipolar agenda. Such shifts bring with them the risk of marginalization for a demographically declining and politically dwarfed Europe.[26] However, contrary to US perceptions of the threat of an emerging Chinese military power, what needs to be stressed according to the EU is the ever-growing need to multilaterally frame the Asia-Pacific hemisphere and its economic and political implications for the global order.

The EU's regional interests and multilateral approach are not to be confused with any traditional or new multipolar world vision of a Westphalian kind. The EU takes for granted that it will never become a classical militarized and nuclear kind of power such as the USA, Russia or China (and maybe Iran as well, or even other middle-range states). If building a multipolar world means reviving in new forms the old system of balance of power, there is evidence that such an asymmetric power politics scenario could only exacerbate the division and marginalization of Europe.

Only a scenario of real progress in multilateral and multilevel global governance is compatible with the emergence of the EU as a regional and global leader, or more exactly as a co-leader. The EU is essentially interested in multilateralizing the multipolar tendencies, by including new and old powers within institutionalized cooperation networks. This fourth scenario has to prove effective in the face of both the main thrusts of an interlinked comprehensive security agenda – addressing the new threats such as environment, climate change, the fight against poverty facing the "bottom billion,"[27] economic crisis, energy shortages, financial imbalances and terrorism, as well as the security challenges and threats to peace, in the Middle East and other flashpoint areas of the planet.

Several chapters of this volume show that the EU is able to assert this multilateral agenda only when it acts, speaks and leads with one voice as a transformative power. In this manner, it can hope to combine new understandings of European and non-European interests, particularism and universalism. This understated meaning of leadership cannot be confused with the phantom of a European world hegemony (including hard and soft power), which is but a dream of a few nostalgics harking back to the age of empires and is far more commonly seen as a nightmare by many

Europeans and non-Europeans alike. There is no substance behind any comparison with whatever empire of the past, be it Roman, British or Dutch. The question is what room is left in the twenty-first century for an even understated but co-leading role for Europe – one that is in line with its values, history and responsibilities. Furthermore, this implies a follow-up question: under what conditions could a demographically declining unique regional entity such as Europe say and implement something significant, legitimate and competent with regard to the multilateral world? The EU would thus act not only by defending the interests of its near 500 million citizens, but also the interests of its 500 million neighbors and even the 6.5 billion inhabitants of the planet.

To become a full co-leading actor, the EU has to further develop its current role as an incipient power of an unprecedented kind. This book details how the EU has already become more than a mere intergovernmental regime or a unique regional entity. It is irrefutably a global player, in several policy fields, and even the first or second global actor in some. The emerging European power is neither the one of an intrinsically hierarchical empire, nor that of a world-running superpower or an emerging hegemonic power.[28] When looking at the next decades, the EU could ultimately only evolve as a form of shared leadership that is a part of a collective multilateral leadership system. In other words, it can only be conceived of as a *collective* power. By this we mean a power acting both on behalf of a multilateral entity as well as globally, so as to strengthen multilateral cooperation, coordination and communication at the regional and global levels.

The communicable dimension of the EU's emerging power depends upon two factors. First, the EU's internal experience of routinized, informal, intergovernmental and transgovernmental gradual convergence within the Brussels-based decision-making and expert community (including national and Commission high-level civil servants, MPs, academics, judges, police investigators and financial regulators – thus a series of actors far beyond those involved in traditional diplomatic relations) is already deepening internal multilateralism. Second, although uneven across policy fields, the EU's internal achievements represent an interesting experiment in the development of government networks[29] and similar epistemic communities at the global, interregional and regional levels. Inner and outer dimensions are thus deeply connected. The Union's internal achievements in conflict prevention, democratic consolidation and fostering prosperity are the foundations of its external credibility as a collective power. And the common external action is a typical feature of a federal kind, offering a positive feedback effect with regard to internal integration.

What will be particularly challenging for the EU during the coming decades is successfully combining, in a distinctive and dynamic way the two levels of its own international and transnational development: its current non-state features, particularly fit for the multiple global civilian agendas (decentralized multilevel governance, transnational social networks, quasi-governmental, civil society approach, etc.) and a new ability to adapt to the rise of other powers within a still state-centred system. While coping with the unstable international context and in the face of hard international crises, the EU is simply not – and will never be – able to act alone, either politically nor militarily, as a superpower.

The public debate about the so-called *Europe puissance* (Europe military power) came back, in an ephemeral way, during the Constitutional momentum of 2002–05. Yet, the EU lacks the will, is for ever deprived of the *jus ad bellum*, and has neither the capacities nor the centralized decision-making system required when going to war which is typically found in classical and newly sovereign states. Whatever hierarchical and asymmetrical elements the international behavior of the EU will contain, and even if its actions imply a limited use of coercion and force – i.e., conditionality, peace-keeping and peace-enforcing missions – these will always be deployed in accordance with the restrictive Treaty provisions, symbolized by the Petersberg Tasks (Treaty of Amsterdam, 1997). Moreover, the structural opposition of national public opinions to any increase of defense budgets will further limit any military ambition even remotely comparable with that of the USA.[30] EU leadership will vary according to different policy fields and external contexts. The choice of the EU and its member states will either be to downgrade their international profile or, when speaking with one voice and acting united, to coherently assert common values and interests within the evolving multilateral regimes, as a leading policy-actor, capable of coalescing its interests and values with those of others.

These internal and external features seriously limit the similarities between the EU's soft power and that of the USA. American soft power is part of a broader political identity and structure wherein soft and hard power are profoundly combined, even if in different ways according to the varying Administration priorities. New concepts are needed to understand the strange form of EU leadership and power which is based on shared values, norm-setting and regime-building orientations, a distinctive social model with consolidated influence, the weight of shared memories, structural power and a deficit of military power, a decentralized decision-making system, and a structural foreign policy. This book highlights for instance that the concepts of "normative power," "quiet power" and "*civilian power*" have all been suggested by the international literature.[31] To what extent do these concepts cope with the internal features and the evolving external environment?

The concept of *normative power* plays an important role in the international debate surrounding the distinctive identity of the EU and its perception by others.[32] However, in order to overcome its idealistic and Eurocentric understandings, this book has chosen to focus on more comprehensive concepts. These broader concepts strive to combine the Union's norm-setting function with both the material, social and institutional backgrounds of the EU's external influence and structural foreign policy. The limits and paradoxes of its international action (mentioned above) are also addressed. The notion of a *civilian power* – contrary to the notions referring to a civilizing or normative power – appears best suited to comprehensively include all crucial variables: the interplay between EU and the various national foreign policies; the constraints on external assertiveness, imposed by internal policies, among which socio-economic cohesion; the memory of past tragedies and defeats; the effective external economic and technological impact; the limits of disposable military capacities; the evolving but highly decentralized institutional framework; the limited concentration of decision-making in foreign policy; or the difficult trade-offs between the open-ended enlargement process and the neighborhood policy.[33]

There is no internal constituency for the EU to emerge as a *normal power* with a military capacity comparable to that of the USA. That is why no single national political leader, whether right wing or left wing, is looking to be elected on a rearmament platform. In one word, the definition of civilian power stresses that the EU is at once more and less than a classical power. The EU is indeed an understated power by default (given the possibility of amassing a classical power through a federal state with appropriated military capabilities) and a provocation for the traditional realist understanding of international relations which linked international power to a hierarchy of capabilities wherein military force maintained a clear primacy.

The EU as a civilian power, just as any other civilian power, could consolidate only within a favorable external context. This context is one where a multilevel multilateralism is not only accepted as a method of governance among others, but increasingly appropriate as a binding framework for major actors in world politics, linking what James Rosenau defines as the two sides of the international system after the cold war: the decentralized system of soft governance and the centralized system of security politics. Or in other words, the liberal world called for throughout the 1990s, and the world beset by security challenges that emerged at the onset of the new century.

The post-hegemonic multilateral network is at a crossroads: either it will further decline as its legitimacy and efficiency deteriorate, or it will go beyond a mere form of global governance and become a leading principle for a new world order. The EU would be weakened and divided by a defensive League of Western democracies oriented towards a new cold war against Russia and China, and equally by a Wesphalian multipolar agenda. Yet according to many observers and in line with past behaviors and achievements, at least a hard core of the EU's member states might be interested in playing a driving role within a collective form of global leadership: in contrast to the unipolar and multipolar scenarios, the great powers, despite differences, would not grow apart, but increasingly cooperate within a reformed institutional multilevel framework. We have come to call this virtuous scenario a *new multilateralism*.[34]

A new multilateralism?

Could multilateralism be conceived of not only as either an instrument or a descriptive analytical tool, but also as an organizing principle of global governance and world order? A multilateral world order never existed in the past and still does not exist. Multilateralism used to be part either of a multipolar UK-led world (until World War One and 1931, the end of the gold standard based on the pound) or a bipolar US-led West (after 1944). The G7 is no longer able to lead the global multilateral network, and the US looks unable to provide the G7 with a consistent and legitimate agenda. A genuine risk exists that multilateralism might become nothing more than a poor second-best option for a would-be unipolar international system or merely be developed along the lines of the instrumental and conservative practices typical of some Asean understanding. The current ambiguity of the concept of multilateralism is confirmed by the huge differences behind the large façade consensus: in the USA, the concept increasingly means an *ad hoc* multilateralism, or one that is *à la carte* in accordance with an openly instrumental understanding. China's recently increased commitment to multilateral cooperation has meant, on the one hand, a conservative approach to the UN Security Council reform process; and on the other, a variety of China-led regional cooperation initiatives in East and Central Asia. In both cases, the challenge for the EU is that these important but quite limited Chinese practices are, both in their scope and their ability to bind the behavior of member states, more akin to American multilateral practices than to those associated with the EU.

What kind of new multilateralism is politically strong and practical enough to successfully frame and limit unipolar and multipolar tendencies? The EU's current practices and dynamics suggest that new multilateralism, which would include both governance and government of world affairs, is to be fostered through a deepening of the current experiences of "diffuse reciprocity" thus allowing for an increased mutual trust among member states. This is essential since, besides the generalized principle of conduct, efficiency and legitimacy can hardly be improved without increasingly sharing national sovereignty,[35] or at least without relevant progress along the concept of "embedded and binding multilateralism" capable of including new issues and influencing the behavior of states.[36]

Given its current achievements and shortcomings, the EU still has a lot to do if it truly wants to play a specific and leading role as one of the main actors underpinning a stronger and deeper rule-based form of multilateral governance within a global multilateral order.

1   In order to limit the efficiency gap, more and better institutionalized interstate cooperation is needed. Enlarging its scope to new issues, through regime-building and organizational settings, even without the driving force of a hegemonic power, is a necessity. With the goal of increasing the outcome legitimacy by providing citizens with true benefits, that which is at stake is to set a reformed network of international organizations that is more *efficient and effective*. For that purpose, it could also look at some of the EU's internal modes of governance for inspiration with regard to the reform of global institutions.[37] Beyond the discourse on effective multilateralism and contrary to the inconsistent practices of member states (i.e., defending privileged positions and over-representation within the IMF and UN), the EU is expected to lead the reform process of the global network and make it strong enough to face both emergencies and structural problems of global governance. Among such challenges, managing the economic crisis: fighting environmental degradation while fostering sustainable development; addressing poverty in the Third World, epidemic diseases, politically corrupted governance; and building up new financial architectures while regulating global competition and the privatization of economic governance (and the emergence of state-controlled Sovereign Wealth Funds). Moreover, what is needed is to improve the coordination among global agencies, since the EU is more likely to understand the link between several agendas (trade and non-trade concerns like labor rights, environment, growth and human rights) and may export several modes of governance which have proven effective

in establishing more constraining rules and monitoring procedures at the regional level.

Furthermore, only a deeper new multilateral form of interaction with recipients and partners is likely to help Europe accommodate to change. Diminishing contradictions and bridging conflicting expectations between actors born from the impact of hierarchies and asymmetries will require renewed communication. The necessary tools to enable post-hegemonic multilateral regimes to work successfully are not only intercultural dialogue about values, but also communication about diverse paths to internal social reforms and innovations. Within the current multicultural world, the new role set out for Europe will fail if it is perceived as a new form of Eurocentrism.[38]

2   The global dimension needs a stronger regional dimension. An enhanced economic and political role for regional associations within a multilevel global regulation system should encompass both economic and political issues and would positively influence UN reform. This evolution should include the transformation of an empirically identifiable regional security *complex* into conscious and institutionalized regional security *communities*. This would call for confidence-building measures and binding of the regimes of former enemies (as between Germany and France; Brazil and Argentina; or even Vietnam and its former regional foes). Regional peaceful conflict-settlement is at stake, even if not yet seriously pursued in Africa, East Asia, South Asia, or the Middle East.

3   Legitimacy is the new frontier of multilateralism in the twenty-first century. This third challenge, the call for a less contingent legitimacy of multilateral governance and government, can only be answered by filling five main criteria: national and supranational accountability of decision-makers; support by the epistemic community; inclusiveness and openness to new members and partnerships; a certain degree of comparability between national democracy (the national and global levels are radically different, but not as radically as two distant planets); an acceptance of some minimum in terms of shared values, namely regarding the protection of human rights (according to the "responsibility to protect" asserted and thus created by the UN in 2005, rather than to the previous optional right to humanitarian intervention).[39]

In this framework, the EU is expected to further implement its distinctive twin role as both the most legitimate international organization, and as an international and internal democratizer. The EU is perceived by external and internal actors to be more credible and legitimate than others when it comes to framing the increasing need for humanitarian interventions in a multilaterally acceptable way. International organizations, often in cooperation with regional ones, are increasingly called to ensure that the responsibility to protect universal values, first and foremost among which human rights, is legitimately carried out following the collection of evidence of the egregious infringements. Including the responsibility to support democratization and the protection of human rights within a new multilateral approach and through multiple conditionalities and actions implies enhancing the level of legitimacy of the global network itself, beyond mere "outcome legitimacy", provided that it works without double standards.

However, two caveats have to be mentioned: first, colonial legacies, diffused external perception of the EU as a protectionist economic fortress, the negative impact of agricultural policy as well as trade policy, and a lack of credible capacities are still limiting the emergence of an enhanced role for the EU. Second, the general process of erosion of national sovereignty is perceived in extremely different ways in view of the varying history and position of each nation. Not only "rogue states" but also weak states have come to perceive sovereignty as a necessary protection. Both the current American unipolarity, as well as the asymmetrical distribution of power (within the global institutions) in favor of the West (which includes Europe) remain major sources of misunderstandings and opposition.

In other words, the question who speaks and acts on behalf of the international community needs to be answered in a credible fashion. When asserting the human rights revolution, the legitimacy of protecting them and the limits to national sovereignty are crucial variables. Europe will fail if it seeks to Europeanize the world in an assertive manner. It must rather learn to better interplay with the non-European world, where the process of limiting national sovereignty is following distinctive alternate paths. Inevitably, new multilateralism will come to affect the entire globe and world politics, or it will fail. But, contrary to assertive and Eurocentric visions, this confirms above all the emergence of the EU into co-leadership, which consequently cannot simply expect others to copy its own past patterns. What will matter is the shared – or missed – perception that limiting national sovereignty within common institutions is a sign of strength and not of weakness.

To what extent is a new multilateral leadership likely to succeed within the next decades? Is it no more than a European utopia, or a contradiction in terms? Of course, what looks likely to occur in the best scenario for the twenty-first century, provided that the EU is able to increase its influence and external impact, is not a post-Westphalian and post-modern world. Rather, it involves a process of deepening and accelerating what has already occurred since World War Two, and more clearly after 1989–91: a gradual revision and transformation of the modern interstate Westphalian system beyond the current heterogeneous and asymmetrical post-cold war transition, towards a more institutionalized, multilevel, pluri-regional, multidimensional, legitimate and rule-based cooperation. Such a system would to a certain extent include a responsibility to protect human rights, provided that the multilateral community underpinned and legitimated it.

Controversy remains regarding the legitimacy and efficiency, as well as the limits, of such controversial interventions. This will have broad implications for both the UN as well as the transatlantic partnership. Where should the line be drawn between the exclusive jurisdiction of the states and the responsibility of the international community for protecting human rights and ensuring the various aspects of comprehensive security? The EU multilateral background and values make it a more credible leading actor in drawing a positive-sum game, balancing the right of individual states and the rights of the collective community of states, by mutually sustaining and pooling their sovereignty, rather than transcending it by new international hierarchies. It is expected to play the role of mediator between the mere defense of the *status quo* and a counterproductive arrogance towards the weak states which provokes demands of stronger sovereignty against Western intrusiveness and double standards.

How will Europe be able to strike a successful and legitimate response in the light of such a historical *rendezvous* with the world, the third one in its history after the time of Ancient Rome and the epoch of modern empires? Europe could fail. Its impact will depend upon both external (already analyzed) and internal variables. Let us focus on the internal variables, since they are crucial in testing whether member states and the EU really want to enhance the coherence and consistency of the European foreign policy complex's external action by combining their more credible international leadership with an enhanced ability to engage and cooperate with minor and major powers, including the USA and emerging actors.

Three internal variables

Having in due course come to the subject of the impact of internal variables on the EU's international actorness and power-in-the-making, we need to address three main factors. First, as clearly shown in the four chapters of the first part of this volume, only the consolidation of the past achievements of the EU's internal multilateral cooperation is and will increasingly be the main background to the EU's external actions; a credit card of sorts, offering the EU bottom-up resources for a new, broader and global multilateralism to emerge. This means that the domestic modernization agenda, the euro, the single market, the multi-tier democratic polity, and the coordination of internal policies, are all essential resources. The second priority is that positive trade-offs born from the enlargement process have to be reassessed. The neighborhood policies are particularly at stake as a middle way between enlargement and foreign policy: they should be neutral on the question of future membership of participants, and more efficient with regard to stable settlements of multidimensional relations with the extremely complex reality of the Union's near abroad.

Third, research has extensively monitored the EU's evolving internal capacities and draws attention to four main points, mentioned in the second part of this volume. The first point refers to material resources, which matter very much when defining the nature and credibility of the EU's power: even if the EU budget will never be comparable with the central budget of a federal state (1 percent of EU states GDP versus 20 percent of US GDP). It must be reoriented, and the CAP's share reassessed, allowing it to be reformed according to internal and international strategic priorities.[40] Furthermore, coordinating and rationalizing national budgetary funding programs, such as in the fields of research and defense, appear to be preconditions for the current expectations–capability gap of the CFSP to be diminished in a realistic manner. Without forgetting the structural limits of the EU's military, which would ultimately only foster inappropriate expectations, it is the Agency for Armaments, the liberalization of the internal arms market, the development of special reaction forces, civilian and military, even at variable geometry (with a changing membership), that may make the EU's role in its near and far abroad more credible without fundamentally changing the nature of the EU's power. The examples of Afghanistan, Kosovo and the Middle East clearly illustrate that new and old threats call the EU to a minimum degree of "security production" in order to be taken seriously by China, the USA, India, the Arab world and so on. In line with the EU's experience, this could be further achieved by regime- and institution-building, notably by binding cooperation, without provoking new security dilemmas for the EU's neighbors.

A second and essential internal capacity is the progress towards a more efficient and legitimate legal basis through a successful Treaty revision. The EU's institutional system expanded over sixty years in response to internal and external challenges. Rather than a stable system, it is still under continuous negotiation, depending on emotional factors and internal diversities. Even if this unique decentralized polity makes classical power politics, statehood and a strong political identity impossible, this book has proven that many policies are working well, including efficient external policies. However, regarding the gradual reform process of the institutional provisions, there is a need for the EU polity to evolve towards enhanced horizontal and vertical cohesion, and more consistency in its external relations, beyond the three-pillar structure set up by the Maastricht Treaty. Foreign policy analysis confirms that three coherences are at stake: first, the coherence between asserted values and practice; second, the coherence between the EU and its member states (taking in loyalty, solidarity in case of aggression, and unity within international organization), although the current two-level polity (EU government and national policy-making) will not change fundamentally for the foreseeable future; third, the horizontal coherence between policies (and Maastricht Treaty pillars), which needs to be strengthened through several institutional changes linking the two centres of external action, the Commission and the Council. However, the EU is unlikely to ever reach the degree of coherence of a state, nor a federal state, because its polity is decentralized and the responsibility for monitoring consistency and coherence will remain shared between several authorities.[41]

The EU's policy coherence cannot reach that displayed by its "communitarized" trade or monetary policy. The limits of inter-pillar coherence, the still emerging Justice and Home Affairs cooperation – notwithstanding the progress achieved after the Amsterdam Treaty – and the imperfect loyalty of bigger member states to the CFSP within the global arena are so many brakes on the EU's chances at international leadership. However, by continuing the step-by-step long-term process of implicit Treaty constitutionalization, despite the numerous problems associated with Treaty revisions, the resulting balance could gradually bring the EU closer to a more integrated and credible international power of a new kind. In spite of growing challenges and oscillations, there is evidence that the EU's role within global governance (financial crisis, environment policy, foreign policy) can play as a driving force for further internal convergence and coherence.

However, the chapters focusing on the EU's legal basis (by Dony, De Bruycker and Weyembergh, and Schrijver) clarify that EU power increases according to the extent it has been awarded competence. This can only result from a free decision by its democratic member states, which confer upon the EU the right to act in certain policy fields. This bottom-up process is the opposite of the one associated with an empire-in-the-making. In case of blockage of the integration process, enhanced cooperation and differentiation within the Union has been possible since the Treaty of Nice, provided there is sufficient political will by at least eight member states to engage in "closer cooperation." This would imply building a kind of hard core (similarly to the Eurozone, but open to latecomers, according to their will and acceptance of the *acquis*[42]), for example as immigration policy and, to some extent, foreign and security policy are concerned.

The EU is the most legitimate international and regional organization in the world. However as a power-in-the-making, its democratic legitimacy is fragile, which has a negative impact on the international projection of its actorness. As is well known, legitimacy and accountability are traditionally weak as far as foreign policies of states are concerned, and that is because of historically rooted factors as well as the remaining influence of the tradition of secret diplomacy and the surviving legacy of non-democratically controlled bodies of the states (secret services, army, etc.), whose origins often pre-date the constitutional state. Furthermore, the electorates are less interested in foreign policy than in local and national politics. However, globalization is provoking changes: the diverse national public opinions are more and more concerned with big global issues such as peace, economic crisis, climate change and underdevelopment. The EU is the object of contradictory feelings at the same time: suspicion and fear on the one hand and yet high expectations on the other. All in all, observers agree that steps towards a common foreign and security policy are not likely to occur without a further enhancement of the controlling powers of both the EU Parliament and the national parliaments.

Last but not least, there is a third point with regard to the internal variables: the changes occurring in practical governance. Beyond and besides the controversial Treaty revision process, what matters are the modes of governance of the EU's external relations, both within partner countries and in Brussels (about 5,000 civil servants in Brussels and Commission delegations abroad). Over several decades, trans-governmental networks and intergovernmental bodies in Brussels have buttressed the building-up of epistemic communities including several actors of external relations, notably within the concerned DGs of the European Commission and the Council secretariat, committees and intergovernmental institutions. What is new is that the deepening coordination among them is going beyond traditional forms of diplomatic cooperation, while remaining within certain limits, and in no manner similar to the radically different supranational forms of integration. On the one hand, through the emerging shared world vision, policy-making and the practices of governance are very much influenced by these processes of socialization. On the other hand, the at times patchy policies are adversely influenced not only by the limits of the legal framework but also, as noted in the chapter of Delcourt and Remacle, by the emerging profile of the first version of the European Security Strategy of 2003 (or Solana Paper).

Developing a new European security strategy would be a relevant precondition for the foreign policy and external policies of a global power EU to emerge. Such a strategy would offer a distinctive analysis and vision of international relations, a perspective on the reform of global governance institutions, and the means to face the threats of the twenty-first century. It would be expected to combine short-term and long-term interests, member states' action and the EU's central orientation. From such an EU security strategy, after the global changes of 1991 and 2001 as well as the current shifts of global power, internal actors and external partners have the right to expect not just wishful calls for more effective multilateralism, but precise answers to the main global emergencies at stake. Among the latter would be hard security issues, and a shared vision of the relations to be entertained between other powers and organizations – first, with the USA (what new partnership might evolve? What new rationale might there be for NATO, beyond its post-cold war identity crisis?) and, second, with each of the main actors of the current heterogeneous and asymmetric world politics, the emerging BRICs and regional groupings abroad – and the inefficient global network. How might a realist logic be reconciled with an idealistic logic when facing the changing distribution of global power, embedding the critical aspects of globalization, engaging with potential enemies, managing the international disorder through stronger common institutions, and exchanging binding cooperation with co-leadership?

This book argues that the most effective instruments of the EU's external action are roughly the International Political Economy (IPE)-related ones: the issues of trade, climate change, poverty and sustainable development represent 80 percent of the EU's agenda (as shown particularly in the chapters by Rodrigues, Dewatripont and Legros, Conconi and Oberthür). Enhanced consistency between internal and external policies is increasingly called a new and necessary mainstreaming tendency within the EU. A vertically and horizontally more coherent understanding of the main external challenges, and the common will to cope with them, with the help of new modes of governance, are preconditions for effecting a better impact on rule-based global governance. Such coherence is also required for an international order where European values and interests are bridging and converging with those of other states, areas and interests. It is a work in progress that both Commission and Council are looking to elaborate as the need for enhanced coherence between the internal modernization agenda and the external relations became ever more pressing.[43] This last issue is one of high salience if one hopes to foster a distinctive European approach to international relations and new multilateralism, through the elaboration of a bottom-up concept of *global politics*. The EU would then be better equipped than others to meet the main civilian agendas facing humankind: sustainable development, balancing technological modernization with social cohesion, and fighting economic and social imbalances at the global level.

Notes

1 The term *acquis communautaire*, deriving from French, refers to the total body of common rights and obligations that bind all the Member States together within the European Union. It is constantly evolving and includes all the treaties, regulations and directives passed by the European institutions as well as judgements laid down by the Court of Justice.
2 See K. Nicolaïdis and R. Howse (eds) (2001).

3 "The community method" entails four main supranational features: the Commission has the monopoly of the law-making initiative; the Council votes by Qualified Majority Voting procedure; the Parliament has a co-decision power; and the Court of Justice is competent (including the application of the "doctrine of primacy" and "direct effect" of European law).

4 Regarding the contradiction between the high regulatory impact at global level and the failures at the level of the near abroad, see A. Sapir (2007).

5 M. Dony and J.-V. Louis (eds) (2005).

6 See TEC Article 131, and S. Woolcock (2005).

7 The Warwick Commission, *The Multilateral Trade Regime: Which Way Forward?*, University of Warwick, directed by R. Higgott, 2007.

8 In the Woody Allen movie *Zelig*, the title character adopts, as in a mirror, the physical features of every person he meets.

9 C. Hill and M. Smith (2005).

10 The Treaty of Westphalia (1648) ended the Thirty-Years War by establishing a new Europe of soveriegn and indpendent states, a successor ro the declining Holy Roman Empire of the Middle Ages.

11 J. L. Quermonne (2008). Close to this institutional research strategy, while with some differences: O. Beaud (2007).

12 See A. Pagden (2002).

13 D. Held and A. McGrew (eds) (2002); A. Prakash and J.A. Hart (eds) (1999); R. Wilkinson (ed.) (2005).

14 By "global governance", after J. Rosenau (*Governance without Government?*, 1992), we mean: both institutionalized and non-institutionalized, formal and informal, public and private modes of regulation and rule-setting at various levels of the globalized world. It can be considered as a useful descriptive tool to cope with the current incipient, multilevel (sub-national, national, regional, global) and multiactor (private, public, hybrid, including or not NGOs, "sovereign funds", etc.), global regulation.

15 For the concept of Europeanization, look at V. Schmidt (2006).

16 See also M. Farrell (ed.) (2005).

17 These are some of the main results of the collective research of the GARNET Network of Excellence focusing on global and regional governance. See the chapters included in M. Telò (ed.) (2007).

18 B. Balassa (1961).

19 For this metaphoric image, see V. Muntharborn (2008).

20 L. Van Langenhove and A. Costea (2007).

21 M. Dony and L. S. Rossi (eds) (2008).

22 By "globalization malaise" we mean the diffused feeling that, contrary to both the expectations and facts of the 1990s, globalization is no longer perceived as a positive sum game by large sectors of European public opinion. The employment problems in sensitive sectors of the labor market and the wages race to the bottom are no longer compensated enough by an enhanced purchasing power, due to gains of free trade – and that happens first of all because of the consequences on family budgets of rapidly growing prices for oil, raw materials, fuel and food. Furthermore, the ECB anti-inflationary policy makes it impossible to fall back on the old-fashioned countermeasures of public deficit and inflation. To what extent this malaise is a structural feature of the EU within the globalized economy is an open question. What is not in question is its political impact on demands for defensive policies, protectionism and even indeed nationalism.

23 J. S. Nye Jr (2008).

24 J. Ikenberry (2006).
25 J. Habermas (2004).
26 For example, K. Mahubani (2008), and, in other terms, Zhemin Chen, (2005).
27 P. Collier (2007).
28 J. McCormick (2007); U. Beck (2004).
29 EU practice is going towards the concept proposed by A.M. Slaughter (2004), though not before a federal-state level of fusion.
30 According to the *SIPRI Yearbook 2008: Armaments, Disarmament and International Security* (Stockholm, 2008), the global military expenditure, after a relevant post-cold war generalized trend to reduction, grew again from 1998 to 2007 by 45%, almost at the level of 1988. In 2007, the USA spent $547 billion, 65% more than in 1998 and 45% of world share ($1,756 per capita and 4.5% of the US GDP in 2006), which accounted for more than the sum of the ten following states: UK, $59.7 billion (5% of world share; in 2006, $990 per capita); China, $58.3 billion (three times more than in 1998, while 2% of GDP and, in 2006, $37 per capita); France, $53.6 billion (in 2006, $875 per capita); Japan, $43.6 billion (in 2006, $341 per capita); Germany, $36.9 billion (in 2006, $447 per capita, 1.1% of GDP); Russia, $35.4 billion (in 2006, $244 per capita); Saudi Arabia, $33.8 billion (in 2006, $1,152 per capita); Italy, $33.1 billion (in 2006, $514 per capita, 1.0% of GDP); and India, $24.2 billion (in 2006, $21 per capita).
31 F. Duchêne (1972); H. Bull (1982); K. Nicolaïdis and R. L. Howse (2002); J. Nye (2004); M. Telò (2006); J. Manners and S. Lucarelli (2007).
32 Furio Cerutti and Sonia Lucarelli (eds) (2008).
33 By the concept of "EU as a civilian power", we mean the collective capacity of exercising an effective external influence on the behavior of public and private actors, through a large array of means, mainly as a "model" and through persuasion, but also, in some spheres of exercise, through following forms of pression, according to the Treaties and the policy fields: from political multi-conditionality, to the use of limited military means by peace enforcing and peace-keeping missions. This complex and unprecedented mix between persuasion and coercion depends upon the EU interaction with both the internal two-level polity, on the one hand (including EU and states, notably welfare states), and, on the other, a still largely Westphalian world politics.
34 By "new multilateralism", we understand a form of multilevel (regional, interregional and global) collective transnational action and cooperation among states, regarding global governance and world politics. It implies generalized principles of conduct and diffuse reciprocity, and includes several degrees and types of institutionalization, from arrangements and regimes to public spheres and established organizations.
35 Which raises the controversial question of the static and rigid interpretation of the respect of the "exclusive jurisdiction of states" (Article 2, clause 7, UN Charter). For the concept of "multilateralism": J.G. Ruggie (ed.) (1993); E. Newmann, R. Thakur, J. Tirman (eds) (2006).
36 Taking into account the literature, by "embedded and binding multilateralism", we understand: agreement among states on principles, norms, expectations, decision-making, standards and rules able to change the behavior of member states. See Ruggie (1998) and R. Keohane in S. Krasner (ed.) (1983).
37 For example, the "open method of coordination" and the spreading of best practice is often considered an example of possible exporting potential to regional and global organizations, and the EU soft law experience as an example of "smooth governance". However, the absence of an institution like the Commission at global level (and at regional level elsewhere) suggests some prudence when stressing similarities.

38   J.G. Ruggie (1998); A. Wiener (2007).
39   R. O. Keohane (2007).
40   A. Sapir, *et al.* (coord.) (2004).
41   According to the Constitutional Treaty of 2004 and the Lisbon Treaty of 2007, the President of the EU Council, the High Representative for Foreign Policy, and the rotating Presidency of the Council (who will chair the General Affairs Council). See the chapter in this volume by M. Dony.
42   Treaty of the European Union, Section VII, Articles 43–5.
43   See Commission Communication to the Council, *Europe in the World*, June 2006, Comm. 2006/278. Portuguese Presidency 2007, Program "Sustainable Development" and EU Council, *Declaration on Globalization*, 13 December 2007.

Bibliography

Balassa, B. (1961), *The Theory of Economic Integration*, London: Greenwood.

Beaud, O. (2007), *Théorie de la fédération*, Paris: Presses Universitaires de France.

Beck, U. (2004) *Das Kosmopolitische Europa*, Frankfurt-am-Main: Suhrkamp Verlag.

Bull, H. (1982), "Civilian power Europe: a contradiction in terms?," *Journal of Common Market Studies*, Vols 1–2: pp. 149–64.

Cerutti, Furio and Sonia Lucarelli (eds) (2008) *The Search for a European Identity: Values, Policies and Legitimacy of the European Union*, London: Routledge.

Chen, Z. (2005) "NATO, APEC and ASEM: triadic interregionalism and global order," *Asia Europe Journal*, No. 3: pp. 361–78.

Collier, P. (2007) *The Bottom Billion*, Oxford: Oxford University Press.

Dony, M. and J.-V. Louis (eds) (2005), *Relations extérieures*, Commentaire J. Mégret on the Law of the European Community, vol. 12, second edition, Editions de l'Université de Bruxelles.

Dony, M. and L. S. Rossi (eds) (2008), *Démocratie, cohérence et transparence: vers une constitutionnalisation de l'Union européenne?*, Editions de l'Université de Bruxelles.

Duchêne, F. (1972), "Europe's role in world's peace," in R. Mayne (ed.), *Europe Tomorrow*, London: Fontana.

Farrell, M. (ed.) (2005), "EU external relations: exporting the EU model of governance?," special issue of *European Foreign Affairs Review*, 4, Vol. 10, Winter, 2005.

Habermas, J. (2004) *Der gespaltene Westen* [The Divided West], Frankfurt-am-Main: Suhrkamp Verlag.

Held, D. and A. McGrew (eds) (2002), *Governing Globalization*, Polity Press.

Hill, C. and M. Smith (2005), *International Relations and the European Union*, Oxford University Press, p. 396.

Ikenberry, J. (2006), *Liberal Order and Imperial Ambition: American Power and International Order*, Polity Press.

Keohane, R.O. (2007), *Key lecture at the Garnet Annual Conference*, Warwick, September 2007, in R. Higgott (ed.), *Paths to Legitimacy*, Routledge, 2008.

Krasner, S. (ed.) (1983), *International Regimes*, Ithaca: Cornell University Press.

McCormick, J. (2007), *The European Superpower*, London: Palgrave.

Manners, J. and S. Lucarelli (2007), *Values and Principles in EU Foreign Policy*, London: Routledge.

Mahubani, K. (2008), *The New Asian Hemisphere: The Irresistible Shift of Global Power to the East*.

Muntharbor, V. (2008), "Regional Integration and Human rights," NESCA Conference on Regional Integration and Human Rights, Chulalongkorn University, February 2008.

Newmann, E., R. Thakur and J. Tirman (eds) (2006), *Multilateralism Under Challenge?*, Tokyo: UN.

Nicolaïdis, K. and R. L. Howse (eds) (2001), *The Federal Vision*, Oxford:, Oxford University Press.

Nicolaïdis and R. L. Howse (2002), "This is my Eutopia ...: narrative as power," in *Journal of Common Market Studies*, 2002, Vol. 40: pp. 767–92.

Nye Jr, J.S. (2004) *Soft Power*.

Nye Jr, J.S. (2008), *The Power to Lead*, Oxford: Oxford University Press.

Pagden, A. (2002), *The Idea of Europe*, Cambridge: Cambridge University Press.

Prakash, A. and J.A. Hart (eds) (1999), *Globalization and Governance*, Routledge.

Quermonne, J.L. (2008), *L'Union Européenne dans le temps long. Vers une Fédération d'Etats-nation?*, Paris.

Ruggie, J.G. (ed.) (1993), *Multilateralism Matters*, New York: Columbia University Press.

Ruggie, J.G. (1998) *Constructing the World Polity: Essays in International Institutionalization*, London and New York: Routledge, 107.

Sapir, A., *et al.* (coord.) (2004), *An Agenda for a Growing Europe: The Sapir Report*, Oxford: Oxford University Press.

Sapir, A. (2007), *Fragmented Power*, Brussels: Bruegel.

Schmidt, V. (2006) *Democracy in Europe*, Oxford: Oxford University Press.

Slaughter, A.M. (2004) *A New World Order*, Princeton: Princeton University Press.

Telò, M. (2006), *Europe: A Civilian Power?*, London: Palgrave.

Telò, M. (ed.) (2007), *EU and New Regionalism*, Ashgate.

Van Langenhove, L. and A. Costea, "The EU as a global actor and the emergence of 'third-generation' regionalism," in P. Foradori, P. Rosa and R. Scartezzini (eds), *Managing Multilevel Foreign Policy*, Lanham: Lexington Books, 2007, pp. 63–86.

Wiener, A. (2007), "The dual quality of norms and governance beyond the state," *Critical Review of International Social and Political Philosophy*, 10/1.

Wilkinson, R. (ed.) (2005), *The Global Governance Reader*, London: Routledge.

Woolcock, S. (2005) "Trade policy," in H. Wallace, W. Wallace and S. Pollack (eds), *Policy-Making in the European Union*, Oxford University Press, pp. 377–99.

Part I

The impact of the EU on global governance

2　The European Union's democratic agenda

Paul Magnette and Kalypso Nicolaïdis

Summary[*]

This chapter asks whether and if so how the EU is able to export, promote or simply showcase its system of democratic governance to the rest of the world. It is organised around a twofold distinction between the EU's external influence applied to states or to relations between states – that is, to democracy *within* states or democracy *between* states. These dimensions are to be related to the three legal orders of a federation of states as identified by Immanuel Kant: (i) relations between citizens and state as established by *ius civitatis*, (ii) relations between states as governed by *ius gentium*, and (iii) relations between nationals and a foreign state as defined by *ius cosmopoliticum*. The first category has to do with political order *within* states, while the last two categories concern relations *between* states. We argue that while the same principles underlie the EU's internal and external action, much is lost in translation: the conditions that gave rise to the construction of an integrated Europe cannot generally be replicated elsewhere. But the intra-state vs inter-state distinction is crucial in this regard. While the agenda of 'democracy promotion' within other states (and the problems it encounters) is shared by many actors in the international system, the second agenda, that of democracy *between* polities (as states or as citizens) is more specific to the EU, at least to the extent that the EU alone can claim to provide a model for such an agenda. It is in this second dimension that the EU might have the most relevant lessons to offer – positive or negative – to the rest of the world.

Introduction

From Athenian democracy to Westminster parliamentarism, Europeans claim not only to have invented the democratic form of government but to have explored most of its variants in the last two thousand years. Indeed, through the EU they are now hoping to explore new frontiers of democracy *across* states rather than *within* states or other sub-state polities. Yet Europe's brand of traditional representative democracy is serially challenged today: by the classical (or direct democracy) variant, but also by bold experiments of the deliberative, participatory, grassroots and, of late, e-democracy kind. Conversely, here as elsewhere, democratic life is challenged by generalised apathy, media overload and collapsing trust. This is happening not only within individual countries, but most interestingly at the supranational EU level, whether we conceptualise it as a set of political institutions, an emerging public space or a polity-in-the-making. European publics have become accustomed to hearing their two main political families, Democrats of the Social or Christian kind, talk of a crisis as well as a renewal or reinvention of democracy, almost in the same programmatic breath. And pundits everywhere speak of the EU's democratic deficit and of its democratic process in the same breath.

But in the mist of such confusion, such effervescence, a bold new project has taken shape for Europe since the end of the cold war: to represent a model of democracy beyond Europe's confines, to be showcased or exported to the rest of the globe. No matter that *what* exactly is to be exported is itself intensely contested within the confines of Europe. The idea that democracy is increasingly part and parcel of the political repertoire of the EU, the brand-mark of its message in the world, is in keeping with its historical trajectory. Democratising the European continent was seen, from the start, as a way of pacifying world order to atone perhaps for Europe's prior worldwide export of its internal conflicts. When Jean Monnet wrote at the end of his memoirs that the European Community (EC) was not an end in itself but a means towards a better world, he may have been trying to assuage the misgivings of the old functionalists like David Mitrany (who pioneered modern integrative theory) for whom region-limited integration would serve only to recreate the barriers that functional integration was meant to tear down at the global level. The European project could be viewed as a building block for the kind of world the founding fathers had in mind. Paradoxically perhaps, the fact that the EC had little room to flourish as an *actor* during the cold war meant that while the EU's external policy stayed modest, the idea of its standing as a model took root. France never managed to convince its partners that a *political* Europe, maintaining equal distance from the USA and the USSR, could be a pacifying device. So the EC came to see and brand itself as a *civilian power*.

There are obviously limits and pitfalls in such an agenda. For one, Europeans are confronted by the same paradox as everyone else involved in this game among the society of nations, namely that of the contradiction between the very essence of democracy, collective self-rule, and the idea that it can be *imported* from another *collective*, thus bypassing the *self* to be ruled. Be it as invaders, colonisers or traders, great powers have long viewed bringing some version of *their* system of government to other peoples as a mark of greatness. Is exporting democracy and the rule of law a by-product and late echo of conquest and domination, or a mark of transnational responsibility and cosmopolitan solidarity? In a post-colonial but also a post-Iraq War era, can the EU give a good name to the project of expanding the global reach of democracy in ways which can be distinguished from that of the USA? Is there an EU-specific response to the *democracy export* paradox? And even if we accept that democracy is not merely an internal EU affair, to what extent can such EU internal precepts and approaches be translated for the rest of the world? The EU must operate in a world which does not look like it, probably a world that looks less and less like it, definitely a non-European world. Why or to what extent can we assume that European recipes are translatable?

We will not provide in this chapter a review of the extensive literature pertaining to this last question. Rather, we propose relevant categories to explore some of these signalled questions and navigate this rugged landscape. We distinguish between two dimensions.

First and foremost, we need to distinguish between levels of analysis. Is the EU's external influence applied to states or to relations between states; democracy *within* states or democracy *between* states? These are obviously two very different agendas. It can be argued that the three democratic aspects of the EU correspond to the three legal orders of a federation of states as identified by Kant (1795): (i) relations between citizens and state as established by *ius civitatis*, (ii) relations between states as governed by *ius gentium*, and (iii) relations between nationals and a foreign state as defined by *ius cosmopoliticum* (Ferry 2000; Magnette 2000; Cheneval 2005). The first category has to do with political order *within* states, while the last two concern relations *between* states.[1] We will argue that while the same principles underlie the EU's external action (internal democratisation, multilateralism and transnational citizenship), much is lost in translation: the conditions that gave rise to the construction of an integrated Europe cannot generally be replicated elsewhere. But the intra-state vs inter-state distinction is crucial in this regard. While the agenda of 'democracy promotion' within other states (and the problems it encounters) is shared by many other actors in the international system (be these actors other countries like the USA or Canada or international organisations like the World Bank or United Nations Development Programme), the second agenda, that of democracy *between* polities (as states or as citizens) is more specific to the EU, at least to the extent that the EU alone can claim to provide a model for such an agenda. It is in this second dimension that the EU might have relevant lessons to offer – positive or negative – to the rest of the world.

As detailed above, in addition to this first dimension a second dimension must be taken into consideration. The EU influences governance beyond its borders in two ideal-typical ways: as a *model* and as an *actor*. The first is what the editor of this volume refers to as the 'spontaneous' democratic influence and the external democratisation policies. Many would argue that, as a new kind of non-state supranational political system, the EU has become an international reference for its near and far abroad. In this light, it is alternatively referred to not only as a model but also as a blueprint, a lighthouse, a toolbox of governance, an experiment and so on. Against the backdrop of our non-European world, it is important to consider how the EU's internal features, including its democratic credentials, affect the relevance, credibility and legitimacy of its claim to 'modelhood', although such a *passive* impact is extremely difficult to assess. Indeed, in practice, its impact as a model is increasingly hard to distinguish from its impact as an *actor*. One of the central goals of the EU as actor is to promote the *European model*, whether that of its member states or the EU system itself. The EU's slide from *democracy experimenter* to *democratiser* has been progressive and multifaceted. It has expressed itself through the externalisation of democracy conditions from internal (TEU, Articles 6–7) to membership conditionality (e.g., the 1993 Copenhagen Criteria) to generic conditionality. Indeed, as we shift from general roles (model vs actor) to actual means, we find a gradation of tools or policy instruments, from least to most coercive: learning, socialisation or enmeshment;

indirect support for actors abroad; provision of financial and technical support; coercive diplomacy and conditionality; sanctions and the use of force.

This chapter is divided in two parts. The first part considers the impact of the EU on democracy *within* states and distinguishes between democracy as a pre- and post-*condition* for membership and democracy as a goal beyond membership. The second part starts by arguing that the EU is best understood as a political regime designed to democratise inter-state relations on the European continent both through the formal institutions that organise these relations (multilateralism) and through rules pertaining to the treatment of citizens (Kant's second and third orders). Its attempts to externalise its own inter-state order have applied both to regional and global governance, raising the question of the compatibility between 'a world of regions' and multilateralism. In spite of its potential contradictions, the narrative and practice of projection is becoming a significant feature of world order. The chapter ultimately concludes by identifying the promise and limits of promoting or showcasing democracy.

Democracy within states: the political order of the component units

Members: the democratic sine qua non condition

Today's democratic peace theory found its earliest incarnation in the creation of the EC as the lessons of the interwar period were drawn and learnt. After World War One, the creation of the League of Nations – European nations, in fact – had seemingly been the crowning achievement of Europe's democratic transition. President Woodrow Wilson's Kantianism had seemed to govern the new Europe when, for a few years, the democratic process seemed the harbinger of a new inter-state order to come, based on cooperation and litigation. But the collapse of the young parliamentary regimes in Southern and Eastern Europe had crushed these hopes and the failure of Munich in 1938 was some time later to symbolise the impossibility of cooperation between democratic and authoritarian regimes. The European experience seemed to confirm Montesquieu's theory – taken up by Rousseau – according to which a federative league could exist only between republics, i.e., regimes founded on the principles of the separation of powers and civic representation.

The years immediately following World War Two were marked, in Europe, by the blossoming of projects aimed at erecting a federal and democratic order on the continent, radically breaking with both fascist experiences and the international anarchy of the inter-war period. Yet, these hopes proved fragile. The Summit of The Hague in 1948, heralded as a moment of federal euphoria, only revealed the inner contradictions within the pro-European movements. As the great expectations attached to the creation of the Council of Europe were dashed on account of its complex and confused organisation, it was clear from the start that Europe would not follow the American constitutional model. Instead, Europe's model was to be functional, based on international treaties negotiated *in camera* by government officials and diplomats. It was not to be a federation but a *community* – a neologism that referred to a mix of classic intergovernmental procedures and a carefully measured dose of supranational incentives and controls. Europe from then on would be a more modest and indirect form of government in charge of market regulation and commercial policies. The democratic issue was thus confined at the state level – the locus of solidarity policies and political links.

As a result, the EU's first and core democratic pillar relates to the political regimes of the member states.[2] The EU has been a community of democracies since its very beginning. Unlike other international organisations set up in Europe at the same time (OECD, NATO), there have only been democracies within the EU. This *democratic condition* was not explicitly mentioned in the founding treaties and the reasons why the Europe of the Six never started actual membership negotiations with authoritarian regimes have not been thoroughly studied. Clearly, geopolitics mattered. Eastern European countries – prevented by Moscow from receiving aid under the Marshall Plan – remained cut off from the European project as early as 1947. But democratic ideology cast a much bigger net. While commercial reasons may also have accounted for Europe's decision not to open membership negotiations with Spain and Portugal, the reasons for keeping out autocracies were not merely material. Indeed from the start the Six were caught in their own rhetoric. As the champions of the 'free West' in their struggle against communism, they could not cooperate with autocracies without contradicting themselves. (Even Greece did not manage to gain admission in the early 1970s with dictators in power.) Nor could they, therefore, reasonably refuse to incorporate the new Southern European democracies in the 1980s or the post-communist regimes in Central Europe after the fall of the Berlin Wall.

From a conceptual standpoint, the EU may thus be apprehended as a countervailing power that balances any potential excesses stemming from national democracies – completing and strengthening the institution of the rule of law. It draws its legitimacy from the lessons of the past. If they are left to themselves, democracies may become xenophobic, nationalistic and bellicose. In the light of the experience of the twentieth century, the project of European integration appears, in Joseph Weiler's formula, as 'an attempt to control the excesses of the modern nation-state in Europe' (Weiler 1998). The twentieth century witnessed the excesses of both nationalism and formalism. Indeed a modernist, bureaucratic and impersonal political system may well cause similar abuses or create a feeling of anomie that might eventually lead a country to withdraw into itself and have aggressive reactions. As stated by John Rawls, an EU freed from the supervision of the nation states might well sacrifice – in the name of profitability and legal standardisation – the rights enjoyed by citizens that stem from 'individual nation-states, each with their own political and social institutions, history, forms and traditions of social policy' which are so many 'achievements of great value for their citizens, [that] give sense to their lives' (Rawls 1999: 9). The constant confrontation between the two 'most elemental, alluring and frightening social and psychological poles of our cultural heritage' (Weiler 1998: 347) is the greatest achievement of the federation of European states. In short, the relationship goes both ways: not only is the democratic character of its member states the best safeguard against the bureaucratic drift of the EU itself, but the EU's function is also to sustain and deepen national democracies.

Even within the EU it is possible to distinguish between passive and active influence. It took decades for the EU to formalise its 'democratic core'. Only in 1997 did the Treaty of Amsterdam codify the democratic nature of a state as a necessary condition for EU membership – thus echoing one of the oldest claims from the federalist movements – and accompanied it with the creation of a multilateral surveillance mechanism of the members themselves. (The Treaty of Amsterdam symbolically mentioned the democratic principles before 'the respect of the states' national identities', thus reversing the order established in the Maastricht Treaty.) The *constitutionalisation* of this process – intended to consolidate member state democracies and prevent any authoritarian drifts – was first perceived with suspicion because it coincided with the opening of membership negotiations with Central and Eastern European countries. Some went as far as to regard it as reminiscent of Brezhnev's doctrine of 'limited sovereignty'. Nevertheless, member states have progressively sought to assert what we could call a *responsibility of democratic interference* – an evolution first brought to light on the occasion of the formation of an Austrian government coalition that included Joerg Haider's FPO (Austrian Freedom Party) and the subsequent sanctions adopted by the other fourteen states against Austria and implemented on an intergovernmental basis. These were seen by some as a sign that Europe was confirming its role as 'a community of values', based on the rule of law and entitled to pass judgement in matters of national domestic policies. But there was no real consensus over such a vision. Others were shocked by what they regarded as pure interference or criticised the counter-productive consequences of such a move. In their views, these sanctions could lead to the re-emergence of excessive national pride and potential nationalistic drifts. In any case, such sanctions won the day and were eventually 'constitutionised' at Nice (2000). Yet, both the Austrian episode and the subsequent negotiations over appropriate constitutional arrangements revealed the ambivalence of the mechanism of democratic interference as well as the difficulties in defining precisely the democratic criteria. The fact that the European Constitutional Treaty signed by the heads of state and government in Rome in 2004 (and confirmed by the Lisbon Treaty) codified this mechanism at least demonstrates that the principle of multilateral democratic surveillance is nevertheless widely accepted in the EU today. It remains to be seen, however, whether such a principle would ever be extended to a more radical responsibility to protect within the European space.

Candidates: the democratic lighthouse

Whereas the democratic nature of political regimes may be perceived as the condition *sine qua non* for a regional/international order based on cooperation, such an order in turn can contribute to consolidating democracy within states. Nowhere is this two-directional causality clearer than in the context of EU enlargement. This was true for the Mediterranean enlargement of the 1980s and even more starkly for the EU's fifth enlargement to post-communist Central and Eastern Europe. In both instances, by ruling out or in certain reform options the prospect of EU membership provided a focal point for modernisers, around which broad coalitions could form, and facilitated the implementation of some hard but necessary democratic reforms in the name of the superior objective of becoming a member of this exclusive club. At the same time, as exemplified by the cases of Greece, Spain and today Turkey, the prospect of peaceful interstate relations under the EU umbrella is thought to weaken the power of the armed forces, thus bringing states in conformity with the principle of civilian control of the military, one of the hallmarks of democracy.

Before being formalised internally in 1997, democratic conditionality was introduced for the first time as a formal condition for accession through the so-called Copenhagen Criteria of 1993. There, in addition to the classic *acquis* (corpus of European Law), the EU set out political and economic criteria for accession – with the former stated as 'membership requires that candidate country has achieved stability of institutions guaranteeing democracy, the rule of law, human rights'. No definition was given of these terms, no benchmarks were provided, and indeed they have been the object of varying interpretation on the part of the EU Commission and the member states. Since conditionality usually needs measurable variables, it can be argued that the EU could not really target the quality of democracy. In spite of its vagueness, political conditionality became a pre-condition for candidate status rather than ultimate membership after 1999. The Balkan states and Turkey were thus deemed to have passed the democracy test when allowed to start negotiations with the EU in 1999 and 2004 respectively. But what does this tell us about EU influence?

While there is little doubt that the EU has some impact on the democratic make-up of aspiring members, the question which occupies academics these days is how – or through which mechanisms and under which conditions – the EU's influence is effective. Is democratic convergence about the EU as a model or an actor, or is it yet a phenomenon unrelated to the EU altogether? And if the EU matters, are we in the presence of a logic of appropriateness grounded in learning and socialisation, or a logic of consequence grounded in cost–benefit calculations stemming from external incentives? In other words, how direct and *coercive* is democratic conditionality?

The answer is: it depends. Schimmelfennig and Sedelmeier (2005) have argued for instance that the logic of consequences and external incentives is most likely if EU conditions are clear and the domestic (political) adoption costs low. Social learning is more likely when mainstream domestic players are persuaded by the legitimacy of EU rules. In the latter case, the EU might set (democratic) conditions, but we should not make any causal inference from this fact. More generally, the EU would not be expected to have much influence either on democratic frontrunners or on authoritarian/nationalist governments (e.g., Slovakia) for whom adoption would threaten their power base. The most credible setting for EU influence would be in the case of fragile democracies after a change of government through the lock-in effect afforded by commitments made to the EU – although analysts agree on the difficulty of disentangling the EU's influence, whether through conditionality or socialisation and the autonomous impact of domestic politics.

The downplaying of a direct effect of democratic conditionality in turn stems from the difference between the two types (hard and soft) of conditionalities in the EU's enlargement process. The logic of consequence is more likely to obtain for the so-called *acquis*, not only because these rules are clear and straightforward but perhaps most importantly because they apply equally to existing member states. When it comes to the softer democratic conditionality, and not withstanding the one-off application to Austria discussed above, existing members of the club do not seem to be bound by the same rules. Indeed, throughout the late 1990s and early 2000s, the EU Commission progressively introduced conditions in realms where it had little or no competence internally, from minority rights to devolution to the independence of the judiciary; this is unsurprising, as these realms are intensely contested and the object of divergent political bargains across member states. What does compliance mean against a norm that is constructed, lacks a firm internal basis and is used flexibly over time?

The response of aspiring members seemed schizophrenic at best. While formal legislative change has definitely been observed, it has often not been accompanied by behavioural change: formal reforms may simply not filter through deeper normative structures of society. Indeed, Sasse (2008) has argued that EU pressure and monitoring has actually had an inverse effect when we consider the political dynamics that have accompanied enlargement: in Latvia and Estonia, the ethnic majorities represented in the parliaments have failed to follow through on citizenship reform for instance, and the implementation of these reforms has been frustratingly patchy. Moreover, conditionality in this case is more a framing device than a direct cause of transformation. It can even have perverse effects by mobilising 'true' domestic actors against its deeper precepts (e.g., integration of Russian minorities). At the very least, as many observers have argued, the need to converge with the EU in general (e.g., not just with regard to the democracy criteria) can infantilise and constrain the extent of democratic debate.

Thus, we must assess the impact of the EU model on the quality of democracy in aspiring member states, which can arguably be restricted through EU intervention. Let us ask to what extent, for instance, the content of the conditions or norms conveyed by the EU fit with the democratic debates of the targeted states – it is arguable that negative conditionality, against certain state behaviours, is more respectful of democracy than the promotion of positive solutions prescribing, say, the territorial autonomy for a minority. More generally, the nature of democracy is especially contested when it comes to the ways in which countries choose to avoid the tyranny of the majority and the tyranny of the minority – the same challenge is seen very differently from Latvia, Romania or France. Indeed, it has not always been clear to external observers why in some cases the EU has pushed for democracy through integration and in other cases for democratisation through partition – here Bosnia, Serbia or Cyprus come to mind.

The impact of democratic conditionality also depends on the phases considered, e.g., regime change prior to the onset of EU accession negotiations; the accession negotiation phase itself; the post-accession period. With the initial impact of the EU on regime change in the early 1990s (with parties advocating different versions of a *return to Europe*), it is harder to demonstrate that the EU had a significant impact on regime features as a whole (except perhaps for the case of Meciar's Slovakia). Indeed, once negotiations have started the credibility of the threat to withdraw the membership offer decreases dramatically, so incentives thereafter relate to timing of entry, length of transition periods and the like. After accession, the EU loses its sanctioning power, especially given the extreme character of the ill-fated Article 6 and the Austrian affair. While early findings on the post-accession implementation of EU rules and infringement procedures seem to show that as of 2008 the EU-10 (that is, the new member states) outperform the EU-15 for the hard *acquis*, the democratic ethos seems less entrenched from the independence of the judiciary to democratic inclusion. The legacy of conditionality is thus very different for hard (*acquis*) vs soft (democracy) conditions. It may be that new members have a greater susceptibility to shaming when it comes to concrete measures, which would be ironic given their extreme negativity towards conditionality. In short, heavy pre-accession institutional investment in legislative capacity, as well as socialisation into appropriateness of good compliance, does not automatically translate into structural change across areas. The question remains open, however, as to whether the *threat of enhanced cooperation* – e.g. whether the state can enter the Schengen area of free movement, the European MU as well as future additional potential areas – might also act as post-accession conditionality.

Finally, it is important to stress that when it comes to democracy and the connected norms of human rights and the rule of law, the EU does not exert influence in a vacuum but through borrowed legal tools and policy recommendations from other institutions, among which the Council of Europe and the OSCE in particular.

If we ask therefore about the democratic legacy of enlargement, we need to come back to the dynamics internal to the EU itself. We see for instance today how the Hungarians have become the champions of minorities in the EU, especially within the European Parliament. Are we likely to witness a feedback loop, whereby the practices and scope for jurisdiction or involvement of Brussels in democratic matters within the EU comes in turn to be affected by the EU stance during enlargement? Perhaps taking such a feedback loop seriously is a pre-condition for loosening the limitation of democratisation through Europeanisation outside the context of enlargement.

Neighbours and partners beyond: democratic conditionality, the European way

It is clear from the above that enlargement provides a unique albeit contested setting for democratic influence. But what is the EU influence without the promise and prospect of membership? This is the realm where EU influence can be directly contrasted with that of the USA or other Western powers as well as international organisations like the World Bank, the OSCE or United Nations Development Programme. Indeed, following the third wave of democratisation around the world, democracy-promotion became a huge industry in the 1990s and the EU a powerful actor within it.[3]

To be sure, there is an intermediary area, dubbed by the EU as its 'neighbourhood', where the lack of membership prospect may only be temporary and where the EU has actually reproduced some of the same patterns of influence as in the enlargement context (the original 2004 European neighbourhood policy was drafted by the same EU Commission staff who managed enlargement). The sixteen countries which take part in the European neighbourhood policy (ENP) as of 2008 can be said to be under the purview of 'conditionality-lite', whereby both the incentives provided and the convergence engineered are much less ambitious than those applying within the EU. If the EU is to be seen as a democratic empire, some of the architects of the ENP may argue that it is already overextended. It is an erroneous myth, they would say, that further enlargement would increase security; instead the ENP can be a functional equivalent by contributing to stabilising the belt of democracies around the EU, which can then strike privileged partnerships with them.

Beyond its immediate neighbourhood, the EC has long hesitated to introduce any sort of conditionality in its bilateral relationships, especially when it came to former colonies. Anticipating decolonisation, the chapter of the Rome Treaty dedicated to cooperation with developing countries was meant to manage a post-colonial order, including asymmetric rights of market access and not interfering in the affairs of other countries. The EU's complex series of external trade preferences either followed pragmatic economic lines or were based on post-colonial ties. Until the 1980s, the EC/EU had no tradition of granting trade or aid privileges strategically as rewards for allies or to entice governments to reform. Its reluctance to use carrots and sticks to affect democracy may have been grounded in sensitivity to the colonial legacy of its member states, in scepticism about the effectiveness of aid or trade conditionality in political matters or in an ingrained culture of diplomatic engagement (as opposed to US balancing or containment). As a result, it has traditionally baulked at using instruments which might involve elements of coercion, suasion or arm-twisting and has often let geostrategic, historical or symbolic imperatives outweigh failings in domestic reform.

But this ethos began to change in the post-cold war era with significant variance across issue areas and regions – e.g., less emphasis on judicial independence or corruption, more on minority or human rights laws or freedom of the press; less in Asia or Latin America than in Africa. This may have been due to the EU's growing sense of its legitimacy and weight as an international actor as well as the spill-over from enlargement dynamics. The European Parliament has been instrumental in this evolution, especially as it gained the power to veto agreements with third parties following the 1987 *Single European Act*. Specifically, in 1995, the EU turned what was to be a quick mid-term review of the Lomé IV Convention, which governed aid to the Africa, Caribbean and the Pacific regions (ACP), into a fundamental rethinking of its aid provisions – introducing broad political conditionality, including support for democratic government. The EU enforced the threat during the 1990s as aid was suspended to Nigeria, Rwanda, Burundi, Niger and Sierra Leone – although the EU tends to resort increasingly to positive rather than negative forms of conditionality (e.g., promises rather than threats). By the beginning of the new millennium, the EU had three diplomatic voices – the Parliament, Council and Commission – all promoting democracy and the rule of law abroad.

One of the greatest challenges recently addressed to the democracy-promotion agenda can be called the sequencing controversy. The argument especially pertinent to Europe, but which applies to the USA and other democracies as well, is that the promotion of only some features of democracy, i.e., electoral democracy, is highly distorting and conflict-inducing if polities are not yet ready through stable rule of law institutions to protect against an appropriation of the spoils of power by the majority or a clique. The argument was best encapsulated by Fareed Zakaria (1997) in his denunciation of 'illiberal democracies'. Accordingly, the rule of law rather than democracy should be the aim of outside intervention: better not to micromanage but instead to create an environment that might eventually be conducive to democratisation. Others like Carothers (2003), however, have argued that the sequencing argument is a fallacy and that countries generally need elections to create the kind of incentives that will lead to the upholding of the rule of law. The controversy persists and will shape European strategies for years to come in places from Afghanistan to Bosnia or Nigeria and, most controversially perhaps given the economic interests at stake, to China.

A second challenge has to do with the EU's acceptance of 'reciprocal intrusion' that could well be the hallmark of a truly democratic post-colonial power. If sovereignty is to be redefined as 'sovereignty as responsibility', justifying intervention in the domestic affairs of other countries, to what extent will the EU accept scrutiny of its own consistency between the application of internal practices and external prescriptions? In the last few years, the EU has refused for instance to let the UN debate certain issues pertaining to human rights and democracy in its own member states, avowedly issues that are partially under the purview of the European Court of Justice (e.g., gay rights in Poland or women's rights in Malta). While the reason given is the UN's unanimity principle and the reluctance to let non-democratic countries sit in judgement on the EU, one also gets a sense from EU diplomats that the EU will not be lectured on democracy by outsiders.

Democracy beyond the state: towards a post-hegemonic state system?

It may be argued that aside from the enlargement process, the EU's most significant influence beyond its borders does not have to do with the (democratic) make-up of individual countries but instead with international society itself – in other words, democracy *beyond* the state. In this section, we will first consider the features of the EU itself as a supranational democracy, then turn to the concept of *civilian power* as a translation device between internal and external action. Finally we will quickly review such translations as they actually exist at the regional and global levels.

From multilateralism to transnational citizenship: the two pillars of the EU as democracy

Obviously, the EU does not look anything like a national democracy, with the ability of its citizenry to 'kick the rascals out' through periodic majority voting. But if we come back to the very concept of democracy rather than comparing the EU with given historical forms of democracy, we may agree that while the EU will never look like a continental democratic state, it does embody a peculiar form of democracy. The concept of democracy, Bobbio reminded us, echoes the idea of autonomy, defined in opposition to both anarchy (the absence of norms) and heteronomy (a set of imposed norms). In this sense, democracy at the international level may be apprehended not as the reproduction of state mechanisms on a wider scale, but rather as the diffusion of mutually negotiated norms in inter-state relations (Bobbio 2006).

If we accept the idea that the building of national democracy has meant that the rule of law and negotiations have progressively replaced power struggle between social groups, we may contend that democracy will spread in international and trans-national relations through the replacement of force by law and peaceful negotiations among equal states. Bobbio did not study the EU, but those who, like him, take their inspiration from Kant's cosmopolitanism have all stressed the essential dimension of the making of a European democracy. In fact, the formation of the EU is a long process of legalisation of conflicts and substitution of civilised negotiations to power relations, and this amounts to an extension of the democratic principle to the inter-state order (Cheneval 2005; Ferry 2005).

Coming back to our initial framing through Kantian categories, the last two of these categories help us to distinguish between two features of European democracy beyond the state: multilateralism and transnational citizenship. Both of them are incomplete and projects-in-the-making.

Multilateralism at the regional level has been Europe's way of dealing with a conflict-prone past where one group or state consistently sought over the centuries to dominate others. The EU has been first and foremost an anti-hegemony structure, due to its use of treaties to organise power relations between states as well as between central institutions. Contrary to all the historical examples of multinational entities throughout European history (the Austro-Hungarian Empire, the German Reich, the United Kingdom, the Soviet Union or Yugoslavia), the EU has not been dominated by any majority ethnic group. From its very origin, it has been based on a 'balance of unbalances', to quote Stanley Hoffmann, a balance that has been regularly confirmed by the successive enlargement processes. The six founding member states were composed of three larger states and three smaller ones, with various configurations: some were rural while others were essentially urban and industrialised; some had been on the winning side in World War Two while others had been defeated; some were old centralised states while others were younger and more fragile; some were colonial powers while others were without any empire; some were countries of immigration while others were countries of emigration; some were free-traders while others were protectionist. There were enough intersecting differences between the states to make the creation of stable fronts and domination of one group over another very unlikely.

As a result, the EU developed a new form of 'multi-level multilateralism' as argued by Mario Telò in the introduction to this volume. The great achievement of the Community method was to overcome the reluctance of some countries that feared the hegemony of France or the Big Three (France, Britain and Germany) by suppressing any potential risk of solitary leadership. Shared leadership was embodied in the combined monopoly of initiative out of the hands of big states (to the High Authority and later the Commission), the system of rotating presidency in the Council of Ministers, and the qualified majority voting system based on a subtle system of weighing votes. Unlike other international organisations in which inter-state equality remained a virtual principle, the EU thus efficiently prohibited the possibility of a state's occupying a hegemonic position. (A great deal of the acrimony stemming from the negotiations over the failed Constitutional Treaty (2002–03) and later the Lisbon Treaty (2007) was due to the attempt to alter this balance on the part of the bigger states.) With time, negotiations based on mutual respect became the rule and spread to every part of the institutional system, even into the bureaucratic and diplomatic spheres which were the foundation of the EU's political system. The most remarkable aspect of such a development process is that – contrary to what happened in federal regimes – the EU was not obliged to establish a new hegemonic centre that would rule *super partes* in order to achieve the repudiation of hegemonic relations among states. Unlike the American, German or Swiss federal models, the EU's political regime remains essentially headless (Magnette 2000).

Beyond the management of power relations between states through multilateral regionalism, the EU has deepened democracy beyond the state by exploring Kant's third dimension of international law, namely transnationalism, which in turn is related to the progressive emergence of the notion of citizenship of the Union. This notion had existed *in nuce* since the very beginning. The cardinal principle of the free movement of persons, together with the essential principle of non-discrimination on the ground of nationality, gave citizens new rights *vis-à-vis* the states where they resided whether or not they were nationals of these states. From then on, the concept of EU citizenship could progressively evolve from its essentially functionalist origins through Court challenges as well as Commission and European Parliament activism, incorporating new rights other than those directly attached to the economic status. The principle of European citizenship, separated from its purely socio-economic dimension, was finally established – with a few restrictions – in the Treaty of Maastricht.

The meaning of the notion of citizenship of the EU is still blurred by the fact that it is often apprehended through the national prism. In other words, being a citizen of the EU is commonly related to the idea of a direct link between citizens and the EU, some form of legal and political vertical relation. But such a relation, though not absent in the European citizen's status, remains embryonic. As early as 1979, citizens were given the right to elect their representatives in the European Parliament, and were, some time later, granted the right of petition and appeal to the European Ombudsman. The Charter also endows all residents with further rights. However, the direct link with the Union stops here.

The horizontal dimension of European citizenship is much more substantial. From a legal point of view, the constant enhancement of the right to travel freely and the banning of any form of discrimination based on nationality have profoundly affected national law. Migrant citizens have been granted civil and social rights, economic freedom and even political rights that they were denied before. In that respect, the Union has gone further than Kant's recommendation of a 'right of access' across nations, considerably deepening his notion of universal hospitality to retain the possibility of civil relations. In the EU, national legal systems are now expurgated of most references to 'national preferences' which once characterised them.

In today's EU, the enlargement of the notion of citizenship to the European-other is not a mere legal issue. As Joseph Weiler rightfully noted, the changes of attitude implied by these legal dispositions are perceptible in social reality and are 'most present in the sphere of public administration, in the habits and practices it instils in the purveyors of public power in European polities, from the most mundane to the most august' and extend to the legislative and judiciary spheres where many policies in the public realm can no longer be adopted without examining their consonance with the interest of others (Weiler *inter alia* 1998). Beyond political, judiciary and bureaucratic practices, collective representations are also being transformed. The growing number of exchanges – professional migrations, tourism, twinning programmes, agreements, networks – has helped to lessen the feeling of mistrust that long prevailed in relations between Europeans, facilitating better understanding and creating some form of mutual curiosity.

The lifting of legal and administrative discrimination practices has also contributed to arousing a community feeling among Europeans, but not as the great 'melting pot' of the American model. Instead, Europeans seem to be engaged in constructing an area of mutual recognition of each other's individual collective identity, creating as it were a 'demoi-cracy'-in-the-making (Nicolaïdis 2004). Public opinion polls show that national identities remain strong among people who are still attached to national habits and practices inherited from history, and are often reflected in some apolitical form of nationalism, be it about food, sports or arts. But their attachment to the nation has become somewhat looser and less exclusive. As sociologists have recently demonstrated, it is complemented by similar attachment to Europe and greater interest for the culture of other European nations.

There are limits, however, to the progress of transnational citizenship in the EU, not least tangible in the fact that citizens to this day do not have the right to vote in their country of residence (except in European or municipal elections), thereby doing away with the ultimate measure of democracy. Most importantly, the question remains of how these new rights for nationals coming from other member states will affect non-European citizens. At the moment, while non-discrimination is progressively being extended, the diagnosis remains mixed on grounds of social representation: as Balibar, Shaw and others have argued, closer solidarity between European citizens inevitably leads to heightened discrimination towards third countries, but at the same time a non-discrimination ethos may also herald more tolerance towards non-Europeans on account of the 'denationalisation' of the notion of citizenship. But of course, the EU is still and only a transnational democracy-in-the-making.

From regional to global integration: promoting the 'single market model'

The earliest and most straightforward way to project the EU model of inter-state relations outside its borders has been through its functional core, e.g. the common or single market. The creation of the *Journal of Common Market Studies* in 1962 testifies to this explicit vision at the outset inside European circles. There was at the time a sense that if mimetic regional integration could be engineered, we might witness the creation of an international society of regions that would constitute the underpinning of a functioning multilateral economic order. Article 24 of the General Agreement on Tariffs and Trade (GATT) had foreseen this vision by setting out the legal conditions under which the two 'multilateral' logics – regional and global – could be compatible.

Yet, the combined factors of the cold war and decolonisation postponed the onset of regionalism by three decades (Fawcett and Hurrell 1995). Clearly, given the specific conditions that gave rise to the creation and deepening of the EC/EU, it seemed improbable that its model could be reproduced whole in other regions. Indeed, most of the countries emerging as former colonies/quasi-colonies/occupied territories on the world scene after World War Two and decolonisation were not keen on turning around right away and sharing their sovereignty with their neighbours.

The pursuit of even only regional integration through trade clearly entailed such transfers where the democratic ethos is upheld the two ways outlined above. For one, most potential regions of the world exhibit much greater structural power asymmetries than does Europe, with big countries potentially or actually acting as regional hegemons (India, Brazil, South Africa, Nigeria, Indonesia and of course China). For symmetric reasons, neither these countries nor their smaller neighbours could comfortably envisage the kind of regional multilateralism based on formal equality between member states practised in the EU. In the EU's case at least, trade liberalisation was practised not only for its own sake or as a vector of (democratic) peace and material interdependence but also as a vector of political interdependence through the pooling of institutions and rights. It could be argued that this was all the more true that the original EC chose to create a customs union rather than a free-trade area, the option which has come to be favoured by the rest of the world. But the distinct implications of the two models have become blurred. In an era of globalisation, a regional economic entity needs to speak with one voice in global economic institutions from the International Monetary Fund (IMF) to the World Trade Organization (WTO). Crucially, supranational institutions need to be entrusted with the mandatory resolution of internal and external trade disputes. Without a Court to adjudicate and a Commission-like entity to monitor and evaluate, the political economy of market integration in a regulated world quickly takes over. And last but not least, in order to function properly, the mutual granting of free movement or economic citizenship through non-discrimination necessarily entails a degree of direct effect. Non-national citizens or companies will come to seek redress if their freedom is curbed not with the state on whose territory they operate but either with their home state as upholder of their rights or with the supranational dispute resolution entity. In all cases, regional integration implies accepting some degree of extraterritorial rights.

In spite of these exacting prospects, regional integration experiments began to flourish around the world after the cold war. Whether in Latin America, Africa or Asia; the EU has for the last decade or more been spontaneously invoked as an integration model (famously the African Union made democracy a goal rather than a prerequisite for membership, explaining that this was its only difference with the EU). Nevertheless, the EU has not been passive but thought to sustain and reinforce such a trend. Persuaded that the end of the cold war marked the hour of Europe, EU leaders have argued in all manner of fora that the spread of the EU model would serve to avoid two dreaded outcomes: global anarchy or US hegemony.

The vision that seems to prevail is that of a new multilateralism, predicated on negotiations between regional groupings over minimal common standards alongside sustained regional political, cultural and economic diversity. Some have even argued for the reorganisation of the UN along regional lines. As building blocks, regions would be best placed to sustain an international order based on negotiation and judicial arbitration rather than the use of force. Indeed, negotiations over global economic integration in the WTO are already regionalised to a great extent – so advocates argue, if trade why not defence? But the crisis of the UN and international economic and financial institutions (and the incapacity of the members of the EU to share views on their reforms) lead to rather pessimistic scenarios.

Ultimately, however, the limitations of the world of regions scenario can be found at the level of the regions themselves. Regional economic integration is first and foremost driven by rational calculations by states that the negative effects of global liberalisation can be (partially) offset or cushioned through more localised preferential regimes. The geopolitical context, and US support for preferences upheld against itself (through the Marshall Plan) also helped in the case of the EU. But such trade interdependence, backed up by perspicuous geopolitical factors, no longer seems to obtain at least to the same extent today and outside Europe. The WTO-led global management of trade liberalisation progressively erodes the comparative advantage of customs unions. And with the collapse of bipolarity, the geopolitics of regional integration have also changed dramatically.

Moreover, as functionalists like Karl Deutsch have long argued, cultural proximity and the intensification of social contacts play a significant role in the dynamics of integration. Yet, like Europe itself other regional groupings are embedded in sociocultural settings at least as diverse, thereby challenging convergence around the idea of polity-formation beyond economic integration. It is not surprising that all regional groupings other than the EU rely exclusively on intergovernmental methods, which in turn renders integration harder. The trade area between Argentina, Brazil, Paraguay and Uruguay (MERCOSUR), the only possible exception, has been floundering exactly on this point.

So whether or not the EU model is reproducible, in part or in whole, in the short term or with a long time lag, the integration game to a great extent today has shifted to the global level. It is not surprising therefore that EU diplomats and politicians have increasingly argued that the EU model is also relevant on a global scale (see Chapter 7 on global trade governance in this volume). In the WTO, as early as the late 1980s with the Uruguay Round, European negotiators were upholding the 'new approach' to trade liberalisation, combining national treatment, harmonisation and mutual recognition as the long-term template for the liberalisation of services, or for dealing with non-tariff barriers in general. By the late 1990s, this discourse of projection had taken on a new momentum as the USA agreed with the EU (somewhat reluctantly) to include the so-called Singapore Agenda on the Doha Round Agenda. That meant designing global rules regarding domestic public procurement and competition laws (as has been done within the EU) – two realms which, if globalised, would involve deep incursions within the domestic sphere of governance and the precinct of the welfare state. Similarly, linking labour or environmental conditions to trade liberalisation would also be inspired by the EU model.

How is this drive to export the EU's brand of inter-state management of markets perceived in the rest of the world? While it may rest on strong economic grounds, this EU defence of its model flounders on a deep divide between the EU and other WTO members. For the EU, and according to its own model, trade liberalisation ought to be about agreed-upon principles and rules to govern trans-border exchanges that are legitimate as *norms*, and thus defensible as something other than concessions that some members have traded away in order to get some benefits in other areas. For most other WTO members, however, this is not what multilateral trade governance should be about. Negotiations are about exchanging concessions estimated on the basis of the expected impact of market access provisions. Everyone needs to be reassured that they will be net winners, so principles alone won't do, especially when suspected to disproportionally serve the interests of certain members. What we have seen with the Doha Round, however, is that while the first approach has been rejected by a wide array of the membership, the second is increasingly unmanageable with the growing number of veto players and veto coalitions. Meanwhile, short of the EU model, the global trade regime is in crisis – or maybe such crisis is seen as preferable to what is sometimes viewed as Euro-imperialism or the unilateral imposition of EU norms through market power.

The next frontier of global democracy in this light is Kant's third dimension, or applying the EU notion of citizenship, with economic rights bestowed directly to citizens in each other's state to the global level through WTO and UN rules. While the WTO appellate body or the International Court of Justice are still cautious in doing so, some argue that such developments are coming from the bottom up, through the application of what can be called globalised administrative law.

From model to actor: the exercise of civilian power

The question we are left with then is how the EU has managed the transition from model to actor, from influence-through-example or persuasion to influence-through-action. While being a model *per se* can be a source of power (the power of induction or attraction), for many it is not enough. Real power involves the capacity to capitalise and extract 'goods' from such passive influence. Indeed, at the regional level, the EU has not simply let its model speak for itself. Instead it has engaged in negotiations over interregional agreements with MERCOSUR and the Association South-East Asian Nations (ASEAN), and by 2002 with the six regions constituting of the ACP. With each of the plans to create regions modelled after the EU, from North East Asia to the Horn of Africa, one can identify the hand of the EU at work (Telò 2007). A common pattern is for the EU to make access to its own market conditional on the adoption of standards and rules in these regions which are said to be 'compatible' with that of the EU. In short, a single passport for Brazilian firms in the EU must be matched by a single passport there for EU firms.

As a result, such interregionalism underpinned by the promotion of the EU model is proving contested precisely because outsiders are made to negotiate over the fine line between the EU's promotion of a systemic vision of a world of interrelated visions and the pursuit of its narrow self-interest. Buy our court of justice and our standard-setting agencies, the EU seems to say, and we will give you Ikea as a bonus. For the EU's partners, more often than not, the promotion of interstate democracy and the rule of law defined as a political ethos seem to give way to the promotion of 'our' institutions, with which we can easily do business, and 'our' standards which grant market power to 'our' businesses. The same may arguably be true at the global level, where the adoption of the EU's own governance and regulative standards obviously promotes the interests of its firms.

One of the keys to this tension between the promotion of one's model and its legitimacy to the rest of the world has to do with consistency both between the ends promoted and the means adopted for promotion; and between internal policies and discourse and their external translation. Indeed, this broad ontological connection has long been made between the EU's internal features and the very special and idiosyncratic way it is supposed to act on the world scene. This is what is at stake today with the refinement and reformulation of the old idea of civilian powerhood. While lacking any precise definition, the notion has less to do with the means the EU might use to influence individual countries, and more to do with the idea of *peaceful* translation of its internal features as an interstate organisation onto the international society of state.

It is of course tempting to dismiss the idea of civilian power as an oxymoron based on myth (peace through trade) and colonial nostalgia, as well as born of frustration at Europe's inability to become a third superpower during the cold war. Yet the idea that the EU could lead by example and project its relevance worldwide has proved resilient, precisely because of its connotation as a link between means and ends – *civilian* as *civil* means (e.g., non-military) and as *civilising* objectives (e.g., diffusing habits of peaceful change). There is, however, considerable fuzziness in the literature over where to draw the line between civilian and military power: for example, peacekeeping forces are frequently considered to be a 'civilian foreign policy instrument' (Smith 2004). But the debate as to whether the occasional use of military means disqualifies the EU claim to civilian powerhood rests on narrow focus on *exercising* civilian power. *Being* a civilian power, however, entails not only the relation between means and ends, but also the use of persuasion and the prevalence of civilian control over foreign (and defence) policy-making (Smith 2004). Combined with the horizontal and vertical transfer of sovereignty discussed above, this set of factors allows the development of the rule of law in international relations, which pushes forward a process of *civilising* international politics. The *civilian ends* most often cited as relevant to this agenda are international cooperation, solidarity, domestication of international relations (or strengthening the rule of law in international relations), responsibility for the global environment, and the diffusion of equality, justice and tolerance. These are '*milieu* goals' which aim to shape the environment in which the state – or the EU, in this case – operates, rather than 'possession goals' which further national interests (Wolfers 1962).

So the question we are left with beyond the realm of trade is whether the EU can be credible in the forceful promotion of its model when the method and the content of such promotion fails to transcend its own interests (say, by advocating discrimination against itself in the formation of new regions). The recent and heated negotiations over Economic Partnership Agreements (EPAs) between the EU and the successor regions to ACP countries seem to exemplify more strongly than before this tension between altruistic systemic goals (promotion of development) and the pursuit of corporate and other interests.

Part of the problem and perhaps the solution in this vein comes back to internal/ external consistency (Weiler 1998; Nicolaïdis 2004). Are EU internal strategies such as in the realm of agriculture or justice and home affairs congruent with the EU's external agenda? If inter-state democratisation means the de-linkage between citizenship rights and nationality, how should the EU relate the treatment of European and non-European others? Instead of fighting for openness, free movement and non-discrimination, it may be necessary to fight against illegal immigration and labour market distortions, but the price to pay lies with the credibility of civilian powerhood as a commitment to promoting a world compatible with one's own internal values.

Conclusion

In the end, is the EU's brand of democracy lost in translation with attempts to export it to the rest of the world? To be sure, Europeans need to learn to live with the contradiction of a non-European world where their influence is dwindling and yet their model continues to be relevant through attraction, symbiosis and fashion. The EU is an unprecedented experience combining intra-state, inter-state and transnational democratisation. To some extent, these principles already apply to the EU's external action: democratic conditionality, rhetorical defence of multilateralism, promotion of the EU model in various regional and global fora. But it is clear that in a Hobbesian world, such a strategy of projection encounters serious limits, from the non-translatability of the EU model to its internal contestation; from accusations of double standards to the lack of internal/external consistency; from the tension between coercion and contract or means and ends to the contradiction involved in the promoting of democracy through (coercive) conditionality. The most radical critics of the EU's global democracy agenda argue that the very idea of promoting democracy or a European model of governance is inherently flawed, laden as it is with echoes of imperialism. For budding scholars of the EU and its role in the world, it is worth critically asking under what conditions this tension can be overcome, for the EU to truly leave behind Eurocentric approaches to global governance while nevertheless making a difference beyond its own tentative experiment of democracy beyond the state.

Acknowledgement

*   We are grateful to Tobias Lenz and Stefan Szwed for previous research assistance, as well as to Jean-Marc Ferry, Justine Lacroix, Louis Scheek and Mario Telò for their precious feedback.

Notes

1 See 'The three definitive articles' in Immanuel Kant (1795). Each of the three founding principles can be seen as a necessary condition for the existence of the other two. (i) The democratic peace argument may be contested but there is little doubt that internal democracy makes inter-state cooperation easier while also making the principle of non-discrimination plausible – dictatorships have always tended to victimise foreigners first. (ii) The 'federalism of free states' exemplified by the European legal and political mechanisms of non-hegemonic cooperation – Kant's second condition – consolidates the states' democratic foundations and forces them to respect the principle of non-discrimination. (iii) A principle that guarantees equal treatment between nationals and citizens of the other member states – Kant's *ius cosmopoliticum* – consolidates democracies by protecting them against their own nationalistic drifts while furthering peaceful relations between states (as potential diplomatic disputes over expatriates' status are avoided).

2 There is no agreed definition of 'democracy'. For our purposes, democracy requires *inter alia* the self-government of citizens within a given territory, which in turn entails: free elections with secret balloting; the right to establish political parties without hindrance from the state; free and equal access to a free press; free trade union organisations; freedom of opinion; executive powers restricted by laws; and an independent judiciary. This is, of course, an expansive definition.

3 Samuel P. Huntington in *The Third Wave*, defined three historical waves of democratisation. The first one bought democracy to Western Europe and Northern America in the 19th century, followed by a rise if dictatorships during the Interwar period. The second began after World War II, but lost steam between 1962 and the mid-1970s. The latest wave has seen more than 60 countries experience democratic transitions since 1974, notably in Latin America and post-Communist countries of Eastern Europe.

Bibliography

Balibar, Étienne (2004), *We, the people of Europe? Reflections on Transnational Citizenship*, Princeton University Press.

Bellamy, Richard, Dario Castiglione and Jo Shaw (2006), *Making European Citizens*, Palgrave.

Bobbio, Norberto (2006), *Liberalism and Democracy (Radical Thinkers)*, London: Verso.

Carothers, Thomas (2003), *Is Gradualism Possible? Choosing a Strategy for Promoting Democracy in the Middle East* [Working Document No. 39], Washington DC: Carnegie Endowment for International Peace.

Cheneval, Francis (2005), *La Cité des peuples*, Paris: Cerf.

Cowles, Maria Green, James Caporaso, and Thomas Risse (eds) (2001), *Transforming Europe: Europeanization and Domestic Change*, Ithaca NY and London: Cornell University Press.

Del Sarto, Schumacher, Lannon, Driss (2007), 'Benchmarking democratic development in the Euro-Mediterranean area: conceptualising ends, means and stategies', *EuroMesco Annual Report 2006*, May 2007.

Emerson, Michael, Senem Aydın, Gergana Noutcheva, Nathalie Tocci, Marius Vahl and Richard Youngs (2005), *The Reluctant Debutante: The European Union as Promoter of Democracy in Its Neighbourhood* [Working Document No. 223], Brussels: Centre for European Policy Studies.

Ellis, Elisabeth (2005), *Kant's Politics: Provisional Theory for an Uncertain World*, New Haven CN: Yale University Press.

Fawcett, Louise and Andrew Hurrell (1995), *Regionalism in World Politics: Regional Organization and International Order*, Oxford: Oxford University Press.

Ferry, J.-M. (2000), *La Question de l'Etat Européen*, Paris: Éditions Gallimard, Collection "NRF-essais".

Ferry, J.-M. (2005), *Europe: La voie kantienne. Essai sur l'identité postnationale*, Paris: Cerf.

Huntington, Samuel (1991), *The Third Wave : Democratization in the Late Twentieth Century*, Norman University of Oklahoma Press.

Kant, Immanuel (1795), *Perpetual Peace: A Philosophical Sketch*.

Magnette, Paul (2000), *Le souverain apprivoisé, l'Europe, L'Etat et la démocratie*, Collection Etudes européennes, Brussels: Complexe.

Nicolaïdis, Kalypso (2004), 'We, the Peoples of Europe ...', in *Foreign Affairs*, November/December 2004, pp. 97–110.

Rawls, John (1999), *The Laws of Peoples*, Boston: Harvard University Press.

Sasse, Gwendolyn (2008) 'The politics of EU conditionality: the norm of minority protection during and beyond EU accession', Journal of European Public Policy, 15: 6, 842–60.

Schimmelfennig, Frank and Ulrich Sedelmeier (2005), *The Politics of European Union Enlargement: Theoretical Approaches*, London: Routledge.

Smith, Karen E. (2004), *The Making of EU Foreign Policy: The Case of Eastern Europe*, London: Palgrave.

Telò, Mario (2007), *The EU and New Regionalism*, London: Ashgate.

Weiler, Joseph (1998), *The Constitution of Europe: Do the New Clothes Have an Emperor?*, Cambridge: Cambridge University Press.

Wolfers, Arnold (1962), *Discord and Collaboration: Essays on International Politics*, Baltimore: The Johns Hopkins Press.

Youngs, Richard (2001), *The European Union and the Promotion of Democracy*, Oxford: Oxford University Press.

Zakaria, Fareed (1997), 'The rise of illiberal democracy', *Foreign Affairs*, Vol. 76, No. 6, pp. 22–43.

3   The international projection of the euro and the international monetary system

Jean-Victor Louis

Summary

Born in 1999, the euro has rapidly become an international currency. It has become the second international currency used in all the functions classically attributed to a currency and its role is now more important than that of the legacy currencies. However, the US dollar although in a position of decline, is still the most widely used currency.

The euro is a currency without a state. This means that it is in a very specific position with respect to other currencies in a world still mostly designed for and by states. In order to evaluate the way the euro has fitted into the international monetary and financial system, it seems necessary to get a broad view of the components and workings of the main institutions and groupings in charge of monetary and financial stability. Despite the focus on the International Monetary Fund (IMF), one cannot neglect the G7, which has been defined as the screening committee of the IMF, and other entities, like the G20 (which has grown in importance since the Washington Summit of November 15, 2008), the G10 and the Basle institutions (Bank of International Settlements (BIS), Basle Committee for Banking Supervision (BCBS), Financial Stability Forum (FSF)).

The European Community Treaty includes provisions concerning the participation and representation of the euro area in international financial institutions. The Lisbon Treaty confirms these provisions and establishes a stable presidency for the Eurogroup, which plays an increasing role in the external representation of the euro area along with the European Central Bank President and the Economic and Monetary Union Commissioner. Practises have developed to coordinate the positions of the member states in the international context. But pragmatism cannot allow for the euro to be effectively represented on an equal footing with the other international currencies.

Taking into account the specific features of the IMF, and the ongoing reform of this institution as well as the pressures exercised on the EU, and Europe in general, by its partners, various scenarios are presented and evaluated with regard to the representation of the euro area within the Fund. The question of the inclusion of the euro area is directly connected to a move towards more legitimacy and effectiveness for the Fund. The future of a universal institution for monetary and financial stability is at stake.

The euro as an international currency

The euro, adopted on January 1, 1999 as the single currency of eleven within the EU, has been legal tender in fifteen of its twenty-seven member states since January 1, 2008, following the adoption of the single currency by Cyprus and Malta.

There is in the euro area a single monetary policy in the Eurosystem, itself composed of the European Central Bank (ECB) and the national central banks of the states that adopted the euro. The exchange rate policy is the joint responsibility of the Council of the EU and the ECB. The euro is a substitute for the former currencies of the states that have adopted it, of which two so-called legacy currencies – the Deutsche Mark (DM) and the French franc (FRF) – were *international* currencies. An international currency is used not only inside but also outside the borders of its originating country. As a "widely accepted" currency, it could serve for paying the subscription to the IMF. The DM and the FRF were, up to January 1, 1999,[1] included in the basket defining the value of the SDR, the IMF's accounting unit, with the US dollar, the pound sterling and the Japanese yen. The euro has since replaced the DM and the FRF in this basket.

Right from the beginning, the euro has become an international currency on its own, and it has immediately affirmed itself as the second international currency after the US dollar. It exercizes internationally the three functions of money – both official and private – which makes it a store of value, a medium of exchange, and a

Table 3.1 Member states of the EU having adopted the euro (as of January 1, 2009)

Belgium	(Jan. 1, 1999)
Germany	(Jan. 1, 1999)
Spain	(Jan. 1, 1999)
France	(Jan. 1, 1999)
Ireland	(Jan. 1, 1999)
Italy	(Jan. 1, 1999)
Luxembourg	(Jan. 1, 1999)
The Netherlands	(Jan. 1, 1999)
Austria	(Jan. 1, 1999)
Portugal	(Jan. 1, 1999)
Finland	(Jan. 1, 1999)
Greece	(Jan. 1, 2001)
Slovenia	(Jan. 1, 2007)
Cyprus	(Jan. 1, 2008)
Malta	(Jan. 1, 2008)
Slovakia	(Jan. 1, 2009)

Note
The UK and Denmark have an exemption under specific protocols to the Maastricht Treaty; Sweden will participate after a positive referendum (a unilateral *de facto* opt-out of sorts) but it legally has the obligation to adopt the euro and hence has the temporary status of a 'member state with a derogation'; the other EU countries with a status of derogation are: Bulgaria, Czech Republic, Estonia, Latvia, Lithuania, Hungary, Poland, Romania, Slovakia.

unit of account (Bertuch-Samuels 2006: 147).[2] For example, as far as the official use is concerned, when the euro appears as an anchor for another currency, in pegging arrangements or otherwise, alone or with other currencies (like the US dollar), in the definition of the parity of a currency, it refers to its *unit of account function*. Interventions on the foreign exchange markets relate to its *medium of exchange function* and the accumulation of euro in the foreign exchange reserves is a manifestation of the role of the currency as a *store of value*. The same grid can be used to analyze the private uses of the euro. It serves as a vehicle to purchase foreign currencies, as a *medium of exchange*; it is used in deposits or in debt operations, in its *store of value* function; and when it serves as an invoicing currency in international trade, it plays the role of a *unit of account* and of payment.

The ECB, the Bank for International Settlements (BIS) and the IMF all produce, more or less regularly, sophisticated statistics on the international role of the euro. They give precious information but, for some data, precise information is difficult to collect. And neither the methods for collecting data nor the categories of data covered by each organization are identical. So the range of information offers "clear" and reliable orientations rather than a totally accurate picture. It is especially the case, for example, with figures about the currency composition of the official reserves or the use of the euro in invoicing. Furthermore, a large part of the reserves of emergent countries, especially oil producers, is located in the so-called Sovereign Wealth Funds (SWF), which started to emerge in the 1990s[3]. These amounts are not counted in the official foreign exchange reserves.

The ECB and the EU, in general, affect a neutral attitude concerning the evolution of the international role of the euro. Their standpoint is that it is for the market to decide. This policy could seem strange to those who rightly considered the move to the single currency as being politically motivated by the ambition to get rid of the dollar supremacy. This consideration clearly was present among a series of motives, some of which were political, behind the decision to build a monetary union. Within most European countries there was an interest in moving towards a multilateral system capable of replacing the former Bretton Woods system, characterized by a system of parities or the intention to support the European vocation of Germany in the perspective of the reunification of the country. But the role of a top international currency presents challenges as well as advantages. For example, if a currency becomes a reserve currency, the value of this currency will depend on decisions taken by other states, i.e., official and not market-led decisions, for economic as well

Table 3.2 The role of the euro as an international currency: statistical data

The ECB publishes a *Review of the International Role of the Euro*. The sixth version was published in June 2007; from this issue onward it has been published on a bi-annual basis.
The BIS produces a *Triennial Central Bank Survey*. The December 2007 one focused on "Foreign exchange and derivatives market activities".
The IMF has a database on Currency Composition of Official Foreign Exchange Reserves (COFER), and an IMF Data Template on International Reserves and Foreign Currency Liquidity, regularly updated on the Fund's website.

as political reasons. The will to control the use by others of its own currency is not a rare attitude. The EU objects to unilateral euroization, i.e., the use of the euro by third countries. The "neutrality" of the authorities respecting the international role of the euro is not in conflict with the expression of satisfaction of the same authorities when analyzing the developments in this context. It means that the euro is considered as a solid and stable currency.

If the euro is clearly the second international currency, and if all statistics concur to demonstrate that its role is greater than the one played by legacy currencies before 1999, the US dollar remains by far the most important currency in the world.[4] In many cases, the euro appears to be used in the context of special relations with the EU, either by candidate, neighboring states or by countries linked to the EU by historical or special links, like African countries.

As far as the *official international role of the euro* is concerned, the euro has become the anchor currency in countries of Europe, Africa and the Mediterranean, as part of a pegging arrangement to the euro alone or in a basket of currencies or in relation with the establishment of a currency board (i.e., a fixed and exclusive relation between a currency and the euro). It concerns between forty and fifty states. 'The euro has become a regional hub for currencies in a formal or informal peg with it' (Pisani-Ferry, *et al.* 2008: 95). The weight of the euro in the operational basket for the rouble used by the Central Bank of the Russian Federation has gone from 35 to 40 percent in 2005 (see Lucas Papademos, "The global importance of the euro," *Speech*, November 17, 2006, www.ecb.int). The Gulf Emirates also include the euro in their basket (Handelsblatt, February 1, 2007). By contrast, sixty to seventy-five countries have an exchange rate policy based on the dollar. Others use a mixed basket (dollar/euro). (See the sources in Table 4.2.)

The euro served as a currency of intervention on foreign exchange markets in September and November 2000, first in a multilateral operation with other central banks, and then unilaterally by the Eurosystem, led by the ECB.

As a reserve currency, the distribution between major currencies is as follows: two-thirds of total global reserves in US dollars, one-quarter in the euro and 7 percent in the yen. Before the monetary union, the legacy currencies accounted for 18 percent; in 2003, the euro was at 25 percent and in December 2006, it accounted for 25.8 percent. In December 2007, the figure has increased to 26.4 percent (FT.com, December 31, 2007). The dollar's share fell to 63.8 percent. The role of the euro is clearly bigger than the one played by the legacy currencies. But this increase is not spectacular considering the seven- to eight-year period.

The *private international use of the euro* is illustrated by its role as exchange currency in payments and exchange operations. The value of the circulating banknotes denominated in euro exceeds the value of US dollar bills. This difference results from the payment uses and from the existence of high-denomination banknotes in euro, like the 200 and the 500 ones, in comparison with the 100-dollar bill, the highest US denomination in circulation. On the other hand, the use of euro banknotes is geographically limited: 10–20 percent are used out of the area, following figures given by the Deutsche Bank Research (*EU Monitor* 46, May 4, 2007), in comparison with 50–70 percent for the US dollar bills.

The euro/US dollar pair (calculations go per pair for exchange operations because there are always two currencies involved – the total is not therefore 100 but 200 percent) is the most used in exchange operations: it appears in 27 percent of the exchange transactions. The US dollar remains by far the most used currency in exchange operations, although this share is (slightly) diminishing (from 90.3 percent in 2001 to 86.3 percent in 2006, in some statistics, but for the ECB, the share of the dollar remains stable at more or less 93 percent). The euro share for its part remains more or less stable at 37 percent (39 percent for the BIS or 41 percent in 2001 for the ECB). The yen is used in 16.5 percent (21 percent for the ECB) of the operations (down from 23.4 in 1992, when the Maastricht Treaty was signed) and the pound sterling in 15 percent. Either the dollar or the euro appears in 98 percent of operations.

In international trade, the US dollar has a share of 50 percent for both invoicing and settlement. As for the euro area, according to the ECB, the euro appears in more or less 50 percent of exports and more or less 35 percent of imports.

The success of the euro is clear in the international debt market. The stock of debt denominated in euro represented 31.4 percent in December 2006 (ECB June 2007 report quoted in Table 4.2); in parallel, the US dollar has decreased from 50 to 43 percent from 1999 to 2006. Of the new international obligations, 46 percent are issued in euro (39 percent in US dollar). On the loan and deposit markets, the part of the euro, in cases where it is not the currency of any of the parties concerned, is respectively more or less 17 and 18 percent.

We may conclude from these rough data that the dollar remains prominent on the international scene but its part is declining, and maybe this evolution could accelerate. The euro progresses without spectacular moves. Both the yen and the pound sterling remain interesting, though the yen retains a smaller position. "The US, Europe and to a diminishing extent Japan are still the unrivalled issuers of the world's key currencies but they represent a much smaller share of world GDP than at the time of Maastricht" (Pisani-Ferry, et al. 2008: 93).

As a currency without a state, the euro is in a specific position in the international monetary system, compared to its competitors. There is no Finance Minister in the EU and this organization is based on the principle of conferred powers and not on general powers like a state. International institutions and caucuses are country-based and not currency-based entities. Furthermore they have been built in a deeply different context. It is banal to observe that the Bretton Woods environment no longer prevails. Political and economic weight in the international economy is shifting. Is the present institutional framework still relevant? Is it able to cope with the global imbalances? How should the representation of the euro be organized? Those are the main questions we will look at in the next sections.

The relevance of the present international system in a changing global world

The present constellation and the composition of groups and institutions in the global financial order reflect a different world than the one of the Bretton Woods order (Ahearne and Eichengreen 2007). Studies in this field generally conclude that there is an over-representation of Europe, not of 'Europe' as the EU or the euro area but as various states with a spread representation. This paragraph's objective is nevertheless quite different. Before discussing the modalities of representation of the EU or the euro area within the IMF and the groups, it is necessary to answer the questions: Do we still need the IMF, as the main organization in charge of financial stability? and What would be its role in the future international system?

The IMF

Until the financial crisis beginning in 2007 with the subprime loans crisis in the US housing sector, which degenerated into a huge financial crisis and global economic slowdown in 2008, there was doubt among many nations, especially in emerging areas, about the role of the IMF in the future. Considering the overwhelming amount of global foreign exchange reserves and their steady growth, many questioned the usefulness of a central organization in charge of providing financing in order to remedy balance of payments problems. After the strong criticism of the way the IMF resolved the Asian crisis at the end of the 1990s, for having applied its classic recipes of budgetary rigor and inflation-fighting, and the reaction in Latin America to the management of the Argentine crisis at the beginning of this century, one could observe a clear trend towards regionalism in this field. The envisaged creation of an Asian Monetary Fund by the ASEAN + 3 grouping with an endowment of 80 billion US dollars is another example of that trend, in parallel with a network of swaps established among these countries in order to address asymmetrical shocks. Following similar concerns are the repeated calls by Vladimir Putin for regionalization. The reaction of Argentina, which was in a hurry to reimburse its IMF debt after a terrible crisis, in a gesture of protestation against the conditionality of the Fund, is typical of bad relations between Third World countries and the global institution. The budget of the Fund has been affected by the impressive diminution of its credits, creating an important problem of resources. On the other hand, China offers unconditional loans to African countries, to a point that the intervention of the Fund could appear as redundant.[5]

All this contributed to create the impression that the Fund had become obsolete. Nevertheless European leaders always were of the opinion that the Fund could keep an important role in the future and, with the development of the crisis, the request for a 'new Bretton Woods' (referring to the place in New Hampshire where the conference which created the IMF and the World Bank was held in 1944) became common to many countries of the EU. The crisis of 2008, the most severe since the Great Depression of the 1930s, demonstrated that the global objectives of the institution are currently still relevant, and will remain so in a rapidly changing world. We will describe what the IMF was built for and look at the end of this chapter on the perspectives open for the future by the G20 'Washington Declaration' of November 15, 2008.

In an overview, the general manager of the Fund, Dominique Strauss Kahn, summed up the objectives of the IMF in his presentation speech to the Board of

Directors in the summer of 2007. For him, the Fund had to facilitate growth and promote employment while ensuring monetary stability.

In order to implement these objectives, the Fund has to accomplish diverse functions. To quote a former general manager of the Fund, Rodrigo de Rato, the *work of surveillance* in "monitoring the global economy, advising individual members on their economies and assessing their policies, is perhaps the greatest single service the Fund can provide"[6]. It includes an impressive list of actions, such as: the publication – each semester – of the *World Economic Outlook*; consultations on exchange rates under Article IV; multilateral assessments of, and bilateral consultations on, the economic situation of members; the Financial Sector Assessment Program (FSAP); anti-money-laundering efforts; the Reports on the Observance of Standards and Codes (ROSCs); technical assistance, especially in the field of central banking; advising low-income countries on appropriate macro-economic policy in the face of high and volatile aid inflows, etc.

However, besides these functions, the Fund has an important responsibility in the *prevention and resolution of financial crisis*. An important number of countries do not have access to international capital markets (Eichengreen and Hausman 2005)[7] and do not have extensive export revenues. Furthermore, the crisis of 2007/2008 has demonstrated how reversible the financial situation of a country is. Emerging countries were not immune from the economic slowdown in the industrial world.[8] Developed countries have repatriated a number of their assets and exporting countries have seen their income lowering. Many countries with fragile economies have experienced a fall in their currency's worth in response to the fall of international currencies like the dollar and the euro, and have accumulated fiscal deficits. These developments have lead the Fund to create in October 2008 a new short term facility open to sound economies but without imposing the strong conditionality that the IMF used to impose on its debtors[9]. Some countries like Hungary, Iceland, Ukraine and Pakistan benefited from loans of the Fund in 2008. It rapidly became apparent that the resources available to the IMF would not be sufficient in order to cope with the large number of demands for financial support.

The Fund did not await the development of the crisis to undertake efforts in order to remain at the center of the public monetary system with a universal vocation. But from the beginning of the century, the steps made in this direction were more symbolic than effective. The Medium-Term Strategy reflects this will, although still in an unambitious way. Three significant elements were going in this direction: the establishment in 2006 of a consultative group for multilateral consultations on global imbalances; the adoption by the Executive Board of the Bilateral Surveillance decision in June 2007 as an element of the strengthening of multilateral surveillance; and the decision in 2006 to start the reform by increasing the quotas of four countries: China, South Korea, Mexico and Turkey. We will underline the meaning of the first two elements and come back on the third one in the next section.

The setting-up of an unprecedented *multilateral consultation* in a group including the USA, the euro area, Japan, China and Saudi Arabia has, for our subject, a symbolic importance. For the first time, within the IMF, a troika including the President of the Eurogroup, the President of the ECB and the member of the Commission in charge of the Economic and Monetary Union (EMU) represented the euro area as such. For evident reasons, and significantly, the situation of the UK outside the monetary union excluded this country from this consultation process. The group was intended to provide a forum for improving understanding and sharing views on global imbalances (a large deficit on the part of the USA and a huge surplus on the part of China are among the most important elements of these imbalances) and on how best to reduce them in the context of sustainable robust global growth. The composition of the group allowed for a first multilateral dialogue on this topic with the participation of the countries and regions representing a very large share of global output; the dialogue was thus able to contribute to a more balanced situation where demand and savings patterns would adjust.[10] It was the first time that China was involved in a multilateral discussion of these questions. And that is perhaps the most important result of this experience in multilateralism. At least the multilateral consultation seems to have created the conviction among the participants that they were confronting a "multilateral challenge" and that it was their "joint responsibility" to work to a solution (as underlined in the report on the consultation of April 14, 2007).[11] It is remarkable that, at least formally, IMF institutions do not play a role in this matter.

Interesting in this context is the Executive Board Decision on bilateral surveillance over members' policies of June 15, 2007, repealing and replacing a 1977 decision. The new Decision, in the terms of the IMF Public Information Notice, "crystallizes a common vision of the best practise of surveillance." It introduces a new concept of external stability that encompasses the current account (trade balance) and the capital account of the balance of payments and clarifies the concept of "exchange rate manipulation" aiming at gaining an "unfair competitive advantage" over other members, which is prohibited under Article IV. "In particular, the new Decision relates such behavior to the concept of fundamental exchange rate misalignment." In fact, the Decision describes seven "developments" as being "among those which would require thorough review and might indicate the need for discussion with a member". But the precautionary wording, especially that used in the traditional chairman's summing up, did not prevent China from protesting against this surveillance that will put emerging countries under greater pressure, accusing the IMF of echoing the recriminations of the US Congress on the sub-evaluation of the yuan (*LA Tribune*, July 2, 2007).[12] The Declaration underlines the limits of its powers. The reference to "best practise" and the insistence on persuasion and dialogue are more appropriate to peer control than to effective legal powers. But it is an undeniable step in the right direction, although the initiative of this reform appeared to some as a sign of the predominant influence of the US on the IMF policies.

The G7 (G8) and the G20

The limited effectiveness of the Fund is due in part to its lack of binding powers but also to the ineffectiveness of the G7 (G8 when Russia joins), the would-be steering committee of a globalized world that includes the USA, Japan, Germany, France, the UK, Canada and Italy. In Fred Bergsten's words, "A fundamental reason for the increasing ineffectiveness of the IMF during the past decade or so has been the ineffectiveness of its steering committee" (Bergsten 2006: 180–91). "Such kind of grouping was created in order to get a global view on the challenges that the international community and in particular, the various international institutions (UN, IMF, World Bank, WTO, ILO, WHO, OECD ...) are confronted with in their respective field of action without a comprehensive system of oversight" (Boughton and Bradford 2007). In the absence of such a structure, the G7 has exercised an important influence on the decisions or the lack of them by the IMF, at the expense of the role of the formal structure and the voices of emerging and smaller states.

The chief problem of the G7 is probably what Bergsten calls "a mutual non aggression pact". Delicate problems are the subject of well-balanced declarations that still cannot solve the global problems, while the G7 members do not follow the same advice they so freely give to the rest of the world.

The second problem of the G7 is its lack of legitimacy. It does not represent the world as it is now. The lack of representativeness of the G7 is also pointed out by Alan Ahearne and Barry Eichengreen, who insist that the over-representation of European countries[13] "bears only a loose relationship to the current condition of world economy" (Ahearne and Eichengreen 2007: 128). These observations reflect the non-representation of emerging countries, the presence of which is necessary to cope with such problems as international global imbalances or energy. An organization like the IMF, considering its quasi-universal membership, could offer more than a grouping with a limited composition and provide more direction at the political level. But this fact should not deter attention from the need to strengthen the mechanisms of the Fund itself. In this perspective, a structure such as the G20, the composition[14] of which allows for a better representation of the world economy (some 85 percent of the world GDP and two thirds of the world population), could certainly act as a kind of (useful) interim grouping. This group was created in 1999, after the short-lived G22, for providing a place for a regular dialogue in order to reduce the "world economy's susceptibility to crises". For the first time the G20 met at the level of heads of state and government in Washington on November 15, 2008 at the invitation of the US President and at the request of President Sarkozy, acting president of the EU Council, and UK Prime Minister Gordon Brown, in order to cope with both the economic and financial crises. It was decided to meet again in London on April 30, 2009 to ensure the following up of the 'Washington Declaration' that provides for an Action Plan including immediate and medium-term actions on Financial Markets and World Economy.

The G10 and the BIS framework

The G10 is an older group, which finds its origin in the General Arrangements to Borrow of 1962 (the GAB have been renewed for a period of five years from December 26, 2008) by which ten (now eleven) industrialized countries (Belgium, Canada, France, Germany, Italy, Japan, the Netherlands, Sweden, Switzerland, the UK and the USA) agreed to put at the disposition of the Fund complementary resources to remedy balance of payment problems. Its members play a central role in the management of the BIS in Basle, of which more than fifty national central banks, and the ECB, are members. This institution, created in 1930, offers a framework for enhancing international financial stability and plays an important role in central banks' collaboration. The composition of the G10 is the result of historic factors, but its mainly technical features, the range of its activities and the excellence of the services it delivers to the international community have up to now left it more or less outside the debate. The Statute of the European System of Central Banks (ESCB) and the ECB (Article 6), and the continuing participation in the BIS, allow to the Central Banks of countries of the euro area to remain members of the BIS, with the authorization of the ECB. The ECB has become a member of the BIS by subscribing to an increase of the capital of the Basle institution. In parallel with the creation of the EMU and the ECB, the BIS has increased its role as a service provider of sorts for international cooperation in the field of financial stability. A Financial Stability Forum (FSF)[15] was established in 1999 in the aftermath of the Asian crisis, "for enhancing co-operation between the various national and international supervisory bodies and international financial institutions so as to promote stability in the international financial system" (Giovanoli 2000: 25). The BIS provides for the secretariat of these groupings and shares its experience with them. The cooperation within the Basle structures is not conceived as an alternative to the role of the IMF. The Forum coexists with the famous Basle Committee on Banking Supervision (BCBS), including G10 representatives and the EU Commission, which has been playing an important role in banking regulation since 1974 and reorganized its structure in 2006. The accent in Basle is more about financial regulation and cooperation among regulators and supervisors. And there is also a legitimacy problem in the Basle institutions. As we will see, the FSF membership will be expended in order to include representatives of emerging countries and has been asked to work in close cooperation with the IMF. The same request has not been made to the other so-called 'Basle institutions'.

The external projection of the euro under the EU Treaty and in practise

Neither the Treaty of the European Economic Community at its origin, nor the Treaty of the European Community (TEC) as reformed by the Maastricht Treaty, includes any explicit reference to the IMF or to other international financial institutions. If the silence of the original treaty was understandable in 1957 because it only provided for a modest monetary cooperation among the member states, it was more surprising to find no reference to the IMF in the context of the realization of the EMU. But there was a provision that could have been used for determining the participation and the representation of the euro area in the IMF. Article 111, paragraph 4, of the TEC provided, in the version of the Treaty of Nice, that:

> [T]he Council, acting by a qualified majority on a proposal from the Commission and after consulting the ECB, shall decide on the position of the Community at international level as regards issues of particular relevance to economic and monetary union and on its representation, in compliance with the allocation of powers laid down in Articles 99 and 105.

Only the member states of the euro area have the right to vote under this article.

Articles 99 and 105 of the TEC respectively refer to economic policy (a matter where the Community has limited powers) and to monetary policy (a matter of the exclusive competence of the Community, and in particular of its Central Bank). This asymmetry between economic and monetary policy has an impact in shaping the participation of the euro area and the EU in international institutions. Another element is the difference of status of the member states towards the euro (see Table 3.1). This means that, in the present EU, twelve member states retain control over their monetary policy. Other problems derive from the present structure of the international monetary system. We will come back to these points in the next section.

Article 138 of the Lisbon Treaty (the Treaty on the Functioning of the European Union or TFEU) is part of a chapter on provisions specific to member states that have adopted the euro:

1 In order to secure the euro's place in the international monetary system, the Council, on a proposal from the Commission, shall adopt a decision establishing common positions on matters of particular interest for economic and monetary union within the competent international financial institutions and conferences. The Council shall act after consulting the European Central Bank.
2 The Council, on a proposal from the Commission, may adopt appropriate measures to ensure unified representation within the international financial institutions and conferences. The Council shall act after consulting the European Central Bank.
3 For the measures referred to in paragraphs 1 and 2, only members of the Council representing Member States whose currency is the euro shall take part in the vote.

   A qualified majority of the said members shall be defined in accordance with Article 205(3)(a).

In contrast with the previous Article 111, paragraph 4, of the TEC, this provision clearly states that the objective of paragraph 1 is to promote common positions in order to secure the euro's place in the international monetary system. Furthermore, paragraph 1 of the new provision is more specific when it points to "common positions [...] within the international institutions and conferences" and not generally as does Article 111, paragraph 4, to "the position of the Community at international level". It is obvious that paragraph 2 of Article 138 TFEU has the same objective, although this reference is lacking. The authors of this provision were aware of the fact that unified representation does not only depend on the will of the Union. The first paragraph comprises a "shall" provision while the second appears as an enabling clause: the Council "may" adopt appropriate measures. It does not mean that the Union has a discretionary power in this respect. The existence of a monetary union, with a single monetary and exchange rate policy, should have a reflection on the international sphere.

The European Council meeting at Luxembourg in December 1997 created a formation initially called the Euro-11, and thereafter, the Eurogroup. This informal grouping includes the Finance Ministers of the states of the euro area, alongside the Commissioner in charge of the EMU, and the President of the ECB. According to the Lisbon Treaty, the existence of this group would be formally recognized, thus providing for the appointment of a "stable" President for renewable terms of two-and-a-half years, while preserving its overall informal feature.

The procedure detailed in Article 111, paragraph 4, of the TEC was never used. The European Council disregarded a proposal by the Commission in this matter and opted for pragmatism. There is no official legally binding decision on this topic. The European Council only approved a report of the ECOFIN Council, on December 11 and 12, 1998, in Vienna. It preferred to rely upon informal procedures in lieu of being linked to the terms of Article 111, paragraph 4, and without needing possible modification to the IMF's Articles of Agreement. It was decided that the position of the euro area or the EU would be expressed by the "competent member" of the office of the executive director (ED) of the member state (ideally the ED himself) exercising the presidency of the Eurogroup (called at the time Euro-11), assisted by a representative of the Commission. The IMF Board did not accept the participation of an official of the Commission in its work. Furthermore, the ECB has been represented under a decision of the Board of December 1998, by an observer who can attend the Board when subjects listed in a specific but rather comprehensive series are on the agenda. The appointment of an observer of the ECB to the Board is sure to be insufficient to warrant a correct projection of the euro. The representative of the Commission in Washington organizes regular meetings with the European Executive Directors (IMF) and the ECB observer. These meetings are called EURIMF (Ahearne and Eichengreen 2007: 135).[16] Nevertheless, these measures could not guarantee the expression of common positions by the euro area or the EU Executive directors. The situation has improved somewhat with time, at least in the preparation of EU common positions. A coordination of positions to be defended within the IMF is organized in an IMF sub-committee of the Economic and Financial Committee[17] (SCIMF of the EFC), with the active participation of the director-general (DG) ECOFIN of the Commission and of the ED chairing the EURIMF. This coordination does not involve an undertaking to reach an agreement. As the former sub-committee President, Lorenzo Bini-Smaghi, underlines, it is apparently not understood as being legally binding for the ED (another solution would create problems for the ED in view of its mixed constituency – see the next section of this chapter) and it bears on strategic issues such as at the level of the G7 and not on specific questions (Bini-Smaghi 2006: 267). Positions are notified to the euro area ED. Bini-Smaghi observes that euro area positions, be it for the IMF, the G7 or other meetings, are prepared at meetings of the Eurogroup after a preparation at the technical and deputy level.[18] These non-binding arrangements cannot substitute for a more elaborate institutional solution that could warrant a correct projection in the international monetary system of the single currency regime built within the euro area.

The President of the Eurogroup and the President of the ECB now regularly take part in the G7 meetings. As Bini-Smaghi pointed out, both have signed all the communiqués of the group since 1999 (Pisani-Ferry *et al.* 2008: 91). By contrast, the EMU Commissioner is not systematically involved. The chairman of the Euro Working Group (a euro sub-committee of the EFC which prepares the Eurogroup meetings and is composed of high-level representatives of the Finance Ministers of the euro area), plus the Commission, and the member of the ECB in charge of international relations, act as deputies respectively for the Eurogroup President and the President of the ECB (Pisani-Ferry, *et al.* 2008: 91).

As we have previously noted, a troika including the President of the Eurogroup, the President of the ECB and the Commissioner in charge of EMU took part in the multilateral consultations organized by the IMF. The same troika had bilateral contacts with Chinese authorities in November 2007 concerning the problems caused to Europe by the exchange rate of the yuan, and a bilateral working party was established in order to follow the matter. The EU is not alone in preferring bilateral dialogue over multilateral discussions. There is no doubt that the increasing role of the Eurogroup and the appointment (in anticipation of the entry into force of the provisions and stipulations of the Lisbon Treaty) of a stable President of the Eurogroup created a strong incentive for bilateral dialogue and action within groups such as the G20, considering the present crisis of the IMF. There exists a parallel bilateral US–China group on the relation between the dollar and the yuan.

Despite the developments outlined above, *the euro area is not, as such, a proactive participant in the international financial scene.* Notwithstanding the progress achieved in the coordination of positions in the framework of the IMF and the groups, the present status of the euro area does not allow for the expression of a single voice and an optimal projection of the euro in multilateral frameworks; hence, the development of bilateral dialogues. Whether it is a permanent phenomenon is a question that cannot be seen in isolation from the larger problem of the future structure of the international monetary and financial system.

We have alluded to the importance of the ongoing reform of the IMF, to which, as we will see, the Washington Declaration gives a new impulse. We will now turn to the reform, taking into account the specific problems raised by the establishment of a single chair for the euro area in this organization in the context of the institution's reshuffling.

The main features of the IMF and the representation of the euro area: possible scenarios

Before looking at the specific questions related to the representation of the euro area in the IMF, we should call attention to important features concerning this organization.

Main features of the Fund

1 Under Article II of its Articles of Agreement, the Fund is a country-based and not a currency-based organization. If the euro area (EU) wants to be admitted as such into the IMF, either the Articles of Agreement should be changed or it

would be necessary to make recourse to an interpretation of Article II permitting its accession. Various authors have advanced this latter possibility, taking into consideration the fact that member states have transferred their competences to the EU in monetary and exchange rate matters, and are no longer the objects of specific obligations imposed on members by the Articles of Agreement (Smits 1997: 209).

2   The IMF is based on a system of quotas. Members' quota subscriptions determine the maximum of financial resources that the 185 members are due to contribute to the Fund, the voting power in IMF decisions, the access to financing by the Fund, and the share of SDR (the special unit of account of the Fund) allocations to which they are entitled. Quotas express the place of a state in the world economy. A country's GDP, current accounts transactions, and official reserves are taken into account in calculating each member state's quota.[19]

3   There are three organs in the Fund: the *Board of Governors*, meeting at the level of Finance Ministers and (not frequently) Central Bank Governors in an Annual General Assembly (and when necessary, in writing), is the highest organ of the Fund, and decides, for example, on the revision of the Articles of Agreement and on delegation of powers to the other organs of the Fund; the *Executive Board*, chaired by the General Manager and conducting the day-to-day business of the Fund; a political organ, the *International Monetary and Financial Committee*, a consultative committee of the Board of Governors, composed of Finance Ministers and Central Bank Governors, meets twice a year.

4   The Executive Board now includes twenty-four appointed and elected members. The USA, Japan, Germany, France and the UK designate the five appointed EDs. The nineteen others are elected by and represent so-called constituencies that are linked by geographical or other connections. China, Saudi Arabia and Russia each elect their own ED.

5   If, as a matter of principle, the simple majority rule applies, some decisions require 70 percent of the voting rights but major decisions, for example on the revision of the Articles of Agreement, need 85 percent of the votes. The USA, which at present has the largest quota (17.14 percent) has a right to veto major decisions.

6   The seat of the IMF is located in the country with the largest quota pursuant from a prescription of Article XIII, section 1 of the Articles of Agreement. It is undoubtedly a very sensitive and symbolic issue.

7   Traditionally, the general manager of the Fund is elected among European candidates and the US proposes the President of the World Bank, a practice very commonly criticized but so far respected.

The 'representation' of the EU in the Executive Board (EB) is spread among a number of EDs. There are three appointed (France, the UK and Germany) and four elected EDs (Belgium, Netherlands, Italy, Finland) from EU countries, of which six are from the euro area. There is also a Swiss ED, not an EU member but linked by many ties and international agreements to the EU and part of the G10. Spain could have an ED through the rotation at the head of a Latin American constituency. The same is true of Norway, a non-EU member that could from time to time chair a Nordic constituency. So Europe is well represented and, for many, over-represented, but in an incoherent and fragmented manner (Ahearne and Eichengreen 2007: 128–30).

Before the 2008 reform (see note 19), the total of the quotas allocated to euro area members exceeded 31 percent, in comparison with 17.09 percent for the USA, and 3.72 percent for China or 1.91 percent for India. The constituencies respectively chaired by Belgium (ten countries) and by the Netherlands (twelve) were very often pointed out for their respective 5.15 and 4.76 percent share of the voting rights. There were escalating demands from developing and emerging countries for a better representation within the IMF.[20] It is in this context that the representation of the euro area in the future has to be looked at, not just as a question of the balance of power between the USA and the Europeans.

Coordination alone cannot ensure the defense of a single euro area position. A variety of voices for expressing euro area opinions, when they exist, cannot be assimilated, whatever the quality of the coordination of views, to the euro area expressing itself with one voice. There could be some strength in the multiplication of the expression of the same position, if one exists. Then again, on the one hand, there is no inbuilt mechanism for the repeated expression of such converging views; and on the other, the partners are not necessarily able or willing to appreciate this demonstration of power.

The composition of the constituencies raises an important problem. Constituencies chaired by euro area ED include a variety of European and other nationalities, industrialized and developing countries, while some euro area members are part of non-European-led constituencies. That makes the smooth defense of common standpoints difficult in the Board and the Governing Council because, if there are divisions among a constituency, the head of the constituency must abstain in the vote. In other words, votes are not divisible. It is also politically and psychologically difficult for euro area Executive Directors to press for the adoption of the euro area position by the members of their own constituency. Of course, every single point on the agenda of the Executive Board does not ask for a single euro area position, let alone a perfect coordination. Furthermore, the position of the ED is not to be compared with that of a diplomat acting on instructions. EDs have a dual loyalty to their state and to the Fund they manage. But decisions that might have a system impact on the working of the Fund or on the world economy[21] do need a single euro area view. Obviously, the present spread of voices has not helped European views on important dossiers to be adequately defended (Ahearne and Eichengreen 2007: 188–42).

The quota reform and a new definition of quotas are in this perspective an important exercise. It started in September 2006 at the General Assembly in Singapore with an increase in the quotas allocated to China, Korea, Turkey and Mexico (the so-called Singapore 4). The work for a new definition and a further allocation continued and it was decided that conclusions should be drawn at the 2008 annual General Assembly. The International Monetary and Financial Committee meeting in October 2007 gave some orientations to the Executive Board. GDP is to be considered as the most important variable. Purchasing power parity calculates the GDP in US dollars, not on the basis of exchange rates of the currency with the

US dollar but on the purchasing power of currencies for a same basket of goods, and should play a role along with a compression factor. The total increase of quotas should not exceed 10 percent. "An outcome of the second round of reforms should be a further increase in the voting share of emerging market and developing economies as a whole. The Committee also stresses the importance of the voting share of low-income countries."[22] This can be realized through an increase of so-called basic votes[23] allocated to each member. They presently amount to 250 votes plus one vote for each SDR 100.000 of quota. In 2008, it was decided to triple this figure.

There are other elements taken into account for the calculation of quotas, like variability (or sustainability) and openness, two criteria that industrialized countries, and among them some Europeans, insisted upon. Developing and especially emerging countries did not succeed in promoting the criterion of population as an important variable associated to the requirement of a more democratic institution. The Fund as a financial institution has to be accepted by both creditor and debtor countries. But traditional debtor countries have become creditors and the call for more democracy is overwhelming.

If the question of the definition of quotas mobilizes energies, the Europeans have apparently adopted a reactive and defensive attitude on reform. The need to strive for a European representation that would inevitably reduce individual participation in the IMF is considered premature. The lack of progress in the field of European political union would impede the adoption of meaningful EU single positions. Some countries leading important constituencies point to the mixed composition of their constituencies that provides for a dialogue between advanced and developing economies, and in this way serves the overall cohesion of the Fund by avoiding a polarization of viewpoints. Many observers point out that the more Europeans wait, the less their influence will be in the Fund, considering the progressive diminution of Europe's part of world GDP.

Some scenarios

Various scenarios have been suggested that should be analyzed from legal, political and practical points of view.

1 The first scenario is *the status quo* in the system of representation, which is often presented as the only realistic formula in the short term. But the *status quo* is damaging because member states of the euro area in the Fund have lost their power to intervene without having been replaced by any authority having the same powers that they had before, when they managed the so-called legacy currencies. There is in other terms a vacuum that cannot be filled by a coordination which has proven its limits. The international community expects a clear view to be expressed by the EU, in line with the provisions of its own charter (see article 138 TFEU, analyzed above).

    The Court of Justice has said, in the context of another international organization (the International Labor Organization, see opinion 2/91 of March 19, 2003, ECR, 1993: 1–1061), that member states are in charge of defending the common interest of the Community in the absence of its representation. This is a pragmatic response to a delicate situation. It is a second best solution for the IMF, considering that monetary and exchange rate policy is an exclusive competence of the Union for the member states having adopted the single currency. Member states cannot intervene except with a delegation of the Union in a field of exclusive competence. This principle is not only valid in the internal sphere of the Union but also in international relations. Unfavorable to the euro area, the *status quo* does not solve the legitimacy, democracy and effectiveness problems of the Fund.

2   Another hypothesis is based on the mixed competences of the Fund, both monetary and economic. In this scenario, the member states and the Union (euro area) would both be members of the Fund. This scenario takes into consideration the remaining responsibilities of the member states in economic policy and is based on the mixed feature, both monetary and economic, of the Fund's competences. Those who back this "solution" refer to the example of other organizations in which the Union and its member states are both represented, such as the World Trade Organization (WTO), the European Bank for Development and Reconstruction (EBRD) or the Food and Agriculture Organisation (FAO).

Objections to this thesis have included that the economic perspective in the Fund is limited by the main objective of monetary and financial stability that, in turn, has to contribute to growth and jobs. On the other hand, the joint participation of the EU and its member states raises problems because the IMF is a very specific financial institution based on quotas that are intended to express, by the use of objective data, the relative ranking of any country in the world economy. Nothing similar is to be found in other international institutions.

The example of the EBRD, a financial institution, is interesting in this respect. The EU member states participate with some third countries and the EU in this bank. Established in 1991, the EBRD strives to help countries from Central and Eastern Europe – which had remained, up to the beginning of the 1990s, on the other side of the Iron Curtain – in their transition towards a market economy. The Commission and the European Investment Bank (EIB) participate in the EBRD on account of the EU. The Commission has a share in the capital, as have the other members, which gives to the bloc composed by the EU and the member states a total of 51 percent of the shares and of the votes. The Commission pays its contribution from the Community budget. It is a very different financing system from the one existing at the IMF, where quotas are calculated on the basis of macroeconomic data. The Commission organizes coordination of member states within the EBRD, but apparently it does not prevent the expression of different opinions in the Board on sometimes strategic issues.

The case of the FAO, which was also presented as a model, serves as an example of the difficulties associated with the expression of a Union position in a mixed system of representation. The Community has become an "organization member" of this organization, with a status which differs slightly from that of member states. Before each meeting of an organ of the FAO, the Union has to decide, through sophisticated procedures, on the basis of the proposed agenda, which issues pertain to the (shared or exclusive) competence of the Union and which are among the retained competences of its member states. From this "allocation of competences" is decided the manner in which speaking and voting rights are assigned. This system has already led the EU Council before the Court of Justice at the request of the Commission (Judgment of March 19, 199, case 25/94, *Commission v Council*, ECR 1996: I–1469). This arrangement is therefore far from ideal, and it is inadequate for an institution such as the IMF, in light of both its workings and mode of representation.

3 Another scenario opens the way for the EU, or at least an EU delegation, to express with one voice the positions of the EU or the euro area.

  a Under one conception, a single EU delegation would represent the euro area, but without the EU becoming an IMF member. EU member states from within or outside the euro area would continue to be parties to the Articles of Agreement of the IMF, with possibly those outside it preserving their representation in the IMF. This formula would present the advantage of a single voice being expressed by the euro area but is not legally satisfying because it allows for member states to exercise a competence in fields that pertain at least partially to the exclusive competence of the Union.

  b Another proposal is based on the EU becoming a single member of the IMF (and the World Bank), after a transitory period where two chairs would exist, one for the euro area, and another for those outside it. Perhaps one could include in the first group the quotas corresponding to those of the EU member states participating in the Exchange Rate Mechanism II (in 2008, Denmark, Estonia, Latvia, Lithuania and Slovakia), which is a convergence criterion leading to the adoption of the euro.

The limits of this chapter make it impossible to provide an exhaustive analysis of the legal and political aspects of each scenario. The TEC as well as the TFEU offer different possibilities that should be checked, including Article 352 of the TFEU, a clause that provides for a procedure allowing for the adoption of appropriate measures if the competences are not provided or are insufficient in order to realize an objective of the Treaty. Let us also observe that a single voice for the EU (euro area), be it under the first or the second form, presupposes a better internal management of questions related to the IMF than is presently the case. By no means is there any question of organizing an understudy of sorts to the Fund in order to follow the work of its organs. Nonetheless, relations with the Fund require a smooth relationship between the ECOFIN/Eurogroup, the ECB and the Commission. We have seen that this troika is already playing a role in bilateral (with China) and some multilateral gatherings. (For example, the IMF organized 2006 consultation but not G20, where the President of the ECOFIN EU Council is participating when the G20 meets at the level of Finance Ministers and not the Eurogroup President.) However, this troika is only an informal creation. For a permanent system, formal procedures should be adopted. The ECOFIN (with the votes of only the euro area members) is in charge, under Article 138, paragraph 2, of the TFEU of proposing or appointing the "representative(s)" of the EU/euro area (and, if the case should arise, its member states) in the organs of the Fund. Member states should have the guarantee that their views would be expressed within the Union in the fields where it has only coordinating competences. Formulas of mandate could be imagined in this respect. At some point,[24] the kind of double-hatting contemplated with regard to the common foreign and security policy (CFSP) and common defense and security policy (CDSP), where the High Representative for Foreign Affairs and Security Policy is also Vice-President of the Commission, could possibly be used for EMU if the experience in the external action of the Union is positive. Political accountability of the EU/euro area representative(s) to the European Parliament should be organized in a similar way to the monetary dialogue established between the European Parliament and the ECB.[25] The dual nature of the mandate of the ED must, as we have stated, be respected.

Some authors insist that "Consolidating Europe's representation would also enhance the continent's influence. Voting as a group, the EU or even the euro area would have the single largest block of votes in the IMF and the World Bank. A single EU chair would not need the support of many other members to form a winning coalition" (Ahearne and Eichengreen 2007: 142) Others, such as the Belgian Executive Director Willy Kiekens,[26] are not favorably inclined towards to such a perspective, or at least insist upon the limits to such an approach. They underline that if the global quota of the EU were to decrease, all the others, including the USA, would increase. In addition to Japan's quota, this would secure a majority for three ED traditional power blocs within the IMF. Adversely, the increase in the quotas of emerging and other developing countries would be of little use for these countries. Their EDs would be marginalized and "seriously out of balance with the Directors of the group of three" and the quoted author continues: "Instead of accepting a continued fragmentation of their representation, the developing countries should reflect on how they might also combine their forces to make the Board better balanced, probably by reducing the number of Directors to between 12 to 15" (Kiekens 2003).

Conclusion

The euro has rapidly become the second international currency. The US dollar preserves an important position but new partners are coming to the fore. Relations with China are essential in this respect.

The EU and its member states, which repeatedly affirm their commitment to multilateralism and have inscribed these principles in the objectives of the external action of the Union,[27] should actively support a renewed IMF. The EU must strive to give it a more proactive role with regard to the stability of the international system. Both Europe and the international community have a clear self-interest in promoting IMF reform. Such reform would increase the effectiveness, legitimacy and internal democracy of an institution that still has an important role to play in global financial stability. Some European countries, big or small, played an important role in shaping the Bretton Woods system. Now it has to be renovated. The alternatives to this renovation are either the creation of regional financial institutions that would try to resolve on a local basis problems that are global by nature, or the shift of responsibilities towards informal groups without legal power and lacking legitimacy.

The reform of the IMF should not be limited to the definition and allocation of quotas and some minor points of governance. The interest must extend to the composition and functioning of the organs, and among them the Executive Board. It is not for the EU, the USA and Japan to affect dominance over the institution. The challenges ahead are political and economic. The question should receive more attention than it has up to now. A satisfactory institutionalized participation of the euro area is necessary for a better international projection of the euro. This represents a major challenge, the solution of which cannot indefinitely be postponed in light of anticipated future progress in the political construction of Europe. It is not an easy question, yet it requires a clear sense of the significance and weight of what is at stake and the political will to take good and necessary decisions. Perhaps the multiplication of monetary unions in the world could be an incentive to find a solution to this problem. But more impulse could derive from the 'Action Plan' devised by the G20 Washington Declaration. This Declaration has called for 'Reviewing the mandates, governance, and resource requirements of the IFIs (International Financial Institutions).' As a part of the 'immediate actions by March 31, 2009', the G20 leaders asked for the FSF to expand 'to a broader membership of emerging countries' and for the IMF and the FSF to 'strengthen their collaboration, enhancing efforts to better integrate regulatory and supervisory responses into the macro-prudential policy framework and conduct early warning exercises.' For the EU and/or the euro area, it would raise the question of a more coherent representation within the FSF.

For the medium-term, the G-20 leaders 'underscored that the Bretton Woods institutions must be comprehensively reformed so that they can more adequately reflect changing economic weights in the world economy and be more responsive to future challenges. Emerging and developing economies should have greater voice and representation in these institutions.'

The pressure of emerging and developing countries will, no doubt, be important, above all from those that have declared their intention to contribute more to the IMF and World Bank resources. This inevitably will raise the questions of governance of the Fund (and the Bank) we evoked supra. The EU will no longer be able to postpone answering the question of its weight in the emerging new global system.

Notes

1 At which point the euro replaced them in the Special Drawing Rights (SDR) basket.
2 Also see Peter Kenen, *The Role of the Dollar as an International Currency*, Group of Thirty Occasional Papers: No. 13, New York, 1983.
3 Sovereign Wealth Funds (SWF) are investment companies owned by official authorities created at the beginning of the 1980s by some oil-producing countries but now present in most emerging countries, from Russia to Brazil. China has recently established a China Investment Corporation. In 2007, the amount of funds managed by SWFs were evaluated at 2,500 billion US dollars and could soar in an estimation of Morgan Stanley

to 12,000 billion US dollars in 2015. The G7, the IMF and the EU have taken steps for insuring a greater transparency of the SWFs. See Jeffrey Garten, "We need rules for sovereign funds," *Financial Times*, August 8, 2007; Edwin Truman, *Sovereign Wealth Funds: The Need for Greater Transparency and Accountability*, Peterson Institute for International Economics, Washington DC, PB07-6, August 2007.

4 Many voices predict a more or less rapid fall of the US dollar. See Jeffrey Frankel, "The euro could surpass the dollar within ten years," March 18, 2008, http://www.voxeu.org/index.php?q=node/989, with the reference to a larger study by Chin and Frankel (2008).

5 The policy of China has been seen as counterproductive by the Fund at the time when the international community is engaged in a process of debt relief under the Heavily Indebted Poor Countries (HIPC) Program and the Multilateral Debt Relief Initiative (MDRI). But recently China decided to contribute to an action of the World Bank in favor of low-income countries. This has been seen as another (modest) mark of the will of China to be involved in the multilateral system. Later on, it seemed that China wanted to swap a more significant contribution to multilateral institutions for a better representation inside these institutions.

6 See Remarks made by Rodrigo de Rato to the Board of Governors of the IMF at the joint Annual Discussion, 2006 Annual Meeting of the IMF and the World Bank Group, Singapore, September 19, 2006, http://www.imf.org/external/np/speeches/2006/091906.htm

7 Quoted by Geoffrey R.D. Underhill, "Global financial architecture, legitimacy, and representation: voice for emerging markets," *GARNET Policy Brief*, No. 3, January 2007: ii, mentioning "the inability of emerging markets to borrow abroad in their own currency".

8 See the communiqué of the G-20 meeting of ministers and governors, São Paolo, Brazil, November 8–9, 2008, www.g20.org

9 On the coming back of the IMF, see Jean Pisani-Ferry, "Will the crisis trigger a revival of the IMF", Bruegel; Brussel, October 30, 2008, www.bruegel.org

10 See IMF Press release No. 07/72 of April 14, 2007.

11 See Edwin M. Truman (2007), "What should the Fund's role be now?," Remarks to the Bretton Woods Committee's Annual Meeting on June 12, 2007: 3. While it considers the initiative as welcome, it is very critical of its result: "Its accomplishments have been limited because of excessive timidity, unsound analysis, or lack of cooperation by the participants." It is characteristic that the dialogue was continued bilaterally without any extraordinary success either.

12 There were bills proposed by congressmen in order to relax the concept of exchange rate illegal manipulation. The law would empower the government to limit or stop the imports from the concerned countries. Under this proposal, the sheer fact that a country would intervene to have its exchange rate go down while accumulating a trade surplus would be sufficient to warrant such an action against that country's imports.

13 This comes from the fact that European countries were the obvious candidates for the steering committee of the international monetary and financial system when the latter entered in a period of flux in the 1970s. Lorenzo Bini-Smaghi notes in a speech on March 26, 2007 – ʻL'Union économique et monétaire: quelle place pour la zone euro sur la scène internationale?ʼ – that in 1980, the three great founding countries of the EC represented respectively 6% (Germany), 5% (France) and 3.5% (Italy) of the world GDP. These figures have already been reduced with one point each. In twenty-five years from now, the three countries will only represent together a total of 6% of the world GDP, the part of Germany alone twenty-five years ago.

14 "The members of the G20 are the finance ministers and central bank governors of 19 countries: Argentina, Australia, Brazil, Canada, China, France, Germany, India,

Indonesia, Italy, Japan, Mexico, Russia, Saudi Arabia, South Africa, South Korea, Turkey, the United Kingdom and the United States of America. The European Union is also a member, represented by the rotating Council presidency and the European Central Bank. To ensure global economic fora and institutions work together, the Managing Director of the International Monetary Fund (IMF) and the President of the World Bank, plus the chairs of the International Monetary and Financial Committee and Development Committee of the IMF and World Bank, also participate in G20 meetings on an ex-officio basis." quoted from the official Web site of the G20: www.G20.org

15 Most important financial centres of the world are represented in the FSF.

16 These authors note that the executive director chairing the EURIMF may make an introductory statement at IMF Board meetings on issues relating to the world economy that reflect the common European view.

17 The EFC is a consultative committee comprising high-level Treasury and Central Banks representatives, with a secretariat organized by the Commission. The previously quoted authors observe that there is a problem of timelessness in the organization of meetings of the SCIMF. It meets more or less eight times a year, which does not always allow following the agenda of the Executive Board of the Fund. M. Willy Kiekens, an executive director, notes in "What kind of representation for the IMF?,"*OeNB*, June 2, 2003, www.oenb.at; that in contrast to the G7 procedure, the consultations in Brussels do not concern individual questions. Bini-Smaghi (2006) adds that "Euro area coordination usually reacts to IMF and G7 agendas rather than the other way round": 273.

18 Lorenzo Bini-Smaghi in his July 2, 2007 speech – "The euro as an international currency: implications for exchange rate policy" – highlights a lack of discipline on the part of Ministers who express individual positions prior to – and sometimes after – the meeting. This is especially true on exchange rates. This could weaken the significance of the possible common position adopted by the Eurogroup. The Bruegel 2008 report mentions that "markets continue to be puzzled by publicly expressed official disagreements over the exchange rate of the euro": 91.

19 A new quota formula was voted by a majority of 92.93% of the votes on April 29, 2008. It contains four variables expressed in shares – GDP, openness, variability and reserves – with weights of 50%, 30%, 15% and 5% respectively. The GDP variable is a blend of 60% of GDP at market exchange rates and 40% of GDP at purchasing power parity (PPP). The reform is intended to be based on "a simpler and more transparent quota formula." The reform includes also an increase of quotas of emergent and developing economies. The change for the euro area is marginal. Germany, Italy, Ireland and Luxembourg have with other developed countries agreed to forgo part of the quota increase under the reform. See IMF Survey online, March 28, 2008.

20 See the declaration of the president of the group of the twenty-four representative of a number of developing and emerging countries, http://www.imf.org/external/np/tr/2007/tr070413c.htm

21 See the examples mentioned by A. Ahearne and B. Eichengreen (2007): 138–42. These relate to IMF policy, and to European exchange rate policy and global imbalances; not all directly regard the IMF, since the analysis also relates to the G7.

22 See Communiqué of the International Monetary and Financial Committee of the Board of Governors of the IMF, Press Release No.07/236, October 2007, p. 3, point 10. http;//www.imf.org/external/np/sec/pr/2007/pr07236.htm

23 Basic votes were supposed to prevent the quota, and hence the voting power, of small developing countries from being insignificant. The successive increases of the total amount of quotas have progressively reduced the share of basic votes in the total. The

existence of these basic votes explains why there is a distinction in the shares of voting rights and quotas.

24 Which would still leave unanswered the need for an "independent voice" such as the one provided by the EMU Commissioner. See Pisani-Ferry, *et al.* (2008): 105.

25 It has already been agreed that the president of the Eurogroup will appear before the European Parliament twice a year, in comparison with the appearance of the ECB president four times a year.

26 See presentation by Willy Kiekens (2003), "What kind of representation for the IMF?" given at the Austrian National Bank (www.oenb.at) on June 2, 2003.

27 See Article 22 of the new EU Treaty and the EU Declaration on Globalisation, adopted on December 14, 2007 by the European Council which states: "We must engage our international partners in enhanced strategic cooperation and work together with stronger multilateral organizations."

Bibliography

Ahearne, Alan and Barry Eichengreen (2007), "External monetary and financial policy: a review and a proposal," in André Sapir (ed.), *Fragmented Power: Europe and the Global Economy*, Brussels: Bruegel Books: 128–55.

Bergsten, Fred (2006), "A new steering committee for the world economy?," in Edwin M. Truman (ed.), *Reforming the IMF for the 21st Century*, Special Report No. 19 – April 2006, Washington DC: Institute of International Economics: 279–92.

Bertuch-Samuels, Axel (2006), "The Euro as an international currency," *Conference on Experience with and Preparation for the Euro*, Osterreichische Nationalbank, Linz, 146–74.

Bini-Smaghi, Lorenzo (2006), "Powerless Europe: why is the euro area still a political dwarf?," *International Finance*, 9 (2): 261–79.

Boughton, James M. and Colin I. Bradford Jr. (2007), "Global governance: new players, new rules", *IMF, Finance and Development*, 44 (4), Washington DC: IMF.

Eichengreen, B. and R. Hausman (eds) (2005), *Other People's Money: Debt Denomination and Financial Instability in Emerging Market Economies*, Chicago: University of Chicago.

Giovanoli, Mario (2000), "A new architecture for the global financial market: legal aspects of international financial standard setting", in M. Giovanoli (ed.), *International Monetary Law: Issues for the New Millennium*, Oxford: Oxford University Press: 3–59.

Lastra, Rosa M. (2006), *Legal Foundations of International Monetary Stability*, Oxford: Oxford University Press.

Pisani-Ferry, Jean, Philippe Aghion, Marek Belka, Jürgen von Hagen, Lars Heikensten and André Sapir (2008), *Coming of Age: Report on the Euro Area*, Rapporteur: Alan Ahearne, Brussels: Bruegel.

Smits, René (1997), *The European Central Bank*, Leiden: Kluwer.

Truman, Edwin M. (2006) *Reforming the IMF for the 21st Century*, Special Report No. 19 – April 2006, Washington DC: Institute of International Economics.

4 EU competition policy in a global world

Mathias Dewatripont and Patrick Legros

Summary[1]

This chapter reviews the forces that have shaped current competition laws and initiatives, in particular those that may ease convergence and cooperation between the USA and the EU. Even if convergence is eased when countries are developed, the objectives and the means put in place to attain these objectives may differ across countries. Differences may in turn generate tensions, and therefore shape further developments of the law. Subsequently, this chapter discusses the specific case of state aid control, an EU specificity which has on the one hand helped to ensure the primacy of competition policy over industrial policy, and has prevented potential wasteful "subsidy wars" between member states. However, on the other hand, this policy has been accused at times of hurting the competitiveness of "European champions." Finally, the chapter looks at current challenges facing competition policy; focusing first on new developments as far as state aid control is concerned, namely the State Aid Action Plan, and the special case of aid to innovation. Here, the focus will be on the pros and cons of this policy, namely its potential ability to better address market failures, but also the potential risk of lax enforcement in the name of "aid to innovation." This danger might be particularly problematic in an era which has witnessed the fast rise to prominence of some emerging-economy powers (like Brazil, Russia, India and China) which do not necessarily share the competition-policy philosophy of the EU and USA. While the chapter discusses how the common ground reached by these two players could serve as the basis for a global competition policy, it also stresses the potential tensions that could arise from the assertiveness of state interests by public corporations and sovereign funds from these emerging countries.

Introduction

The introduction summarizes the history and key competition regulations existing in the USA and EU. It subsequently explains how openness to the external world has introduced a tension that competition policy must take into account.

EU and USA: a snapshot[2]

Historically, US competition law arose during the later decades of the nineteenth century. The opening-up of markets and an increase in competitiveness led to the formation of cartels and trusts that brought with them the danger of preventing further expansion and growth. Interestingly, parallel to the desire to create a competitive national market, the USA also went from a free-trade policy to a more protectionist view. Competition laws protected consumers from high prices from local firms while protectionism and high tariffs on imported goods permitted upward pressure on these prices.

While the *Sherman Act 1890* limited their power, cartels and trusts developed mostly free of regulatory constraints in Europe, until the first competition laws were introduced after World War Two. So, from a historical point of view, US competition law was a natural reference point on which to base EU laws and institutions. It is therefore not at all surprising that the main objectives and instruments in the EU and the USA look quite similar. However, despite broad agreement on the core objectives of limiting collusive and unilateral market power, and promoting competition and enhancing welfare, the EU's approach in these matters has developed along specific lines. The main aspects of EU and US laws, in terms of their scope and enforcement, are summarized in the Table and text below.

In the USA, the *Sherman Antitrust Act*, through its Sections 1 and 2, makes it illegal to restrain trade by collusive agreements or by attempts to monopolize an industry. The Act also gave private parties the right to seek (treble) damages in court. The *Clayton Antitrust Act 1914* completed the *Sherman Act* by both prohibiting specific conduct (price discrimination, tie-in sales, mergers and acquisitions, exclusive dealing), and by specifying procedural and remedial actions. This Act in particular extended the reach of competition authorities, since it allows them to prevent mergers and acquisitions if they create a monopoly. The *Federal Trade Commission Act 1914* further allows *preventive* measures to prohibit practices like horizontal or vertical restraints.

In the EU, the Treaty of the European Community (Treaty of Rome 1957, renamed TEC by the Treaty of Maastricht in 1992) Articles 81 and 82 parallel the US laws. Article 81 addresses collusion and other anti-competitive practices (like exclusive

Table 4.1 US and EU anti-trust measures

Object	USA	EU
Cartels	Sherman S1	TEC Art. 81
Monopolization	Sherman S2, Clayton and FTC	TEC Art. 82
Mergers and acquisitions	Sherman, Clayton and FTC	Regulations 139/2004 and 802/2004
State aids	n.a.	TEC Art. 87
Enforcement	FTC, DOJ and courts	EU Commission and courts

dealing, tying, price-fixing), while Article 82 addresses abuses of dominant position (predatory pricing, anti-competitive merger). Article 87 of the treaty addresses state aids and is specific to the EU. This article reflects the need to prevent individual member states from over-internalizing their advantage of having strong national firms, possibly at the expense of the competitiveness of the EU market, or the enforcement of Article 82.

Most notably between 1990 and 2005, some of the basic texts cited above profited from an extensive overhaul. The new Regulation 1/2003 decentralizes enforcement of Articles 81 and 82 of the EU competition law to national authorities and courts. In parallel with this decentralization, coordination is facilitated by the creation of the European Competition Network. Further innovations include the modification of Articles 81 (previously 85) and 82 (previously 86), as well as new guidelines for vertical mergers; and the internal reforms of the Commission's Directorate General for Competition, putting more emphasis on economic analysis.

A double-edged sword

Competition policy is a double-edged sword for a regulator. First, by promoting good practices in markets it prevents incumbent firms from abusing their position and erecting artificial entry barriers, which eventually facilitates entry by more efficient producers and leads to a beneficial use of social resources. One can think of this as a positive *internal effect* of competition policy. But, could competition policy also put local firms at a disadvantage on the international scene if foreign firms are not subject to the same constraints? Individual domestic firms will clearly argue this line, although evidence suggesting that domestic competitive pressures strengthen aggregate competitiveness (an idea underlying the Single Market Program) also exists. However, one cannot exclude *a priori* potential negative *external effects* of competition policy. The costs and benefits of competition policy in Europe must therefore be assessed with respect to the rules set by the bloc's trading partners, or countries having firms with a significant presence in Europe.

Until recently, the external effect seemed mainly relevant with respect to other developed countries, which were the main source of trade flows and cross-border investments; yet this view is no longer valid. The rise to economic predominance of previously developing countries creates new challenges for Europe as for developed countries. History suggests that competition policy is an institutional tool which emerges after countries have reached a sufficient level of development, and there are simple economic explanations for this. When development is low, access to financial markets is difficult and resources are scarce and often unequally distributed: exogenous barriers to entry are high. Putting additional constraints on how firms behave will not remove these exogenous entry barriers but may have the undesirable effect of stifling competition among existing firms, or discouraging even more firms from entering the market. When countries start their development, the main problem is to induce firms to participate in activities conducive to growth, rather than making sure that pricing is competitive. (There is little need to have a level playing field if there are no players.) For developed countries, access to the financial market is eased and infrastructures is such that producers are no longer limited to selling in their local market: exogenous entry barriers are low. However, endogenous entry barriers, enacted by dominant firms, may become problematic and competition policy may start playing a role to ensure that existing players do not enact artificial entry barriers.

If two trading countries develop at the same speed, it is likely that there will be less of a conflict between the internal and external effects and that both countries will eventually converge in adopting competition laws and will even cooperate for enforcement. A leading case would be the USA versus the EU. However, if two trading countries develop at different speeds, a conflict between the internal and the external effects is likely to arise: the country with the low development will have little incentive to put constraints on its firms, so the external effect is potentially large for the developed country and this may put pressure in turn on its desire to enforce strict competition rules. Leading cases would be the EU versus China, or Brazil, Russia, India and China (the BRICs) more generally. (One could also think of the EU-15 versus the latter twelve member states, except for their entry into the EU which implied accepting the *acquis communautaire* – the fundamental principles of the Community – including EU competition policy.) Europe is therefore at a stage where some of its future partners have started their development only recently and have not yet set up competition policies that are similar in scope and spirit to those in Europe or in the USA.

Exploring the forces that have shaped current competition laws and initiatives, in particular those that may ease convergence and cooperation between the USA and the EU, is therefore a first step in understanding EU competition policy within the globalizing world. Even if convergence is eased when countries are developed, the objectives and the means put in place to attain these objectives may differ across countries. These differences may in turn generate tensions, magnify the external effect, and therefore shape further developments of the law. Furthermore, the specific case of state aid control – an EU specificity which has helped to ensure the primacy of competition policy over industrial policy, and has prevented potential wasteful "subsidy wars" between member states – must also be addressed in this chapter. On the other hand, this policy has been accused at times of hurting the competitiveness of "European champions." Finally, a look at the current challenges of competition policy, focusing first on new developments as far as state aid control is concerned, namely the State Aid Action Plan and the special case of aid to innovation, will offer some insights into potential future developments. Here, we look at the pros and cons of this policy, namely its potential ability to better address market failures, but also the potential risk of lax enforcement in the name of "aid to innovation." Such hazards could be particularly problematic in an era which has witnessed the fast rise to prominence of some emerging-economy powers (such as the BRICs) which do not necessarily share the competition-policy philosophy of the EU and USA. How the common ground reached by these two players could serve as the basis for a global competition policy is a further prospective outlook that should be discussed, while also stressing the potential tensions that could arise from the assertiveness of state interests by public corporations and sovereign funds from emerging countries.

Where we are and how we got here

Divergence or convergence?

Despite many similarities, the EU and US competition laws and enforcement diverge in several ways. First, *with regard to the objectives*, the EU focuses on the integration of its member states' markets and prevention of national or private restraints in an environment characterized by strong trade unions and consumer organizations and a balance between business and political communities with a strong history of regulation. By contrast, the USA is more concerned with efficient market operation in an environment where businesses play a strong role and *laissez-faire* is the preferred way to let markets evolve. These historical differences influence the way practices are evaluated. While the USA and the EU seem to converge towards a consumer welfare standard when evaluating mergers, such a coming-together is less clear for other dimensions of competition law (for instance, Article 81 or the guidelines for vertical restraints). Moreover, the threshold for evaluating market dominance is lower in the EU (50 percent) than in the USA (66 percent). Contrary to practice in the EU, US violators of competition law can receive criminal sanctions and can also be the subject of civil suits, and plaintiffs can obtain up to three times the damages caused by the violation.

Furthermore, *with regard to the procedures*, EU enforcement is far more "bureaucratic" than is its US counterpart, and arguably less transparent. In the EU, information is obtained through responses by parties to official requests, while in the USA there is more reliance on interviews and depositions as well as on documents (in particular, papers by experts). At the same time, in the case of merger reviews, the process, being more bureaucratic, has a timing that is also more predictable in the EU. This may explain why in the case of international mergers, firms may prefer to start the process in the EU.

Third, *on the role of economic analysis and its use*, both parties also vary. Microeconomic analysis plays a central role in anti-trust matters in the USA. The Federal Trade Commission (FTC) and the Department of Justice (DOJ) staffs are composed of PhD economists well versed in the latest theoretical and econometric findings. By contrast, until recently, anti-trust enforcement was the domain of lawyers in the EU; the Directorate General Competition (DG Comp) was mainly staffed by lawyers. The EU has been more focused on the legal side of agreements and economists have traditionally not been key players in the implementation of competition policy, even if economic principles have been a cornerstone of its philosophy. However, starting in 2003, the DG Comp included an "office of the chief economist." The creation of this office, and the concomitant increased role played by economic analysis, was triggered in part by the need to justify the benefits of anti-trust scrutiny and recent court decisions suggesting that the Commission needed to base its decision on more thorough economic analysis (see Röller and Buigues 2005 for a description of the role of the economists within the division; see Economic Advisory Group on Competition Policy 2005 for the role of economic analysis for application of Article 82). Despite such innovations, the role of economists in competition law in the EU is still more limited than in the USA.

Some of these divergences are important to understand how the two competition authorities differ in their evaluations of some cases. An illustrative example is that of the *General Electric–Honeywell* merger case (2001). General Electric (GE) was one of the main suppliers of jet engines for large commercial aircraft, and its division General Electric Commercial Aviation Services (GECAS) was one of the biggest buyers of airplanes which it later leased to other companies, as well as offering a variety of related financial services through GE. Honeywell was one of the main suppliers of avionics (electronics used for the piloting the plane) and non-avionics (control systems, power units, brakes, engine starters) products. Both GE and Honeywell competed for the supply of jet engines to regional jet aircraft. The merger had both a manufacturing and a financial market dimension, presenting horizontal and vertical conglomerate dimensions.

The US DoJ approved this conglomerate merger on the basis of its ability to generate significant efficiency gains. But there was significant resistance in Europe where the Commission used a combination of portfolio theory and bundling theory to challenge the merger. In particular, the EU argued that the merger might lead to market foreclosure through two channels: first, through bundling of GE and Honeywell products; second, through the vertical integration of Honeywell with GECAS, GE's leasing arm. On July 3, 2001, the European Commission blocked the $42 billion merger proposal.

In this case, many observers did not find the EU portfolio and bundling arguments convincing, partly because foreclosure is not a theoretical consequence of mixed bundling (when the firm sells both a bundle and the individual components), but also because the economic reasoning did not seem to take into account the reactions of competitors within an equilibrium model. Some reactions also voiced concerns over the argument that the merger may lead to the exit of competitors in the short term since this may open the door to an "efficiency offense." If the merger led to efficiencies, the new company would be at a competitive advantage and by charging lower prices to its customers might indeed force competitors to exit. GE and Honeywell appealed the decision. While the Court of First Instance (CFI) confirmed the decision, the analysis of the conglomerate effects of the Commission was annulled, and the case was therefore reduced to its horizontal dimension, i.e., the jet engine market for large regional jet aircraft.

In another case of conglomerate merger, the *Tetra Laval–Sidel* case, the decision of the Commission to stop the merger was also appealed by the firms. In this case, the CFI overturned the decision and highlighted the need for the Commission to use rigorous economic analysis in their merger decisions. These rebuttals by the CFI eventually led to the creation of the Office of the Chief Economist.

Divergences may be exacerbated or reduced by globalization, opening of trade, and reduction of trade barriers. Indeed, these factors may increase the search by firms for cost-saving or profit-enhancing opportunities. If globalization increases the incentives to merge transnationally, both EU and US competition authorities must rule on the same cases. This may magnify strategic considerations associated with national interests, as for example in the *Boeing–McDonnell Douglas* case. There, the US FTC approved the merger, probably based on industrial policy reasons, while the Commission initially opposed the merger, probably also on the basis of industrial policy reasons (to protect the European firm Airbus). If joint competition authority rulings do not occur, the divergence of EU and US opinions on a same case, as with the *GE–Honeywell* case, may reflect one of the principled divergences we highlighted above.

If globalization increases the incentives of firms to form international cartels, the stakes of the EU and the USA are more balanced and this may result in efforts of cooperation, as for instance when both the EU and the USA adopt leniency programs. The leniency program adopted by the European Commission in 1996 is based on US Corporate Leniency Program (1993). The leniency program was revised in 2002, setting higher fines for anti-trust violation and encouraging leniency arrangements. The "vitamins cartel" illustrates the converging approach of the EU and US authorities since Hoffmann La Roche and BASF received reductions in the order of 50 percent in exchange for their cooperation with the competition authorities. Yet, differences between the two systems remain, for instance the possibility in the US of an "amnesty plus" system whereby a firm benefits from additional reductions for revealing a cartel in another market. Also, given the international nature of cartels, an important barrier to the efficiency of leniency programs is the risk of civil litigation in the US following disclosure in the EU, which creates uncertainty over the costs and benefits of participating in a leniency program in Europe. In addition to such cross-pollinating practices, a new direction has emerged in the external relationships of the EU authorities with other competition authorities, and in particular the USA. There is an advertised desire to cooperate and to reach a level of harmonization in competition laws.

Three bilateral agreements

There are three critical junctures in the cooperation between the EU and the USA: in 1991, 1998 and 2002.

The 1991 US–EU Agreement

The goal of the bilateral agreement signed on September 23, 1991, was to "promote cooperation and coordination and lessen the possibility or impact of differences between the Parties in the application of their competition laws" (EU 1991). The agreement requires notification and assistance to the other party of anti-trust enforcement activities that may affect it. It also provides in Articles V and VI the positive and negative comity principles. The negative comity principle allows a sovereign country in case of a transnational violation to leave the investigation to the authority of another country and more generally to "consider important interest of the other Party in decisions as to whether or not to initiate an investigation or proceeding, the scope of an investigation or proceeding, the nature of the remedies or penalties sought, and in other ways, as appropriate" (Article VI, EU 1991). This possibility is non-binding and does not really solve potential conflicts between EU and US authorities. The positive comity principle consists of acts of cooperation and assistance: "[I]f a party believes that anticompetitive activities carried out in the territory of the other Party are adversely affecting its important interest, the first Party may notify the other Party and may request that the other Party's competition authorities initiate appropriate enforcement."

Intrinsic limitations of this agreement were the non-binding aspect of the comity principles as well as the difficulties in credibly sharing sensitive information. As it were, Article VIII specifies that "neither Party is required to provide information to the other Party if disclosure of that information to the requesting Party (a) is prohibited by the law of the Party possessing the information, or (b) would be incompatible with important interests of the Party possessing the information."

The 1998 US–EU Positive Comity Agreement

This agreement complements the 1991 agreement with regard to the application of the positive comity principle. The new version of the positive comity agreement extends significantly the previous agreement since it allows for instance the European Commission to request the US competition authorities to investigate an act that does not violate US competition laws and even if the US competition authorities have no interest in pursuing the investigation. Nevertheless, the agreement is still voluntary and does not eliminate the confidentiality clauses present in the 1991 agreement. As noted by Alexander Schaub (1998), European Commission Director General of Competition, "procedures of notification and consultation and the principles of traditional and positive comity allow us to bring our respective approaches closer in cases of common interest but there exist no mechanism for resolving conflicts in cases of substantial divergence of the analysis." The attempted merger of GE–Honeywell illustrates the limitations of the comity principles, since the EU and USA both complained about the lack of concern for each other's interests. Finally, the decentralization of some decisions to the national authorities in the EU may reduce the scope of such cooperation agreements, since they are non-binding for competition authorities in the member states.

The 2002 Best Practices on Cooperation in Merger Cases

On 30 October, 2002, the US DoJ and European Commission Directorate General of Competition issued a set of best practices on cooperation in reviewing mergers that require approval on both sides of the Atlantic. Under the best practices cooperation, the investigation is run simultaneously. Companies are encouraged to permit the agencies to exchange information which they have submitted during the course of an investigation and to allow joint EU–US interviews of the companies concerned. The best practices are intended to facilitate coherence in remedies (i.e., deal monetary settlements), to speed up the process (since both competition authorities have to act at the same case) and ideally to avoid conflicting decisions.

Despite these best practices, there have been well-publicized mergers where the USA and the EU disagreed, in particular *Boeing–McDonnell Douglas* and *Oracle–PeopleSoft*. In the first case, the USA allowed the merger but the EU required substantial remedies; in the second, the roles were reversed, with the US litigating and the EU authorizing the merger after the completion of US litigation. As for the application of the negative comity principle, the evaluation of bilateral mergers depends on the quality of information disclosed. The EU Commission can only disclose information to the US authorities with the consent of the firms. Optimistic firms may value disclosure because it speeds up the process and ensures a consistent treatment on both the EU and US sides of their case. Sceptical firms may be reluctant to disclose information to the US authorities in light of the risk of civil litigation. Since the US law permits the disclosure of information as long as it is reciprocal, there may be significant differences in the type and quality of information available to the EU and the US authorities on a given case, which may contribute to differences in evaluation.

EU state aid control in an international perspective

State aid control: the "fighting spillover effects" rationale

State aid control is a paradox: in the name of protecting competition, a public authority intervenes in spending decisions taken by other public authorities, rather than in decisions taken by private firms as within the rest of the domain of competition policy. What is the rationale for such intervention?

The conventional answer to this question points to international spillover effects: when markets are both international and imperfectly competitive, spending by a public authority in one country can subsidize its own economic activity at the expense of lost activity in another country. Therefore, the story goes, supranational intervention, by such appropriate institution such as the EC or the World Trade Organization (WTO), may be needed to ensure that countries do not engage in a collectively wasteful "subsidy war." The problem arises because public authorities make spending decisions on the basis of narrowly national (or regional) interests, and the solution requires intervention by other public authorities that are capable of taking a more collective point of view.

The academic literature on inter-jurisdictional externalities identifies many reasons why government action to support economic activity in their own state will impinge on other states. Most relevant to state aid control is the literature on "strategic trade policy," in which countries compete with each other in a game of individually rational but collectively wasteful subsidies to industry, spurred by the prospect of poaching each other's profits in imperfectly competitive markets. All countries are therefore better off if they can reach and enforce an agreement to forgo such subsidies. In these models, it makes no difference where firms choose to undertake their economic activity, so there is no purpose in governments competing to attract economic activity and there are no benefits from such competition to offset the possible costs. Instead inter-government activity is purely a form of rent shifting. Interpreted in the context of state aids, this means that subsidies to firms will consequently be higher than would be efficient and that the level of subsidized activity will be higher than is efficient.

Matters are very different in models in which mobility of firms between jurisdictions can have efficiency-enhancing properties. In a world without externalities and many jurisdictions, Tiebout (1956) proposed the notion that intergovernmental competition resulted in a virtuous sorting function. The Tiebout literature therefore emphasizes the benefits of decentralization in inducing jurisdictions to compete for sources of tax revenue by inducing citizens and firms to sort themselves into groups on the basis of their preferences for local public goods. Although Tiebout wrote about citizens, others have developed the analysis for firms. The new economic geography has provided a further basis for thinking that there are externalities in the location of economic activity. In these models the location and production decisions of firms may have important external effects (e.g., congestion, job creation) on their host economies, so that government action to internalize these externalities (by taxes, subsidies or other means) is in principle justified even though the public policy conclusions are at best mixed. Regional or national governments can internalize some externalities through their actions, but others (notably those that spill across borders) will remain, and the results of inter-jurisdictional competition might be better or worse than prior to the intervention.

Overall, the most general conclusion that can be drawn from this literature is that, while the gains from intervention by regional or national governments to support private firms may be large or small according to circumstances, the only grounds for preventing such intervention (by state aid control at a supranational level) rest on the presence of a cross-border externality that the normal processes of bargaining between governments and firms fail to internalize. The presumption, however, is that governments are acting to maximize the welfare of their own jurisdictions; or at least that if they are not, then this is a domestic political failure that is at most indirectly related to the international competition between governments to attract firms. If such a presumption is not justified in practice, then the normative conclusions of this literature may not be justified either.

State aid control: the "fighting wasteful spending" rationale[3]

Although there is much to be said for the spillover rationale, it captures rather poorly what competition policy practitioners (both competition agencies and the political authorities to which they are responsible) say when explaining their actions. Explanations are often couched in terms of curbing "wasteful" spending, regardless of whether or not any international spillover effects are involved. The State Aid Action Plan launched in June 2005 by the EC, for example, talks of the need to aim for "less but better targeted" state aid. However, even if much state aid is indeed wasteful, in the absence of international spillover effects it is hard to see why supranational intervention should be justified. Is not the waste of fiscal resources involved simply a matter of domestic political failure to be resolved by strengthening the mechanisms of domestic political accountability?

The evidence that governments often subsidize private firms in ways that do not maximize the welfare of their own jurisdictions comes from a variety of sources. Some of it is frankly anecdotal: expensive prestige projects such as Concorde, or the well-publicized state support to struggling firms such as Crédit Lyonnais, Alstom and MG Rover. Although strongly suggestive, such evidence is hard to evaluate. Does it reflect more than the errors of judgment that frequently happen when industrial decisions are made both within the private and public sectors (as attested by private sector disasters like Vivendi Universal, Enron and WorldCom)? Two more systematic kinds of evidence strengthen the case. First, there is econometric evidence that politicians and public officials tend to favor projects in relatively high-technology sectors, whether or not these are suitable for the comparative advantage of the location in question. A study by Midelfart-Knarvik and Overman (2002) showed that both national state aid and EU regional aid often failed to attract targeted industries to a significant degree because they did not take comparative advantages into account (e.g., whether there was enough skilled labor in the workforce). Citizens therefore often failed to benefit from agglomeration economies. A second bias is that politicians frequently ignore the impact of one project on others. Such impacts can be large: public employment can reduce private employment through general equilibrium effects. The 2003 biennial report of the German Monopolkommission also discusses these harmful inter-project effects at some length.

Overall, it seems highly plausible that political processes driven by the desire for politicians to gain favorable press coverage may lead to spending decisions that incur costs which are out of proportion to the resulting economic benefits. A recent case approved by the EC provides an interesting illustration. The Portuguese government approved aid worth 41.5 million euros (at 2000 prices) to the semiconductor firm Infineon aimed at establishing a plant manufacturing DRAM memory chips in Portugal. According to the firm's own estimates (plausibly erring on the optimistic side), the investment would generate 252 new jobs and safeguard 596 existing ones – a total of 848 at a cost of some 49,000 euros per job. Yet a study by Haskel, *et al.* (2002) estimates that foreign direct investment generates productivity worth around 3,500 euros per job per year, so the project would have to continue for twenty-five years just to pay for itself – even discounting the possibility that Infineon's spillover effects are lower than estimated (since there are no other DRAM manufacturers in Portugal). Does it really seem likely that Portugal's politicians are getting value for money? If not, then what is prompting them to spend money in this way?

Is it therefore true that, without state aid control, there is a risk of having too much – and unwarranted – aid, because firms are typically better politically organized than taxpayers? Can't excessive public funding be curbed by "political accountability"? In fact, the opposite can happen. Dewatripont and Seabright (2006) have shown in a theoretical model how inefficient aid can arise as a result of electoral concerns in an environment where politicians have to demonstrate to voters that they are actively trying to attract investment – which can in the end turn out to be good or bad for the region or country as a whole. This is consistent with the study by Neven and Seabright (1995) which looks at the subsidization of Airbus and Boeing by the EU and the USA – a subsidization which, according to the researchers' computations, seems mostly to benefit countries which buy aircraft and do not produce them, because subsidies translate into lower prices.

Why state aid control in the EU?

At the EU level, reducing state aid is not a new policy. At one level, it merely reflects the idea of the primacy of competition policy over industrial policy, and experience has taught us how tough it is for public authorities to "pick winners." Moreover, state aid controls can be seen as a straightforward consequence of the Single Market Program. Nevertheless, state aid policy is not without its critics. Beyond the obviously embarrassing cases of tiny undertakings that have at times occupied European attention (and which should be cleared automatically in the future thanks to more powerful *de minimis* provisions), there are at least two more substantive arguments that have been put forward.

The first concerns the case where there is only one European firm in the market (e.g., Airbus). In such cases where the "fighting spillover defense" cannot be called upon, isn't Europe hurting its own competitiveness in a world where it is the *only jurisdiction* to have state aid control? It is true that such cases should ideally be dealt with in a forum like the WTO. It is also clear that state aid control works best in the presence of competitors that act as "watchdogs," which means that European state aid control is most seriously enforced in markets with multiple European-based firms. Beyond these contingent considerations, one should keep in mind the general idea (mentioned at the beginning of this chapter) underlying the Single Market Program, i.e., that vigorous competition at home does contribute overall to international competitiveness.

The second question concerns the very wisdom of the "fighting wasteful spending" defense. Even if one recognizes that state aid control is a commitment device against national or regional governmental abuse against its own citizens, that has moreover been agreed upon *ex ante* by member states, one should stress that it leads to an "image problem" for EU institutions, which typically end up playing the role of scapegoat in national politics against the "political pressure of globalization."

To sum up, it is safe to say that state aid policy is on more solid grounds when it focuses explicitly on distortions of competition. This being said, it remains to be argued that it is in the interests of Europe to be the only jurisdiction with state aid control. To understand this, one must try to understand what is different from other jurisdictions. The obvious feature is the high degree of budget decentralization in the EU: the EU budget is of the order of 1 percent of EU GDP, which is tiny in comparison with the federal budget in the USA, for example. And, as a proportion of GDP, member state budgets are substantially much bigger within the EU, than are state budgets in the USA. Therefore, while Alabama and Ohio are allowed to compete by paying subsidies to attract foreign direct investment much more freely than are Germany and France, their very financial ability to do it is much more limited. This is the key reason behind the need for a state aid policy, as a key instrument of the single market.

Summing up

On the one hand, state aid control in the EU is a very useful tool to prevent wasteful "subsidy wars" between member states which enjoy ample fiscal means to potentially engage in such behavior. On the other hand, it is not an easy policy to defend politically, especially when competitors are outside the EU and not subject to such control. This means that the policy has to be transparent and rational, and has to help focus attention on the consistency with other policy initiatives, like the Single Market Program and the Lisbon Strategy. A key question is how this approach to state aid control can help to keep industrial policy under control in the global market environment. This question is among the key challenges facing the EU today.

Challenges to the status quo and what can happen

In this section, a number of questions that will significantly affect competition policy in the future will be addressed. State aid control and considerations with regard to international relations beyond the EU–US relationship can be identified as the two vital questions that EU competition policy will come to face in its future developments.

The current state of play concerning state aid control: the State Aid Action Plan

The current trend in state aid control, embodied in the State Aid Action Plan, is to strengthen the emphasis on economic principles, trading off market failures (which can justify state aid) and competition distortions (which can justify ruling out state aid). This is in fact a very natural way of streamlining the existing – often *ad hoc* – case-by-case approach, since economists have long since developed analyses of these trade-offs. For example, Friederiszik, Roeller and Verouden (2006) offer a detailed discussion of the "roadmap" that can emerge from such an approach. It is consistent with the "pragmatic" idea of compatibility with the Single Market, which means focusing on "equal access" to aid, for example through tendering processes. One can predict that attempting to systematically trade off market failures and distortions of competition will not imply a revolution in state aid policy, but rather a (welcome) streamlining. It will most likely continue to favor Services of General Economic Interest, Small and Medium Entreprises (SMEs), innovation, training, poor regions and environmental measures.

The big question ahead is where will one draw the line? Will "better-targeted aid" necessarily lead to less aid overall (another objective of the State Aid Action Plan)? While economics can help to give guidance concerning the determination of desirable *relative* aid levels, defining the tolerated *overall* level of state aid will remain pretty much pragmatic or *ad hoc*, since economics does not offer any easy, rational way to address this issue. The general question of competition policy versus industrial policy in the global age will therefore become a crucial one.

For example, this question might crystallize within the context of aid to Research,

Development and Innovation (R&D&I), an area where economics has given particular attention to the trade-off between market failures and distortions of competition. Opting for an economic approach as a way to streamline the rules for granting aid is therefore quite natural in such case. Moreover, aid to R&D&I is of course one area where there is a potential tension between the State Aid Action Plan's principle of "less aid" and the Lisbon Strategy, which makes the case for giving preferential treatment to innovation. Such a case can easily be made, as the *Sapir Report* amply testifies (Sapir, *et al.* 2004). "Better targeting" can therefore resolve the tension, by interpreting it to mean less aid overall but more aid to innovation.

However it is important, in this Lisbon context, to be aware of the risk of the (re)emergence of an industrial policy captured by big incumbent firms. If one wants to avoid this, one can focus aid to R&D&I on SMEs, which makes sense given that they are more subject to market failures (e.g., in credit markets) and that there is a lower risk of distortions. Moreover, when thinking about promoting European growth, one should keep in mind the key role of new firms in US growth (which has crucially benefited from the ability of successful young firms to grow very fast). Studies have for instance shown not only that the US stock market recovery of the 1980s and 1990s was driven almost entirely by new firms, but also that incumbent firms of the early 1970s that did not take over or merge with new firms had, by the end of the 1990s, still not recovered their market value relative to US GDP.

Then again, it is fair to acknowledge that European innovation may be less "entrepreneurial" than US innovation. For example, the Nokia of today did not start in a garage like Apple, but emerged from a (drastically restructured) large diversified company. In this sense, ruling out state aid to large companies is not optimal. But it is then crucial to insist on "good practices" for aid provisions: accessibility to new entrants, limited duration provisions, investment in complementary inputs (like human capital). Current guidelines go in this direction, but going about it in an even more systematic way would not hurt, given the potentially excessive enthusiasm for innovation policies in the Lisbon era.

The key challenge is to prevent excessively lenient state aid policy, which would give preferential treatment to "European champions," big incumbents that would, in the name of global competition, prevent market forces from allowing for a dynamic adjustment of industrial structures in Europe. Given the natural tendencies of several European governments to indulge in this direction, it is important that good safeguards be put in place to channel state aid into directions where it can help and prevent it otherwise.

Conclusion[4]

While the EU–US relationships are in the process of being stabilized, with co-operation aimed at fighting well-defined practices (cartels) and potential tensions on decisions benefitting the two differently (transatlantic mergers, for instance), the increase in EU and US trade with the rest of the world and the growth of trade with some emerging economies have all heightened the need to develop competition laws in these trading partners and to reach harmonization. The key players in this endeavor will be the EC in the EU; the FTC and DOJ in the USA; the OECD, WTO and International Competition Network (ICN) at the global level. Both the EU and the USA will be key players in striving to reach harmonization and it is likely that the common principles behind the EU and US laws will serve as reference points in a number of areas:

- commitment to fight high-core cartels
- scope of flexible arrangements
- transparency of rules of regulation
- recourse to judicial review procedures
- non-discrimination between firms based on nationality.

Among these principles, the last two will probably be the hardest to achieve. Recourse to judicial review procedures will be difficult because the quality of institutions within emerging economies, in particular the legal system, are still far from those in the EU and the USA. And non-discrimination on the basis of nationality may give a strong advantage to foreign multinational firms at the expense of local firms and may therefore conflict with the desire to develop national industries. The view that competition law in emerging or developing countries may increase the global power of big corporations is consistent with the resistance in 1999 by Third World countries against the proposal in favor of the WTO's adopting a new agreement on competition policy.

The EU has several bilateral cooperation agreements on competition policy, most notably with the US as we have seen, but also with Canada and Japan. Weaker agreements are also made with important trading partners, such as Korea and China, mainly so as to exchange experience on competition policy matters and for the EU to provide technical assistance. The first such agreement with China was signed in 2003. Since then China has adopted its first *Anti-Monopoly Act* in 2007. Interestingly, while corporations were lobbying the WTO for stronger competition laws in Third World countries, they tended to view the recent *Anti-Monopoly Act* in China as a potential impediment to future takeover activity.

Bilateral agreements are a step towards harmonization, but have obvious limitations if more than a few countries are involved. International organizations like WTO could provide a framework for multilateral agreements, even if attempts at harmonization or development of competition laws may face opposition from developing countries, mainly because the magnitudes of the internal and external effects of competition laws vary significantly from one country to the other.

One key question for the future is whether the speed at which emerging economies and their big corporate players rise in strength will be matched with the speed at which competition rules converge. This is not obvious given that the "primacy of the market" – a philosophy that has come to dominate the developed world in recent decades – is not necessarily the rule in emerging economies. Indeed, there the state may have much more power, either through individual state firms or through "sovereign funds." This can cause worries among developed countries, especially when one is talking about strategic sectors, like energy. This is probably the main challenge to a process of convergence along the lines of what has guided the EU–US relationship in recent times.

Notes

1 Our goal here *is not* to provide a thorough review of EU antitrust measures in a globalized world. There are excellent analyses like Evenett, *et al.* (2000), Bertrand and Ivaldi (2007) to which we refer the interested reader.
2 Work by Bergman, *et al.* (2007) attempts to identify the sources of convergence and divergence in merger evaluations between the EU and the USA; see also Fox (2007).
3 This section is partly based on Dewatripont and Seabright (2006).
4 We abstract largely here from the WTO, which is the subject of the contribution by Conconi in this volume. See also Telò (2007) for a perspective on the interaction between "regionalism" and global governance (especially Part II, which takes a comparative perspective of the relations between the EU and other "regional groupings").

Bibliography

Bergman, M.A., M.B. Coate, M. Jakobsson and S.W. Ulrick (2007), *Comparing Merger Policies: The European Union versus the United States*, Working Paper 07–1.

Bertrand, O. and M. Ivaldi (2007), "Competition policy: Europe in international markets," in A. Sapir, ed., *Fragmented Power: Europe and the Global Economy*, Bruegel Books, 2007, pp. 156–99.

Dewatripont, M. and P. Seabright (2006), "'Wasteful' public spending and state aid control," *Journal of the European Economic Association*, 4: 513–22.

Dony, M. and C. Smits (2005), *Aides d'Etat*, Bruxelles, Editions de l'Université de Bruxelles.

EAGCP (2005), 'An economic approach to Article 82,' report of the Economic Advisory Group on Competition Policy, available online at http://ec.europa.eu/comm/competition/publications/studies/eagcp_july_21_05.pdf

Evenett, S.J., Lehmann, A. and Steil, B. (2000), *Antitrust Goes Global – What Future for Transatlantic Cooperation?*, Brookings Institution Press.

EU (1991), Agreement between the Government of the United States and the Commission of the European Communities regarding the Application of Their Competition Laws, O.J. EUR. COMM. L 95/47, 30 I.L.M. 1487

Fox, E.M. (2007), "The Market Power Element of Abuse of Dominance. Parallels and Differences in Attitudes, US and EU," European University Institute – Robert Schuman Centre for Advanced Studies.

Friederiszik, H., L.-H. Roeller and V. Verouden (2006), "European state aids control: an economic framework," in P. Buccirossi (ed.), *Advances in the Economics of Competition Law.*

Haskel, J., S. Pereira, and M. Slaughter (2002), *Does Inward Foreign Direct Investment Boost the Productivity of Domestic Firms?*, NBER Working Paper No. 8724.

Kovacic, W.E. and C. Shapiro (2000), "Antitrust policy: a century of economic and legal thinking," *Journal of Economic Perspectives*, 14, 43–60.

Midelfart-Knarvik, K.-H. and H. Overman (2002), "Delocation and European integration: is structural spending justified?," *Economic Policy*, 35: 321–59.

Neven, D.J. and P. Seabright (1995), "European industrial policy: the Airbus case," *Economic Policy* 21.

Reynolds, S. (1996), "Comparison of US antitrust law and EC competition law," http://www.antitrust.org/law/EU/intlLaw.html, also appeared as "International antitrust compliance for a company with multinational operations," *International Quarterly* 76.

Röller, L.-H. and P.A. Buigues (2005). The Office of the Chief Competition Economist at the European Commission. May 2005.

Sapir, A., P. Aghion, G. Bertola, M. Hellwig, J. Pisani-Ferry, D. Rosati, J. Vinals and H. Wallace (2004), *An Agenda for a Growing Europe: The Sapir Report*, Oxford University Press.

Schaub, A. (1998);International co-operation in antitrust matters: making the point in the wake of the Boeing/MDD proceedings,' EC Competition Policy/DGVV/speech/eight/en/sp980xx.htm, vol 4(1), February. Available online at http://ec.europa.eu/comm/competition/speeches/text/sp1998_004_en.html

Telò, M. (ed.), (2007) *European Union and New Regionalism*, second edition, Ashgate.

Tiebout, c. (1956), 'A Pure Theory of Local Expenditures', Journal of Political Economy 64(5): 416–24.

5 The influence of the European socio-economic model in the global economy

Maria João Rodrigues

Summary

The EU is a major player in the global economy, due not only to its weight in international trade, foreign direct investment and exchange rate mechanisms, but also to its capacity to influence global standard formation through its single market and its Economic and Monetary Union. In addition, a further more diffuse form of influence stems from the sum of its external policies, as well as from the model provided by its internal socio-economic model. This prominent position poses the question of the extent to which these vectors of influence have been adapted to the new landscape defined by globalisation. First, this chapter starts with a preliminary characterisation of the European economic and social model, and with the challenges arising from a globalised economy. Second, it details the evolution of the Lisbon Strategy (2000–10), the modernisation agenda aimed at preparing Europe for the challenges of globalisation, as well as its implications for the Union's external action.

The Lisbon Strategy, adopted by the European Council in 2000, was designed to address the question of whether it is possible to update Europe's development strategy so that it might rise to the new challenges resulting from globalisation, technological change and population ageing, while still preserving European values. A further core question which emerged was the need to identify under which conditions a win–win game could be fostered at the international level. In other words, the question is how to create global players engaged in a race to the top – not the bottom – with regard to the social and environmental conditions of a transition to a knowledge-intensive economy. What could the specific role of the EU be in this process of international convergence? This chapter argues that the EU can play a very relevant role in spreading a new development agenda through a variety of means: by providing a positive example in implementing a new development agenda, in line with the Lisbon Agenda, in its own member states; by intertwining this new development agenda with its enlargement and neighbourhood policies; and by connecting this new development agenda in the various components of its external action: its cooperation policy; the external projection of its internal policies; its trade policy and foreign policy regarding third countries, other macro-regions and multilateral organisations.

The European economic and social model

The European economic and social model is the outcome of a long and complex historical process striving to combine social cohesion with higher economic performance. This means that the social dimension should be shaped with the purpose of social justice, as well as contributing to growth and competitiveness. Conversely, growth and competitiveness are crucial in supporting the social dimension, and must therefore also be moulded so as to support it. This implies that there are different choices in both economic and social policies which have evolved over time; these remain under constant review through both political debate and social dialogue. This is the European tradition, and it is valued both inside and outside Europe as a method of building prosperity and quality of life. This tradition has been translated into quite different national models. The most renowned typologies (seen in Table 5.1) distinguish between the Scandinavian, Anglo-Saxon, Continental or Central European, and Southern European types (Hall and Soskice 2001; Amable 2003; Esping-Andersen 2002; Sakellaropoulos and Berghman 2004).

The Central European (or Continental) model of capitalism is roughly characterised by (adapted from Amable, Barré and Boyer 1997, and Amable 2000 and 2003):

- high employment protection, limited external flexibility, job stability, conflicting industrial relations, active employment policy, moderately strong unions, coordination of wage bargaining
- strong institutionalisation of employment rules, working hours and social protection
- a high degree of social protection, employment-based social protection, involvement of the state, high importance of social protection in society, contribution-financed social insurance, pay-as-you-go pension systems
- moderate competition, because of public intervention or business associations, even if intensified within the single market
- the importance of banks and relatively low sophistication of financial services
- public basic research being disconnected from new product development within firms, although there are large-scale programmes
- the importance of public impetus for private research
- internal rather than external mobility of the labour force
- a high level of public expenditure, high enrolment rates in secondary education, emphasis on secondary education homogeneity, developed vocational training, and an emphasis on specific skills.

The Anglo-Saxon model of capitalism is characterised by:

- low employment protection, external flexibility, easy use of temporary work and easy recruitment and dismissal policies, no active employment policy, defensive union strategies, decentralisation of wage bargaining
- individualised wage and labour-market segmentation
- weak social protection, low involvement of the state, emphasis on poverty

alleviation (social safety net), means-tested benefits, private-funded pension system
- limits to concentration through legal action, constant evolution of oligopolistic competition
- market-based finance and sophistication of financial services, financial innovation, strong influence of shareholders
- a research system based on competition between researchers and between research institutions
- importance of intellectual property rights protection incentives towards innovation
- a highly segmented labour force, with high skills and innovation on one side, and low skills and production on the other
- low public expenditures, a highly competitive higher education system, non-homogenised secondary education, weak vocational training, emphasis on general skills and lifelong learning.

The Southern European model of capitalism is characterised by:

- high employment protection (large firms) yet dualism: a 'flexible' fringe of employment in temporary and part-time work, possible conflicts in industrial relations, weaker active employment policy, centralisation of wage bargaining
- a moderate level of social protection, expenditures structure oriented towards poverty alleviation and pensions, high involvement of the state
- low public expenditures, low enrolment rates in tertiary education, a weak higher education system, weak vocational training, no lifelong learning but an emphasis on general skills.

The Nordic European model of capitalism is characterised by:

- moderate employment protection, coordinated or centralised wage bargaining, active employment policy, strong unions, cooperative industrial relations
- a high level of social protection, high involvement of the state, high importance of the welfare state in public policy and society
- a small number of large, internationalised firms and networks of small, local suppliers
- a bank-based financial system, no sophistication of financial services
- social needs being important in the definition of research objectives
- gradual evolution towards advanced technologies and new sectors – from natural resources exploitation to information technology
- egalitarian ideals in education and wage-setting, limits through public action to the adverse consequences of technical progress
- a high level of public expenditure, high enrolment rates, emphasis on the quality of primary and secondary education, importance of vocational training, emphasis on specific skills, importance of retraining and lifelong learning.

Table 5.1 The national diversity in the European socio-economic model

Institutional area	Anglo-Saxon capitalism	Central European capitalism	Southern European capitalism	Nordic European capitalism
Wage–labour nexus	Low employment protection, external flexibility: easy recourse to temporary work and easy hire and fire, no active employment policy, defensive union strategies, decentralisation of wage bargaining	High employment protection, limited external flexibility; job stability, conflicting industrial relations, active employment policy, moderately strong unions, coordination of wage bargaining	High employment protection (large firms) but dualism: a 'flexible' fringe of employment in temporary and part-time work, possible conflicts in industrial relations, no active employment policy, centralisation of wage bargaining	Moderate employment protection, coordinated or centralised wage bargaining, active employment policy, strong unions, cooperative industrial relations
Labour markets	Decentralisation of wage bargaining; individualised wage and labour-market segmentation	Strong institutionalisation of employment rules, working hours, and social protection		Centralisation of wage bargaining under the external competitiveness constraint
Social protection	Weak social protection, low involvement of the state, emphasis on poverty alleviation (social safety net), means-tested benefits, private-funded pension system	High degree of social protection, employment-based social protection, involvement of the state, high importance of social protection in society; contribution-financed social insurance, pay-as-you-go pension systems	Moderate level of social protection, expenditures structure oriented towards poverty alleviation and pensions, high involvement of the state	High level of social protection, high involvement of the state, high importance of the welfare state in public policy and society
Competition	Limits to concentration through legal action; constant evolution of oligopolistic competition	Once moderate competition, because of public intervention or business associations, has intensified within the single market; concentration of capital		Small number of large, internationalised firms and networks of small, local suppliers

Table 5.1 (continued)

Table 5.1 (continued)

Institutional area	Market-based economies	Central European capitalism	Southern European capitalism	Nordic European capitalism
Product-market competition	High importance of price competition, non-involvement of the State in product markets, coordination through market (price) signals, openness to foreign competition and investment	Moderate importance of price competition, relatively high importance of quality competition, involvement of public authorities, relatively high non-price "coordination", low protection against foreign firms and investment	Price- rather than quality-based competition, involvement of the State, little "non-price" coordination, moderate protection against foreign trade or investment, importance of small firms	High importance of quality competition, high involvement of the State in product markets, high degree of "coordination" through channels other than market signals, openness to foreign competition and investment
Finance	Market-based finance and sophistication of financial services; financial innovation; strong influence of shareholders	Importance of banks; relatively low sophistication of financial services		Bank-based financial system; no sophistication of financial services
Financial sector	High protection of minority shareholders, low ownership concentration, high importance of institutional investors, active market for corporate control (takeovers, mergers and acquisitions), high sophistication of financial markets, development of venture capital	Low protection of external shareholders, high ownership concentration, no active market for corporate control (takeovers, mergers and acquisitions), low sophistication of financial markets, moderate development of venture capital, high banking concentration, importance of banks in firms' investment funding	Low protection of external shareholders, high ownership concentration, bank-based corporate governance, no active market for corporate control (takeovers, mergers and acquisitions), low sophistication of financial markets, limited development of venture capital, high banking concentration	High ownership concentration, high share of institutional investors, no market for corporate control (takeovers, mergers and acquisitions), no sophistication of financial markets, high degree of banking concentration

Nonetheless, in spite of these differences, the European economic and social model can be defined by some common features, among which:

- a general access to education and training
- regulated labour contracts
- a general access to social protection and health care
- active policies for social inclusion
- social dialogue procedures
- a predominance of public funding of health and education systems via taxes or social contributions, with a redistribution effect
- macro-economic policy marked by the weight of the public budget
- competition policy coupled with industrial, research and regional policy
- regulated financial systems with predominance of the banking system.

Therefore, the European economic and social model is translated not only into a particular policy mix, but, more profoundly, into a particular pattern of institutional features in the fields of education, health, social protection, public administration, finance and even within companies themselves. The European economies are regulated by these particular patterns of institutional features. This model has also been strongly influenced by the very process of the European construction wherein, within the context of an ever-evolving political framework, the combination of the economic and social dimension has been present from the onset.

On the basis of the Treaty of Rome, the creation of the European Common Market involved the establishment of a European competition policy combined with some instruments of industrial and social policy at the European level (see the Treaty of the European Community, signed in 1957). In the 1980s, the deepening of both the single market and the competition policy was combined with new labour directives, the deepening of the European social dialogue, as well as a stronger regional policy. The European research policy was also developed in connection with the pre-existing industrial policy (see the *Single Act*, signed in 1987). In the 1990s, the creation of an Economic and Monetary Union (EMU) led to a single monetary and exchange rate policy, to a more coordinated fiscal policy as well as to a progressive integration of the financial markets. Over this period, the *acquis communautaire* (fundamental principles of the Community) in labour law was also extended and combined with a new open coordination of the national employment policies (see the Maastricht and the Amsterdam Treaties, signed respectively in 1991 and in 1997).

A systematic update of the European economic and social policies equipped to cope with the new challenges that arose from globalisation and demographic change started at the turn of the millennium with the Lisbon Strategy. This process was further partially echoed, some years later, in the Lisbon Treaty, signed in 2007. By the end of the twentieth century, it was clear that the European social model was facing new strategic challenges stemming from: globalisation and its new competitive pressures; the transition to a knowledge-intensive economy; ageing demographic trends; new family models; the latest stages of very process of European integration. The sustainability of the European social model depended on renewing its economic basis, as well as reforming its main components, in order to cope with these key strategic challenges. Against this background, some of the main priorities for these structural reforms were being identified and debated within European circles.

The access to new skills would become crucial in securing new and better jobs. Education and training systems needed to be reformed in order to better cope with globalisation and the transition to a knowledge economy through: a more dynamic identification of the skills needed; the generalisation of lifelong learning opportunities in schools, training centres, companies, public administrations and households, which rely on universal pre-schooling education and the reduction of the numbers of early school leavers; addressing ageing demographic trends by spreading new methods to assess, enhance and use elderly workers' competences; incorporating new family models by providing equal opportunities to career choices and more flexible access to lifelong learning; buttressing European integration by adopting a common framework for key competences and facilitating the recognition of qualifications and labour mobility.

Social protection systems appeared to need structural reforms to cope with global-isation and new competitive pressures. This was to be achieved by giving stronger priority to more effective active labour market policies and careful monitoring benefits, in order to make work pay and to attract more people into the labour market, thus reducing unemployment and strengthening the financial basis of social protection systems. Further requirements were a careful monitoring system of non-wage labour costs, as well as new complementary (public and private) finan-cial resources. Ageing trends were to be met by the promotion of active ageing, the reduction of early retirement, the provision of incentives to remain active and the introduction of more flexibility in the retirement age. Balancing the financial effort to be provided by different generations would also require a careful reconsideration of the balance between the three pillars of the social protection system. New family models called for the broadening of family care services and the facilitation of working time flexibility as important ways to reconcile work and family life. In light of the deepening single market, European integration increasingly required a common legal framework concerning minimum standards and portability, to be complemented with the open coordination of the reforms of the social protection systems.

Labour regulations and human resource management were also to respond to globalisation, by creating more internal labour flexibility (concerning work organi-sation, working time and wage-setting) at the same time as new forms of external flexibility were being combined with security and the management of industrial restructuring was being strengthened. The active promotion of better labour standards at international level also plays a crucial role: in addressing the ageing population through new forms of work organisation, working time management and better working conditions; in supporting new family models with the help of work-time flexibility, parental leave and career breaks; in responding to European integration by regularly updating European directives, removing obstacles to the mobility of workers at the European level, and by defining a European framework for economic migration.

The changes mentioned above were the outcome of an intensive process of experimentation, debate and negotiation which is still ongoing in Europe. Most of these changes were later framed by a new development strategy adopted by the EU, the so-called Lisbon Strategy (2000–10). What was at stake was not only the reform of the European social model, but the entire European socio-economic model. A new engine for growth and competitiveness was to be developed.

Modernising the European socio-economic model within the global economy

The starting point

The European Council in 2000 approved a long-term and comprehensive modernisation strategy, called the Lisbon Strategy. It was designed to address the question of whether it was possible to update Europe's development strategy so that it might rise to meet the new challenges brought about by globalisation, technological change and ageing populations, while preserving Europe's core values. In this new emerging paradigm, knowledge and innovation were the main source of both wealth and divergence between nations, companies and individuals. Europe was considered to be losing ground to the United States, but this did not mean that it must necessarily copy them. The purpose of the Lisbon Strategy was to define a European way of fostering innovation within a knowledge-based economy, by using distinctive attributes ranging from the preservation of social cohesion and cultural diversity to the various available technological options. A critical step in all this was the need to set up, and continuously renew, a competitive socio-economic platform able to sustain the European social model.

If Europe wished to tap into the potential that arose from this new paradigm while avoiding the risks of a growing social divide, then it was required to engage in necessary institutional reforms. Such institutional change would, for example, include innovation regarding the norms underlying the regulation variously of international trade and competition, social models and educational systems. Moreover, in each and every member state of the EU, institutional reforms would need to effectively internalise the level of integration accomplished through the single market and the single currency. This meant that some level of European coordination would be required to carry out institutional reforms, while respecting national custom and practice. A multilevel governance system was needed, enabling the Union's various levels (i.e,. European, national and local) to interact.

In order to find an answer to the initial question, an extensive intellectual and political effort was undertaken to review, in light of the latest innovations in social sciences, Europe's political agenda as well as the main Community policy documents. European politicians, top officials and experts with a broad experience in these fields were involved in this task (Rodrigues, *et al.* 2002). Their purpose was to ascertain which institutional reforms could change the way in which European societies are currently regulated, so as to pave the way for a new development trajectory towards a knowledge-based economy. But key ideas were needed to lead the political decision-taking and action. In 2000, the entire Portuguese Presidency of the EU was tailored towards achieving this goal – throughout its two European Councils, the fourteen meetings of the Councils of Ministers, seven Ministerial Conferences, several sessions of the European Parliament and a high-level Forum grouping the major stakeholders in Europe and the member states. It is important to recall in its exact terms the new strategic goal and overall strategy defined by the Lisbon European Council on 23–4 March 2000. Quoting its own Conclusions:[1]

> The Union has today set itself a new strategic goal for the next decade: to become the most competitive and dynamic knowledge-based economy in the world capable of sustainable economic growth with more and better jobs and greater social cohesion.

This quote is important since it clarifies that, contrary to the general understanding, the strategic goal defined in Lisbon was not 'to become the most competitive', even if this remains a crucial objective, but rather to achieve a particular combination of strong competitiveness and other identified features. Therefore it is by reference to this combination that the European way should be defined, and that Europe can do better than other counterparts such as the USA. This has methodological implications for the indicators to be chosen in order to compare relative performances. Such a complex goal required a particular strategy, which in 2000 was defined in the following terms:

> Achieving this goal requires an overall strategy aimed at:
>
> - preparing the transition to a knowledge-based economy and society by better policies for the information society and R&D, as well as by stepping up the process of structural reform for competitiveness and innovation and by completing the internal market;
> - modernising the European social model, investing in people and combating social exclusion;
> - sustaining the healthy economic outlook and favourable growth prospects by applying an appropriate macro-economic policy mix.

Later, in 2001, the spring European Council in Stockholm emphasised the concerns related to the environment and sustainable development. The implementation of the Lisbon Strategy should therefore be comprehensive, balanced and based on synergies, but also focused on clear priorities while remaining adaptable to diverse situations. One can argue that this seems close to 'squaring a circle', notably because there are too many trade-offs between these different objectives. Most certainly there are difficult trade-offs, requiring difficult political choices in the short run. Nevertheless, it is important to learn from past successful initiatives. Success often depends on the capacity to overcome a specific trade-off by developing a relevant synergy. For instance, to overcome the trade-offs between macroeconomic stability and growth, some fiscal room for manoeuvre can be created by allowing key public investments to enhance the growth potential: balancing productivity and employment by fostering innovation in products and services and not just in technological processes; balancing growth and cohesion by shifting cohesion policies to equip disfavoured people and regions with more capabilities; maintaining flexibility and security in the labour market by negotiating new kinds of 'flexi-curity'; balancing growth and environment by turning sustainable development into new opportunities for investment and growth creation. These examples illustrate that a successful implementation of the Lisbon Strategy required a comprehensive approach with implications for both policies and governance.

Table 5.2 The Lisbon Agenda

a A *policy for the information society* aimed at improving the citizens' standards of living, with concrete applications in the fields of education, public services, electronic commerce, health and urban management; a new impetus to spread information technologies in companies, namely e-commerce and knowledge management tools; an ambition to deploy advanced telecommunications networks and democratise the access to the internet, on the one hand, and to produce contents that add value to Europe's cultural and scientific heritage, on the other.

b An *R&D policy* whereby the existing community programme and the national policies converge into a European research area by networking R&D programmes and institutions.

c A strong priority for an *innovation policy* and the creation of a Community patent.

d An *enterprise policy* going beyond the existing Community programme, combining it with a coordination of national policies in order to create better conditions for entrepreneurship – namely administrative simplification, better regulation, access to venture capital or manager training.

e *Economic reforms* that target the creation of growth and innovation potential, improve financial markets to support new investments, and complete Europe's internal market by liberalising the basic sectors while respecting the public service inherent to the European model.

f New priorities defined for national *education policies*, i.e., turning schools into open learning centres, providing support to each and every population group, using the internet and multimedia; in addition, Europe should adopt a framework of new basic skills and create a European diploma to combat computer illiteracy.

g Active *employment policies* intensified with the aim of making lifelong training generally available and expanding employment in services as a significant source of job creation; improvement of the adaptability and promotion of equal opportunities for women and men. Raising Europe's employment rate was adopted as a key target in order to reduce the unemployment rate and to consolidate the sustainability of social protection systems.

h An organised process of cooperation between the member states to modernise *social protection*, identifying reforms to answer to common problems such as matching pension systems with population ageing.

i National plans to take action against *social exclusion* in each and every dimension of the problem (including education, health, housing) and meeting the requirements of target groups specific to each national situation.

j The *environmental dimension* was added by the European Council of Stockholm in 2001 to the economic and social dimensions defined in Lisbon, providing the EU with a comprehensive strategy for sustainable development.

Reshaping the European economic and social model

The Lisbon Strategy was also translated into new general orientations for the following policies: the information society, research and development, innovation, enterprise, the single market, education, employment, social protection, social inclusion, environment, transport and telecommunications (see Table 5.2).

It is important to keep in mind this list of policies because each of them has a specific institutional basis in the EU, as well as a network of specialised people involved in the public administration and civil societies across all member states. Over the following years, these general orientations were transformed by these key actors into the operational instruments, directives, regulations, community programmes and concrete action plans (see Table 5.2) collectively designated as the Lisbon Agenda (Rodrigues 2003).

A short story of the Lisbon Agenda

The Lisbon Agenda was developed to address the evolving challenges of a global economy, by progressively adapting several existing policies, as well as institutional and financial instruments, to its strategic priorities. The implementation of the Lisbon Strategy has gone through different phases as it progressed towards the 2010 horizon.

The *first phase*, while integrating the environmental dimension, was focused on: translating the European Council's Lisbon conclusions into policy instruments of the EU and defining its approach to sustainable development;[2] preliminary implementation in the member states (a process still very imbalanced among areas and member states); introducing the basic mechanisms for implementation (spring European Council; reorganisation of the Council formations and schedules; involvement of the European Parliament and the other European institutions, the social partners and the organised civil society at European level; development of the open method of coordination tools); introducing stronger mechanisms in the new European Constitutional Treaty which were preserved in the Lisbon Treaty (e.g., the General Affairs Council; the coordination between economic, employment and social policies; the instrument mix in each policy; the basic tools of the open method of coordination).

The *second* phase, following the 2005 mid-term review, put the focus on implementation at the national level, including in the new member states.[3] This new focus would require a stronger interface between the European and the national levels of governance, with major implications for the behaviour of the main actors. This phase would also be used to clarify the financial basis of the implementation of the Lisbon Strategy. Finally, a *third phase* was scheduled in order to fine-tune implementation on the ground, and to take into account the final outcomes of the new European Treaty, adapting to the new context and to prepare the post-2010 era.

In fact, both in 2001 and 2002, the Lisbon Strategy was already turned into an operational agenda by the Commission and the Council, which mobilised several available instruments and developed the open method of coordination in eleven policy fields: from information society, research, innovation and enterprise policy to education, employment, social protection and environment. This process of policy-making and implementation also involved the other European institutions and stakeholders as well as their equivalents at the national level. The new member states were involved from 2002 onwards. Nevertheless, from the start implementation was quite unequal in the various member states and between the different policy fields.

In 2003 there was debate on the possible connections between the Lisbon Agenda and the new Treaty on the future of Europe being compiled within the Convention. In parallel, some cooperation initiatives with partner countries began exchanging experience on development agendas (China, Brazil), with the Lisbon Strategy as reference. In 2004, as the implementation seemed to be hindered by inadequate financial means, another debate emerged on the future profile of the Community budget. The priorities for the next generation of Community Programmes and Structural Funds, the reform of state aids, and, last but not least, the reform of the Stability and Growth Pact (SGP) were all up for debate. In the meantime, the planned mid-term review of the Lisbon Agenda was being prepared.

In 2005, following the mid-term review, major decisions were taken in order to further foster the implementation of this agenda. It was decided to clarify the priorities and launch new political and financial instruments. More specifically, new integrated guidelines were adopted for economic and employment policies and member states were invited to turn them into national reform programmes, adapting the Lisbon Strategy to their national systems. A new set of financial instruments was also adopted, comprising the Community budget, the guidelines for structural funds, the rules for state aids and a revised SGP.

Throughout 2006 the focus was on implementation, which involved the creation of new government structures regarding the Lisbon coordinators, the inclusion of more stakeholders at national level and the mobilisation of new financial means as well the development of new policy measures. A stronger political focus was put on energy and environment because of the increased evidence confirming the risks associated with climate change. By 2007, a positive trend in growth and net employment creation was emerging, but the sustainability of this trend depended on more growth potential being fostered by structural reforms. Several such reforms have thus already taken place in Europe, notably in social protection, health systems, public administration, financial systems, research and education, and labour markets; but these still appear insufficient and, most of all, imbalanced when comparing different policy fields and countries. Nevertheless, it is already possible to conclude that the member states which have been more effective in implementing the Lisbon Agenda are also those reaping more benefits in terms of growth, job creation and sustainable development.

In search of more coherence and consistency

The search for more coherence and consistency of policies is key to understanding the steps taken all over this period and, in particular, the mid-term review in 2004–05, under the Luxembourg Presidency. The Lisbon Agenda was reshaped in an effort to provide answers to the main problems which had been identified (Kok 2004;

Sapir, *et al.* 2004): the blurring of the strategic objectives, the inflation of priorities and measures, the lack of implementation, coordination and participation mechanisms, and the lack of financial incentives. In short, this resulted in a deficit in both coherence and consistency. The political priorities were specified in a list of twenty-four guidelines using the Treaty-based instruments called 'broad economic policy guidelines' and the 'employment guidelines'. Moreover, an additional strand was included dealing with the macroeconomic policies, under the label 'macroeconomic policies for growth and jobs' (see Table 5.3 and CEU 2005).

Hence, for the first time, the EU was equipped with an integrated package of guidelines for its economic and social policies, using Treaty-based instruments, in order to improve the coherence of the economic and social policies and their consistency between the European and the national levels. Behind this major political development a quite long-maturing process had taken place, creating a new strategic consensus on the political priorities, by using the so-called 'open method' of coordination. These guidelines were supposed to play a central role in mobilising the full Lisbon toolbox (Table 5.4).

It is also important to identify the innovations which were introduced within European governance mechanisms to strengthen policy coherence and consistency. In order to foster implementation, the member states committed themselves to turning these integrated guidelines into national reform programmes. These programmes are forward-looking political documents that set out a comprehensive strategy to implement the integrated guidelines and adapt them to the national situation. Besides presenting political priorities and measures, these programmes are also expected to point out the roles of the different stakeholders as well as the budgetary resources to be mobilised, including the structural funds with a link to the stability and convergence programmes. The preparation, implementation and monitoring of the national programmes involves the main political institutions as well as the civil society; and, when appropriate, a national coordinator is be appointed. An annual follow-up report is also provided by all member states, leading to a general report, which the European Commission presents to the European Council at the annual spring meeting.

A final important piece fostering the implementation is the Community's Lisbon Programme, which collects, for the first time, all the regulatory actions, financing actions and policy developments to be launched at the European level regarding the Lisbon Strategy for growth and jobs, and organises them along the three main priorities previously mentioned.[4] Overall, the implementation of the Lisbon Agenda has created a political and social process concerned with improving the coherence and consistency of economic and social policies, thereby progressively involving a series of institutions and actors. First, the European Council gives a particular weight to the Lisbon Agenda at its annual spring meeting. Second, several Council sub-groupings reflect the Lisbon priorities: General Affairs, ECOFIN, Competitiveness, Employment, Education, Environment, Energy and Telecommunications. Also, in the European Commission, fifteen out of the current twenty-seven commissioners and seventeen directorate generals (a smaller group of Lisbon Commissioners meet on a more regular basis) are directly involved in Lisbon agenda matters;

Table 5.3 Lisbon Strategy: the integrated guidelines for growth and jobs

Macroeconomic policies for growth and jobs

1   To secure economic stability for sustainable growth
2   To safeguard economic and fiscal sustainability as a basis for increased employment
3   To promote a growth-and-employment oriented and efficient allocation of resources
4   To ensure that wage developments contribute to macroeconomic stability and growth
5   To promote greater coherence between macroeconomic, structural and employment policies
6   To contribute to a dynamic and well-functioning EMU.

Knowledge and innovation – engines of sustainable growth

7   To increase and improve investment in R&D, in particular by private business
8   To facilitate all forms of innovation
9   To facilitate the spread and effective use of ICT and to build a fully inclusive information society
10 To strengthen the competitive advantages of its industrial base
11 To encourage the sustainable use of resources and strengthen the synergies between environmental protection and growth.

Making Europe a more attractive place to invest and work

12 To extend and deepen the internal market
13 To ensure open and competitive markets inside and outside Europe and to reap the benefits of globalisation
14 To create a more competitive business environment and encourage private initiative through better regulation
15 To promote a more entrepreneurial culture and create a supportive environment for SMEs
16 To expand and improve European infrastructure and complete priority cross-border projects.

More and better jobs

17 To implement employment policies aimed at achieving full employment, improving quality and productivity at work, and strengthening social and territorial cohesion
18 To promote a lifecycle approach to work
19 To ensure inclusive labour markets, enhance work attractiveness and make work pay for job-seekers, including disadvantaged people and the inactive
20 To improve matching of labour market needs
21 To promote flexibility combined with employment security and reduce labour market segmentation, having due regard to the role of the social partners
22 To ensure employment-friendly labour cost developments and wage-setting mechanisms
23 To expand and improve investment in human capital
24 To adapt education and training systems in response to new competence.

Table 5.4 Modes of governance by policy area

Policies Instruments	Monetary (euro area)	Budget	Internal market	Competetiveness	Industrial	Innovation	Environment and energy	Research	Education and learning	Employment	Social protection
Exclusive EU competence	X BCE			X							
Directives, regulations		X	X	X	X		X	X		X	X
Guidelines		X			X	X	X	X	X	X	
Common objectives									X		X
EU programmes					X	X	X	X	X	X	X
Reinforced cooperation						X		X			
Intergovernmental cooperation								X			
National reform programmes		X			X	X	X	X	X	X	
National sectorial programmes							X				X
National budgets		X				X		X	X	X	X
Structural funds					X	X	X	X	X	X	X
European frameworks									X		

in the European Parliament, six of the committees deal with these matters, as do the national parliaments (involved through both their European Affairs Committees, and through an annual Lisbon conference hosted along with the European Parliament). The European Economic and Social Committee, and its Lisbon network of Economic and Social Councils (in the member states where they exist), as well as the Committee of Regions and its Lisbon platform involving more than one hundred regions, are further sets of partners. Obviously, the European confederations of social partners are also on board; representing their counterparts at national level, and meeting regularly with the other European institutions in the Tripartite Social Summit. And finally, the national governments are involved through several ministers and ministries, as well as the prime ministers. A horizontal network of top officials has also emerged in light of the role of the Lisbon Coordinators, who can be either a ministers or a top officials, reporting to a minister or even the head of state.

Beyond this institutional setting, there exists a diverse network of civil society organisations in various areas which have followed and supported in some fashion the development of the Lisbon Agenda. Most of them are only faintly aware of this European agenda; they are more often rather concerned with its various translations at the national levels. Nevertheless, quite a large network of civil society leaders across Europe was explicitly connecting with the Lisbon Agenda (2000–10) in their normal work. In the meantime, the 2007 Lisbon Treaty strives to create the institutional conditions supporting better governance of the Lisbon process; notably by clarifying the Union competences, improving horizontal coordination, streamlining decision-making processes and strengthening the Union's democratic legitimacy. It remains to be seen to what extent this potential will be harnessed.

Key issues for the evolution of the European socio-economic model

Within the institutional framework defined in 2005, the EU member states implemented their national reform programmes, in the largest coordinated process of economic reform ever tried in Europe. The purpose was to adapt to each country a set of common priorities to foster growth and employment and to prepare Europe for globalisation. In the following years, these national programmes have shown that many reforms are underway throughout Europe, addressing education, research, social protection, financial systems, public administrations, infrastructures, as well as labour markets and business organisations.

Despite a wide variety of policy measures, some of them have become quite generalised, such as: improving the conditions for start-ups, strengthening the interface between universities and companies, modernising employment services, delaying the retirement age, spreading e-government. Nevertheless, progress remained slow regarding the reform of universities, access to lifelong learning, 'flexi-curity' within labour markets, and the opening of the energy markets. Regarding key quantitative targets, progress has been substantial on economic growth potential, employment rates, internet coverage and the reduction of administrative burdens; but progress has remained insufficient on investment in research, the number of patents, access to training, and labour productivity.

Hence, a debate across the member states and in the European institutions has continued to question whether these reforms are going in the right direction and whether they enjoy the necessary scope. Consequently, the unmistakable core question remains how to ensure that Europe develops a knowledge-intensive and low-carbon economy while growing faster, creating more and better jobs and keeping social inclusion in a globalised economy. However, meeting this challenge entails tackling a major problem: Europe was at the turn of the century the economic bloc with the slowest growth. The obvious answer was to highlight the need variously to explore new markets, increase competitiveness by investing in knowledge, and expand and train the employed population. From this viewpoint, what overarching conclusions could be drawn within the national reform programmes?

Concerning new markets, there was progress stemming from enlargement as well as from the renewed globalisation strategies adopted by some European countries and corporations. It suffices to mention the growing race to invest in China or India to illustrate this point. Nevertheless, many other steps were to be taken: promoting an agreement in the Doha World Trade Organization (WTO) Round; developing long-term strategic partnerships with key external partners; taking advantage of the services directive; turning structural funds into powerful tools allowing less developed regions to catch up; using the Eurozone for a stronger co-ordination of macroeconomic policies for investment and growth.

As for competitiveness, what was at stake was the redeployment of European economies towards high value-added activities, whatever the sector: from biotech, information technologies or business services to automotive technologies, textiles or tourism. More public and private investment in R&D was crucial to step up this transition to a knowledge-intensive economy. This could be achieved with better infrastructures, more training and mobility of researchers, more fiscal incentives. But this was not enough to turn knowledge into value. What was also missing in many European countries was a more ambitious development of their innovation systems, connecting companies and universities in promising clusters and partnerships.

The European employment policy, for its part, had adopted another focus: not only to reduce unemployment, but also to increase the employed population, who could therefore contribute to sustaining the social protection systems. For this reason, many countries were activating their employment services to make jobs or training proposals as they were expanding child care and testing the first measures for active ageing. Nevertheless, something deeper was at stake: the reorganisation and coordination of employment, training and social protection policies so as to support people over their lifecycle with choices which are increasingly varied. This would make it easier to introduce more flexibility in the labour market, according to the so-called 'flexi-curity' models.

In the meantime, the original mark of the Lisbon Strategy remained clear. The best tool to adapt to change is lifelong learning. Once more, the situation was improving regarding the rate of workers enjoying this possibility or the share of young people concluding secondary education. But, yet again, what was at stake was something broader: building a lifelong learning system with access points in schools, companies and households, providing more tailor-made services for education and training. Universities had a particular responsibility here to respond to much more diversified demands.

A reorientation of national and European policies seemed to be underway. Still, this should be progressed much further and also pass another very important test: re-directing financial means themselves. The review of the Stability and Growth Pact would fall under scrutiny. What was at stake was the continued pursuit of fiscal consolidation, and the strengthening and sustainability of the social protection systems. However, it was also a window of opportunity to reshape the debate on public expenditure, tax systems and structural funds in favour of future-oriented priorities such as investing in research, innovation and human capital.

A conclusion which can be drawn from a review of the national reform programmes is that the differences in implementation of this European strategy, between policy fields or member states, have become increasingly obvious. When comparing member states, the best general performances in growth, jobs, innovation, social inclusion and environmental protection have been booked in those countries which have achieved a better implementation of the Lisbon Strategy, thus often deepening old differences between the member states.

Implications for the external action of the EU

International convergence or divergence?

The Lisbon Strategy aimed at defining a European path towards a knowledge society. Knowledge has become the main source of wealth for nations, companies and people; but it has also turned into the main dividing factor in today's world. Hence, investing in research, innovation and education, developing a knowledge-intensive economy society has been deemed a key lever for competitiveness and prosperity.

Many other countries were making the same choice. Not only the USA and Japan – the first to start – but also India, China, South Korea, Brazil and many others. Around 2006, it became clear there was an international movement in a convergent direction: Japan was preparing a very comprehensive Plan for Innovation focusing on citizens needs; India had created a Knowledge Commission which was elaborating a larger development agenda for India; China had adopted a new Five-Year Plan introduced within the framework of the Chinese concept of 'harmonious development'. This novel concept, functionally akin to the notion of sustainable development, has allowed for new convergent concerns to be raised within the Chinese political debate, such as the role of knowledge and innovation, and the need for social cohesion and environmental sustainability. Similarly, Brazil, after a foresight exercise called 'Brazil 3 Times', adopted an ambitious agenda for development, emphasising the role of knowledge, social inclusion and concern with the environment. And the USA was launching new initiatives to keep the lead in a more competitive knowledge economy.

This international movement towards increased convergence could be deemed to be in the European interest, because Europe could not implement an agenda like the Lisbon one in isolation, but instead needed other partner countries to go in the same direction. Nevertheless, a crucial question has emerged: under which conditions could Europe enjoy a win–win game? How could they ensure a race to the top – not the bottom – with regard to the social and environmental conditions of this transition to a knowledge-intensive economy? In fact, both scenarios should be considered as possible ones. It seems that some conditions should be fulfilled in order to avoid the 'race to the bottom' scenario: developing EU relationships as global partners facing common challenges; setting common basic standards to define a level playing field; turning the strategy for a knowledge-intensive economy of EU partners into a more comprehensive development agenda combining the economic, social and environmental dimensions.

A broader and pro-active approach for the EU external action

What could be the specific role of the EU in this process of international convergence? The Union could play a very relevant role in spreading new references for a new development agenda, by diverse means: by providing a positive example in implementing a new development agenda in its own member states, building on the outcomes of the Lisbon Agenda; by intertwining this new development agenda with its enlargement and neighbourhood policies; by connecting this new development agenda to the various components of its external action – cooperation policy, external projection of its internal policies, trade policy and foreign policy regarding countries, macro-regions and multilateral organisations.

Therefore, the achievements of the Lisbon Agenda depend on stronger action on not only the internal but also the external front. This agenda requires an international convergence towards more open markets with better standards in environmental, social, financial and technological areas. With these concerns in mind, the discussion on the external dimension of the Lisbon Strategy held by the informal European Council in Lisbon on 18–19 October 2007 set the tone. Europe was to take a leading position in this international upward movement. This implied envisaging globalisation as not only a challenge, but also an opportunity to be seized, and a responsibility to be taken.

A *European Declaration on Globalisation* was subsequently prepared and adopted by the December 2007 European Council. The European approach to globalisation would strive for reciprocal market-opening, the improvement of global standards, and the deepening of strategic cooperation with the EU's international partners. Be it in multilateral or bilateral frameworks, this pro-active approach was to inspire the various components of the Union's external action: common foreign and security policy (CFSP); trade policy; cooperation policy; as well as the external dimension of Community policies such as research, education, employment or environment.

The Lisbon Treaty opens up new avenues for these concerns to be more systematically integrated into the subsequent generations of external policies to be developed by the EU. Accordingly, the Union's external action is to be moulded by the following innovations:

Table 5.5 Key issues for a strategic dialogue on the socio-economic model

1 We need to design and implement a new comprehensive agenda for sustainable development combining the economic, social and environmental dimensions. Synergies between these three dimensions should become more important than trade-offs.
2 We should neither sacrifice social conditions to competitiveness nor competitiveness to social conditions. In order to overcome this dilemma, we should renew both.
3 The triangle of knowledge (research, innovation and education) plays a central role in this agenda.
4 It is not enough to invest in research. It is crucial to turn knowledge into added value through innovation.
   Innovation provides a new means for capacity building, which overcomes the protectionist approach to industrial policy.
5 Innovation is:
   · not only in processes but also in products and services;
   · not only technological but also in organisation, management, skills and culture;
   · not only for high-tech companies and highly skilled workers but for all companies and people.
6 Entrepreneurship – taking the initiative to mobilise new resources to address new problems – should be encouraged everywhere, beginning in schools and universities. This will ensure support and seed capital is available for start-ups and help innovative companies to reach their market.
7 The information and communication technologies provide the basic infrastructures for a knowledge society. In order to overcome the risk of digital divide, new technologies should provide better access to all citizens in schools, health care, leisure and all public services.
8 Social policy can become a productive factor provided that:
   · it equips people for change, to move to new jobs by providing new skills and adequate social protection;
   · it increases equal opportunities.
9 A sound basic and secondary education is a key factor in providing better life chances. Nevertheless, learning opportunities should be provided for all over their life cycle.
10 Social protection systems should be built and recalibrated to cope with demographic change.
11 Respecting the environment is not against investment and jobs creation. Rather, it can be turned into new opportunities for investment and jobs creation.
12 Macroeconomic policies should ensure macroeconomic stability, but also a stronger focus on key investments for the future in research, innovation, education, infrastructures and social conditions.
13 Multilevel governance should be reformed for a better implementation of this agenda at local, national, regional and international levels. At all levels, we need more horizontal coordination of the relevant policies and a stronger involvement of the relevant stakeholders.
14 Cultural openness, initiative, participation and partnership are key ingredients for a successful implementation of this agenda.

- a broader approach for the external action of the Union which combines CFSP, trade and cooperation policies with the external projection of the internal policies of the Union. This requires the external action of the EU to integrate the external dimension of such policy areas as research, environment, education and employment[5]
- a new generation of the EU's cooperation programmes based on the new political orientations defined by the European Consensus[6]
- a new approach in trade policy mindful of the Lisbon Agenda, notably aimed at better equipping Europe in the face of globalisation by using trade combined with basic standards as a major lever for growth, as well as more and better jobs.[7]

All these external policies could play a stronger role in developing the external dimension of the Lisbon Agenda, projecting its main strategic priorities to the outside world, notably: trade policy, in opening new markets and improving standards; cooperation policy, in capacity building to improve standards and improve policy coherence regarding the Millennium Development Goals; research, education and culture policies, in improving international cooperation; social policies, in supporting decent work strategies; energy and environmental policies, in spreading the carbon emissions trade and the renewable energies; macroeconomic policies, in ensuring international financial stability.

A new development agenda and the EU trade policy

According to the European Commission's proposals to connect the trade policy with the Lisbon Agenda, the EU should be engaged in developing a social dimension in trade policy. From this point of view, it is unfortunate that basic labour standards have not been included in the Growth and Stability Pact (GSP) and in the Growth and Stability Pact plus (GSP+). This brings with it other broader implications for the EU's stance within the Doha Round.

Nevertheless, the EU could introduce them in its bilateral negotiations. The negotiation of agreements with macro-regions in the process of regional integration could open important windows of opportunity, even if a special effort were required to address new and specific problems regarding the social dimension of the regional integration. The main assumption to be taken is that regional integration could become an important leverage to promote trade with better social and environmental standards.

The EU approach should create an effective environment for this negotiation by combining incentives and sanctions. To improve this combination, it seemed particularly important to strengthen the coordination between trade, cooperation and the other components of the external action of the Union, including the external projection of the EU's internal policies. The role to be played by companies investing abroad in promoting better labour and environmental standards could also be emphasised as a basic component of corporate social responsibility.

The development and the diffusion of a new development agenda crucially depend upon a stronger impetus emanating from the multilateral institutions. The EU has a special responsibility in this regard. Consequently, more effective EU action in this direction is required, notably within the board of directors of the World Bank and International Monetary Fund (IMF), as well as in the UN system, and more specifically in the Economic and Social Council (ECOSOC). Such efforts by the EU must be made in association with the World Trade Organization (WTO) and the International Labor Organization (ILO).

The debate on a new development agenda has also become a debate on the basic rules underlying the process of globalisation. In fact, these rules have proven crucial in supporting the implementation of a new development agenda, and they have consequently emerged in a broad range of policy fields, such as: finance, environment, intellectual property and labour. Nevertheless, they still require further clarification, enforcement and coordination. For instance, when considering the coordination of ILO rules with WTO rules, the following potential policy avenues can still be identified: defining how the WTO could take into account the ILO rules; creating a Committee on Trade and Decent Working Conditions within the WTO; defining the role of specific indicators to introduce into the negotiation process; going even further by deciding that the ratification of the ILO core labour standards be a prerequisite for WTO membership.

Conclusion

In conclusion, the implementation of a new agenda has challenged the *coherence* and the *consistency* of the external action of the EU. The *coherence*, because the Union has been striving to improve this aspect of its internal economic, social and environmental policies within the framework of the Lisbon Agenda and, accordingly, the degree of coherence between policies prompted by the EU's external action in partner countries must also be improved. The *consistency*, because the efforts of the EU to reform the multilateral system, and to improve the basic rules for globalisation, require a much stronger coordination between the EU and its member states within the multilateral arenas. This is a further reason why the Lisbon Treaty provides important new levers for the implementation of the Lisbon Strategy.

This emerging framework grounded in the Lisbon Strategy can help to identify critical points in the various agendas of the EU's external action:

- *within the multilateral agenda*: achieving an agreement in the Doha Round; rebalancing governance provided by the Breton Woods institutions; and strengthening multilateral environmental governance
- *within the regional agenda*: addressing past and future enlargements as well as the EU's neighbourhood, and fostering convergence and catch-up
- *within the development agenda*: providing aid for trade; deepening the strategic dialogue for sustainable development; and improving policy coherence in development strategies
- *within the transatlantic agenda*: securing progress in regulatory convergence on trade-related intellectual property rights (TRIPs) issues, financial markets, and energy

- *with a more global and general agenda, notably regarding strategic partners*: deepening strategic cooperation for sustainable development by encompassing climate change, environment, energy, social inclusion and creating a win–win game in trade
- *within the agenda with other macro-regions*: an agenda similar to the one developed at the general level is to be pursued in conjunction with a deepening dialogue on regional integration.

Even if the EU adopts a more assertive tone regarding its own interests, strategic dialogues are also developed in order to encourage an international convergence towards knowledge-intensive economies with better standards. Such an innovative approach lies at the basis of a renewed push towards strategic cooperation between the EU and partner countries, notably aimed at fostering an optimal use of all these available instruments of external action. In order to develop such strategic dialogue with its partners, some policy initiatives launched by the EU have drawn from the available European experience. As a result, deepening the understanding of the EU partner countries' experiences emerges as a logical move to further the process of mutual understanding and adjustment. This could potentially provide a new basis for the next generation of the Union's external action.

Notes

1 Council of the European Union (2000).
2 European Commission (2003).
3 Council of the European Union (2005).
4 European Commission (2005b).
5 European Commission (2006a).
6 European Commission (2005a).
7 European Commission (2006b).

Bibliography

Amable, Bruno (2003), *The Diversity of Modern Capitalism*, Oxford, Oxford University Press.
Amable, B., R. Barré and R. Boyer (1997), *Les Systemes d'Innovation à l'ère de la Globalistion*, Paris: Economica.
Boyer, Robert (1998), *The Search for Labour Market Flexibility*, Oxford, Oxford University Press.
Council of the European Union (2000), *Conclusions of the Lisbon European Council*, Council of the European Union SN 100/00, 23–4 March 2000.
Council of the European Union (2005), *Conclusions of the Brussels European Council*, Council of the European Union 10255/05, 16–17 June 2005.
Esping-Anderson, G. 2002), 'A New European Social Model for the Twenty-First Century?', in M.J. Rodrigues (ed.), *The New Knowledge Economy in Europe: A Strategy for International Competitiveness and Social Cohesion*, Cheltenham, UK and Northhampton, MA: Edward Elgar pp. 54–94.

European Commission (1994), *Growth, Competitiveness, Employment – The Challenges and Ways Forward into the 21st Century*, Luxembourg, Office for Official Publications of the European Communities.

European Commission (2003), *Choosing to Grow: Knowledge, Innovation and Jobs in a Cohesive Society – Report to the Spring European Council, 21 March 2003 on the Lisbon Strategy of Economic, Social and Environmental Renewal*, COM (2003) 5 final, 14.01.2003.

European Commission (2005a), *Proposal for a Joint Declaration by the Council, the European Parliament and the Commission on the European Union Development Policy 'The European Consensus'*, COM (2005) 311 final, 13.07.2005.

European Commission (2005b), *Common Actions for Growth and Employment: The Community Lisbon Programme*, COM (2005) 330 final, 20.07.2005.

European Commission (2006a), *Europe in the World: Some Practical Proposals for Greater Coherence, Effectiveness and Visibility*, COM (2006) 278 final, 08.06.2006.

European Commission (2006b), *Promoting Decent Work for All: The EU Contribution to the Implementation of the Decent Work Agenda in the World*, COM (2006) 249, 13.07.2006.

European Commission (2006c), *Global Europe Competing in the World: A Contribution to the EU's Growth and Jobs Strategy*, COM (2006) 567 final, 04.10.2006.

Hall, Peter A. and David Soskice (eds) (2001), *Varieties of Capitalism: The Institutional Foundations of Comparative Advantage*, Oxford, Oxford University Press.

Kok, Wim (coord.) (2004), *Facing the Challenge: The Lisbon Strategy for Growth and Employment*, Report from the High Level Group, European Commission.

Lundvall, Bengt-Åke (ed.) (1992), *National Systems of Innovation: Towards a Theory of Innovation and Interactive Learning*, London, Pinter Publishers.

Rodrigues, Maria João, *et al.* (coord.) (2002), *The New Knowledge Economy in Europe: A Strategy for International Competitiveness and Social Cohesion*, Cheltenham, Edward Elgar.

Rodrigues, Maria João (2003), *European Policies for a Knowledge Economy*, Cheltenham, Northhampton MA, Edward Elgar.

Sakellaropoulos, Theodoros and Jos Berghman (eds) (2004), *Connecting Welfare Diversity within the European Social Model*, Social Europe Series, Vol. 9, Schoten, Intersentia.

Sapir, André, *et al.* (coord.) (2004), *An Agenda for a Growing Europe: The Sapir Report*, Oxford: Oxford University Press.

Part II

EU external policies

6   The EU's external relations and their evolving legal framework

Marianne Dony

Summary

The EU has a broad and complex network of external relations, developed both within the context of the European Community (trade relations, development cooperation, etc.) as well as within the framework of the common foreign and security policy. This chapter first details how the Maastricht Treaty laid out the famous three pillars which originally made up the EU. The Lisbon Treaty would ultimately remove this three-tiered structure, thereby affirming the EU's singular and unified legal personality, both domestically and internationally. The EU enjoys important competences in different fields of its external relations. As shown next in this chapter, these competences can be distinguished as being either explicitly or implicitly conferred, as well as exclusive or shared with regard to the member states. The Union's competences include *inter alia* the conclusion of international agreements. To a large extent, the Lisbon Treaty has, along the lines subsequently described, unified the procedures behind the conclusion of such international agreements, while also awarding an ever-increasing role to the European Parliament. The EU also participates to varying degrees in many international organisations. As outlined, such participation is mostly a joint venture with the member states. This implies a necessarily close cooperation between the Union and the member states when acting within these international institutions. In conclusion, the chapter highlights the clear intent on strengthening the coherence between the different fields of the EU's external action, as well as between its internal and external policies. Coherence remains a difficult goal, even though the Lisbon Treaty improves the overall situation through important institutional reforms.

The legal personality of the EU

A pivotal point of the Lisbon Treaty (signed on 13 December 2007[1]) regarding the EU's external relations is the recognition of the single legal personality of the EU that 'shall replace and succeed the European Community'.[2] The Union henceforth becomes a subject of international law, able to avail itself of all means of international action: the right to conclude treaties; to submit claims; to act before an international court or judge; and to become a member of an international organisation. Moreover, the Lisbon Treaty also partially condensed the fundamental 'three pillars system' created by the Maastricht Treaty.

The pillar system of the Maastricht Treaty

The Maastricht Treaty, signed in 1992, established the European Union 'as a new stage in the process of creating an ever closer union among the peoples of Europe' (Article 1, TEU) and identified as one of its objectives 'to assert its identity on the international scene'.

However the Maastricht Treaty did not remove the former Communities, created by the 1951 Paris Treaty and 1957 Rome Treaty, which were endowed with legal personality from the outset. It laid out the fundamental three-pillar system comprised of the supranational Community pillar[3] and the two intergovernmental pillars, one concerned with the common foreign and security policy (CFSP) and the other with justice and home affairs (JHA).[4] However, at that time the EU was not awarded a single, overarching legal personality.

It was widely admitted that the coexistence of the EU and the Communities, with their diverging competences, decision-making powers and instruments, created an ambiguity with regard to their respective competences and would consequently result in confusion on the part of the Union's partners. Furthermore, these ambiguities would also undermine the Union's capacity to affirm its specific identity at the international level, and hamper its ability to efficiently manage the negotiation of international treaties and the representation of the Union in international organisations.

Figure 6.1 The architecture of the EU in the Maastricht Treaty.

During the negotiations leading up to the Amsterdam Treaty signed in 1997, some tabled initiatives suggested that the Union should be given a unified legal personality. However, these efforts failed in the face of determined opposition from certain member states. The Amsterdam Treaty still gave the Union specific treaty-making powers insofar as the EU was empowered to conclude international agreements in the fields of the second and third pillars (Articles 24 and 38, TEU). These powers opened up a new set of questions: on whose behalf were the agreements concluded – that of the Union as such or that of the member states?

The recognition by the Lisbon Treaty of the EU's single legal personality is an important step allowing the Union both to become more transparent and visible in its dealings with third countries, and to operate more effectively internationally. Nevertheless, the merger of the three pillars remains incomplete insofar as the CFSP remains governed by the previously established reformed EU Treaty – and not by the Treaty on the Functioning of the European Union (TFEU). Consequently, the CFSP continues to function according to distinct intergovernmental procedures; the artificial divide between the economic and the strategic aspects of the Union's external relations has therefore not totally disappeared.

The external competences of the EU

The EU's external competences reside primarily in the ability to negotiate and sign international agreements, and to participate in various international organisations. In this section the legal basis of the EU's external powers will be detailed, then, having established the scope of these powers, their nature will be further explored.

Legal basis of the EU's external competences

The EU (like the European Community – hereafter EC – before the Lisbon Treaty) is subject to the principle of competence attribution, also named 'principle of conferral'. This principle, set out in Article 5 of the reformed EU Treaty, governs '[t]he limits of Union competences'. It states that the 'Union shall act only within the limits of the competences conferred upon it by the Member States in the Treaties to attain the objectives set out therein'. Therefore, all 'competences not conferred upon the Union in the Treaties remain with the Member States'. In other words, in order for the EU to act it needs a specific legal basis for its actions. The principle of conferral must be respected in both the internal as well as the international actions of the EU.

Before the Lisbon Treaty, determining the scope of the Union's external competences implied distinguishing between the situation instituted by the EC Treaty governing the first pillar, and the mechanisms established under the second and third pillars. According to the Lisbon Treaty, this distinction would be abolished and some important institutional modifications would be introduced which directly affected the execution of the Union's external competences.

The situation under the EC Treaty before the Lisbon Treaty

No provision of the EC Treaty provided the EC with a general external competence. Article 300 of the TEC stipulated the procedure for concluding international agreements but *only* '[w]here this treaty provides for the conclusion of agreements between the Community and one or more States or international organisations'. And they were only a few articles out of more than 300 articles contained in the EC Treaty that gave explicitly external competences to the EC. However, the question remained whether this implied that in all the other fields, in the absence of an express provision within the Treaty, the Community did not enjoy any external competence.

The European Court of Justice[5] has played a determinant role with regard to this open question. The Court did not accept the restrictive interpretation championed by the member states and established the principle that, when determining in a particular field what the external competences of the Community are, 'regard must be had to the whole scheme of the Treaty no less than to its substantive provisions'.[6] The Rome Treaty, signed in 1957, clearly provided the EC with external powers, yet only in connection with the common commercial policy (CCP) and association agreements. Nonetheless, subsequent Treaty revisions led to the extension of the express sphere of the external competences of the Community. The explicit external powers of the EC include its CCP, its association agreements, as well as a whole host of other explicit external competences aggregated and honed over the years.

THE CCP

Article 133 of the TEC was the legal basis for the CCP. It enabled the Community 'to negotiate, conclude and implement trade agreements with other countries of the world'. The scope of the CCP has been interpreted very broadly by the Court of Justice. It has stated that the said policy cannot be restricted to measures intended to have a direct effect on the traditional aspects of external trade without facing the risk of becoming insignificant over time.[7]

However, up until the Lisbon Treaty important difficulties and ambiguities remained with regard to the trade in services, the commercial aspects of intellectual property and investment. In its Opinion 1/94, the Court had rejected the Commission's argument that all trade in services covered by the General Agreement on Trade in Services (GATS)[8] and intellectual property rights[9] covered by the Trade Related Intellectual Property Rights (TRIPs) were included in the CCP. This very controversial opinion of the Court posed in no uncertain terms the question of the exact scope of the CCP. Accordingly, this issue loomed large in the negotiations leading up to the Amsterdam and Nice Treaties.

In 1997, the Amsterdam Treaty allowed the Council acting unanimously to extend the application of provisions on CCP to services and intellectual property, but the Council never used the said possibility. In 2001, the Nice Treaty saw Article 133 rewritten, which resulted in its becoming one of the most obscure provisions of the EC Treaty.

- In the fields of trade in services and the commercial aspects of intellectual property (but not the intellectual property itself), the negotiation and conclusion of agreements was within the sphere of the CCP.
- However, no agreement could be concluded if it included provisions which went beyond the Community's internal powers, in particular by leading to harmonisation of the laws or regulations of the member states in areas for which the Treaty ruled out such harmonisation.
- Therefore, agreements relating to trade in cultural and audiovisual services, educational services, and social and human health services were placed beyond the reach of the CCP.
- With regard to voting rules, in some cases unanimity was maintained *in lieu* of qualified majority.

ASSOCIATION AGREEMENTS

Article 310 of the TEC enabled the Community to 'conclude with one or more states or international organisations agreements establishing an association involving reciprocal rights and obligations, common action and special procedure'. The Community has entered into association agreements with a large number of third states.

Association agreements create a closer relationship than a simple trade agreement, and usually involve some kind of reciprocal obligations as well as common institutions. They can entail various degrees of commitment and different economic and political purposes: preparing associate countries to accede to the EU,[10] offering an alternative to a non-envisaged accession of the targeted countries,[11] serveing as an instrument of development within associate countries,[12] or supporting interregional cooperation with other regional cooperation organisations.[13]

OTHER EXPLICIT EXTERNAL COMPETENCES OF THE EC

In 1987, with the *Single European Act*, the Community gained the competence 'to engage in international cooperation' and 'to conclude agreements fixing the arrangements for Community cooperation' with third countries and international organisations, within the areas of research policy (Article 170, TEC) and environmental policy (Article 174, TEC). The Court retained a very strict interpretation of the notion of 'agreements fixing the arrangements for Community cooperation', resulting in the Community's inability to lay down substantive rules.

In 1992, the Maastricht Treaty added a new express legal basis for Community external action:

- 'agreements concerning monetary or foreign-exchange regime matters' that only bind the member states having adopted the euro (Article 111, TEC)
- with regard to development cooperation, 'the arrangements for Community cooperation may be the subject of agreements between the Community and the third parties concerned'

- a possibility for the Community to 'cooperate' with third countries or international organisations, without specifying up front what would constitute the exact object and extent of that cooperation, in the fields of education (Article 149, TEC), vocational training (Article 150, TEC), culture (Article 151, TEC), public health (Article 152, TEC) and trans-European networks (Article 155, TEC).

Finally, in 2001, the Nice Treaty extended the CCP's scope and gave the EC the competence to carry out economic, financial and technical cooperation measures with third countries. With regard to these matters, direct cooperation between the EU and relevant third countries, as well as the competent international organisations (Article 181A, TEC), was thus sanctioned.

THE IMPLIED EXTERNAL POWERS OF THE EC BEFORE THE LISBON TREATY

In many fields, the EC Treaty did not mention the external dimension at all (e.g., agriculture, transport, social policy, competition, asylum and immigration), despite the fact these policy fields did have important external implications. The Court of Justice has, through its vital jurisprudential decisions, filled these 'gaps' in light of 'the theory of implied powers'. The Court has enshrined the principle that 'the competence of the Community to conclude international agreements may arise not only from an express conferment by the Treaty but may equally flow implicitly from other provisions of the Treaty and from measures adopted [...] by the Community institutions',[14] adding that 'whenever Community law has created for the institutions of the Community powers within its internal system for the purpose of attaining a specific objective, the Community is empowered to enter into the international commitments necessary for attainment of that objective even in the absence of an express provision to that effect'.[15]

However, besides these broad statements, the Court provided very little general guidance in determining when implied powers were to be reckoned with. The main difficulty arose from the fact that the Court has had to struggle not only with the question of the *existence* of an implied competence of the Community, but also with the issue of the *exclusive nature* of the said competence. Consequently, there was a certain confusion between the scope and the nature of the competence of the Community.

Furthermore, the Court gave only examples, without stipulating general criteria:

- since the Council may lay down common rules applicable 'to international transport to or from the territory of a Member State or passing across the territory of one or more Member States' as well as 'any other appropriate provisions', 'the powers of the Community extend to relationships arising from international law, and hence involve the need [...] for agreements with the third countries concerned'
- an international convention on safety with regard to the use of chemicals falls 'within the Community's area of competence' given that the Community enjoys an internal legislative competence in the area of social policy. Moreover

the subject matter of this convention coincides with that of several directives adopted under Article 137 of the TEC[16]

• Article 175 of the TEC, which provides in general terms that the Council 'shall decide what action is to be taken by the Community in order to achieve the objectives referred to in Article 174', is an 'appropriate legal basis for conclusion, on behalf of the Community, of international agreements on protection of the environment'.[17]

As for the question of whether the Community enjoyed external powers even *in the absence of any exercise* of internal powers, the situation proved more complicated. In one case, the Court stated that, in this hypothesis, the Community nevertheless has external powers to conclude this agreement 'in so far as the participation of the Community in the international agreement is [...] necessary for the attainment of one of the objectives of the Community'. Thereafter the emerging dilemma was that the Court would never come to recognise in any specific cases that such a necessity existed. Deep-seated ambiguities therefore remained. On the one hand, questioned about the existence of an exclusive implied external competence, the Court gave a very strict interpretation of the notion of necessity. On the other hand, in a judgment of 30 June 2006, the Court stated that the Community 'can enter into agreements in the area of environmental protection even if the specific matters covered by those agreements are not yet, or are only very partially, the subject of rules at Community level'.[18]

As a final point, the jurisprudence of the Court concluded that Article 308 of the EC Treaty, which enabled the Council to take the appropriate measures '[i]f action by the Community should prove necessary to attain [...] one of the objectives of the Community, and this Treaty has not provided the necessary powers', could in principle empower the Council to take any 'appropriate measures' equally in the sphere of external relations and thus constituted the necessary legal basis for its external powers.[19]

External action within the second and third pillars of the EU prior to the Lisbon Treaty

The conclusion of international agreements related to the second and third pillars were authorised by Articles 24 and 38 of the EU Treaty, both introduced in Amsterdam and subsequently modified by Nice. Article 24 refers to the conclusion of agreements with one or more states or international organisations in implementation within the CFSP. It clearly authorises the Council to conclude agreements in all matters covered by the said policy. As for the third pillar, Article 38 extends the powers detailed in Article 24 to justice and home affairs by simply stating that '[a]greements referred to in Article 24 may cover matters falling under this title'.

Presumably the exact scope of the said provisions' application was to be circumscribed by the fact that member states maintained constant control over the exercise of these powers through both the generally prevalent rule of unanimity, as well as their overarching right to submit any agreement to their constitutionally defined national checks and safeguards. Nonetheless, Article 47 of the EU Treaty was also to be taken into account in all considered cases. This implied that 'nothing in this Treaty shall affect the Treaties establishing the European Communities or the subsequent Treaties and Acts modifying or supplementing them'. Accordingly, the EC's competences could in no way be jeopardised or even curtailed.

Furthermore, one must keep in mind that Article 24 of the TEU established a specific treaty-making procedure, yet without having granted the EU a distinctive legal personality. It therefore remained unclear whether this meant that it was not the Union as such that concluded the said agreements, but only the Council, acting collectively in the name of the member states. This issue remained very controversial, although most authors concluded that agreements based on Article 24 (and 38) of the TEU should be considered as concluded in name of the Union. These arrangements were reassessed and recalibrated by the Lisbon Treaty signed in 2007, most notably with regard to the scope of the competences of the EU in external affairs.

The aftermath of the Lisbon Treaty signed in December 2007

Four important contributions of the Lisbon Treaty with regard the Union's external competences are to be emphasised.

- The Lisbon Treaty, by removing the three-pillar structure in pillars established by the TEU, also removed the distinction between the competences of the EC and those of the EU.
- The Lisbon Treaty introduced a new specific legal basis upon which the EU's external competence could rest:
  a   agreements with third countries concerning the readmission of third-country nationals to their countries of origin or provenance, when the conditions for entry, presence or residence in the territory of one of the member states are not met
  b   agreements with third countries and competent international organisations aimed at helping to achieve the Union's objectives in humanitarian aid
  c   agreements with neighbouring countries aiming to establish an area of prosperity and good neighbourliness, founded on the values of the Union and characterised by close and peaceful relations based on mutual cooperation.
- The Lisbon Treaty enlarged the scope of the existing legal basis, in particular with regard to the CCP. Article 207 of the TFEU replaced the very convoluted Article 133 of the EC Treaty as amended by the Nice Treaty. The general rule was henceforth to be that the common policy would apply to: the conclusion of tariff and trade agreements relating to trade in goods and services; the commercial aspects of intellectual property; foreign direct investment; the achievement of uniformity in measures aimed at liberalisation; to export policies; and to measures aimed at protecting trade, such as those to be taken in the event of dumping or subsidies. However, the exercise by the Union of its competences relating to the CCP would in no way 'lead to harmonisation of legislative or regulatory provisions of the Member States insofar as the Treaties exclude such harmonisation'. Finally, a supplementary safeguard was that unanimity would

continue to be required in some instances.
- The Lisbon Treaty also introduced two novel general provisions enabling the EU to conclude international agreements. On the one hand, Article 37 of the renovated EU Treaty already enabled the Union, in very general terms, to conclude agreements with one or more states or international organisations with an eye to implementing the CFSP. On the other hand, Article 216 of the TFEU states that '[t]he Union may conclude an international agreement with one or more third countries or international organisations where the Treaties so provide or where the conclusion of an agreement is necessary in order to achieve, within the framework of the Union's policies, one of the objectives referred to in the Treaties, or is provided for in a legally binding act of the Union or is likely to affect common rules or alter their scope'.

To some extent, Article 216 seeks to codify earlier findings and decisions made by the Courts; yet the provision's specific wording raises some new questions:

- 'where [the treaties] so provide' introduces a certain vagueness, as it remains unclear whether this implies an express provision, or whether it is possible for the EU to be implicitly empowered
- where an agreement 'is provided for in a legally binding act' offers no guidance as to the limits of the competence potentially conferred by a legally binding act. It remains questionable whether in a system of conferred power it is sustainable for an act of the institutions to provide something not originally provided by the founding treaties
- 'where the conclusion of an agreement is necessary in order to achieve, within the framework of the Union's policies, one of the objectives referred to in the Treaties' appears to be an application of Article 352 TFEU in the field of international agreements. However, it remains open for debate whether this implies, as with the preceding Article 352, a unanimous decision on the Council's part, as well as the approbation of the European Parliament.
- the Court's jurisprudence appears to indicate that an agreement's likelihood 'to affect common rules or alter their scope' was not to be understood as a condition for the existence of an external competence in the head of the Community, but was to be linked to their exclusive nature (see below). Future potential confusion between the scope and the nature of the Union's competence might thus be fostered.

Nature of the EU's external competences

The scope of the Union's external competences having been described, their exact nature remains to be identified, notably by distinguishing the situations created by the EC Treaty; the one associated with the second and third pillars; and how these have been transformed by the Lisbon Treaty's contribution.

The situation under the EC Treaty before the Lisbon Treaty

The external competences wielded by the EC could be either exclusive or shared with the member states.

THE EC'S EXCLUSIVE COMPETENCES

Two basic and distinct forms of exclusivity can be identified: on the one hand, exclusivity *a priori*; and on the other, pre-emption exclusivity.

- *A priori* exclusivity is associated with an exclusive competence arising from a specific Treaty provision. This was the case in two specific fields: the CCP[20] and the conservation of marine resources.[21] The existence of such exclusive competence excluded any competence on the part of member states, both within the Community sphere, as well as in the broader international sphere and even if the Community abstains from exercising its own powers. In other words, within these two fields, the exclusive nature of the competence of the Community does not depend on the prior exercise of the said competence. It should, nonetheless, be noted that such exclusive competence did not exclude delegations to the member states.
- The Court of Justice once more played a substantial role in defining pre-emption exclusivity by ruling that, beyond the exclusive competences flowing from the provisions of the Treaty, the exclusive nature of the European Community's competence could also 'depend on the scope of the measures which have been adopted by the Community institutions [...] which [were] of such a kind as to deprive the Member States of an area of competence which they were able to exercise previously'.[22]

Where common rules had been adopted, 'the Member States no longer had the right [...] to undertake obligations with non-member countries which affect those rules', even if there was no contradiction between those commitments and the common rules. Given such a situation, the Community alone was to have the right to conclude international agreements; it thus had an exclusive competence in that respect. In this second hypothesis, the exclusivity of the competence was not an *a priori* exclusivity but a 'pre-emption' resulting from the exercise by the Community of the competences conferred upon it. The 'pre-emption' effect related to implied external competences as well as to explicit external competences that had not been qualified as exclusive by the EC Treaty.

Consequently, the question of when an internal Community measure had implications for exclusive external powers became a central bone of contention. In three situations, it was beyond doubt that the Community competence was exclusive both internally and externally:

- when the Community had included in its internal legislative acts provisions relating to the treatment of nationals of non-member countries

- when an internal legislative act had expressly conferred on its institutions powers to negotiate with non-member countries
- when the Community had achieved complete harmonisation in a given area.

However, these cases were only examples, and other unexplored hypotheses remained possible. Moreover, it was not necessary for the areas covered by the international agreement and the Community legislation to coincide fully; it might be sufficient that the agreement covered an area already dealt with to a large extent by Community rules. Subsequent assessments were to be based not only on the scope of the rules in question, but also on their nature and content. Furthermore, when possible, it was also necessary to take into account not only the current state of Community law within the concerned area, but also its potential future developments.

A last hypothesis of exclusive competence with regard to the EC resulted from the occasional case of the Community's finding it impossible to achieve an objective by the sole adoption of internal measures. In such a situation, external powers could be exercised according to the Court, and thus become exclusive without any internal legislation having first been adopted. However, this type of exclusive competence applied only in a very limited range of situations characterised by an inextricable link between the internal and the external competence. Such a link had to result in the fact that the internal competence could exist solely with the external one. This particular scenario therefore remained rather marginal as to its overall political and practical impact. One example was the rationalisation of the economic situation in the Rhine's inland waterways, which could not be achieved solely through internal measures because of the traditional participation of vessels from Switzerland which was not a member of the European Community.

THE COMMUNITY'S EXTERNAL COMPETENCES SHARED WITH MEMBER STATES

Some articles included in the EC Treaty, and strengthened by its successive revisions, safeguard the capacity of member states to 'conclude international agreements' by stating that they 'shall be without prejudice to Member States' competence to negotiate in international bodies and to conclude international agreements' (Articles 111, 174, 181 and 181A, TEC). However, it must be noted that the Tenth Declaration joined to the Maastricht Treaty specified that those provisions did 'not affect the principles resulting from the judgment handed down by the Court of Justice in the AETR case'.[23]

With regard to the EC's implied external competences, most of the Court's decisions were related to the existence of exclusive implied competences. Nonetheless, in Opinion 1/03 the Court ruled that implied competences of the Community 'may be exclusive or shared with the Member States'. In at least two cases, the existence of implied external non-exclusive competences has been recognised:

- the convention on safety in the use of chemicals at work, insofar as *both* the Community provisions and those of the convention lay down minimum standards[24]

- the competence of the Community to conclude the Protocol of Cartagena, since the harmonisation achieved at Community level covers only a very small part of the field of application of the protocol.[25]

In the case of shared competence with the member states, agreements concluded by the member states alone are possible; as well as parallel agreements concluded in a same field by member states and the Community; or mixed agreements concluded by the Community and its member states. Clearly, the nature of the Community competences had an evolving character; from the time the Community decided to exercise its powers in a field, on the domestic plane or through an international agreement, the member states would lose their power to enter into agreements that affected common rules or altered their scope.

The situation in the second and third pillars before the Lisbon Treaty

In the second and third pillars, no clear demarcation line could be drawn between the competences of the Union and those of the member states. However, in the fields of CFSP and police and judicial cooperation in criminal matters, nothing in the EU Treaty seemed to suggest an exclusive competence on the part of the EU – neither *a priori* nor by pre-emption. The Union's treaty-making powers in these fields were therefore shared with the member states.

The Lisbon Treaty (December 2007)

One of the 2004 Constitutional Treaty's main aims was to produce a clarification of the competences of the EU. After the constitution's ratification process faltered, this drive for further clarification was taken over and met by the Lisbon Treaty. It established a distinction between three categories of competences: exclusive competence of the EU; shared competences with the member states; and areas of supporting, coordinating or complementary action.

In addition, Article 4 of the TFEU introduced in its second paragraph a distinct and defined exclusive competence of the EU to conclude – in three circumstances – an international agreement in areas other than those of exclusive competence listed in the first paragraph:

- where the agreement 'is provided for in a legislative act of the Union'
- where the agreement 'is necessary to enable the Union to exercise its internal competence'
- where the agreement 'may affect common rules or alter their scope'.

This second paragraph appears to be a consolidation of the Court of Justice's jurisprudence as detailed above. However, it does not refer to the distinction established by the Court between *a priori* exclusivity and pre-emption exclusivity. Consequently, such exclusivity does not correspond to the general definition of exclusivity given by the Lisbon Treaty. With regard to the conclusion of an

Table 6.1 The share of competence according to the Lisbon Treaty

Exclusive competences	Shared competences	Supporting competence
Only the Union may adopt legally binding acts. The member states are able to do so themselves only if they are empowered by the Union, or for the implementation of Acts proposed by the Union.	Member states may exercise their competence to the extent that the Union has not exercised its competence or decided to cease to employ it.	The Union carries out actions to support, coordinate or supplement the actions of the member states, without superseding their competence. Its legally binding Acts shall not entail harmonisation of member states' laws.
Areas	*Areas (examples)*	*Areas (examples)*
customs union competition rules necessary for the functioning of the internal market monetary policy for the member states having adopted the euro conservation of marine biological resources common commercial policy	internal market social policy agriculture and fisheries environment consumer protection transport energy area of freedom, security and justice.	protection and improvement of human health culture tourism education, vocational training, youth and sport civil protection.

agreement, member states could recover their competences if existing common rules at the Union's level came to be removed.

Since exclusive competence is limited to the cases where the conclusion of an international agreement is provided by a 'legislative act' and not another 'binding act', the possibility of such exclusive competence in the field of the CFSP is limited. As a matter of fact, in this field, the reformed EU Treaty even expressly bans the adoption of legislative acts (Article 31).

Furthermore, the Lisbon Treaty also identifies two areas where the exercise of its competence by the Union does not result in member states being prevented from exercising theirs: research, technological development and space on the one hand; and development cooperation and humanitarian aid on the other. Moreover, the Thirty-Sixth Joint Declaration 'confirms that Member States may negotiate and conclude agreements with third countries or international organisations' in the area of freedom, security and justice 'insofar as such agreements comply with Union law'.

The conclusion of international agreements

One of the most important means for the EU to exercise its external powers is by negotiating and signing international agreements. The following analysis considers how an international agreement is concluded by the EU. The procedure leading up to the conclusion of an international agreement has differed under the EC Treaty, and the second and third pillars, until the Lisbon Treaty. The latter tries to a certain point to unify the procedure. Furthermore, some agreements – called mixed agreements – require the participation of both the Union and the member states.

The conclusion of international agreements under the EC Treaty

Article 300 of the TEC regulated the procedures behind the conclusion of international agreements; derogative rules nevertheless applied with regard to monetary policy and the CCP.

General procedure (Article 300, TEC)

The general procedure was as follows: the Commission presented recommendations to the Council for initiating negotiations. The Commission would conduct the said negotiations after having been authorised by the Council, and on the basis of directives received from the Council. The Council would ultimately conclude the agreement. As a rule, Council adopted agreements by qualified majority, although unanimity remained necessary for association agreements, as well as for cases where the covered field required unanimous decision when adopting internal rules. The European Parliament was to be consulted but only had to give its assent on:

- association agreements
- other agreements establishing a specific institutional framework by organising cooperation procedures

- agreements having important budgetary implications for the Community
- agreements entailing amendment of an act adopted under the co-decision procedure.

Derogative procedures

MONETARY AND EXCHANGE RATE AGREEMENTS (ARTICLE 111, TEC)

The Council was to decide the arrangements for the negotiation, as well as for the conclusion of such agreements. Such agreements were approved by a qualified majority, following a recommendation from the Commission, and after consultation with the European Central Bank. Whereas the Commission was to be fully associated with the negotiations, the European Parliament was not even to be consulted.

AGREEMENTS IN THE FIELD OF COMMON COMMERCIAL POLICY (ARTICLE 133, TEC)

The Commission made recommendations to the Council, which authorised it to open the necessary negotiations. The Commission conducted these negotiations in consultation with a special committee appointed by the Council, and within the framework of such directives as the Council might issue to it. The Council, voting under qualified majority, concluded the agreement. Nevertheless, unanimity was needed when agreements included provisions for which unanimity was required for internal rules, or related to a field in which the Community had not yet adopted internal rules. Once more, the European Parliament was not to be consulted.

Procedure associated with international agreements in the second and third pillars of the EU before the Lisbon Treaty

The procedure was defined in Article 24 of the TEU. The Council authorised the Presidency, assisted by the Commission as appropriate, to open negotiations aimed at concluding an agreement with one or more states or international organisations. The Council concluded the agreements following a recommendation from the Presidency. The Council had to act unanimously when the considered agreement covered issues for which unanimity was required in the adoption of internal decisions. The prevailing unanimity requirement clearly reduced the effectiveness of the EU as an international negotiator in these fields. As for the European Parliament, it was only to be indirectly involved by virtue of its general right to be regularly informed by the Presidency and the Commission of developments within the second and third pillars.

The conclusion of international agreements as defined by the Lisbon Treaty

With the Lisbon Treaty, a single provision (Article 218, TFEU) covers all international agreements concluded by the EU, except agreements within the monetary field.[26] Overall, the procedures previously detailed by Article 300 of the EC are retained, save a few pointed changes aimed at streamlining the procedure.

In the case of international negotiations aimed at concluding a given agreement, recommendations are to be submitted to the Council either by the Commission or, when the considered agreement relates exclusively or principally to the CFSP, by the High Representative of the Union for Foreign Affairs and Security Policy. The Council subsequently adopts 'a decision authorising the opening of negotiations and, depending on the subject of the agreement envisaged, nominating the Union's negotiator or the head of the Union's negotiating team'. The mobilisation of a negotiator, or a negotiating team, is a novelty with regard to previous practices.

With respect to the conclusion of the agreements, overall the previously established rules and principles are maintained. However, as the field of qualified majority voting is broadened, the scope of agreements likely to be concluded is sensibly increased. Furthermore, it should also be noted that, for the conclusion of agreements in the fields of trade in services and the commercial aspects of intellectual property, as well as foreign direct investment, the Council has to act unanimously when brokering any agreement:

- in the field of trade in cultural and audiovisual services, as they risk prejudicing the Union's cultural and linguistic diversity
- in the field of trade in social, education and health services, as they risk seriously disturbing the national organisation of these services.

The main revolution concerns the role of the European Parliament. The range of agreements that may be concluded without the Parliament having been consulted is limited to those agreements 'relat[ing] exclusively to the common foreign and security policy'. Moreover, the number of cases where the European Parliament has to give its express assent is notably increased. In particular, its assent is required for all agreements covering fields in which the ordinary legislative procedure applies. Given the increasing scope of the ordinary legislative procedure, which has replaced the co-decision procedure, it represents an important enlargement of the European Parliament's powers. The change has particular consequences in the field of the CCP, where, under the EC Treaty, the Council did not even have to consult the European Parliament.

Table 6.2 Agreements subject to European Parliament assent

- Association agreements
- agreement on Union accession to the European Convention for the Protection of Human Rights and Fundamental Freedoms
- agreements establishing a specific institutional framework by organising cooperation procedures
- agreements with important budgetary implications for the Union
- agreements covering fields to which either the ordinary legislative procedure applies, or the special legislative procedure where consent by the European Parliament is required.

Mixed agreements

Mixed agreements are concluded with a third state, and are ones to which the EU as well as its member states are contractual parties. The main rationale for concluding a mixed agreement is the non-exclusive character of the competences engaging the EU within the field of the agreement. Consequently, a need for close cooperation is systematically imposed within the process of negotiation, conclusion and execution of such mixed agreements.

Mixed agreements are negotiated and concluded along the same procedures as 'pure' Union agreements. However, in addition the Union's decisions with regard to these matters have to be taken in accordance with the relevant provisions of the Treaties, as well as being concurrently fully concluded by the member states themselves. These agreements therefore require ratification by all the member states in accordance with their respective national constitutional requirements. This means that common accord of the member states is required even for provisions covered by the Union's competence and approved by a qualified majority voting in the Council. Failure by one member state to ratify the provisions falling within its competence means that the entire agreement, including the provisions falling within the Community's competence, is prevented from entering into force. In addition, the conclusion of the agreement by the EU comes only after all member states have ratified it. Accordingly, it may take several years before a mixed agreement can enter into force, even if the Union often opts for a provisional application of the Union's part of the agreement.

Participation of the EU in international organisations

One of the most significant recent developments with regard to the EU's external relations is that its external powers have increasingly been exercised through its participation in a range of international organisations. The following discussion details the Union's status within international organisations, and the necessary cooperation between the EU and its member states when functioning within those organisations.

EU status in international organisations: observer or participant

The EU's standing and status with different international organisations varies greatly, ranging from mere observer to fully fledged member.

The status of observer, which does not impose any significant strains or hindrances upon the host international organisation's functioning, is the most common status. It comes into play in such organisations as the World Health Organization, UNESCO, the International Monetary Fund (IMF), the World Bank and the International Labour Organisation (ILO). Occasionally, the Union's observer status is enhanced. In those cases the EU's position can be described as that of a 'guest', a 'participant', a 'participant with special rights' or even a 'full participant'. Such enhanced positions allow the EU not only to be present but also actively to participate in the debates by taking the floor; still, this does not give the Union voting rights.

Exceptionally the EU is awarded full member status. Most international organisations only allow for accession by states. Any form of accession on the EU's part therefore more often than not requires a series of modifications of the constitutive charter of a given organisation. This readily explains why the EU is a member of only a few organisations. Significantly, the EU is not a member of the United Nations or of any major UN organisation.

Prior to the Lisbon Treaty, distinct accession to international organisations concerned only the EC, because the competences involved and organisations petitioned were economic in nature. The EC was a member of several regional fishing organisations; it was one of the founding members of the European Bank for Reconstruction and Development, and one of the original members of the World Trade Organization (WTO) following the April 1994 Marrakech Agreement. In all of the above cases, the Union's membership was the by-product of the creation of international organisations through founding agreements to which the Community itself was an original party. Furthermore, the EC was admitted as an 'organisation member' of the United Nations' Organisation for Food and Agriculture (FAO), yet with a specific status.

Where membership of the EC – and now, following the Lisbon Treaty, the EU – is possible, two different situations can unfold. In a very limited number of situations, the EC/EU acts alone within the framework of a given international organisation. Only a very few examples of this can be found, one being the regional fisheries organisations, insofar as the EU enjoys an exclusive competence for the conservation of marine biological resources. In such a case, the EC substitutes itself entirely in place of its member states, notably in exercising the right to vote. The more general formula is that of joint participation of the EU and its member states.

The representation of the EU in international organisations

As for the representation of the EU in international organisations, a necessary distinction was to be made before the Lisbon Treaty between organisations of a mainly economic make-up and those of a mainly political make-up. In the first case, it was the EC that was either an observer or a member, hence it was up to the Commission to set out the unitary position of the Community. In the second case, the status, which was always that of observer, fell outside of the competence of the EC and it was up to the Presidency to express the EU's positions, with the support of the High Representative, and in full association with the Commission. Managing these distinctions became increasingly complicated in multi-issue organisations which span both political and economic areas. The Lisbon Treaty provided for a more streamlined representation as detailed in the subsequent section.

Where the EU and its member states are both members of an organisation, it is imperative to reconcile coherence with the plurality of actors involved in the organisation. Such a plurality brings with it an overriding need for cooperation between the EU and its member states. To this end, informal and *ad hoc* arrangements are frequently concluded between the EU institutions and the member states.

The coherence of the external action of the EU

Under the Maastricht Treaty, the external action of the EU could be viewed as the outcome of the interactions between the EC (acting within the context of the first pillar), the EU (acting on the basis of the second and third pillars) and the member states (acting within their own competences). Article 3 of the EU Treaty stated that '[t]he Union shall in particular ensure the consistency of its external activities as a whole in the context of its external relations, security, economic and development policies. The Council and the Commission shall be responsible for ensuring such consistency. They shall ensure the implementation of these policies, each in accordance with its respective powers.' Article 13 reiterates that the Council is responsible for ensuring the 'unity, consistency and effectiveness of action by the Union'.[27]

With the Maastricht Treaty, the principle of coherence had become a central exhortation of sorts, but it proved very difficult to attain. The overlap between the Union's constituent pillars had often been stressed as the main obstacle hampering the promotion of improved coherence. Up until the entry into force of the Lisbon Treaty, provisions for external action were scattered throughout the European treaties. The CFSP was the subject of Title V in the EU Treaty, whereas the EC Treaty generally covered trade policy, development aid and economic, financial and technical cooperation with third countries. Finally, the Union's economic and political relations with third countries/regions and its action within international organisations were governed by different rules and decision-making procedures. Such a composite system made it difficult to guarantee that the multiple instruments were used harmoniously and in pursuit of common strategic objectives.

The Lisbon Treaty sought to improve the coherence of the EU's external action, notably by systematically addressing these complexities. However, despite the EU's single legal personality and the removal of the so-called pillar system, the CFSP remains in the renovated EU Treaty, while all other provisions ruling the external action of the EU[28] are grouped under a single part of the TFEU. Nonetheless, there are two different factors within this Treaty capable of fostering increased coherence: the establishment of common principles and objectives for the Union's external action and the proposed institutional reforms.

A common set of objectives for the EU's external action

The former treaties did not state explicit overarching and transversal objectives with regard to the Union's external action. Identifiable objectives within the treaties prior to the TFEU were either explicitly linked to specific policy fields (e.g., CCP, development, and CFSP), or singularly focused on the links between the internal and the external policies of the EU.

The Lisbon Treaty provides a common set of objectives which are to be achieved through all the aspects of the EU's external action. Such a common set of goals is a prerequisite for a coherent external policy. There can be no doubt that this set will support both the coherence of external action, as well as consistency between external and internal policy fields. The list of objectives is largely taken from the

Table 6.3 Objectives of the EU's external action

'In its relations with the wider world, the Union shall uphold and promote its values and contribute to the protection if its citizens. It shall contribute to peace, security, the sustainable development of the Earth, solidarity and mutual respect among peoples, free and fair trade, eradication of poverty and the protection of human rights, in particular the rights of the child, as well as to the strict observance and the development of international law, including respect for the principles of the United Nations Charter.'

(Article 3(5), reformed TEU)

former treaties' provisions, but by clearly stating them the TFEU compels each external policy to take into account a wider set of objectives than those specifically formulated within its own field. For instance, the Lisbon Treaty thus allows for the CCP to open itself up and even contribute to other dimensions, such as human rights and sustainable development.

Within the reformed TEU, these objectives are elaborated upon further in the second paragraph of Article 21, which lists eight specific objectives that, according to the third paragraph, should be respected and pursued in developing and implementing the different areas of the Union's external action:

  i   safeguard its values, fundamental interests, security, independence and integrity;
  ii consolidate and support democracy, the rule of law, human rights and the principles of international law;
  iii preserve peace, prevent conflicts and strengthen international security, in accordance with the purposes and principles of the United Nations Charter;
  iv foster the sustainable economic, social and environmental development of developing countries, with the primary aim of eradicating poverty;
  v   encourage the integration of all countries into the world economy, including through the progressive abolition of restrictions on international trade;
  vi help develop international measures to preserve and improve the quality of the environment and the sustainable management of global natural resources, in order to ensure sustainable development;
  vii assist populations, countries and regions confronting natural or man-made disasters;
  viii promote an international system based on stronger multilateral cooperation and good global governance.

However, the Lisbon Treaty only lists the different objectives, without linking them to one another and without offering any hierarchy, prioritising mechanism or general means for resolving (potential) conflicts between the different objectives. Even so, within this set of objectives, the aspirational coherence or consistency of the EU's action occupies a central place. The Union shall 'ensure consistency between the different areas of its external action and between these and its other policies' (Article 21, renovated TFEU); it shall also 'ensure consistency between its policies and activities, taking all of its objectives into account' (Article 7, TFEU).

Furthermore, the TFEU contains some general principles which have to be integrated or taken into account across all policy fields of the EU, including its external action: equality between men and women (Article 8); the promotion of a high level of employment, the guarantee of adequate social protection, the fight against social exclusion, and a high level of education, training and protection of human health (Article 9); combating discrimination based on sex, racial or ethnic origin, religion or belief, disability, age or sexual orientation (Article 10); environmental protection (Article 11); and consumer protection (Article 12). Therefore, these principles aim to further guide the development policy and the trade negotiations.

Institutional reforms introduced by the Lisbon Treaty

Several institutional reforms aimed at improving the coherence of the Union's external action were formulated. As a result, the TFEU unequivocally identifies the European Council as being responsible for defining the strategic interests and objectives of the Union, requiring the Council to concern itself with the CFSP as well as other areas of the Union's external action. This means that the European Council's role in the Union's external action is augmented, but also that it can thus contribute to ensuring better consistency.

The TFEU also brings into being a specific Foreign Affairs Council, formally distinct from the General Affairs formation. It is charged with elaborating the Union's external action on the basis of the strategic guidelines laid down by the European Council, thereby further strengthening the consistency of the Union's actions. Meanwhile, the Council and the Commission, assisted by the High Representative of the Union for Foreign Affairs and Security Policy, remain responsible for ensuring consistency between the different areas of the EU's external action and between these and its other policies. The roles of all parties involved are clarified with an eye to increased coherence; fittingly, all relevant actors are also invited to cooperate to that effect.

The creation of a High Representative of the Union for Foreign Affairs and Security Policy is a direct product of the Union's search for improved coherence. Following Article 19 of the renovated EU Treaty, he (or she) will have the express responsibility for ensuring the consistency of the Union's external action. Yet, which tools he (or she) will call upon to fulfil this task remains unspecified in the TFEU, and thus several questions concerning the exact long-term development of such a novel institutional actor remain unanswered.

The High Representative of the Union for Foreign Affairs and Security Policy is to conduct the Union's CFSP but also to be one of the Commission's Vice-Presidents: as such, he (or she) will be charged both with the responsibilities incumbent on the Commission in external relations, as well as with need to coordinate them with the other aspects of the Union's external action. This post combines those previously held by the former Council and Commission representatives in external relations. It tries to pragmatically defuse the underlying rivalries by introducing a 'double hat' system. Such a unifying system is also an attempt to bring together within the same hands all the instruments of external action at the EU's disposal so as to offer a better outline of the EU's overall external relations, while once again promoting greater consistency between the CFSP and the other aspects of its external relations.

In the CFSP, the new High Representative has more powers than the former High Representative. Most significant is his new right, along the same lines as the member states, to formulate and submit proposals for action to the European Council or the Council. He also chairs the Foreign Affairs Council which, unlike the other formats of the Council, is not be subject to a (revised) rotating Presidency. The High Representative, jointly with the Commission, also has extensive representational duties. Before the Lisbon Treaty, the treaties provided for a separate international representation of the EC and the EU. The Community was represented abroad by the Commission delegations, while it was the country holding the Presidency of the Council and its diplomatic representation that represented the EU. The Lisbon Treaty provides that the Commission 'with the exception of the common foreign and security policy [...] shall ensure the Union's external representation' (Article 17, reformed TEU). As for matters relating to the CFSP, the High Representative shall represent the Union (Article 27, reformed TEU). He (or she) shall express the Union's position in international organisations and at international conferences, for matters relating to the CFSP, while the Commission will fulfil this role with regard to all tother matters. It is important to note that a declaration adopted at Lisbon specifies that the creation of the office of High Representative of the Union for Foreign Affairs and Security Policy cannot affect the national representation of member states in international organisations.

Finally, pursuant to Article 27 of the renovated EU Treaty, the High Representative will be assisted by a European External Action Service, which have to 'work in cooperation with the diplomatic services of the Member States' and comprises 'officials from relevant departments of the General Secretariat of the Council and of the Commission as well as staff seconded from national diplomatic services of the Member States'. This provision is included in the chapter on the CFSP; however, the European External Action Service should bridge all the different components of the Union's external action. The Commission delegations are to be converted into 'Union delegations in third countries and at international organisations' and will represent the Union. They are 'placed under the authority of the High Representative of the Union for Foreign Affairs and Security Policy' and 'shall act in close cooperation with Member States' diplomatic and consular missions' (Article 221, TFEU).

In spite of all these innovations, and at times because of them, several questions concerning the long-term performance and impact of such a High Representative of the Union for Foreign Affairs and Security Policy remain open.

- One question is to discern whether a single person can take on the inevitably crippling workload, especially considering that the details of the supporting European External Action Service remain murky. Much of his (or her) ability to carry out the demanding role will inevitably depend upon the complementary emergence of a seasoned and professional European diplomatic service.
- The second general concern is whether the collegial nature of the Commission will be compromised, or even significantly damaged, by the presence of the High

Representative within its midst. Commission procedures will only be binding for him or her when exercising responsibilities within the Commission, and even then only to the extent they remain compatible with his or her CFSP and Council-related functions.

• A third more pressing concern is what relationship the High Representative should establish with the other two individuals also entrusted with a legitimate right to speak authoritatively on the external relations of the EU. First, the 'permanent' President of the European Council, who shall in 'that capacity' and 'at his level' ensure the 'representation' of the Union on issues related to its CFSP, without prejudice to the responsibilities of the High Representative. It remains unclear how the division of labour will work out. The second potential source of friction is the relationship with the President of the Commission. One of the tasks of this President is to 'ensure that [the Commission] acts consistently, efficiently and on a collegiate basis'. The degree to which the High Representative will be able, as a member of the College of Commissioners, to conform to this is unclear. Finally, it is also unclear whether the rotating Presidency of the Council may feel frustrated at its loss of voice in external relations.

Notes

1 The Lisbon Treaty was signed by the twenty-seven member states in December 2007. It aims to resolve the constitutional reform process that had stalled since France and the Netherlands voted by referendum against the Treaty Establishing a Constitution for Europe in 2005, by means of amendments to the Treaty on European Union (EU Treaty or TEU) and the Treaty Establishing the European Community (EC Treaty or TEC) that remain into force. The former retains its title, while the latter becomes the Treaty on the Functioning of the European Union (FEU Treaty or TFEU). When writing this chapter, we did not know whether the Lisbon Treaty would be ratified by all member states and enter into force, but we have still analysed the (important) contribution of this treaty in the fields of external relations of the EU. When we refer to the Treaty on European Union in its version amended by the Lisbon Treaty, we will use the expressions 'reformed EU Treaty' or 'reformed TEU'.

2 But not the European Atomic Energy Community.

3 Consisting of the three Communities: the European Community; the European Coal and Steel Community and the European Atomic Energy Community. The ECSC expired on 23 July 2002.

4 After the Treaty of Amsterdam, only judicial and police cooperation remained in this third pillar.

5 The vast number of opinions of the Court of Justice on this matter is the result of procedure established in Article 300 (6) EC, (Article 218, TFEU), which enables the Court to rule on the compatibility of an envisaged agreement with the Treaty, and on matters of competence, if an institution or a member state feels that the case may be disputable.

6 CJ, Judgment of 31 March 1971, *Commission v Council*, Case 22/70, named ERTA or AETR case. This case concerned the conclusion of the European Agreement concerning the work of crews and vehicles engaged in international road transport and the question was to know if this conclusion fell within either of the EEC's of the Member State's competence.

7 Opinion 1/78 of 4 October 1979. The Court decided, therefore, that the fact that an agreement having as its main aim to regulate trade on natural rubber had links to general economic policy did not exclude the application of Article 133 TEC. However, in Opinion 2/00 of 18 April 2002, the Court specified that an agreement which, in the light of its context, aim and content, principally concerned environmental protection and which was liable to have incidental effects on trade could not be adopted on the legal basis of common commercial policy.

8 With regard to trade in services, the Court only admitted that the cross-frontier supply of services not involving any movement of persons was similar to trade in goods, but not the other modes of service supply, namely: consumption abroad, commercial presence of a subsidiary or a branch and the presence of natural persons from a WTO member country.

9 The Court considered that only the measures intended to prohibit the release for free circulation of counterfeit goods fell 'within the Community's competence in matters of commercial policy'.

10 For example, the Stabilisation and Association Agreements concluded or to be concluded with the countries of the Western Balkans.

11 For example, the European Economic Area agreements or the agreements concluded in the framework of the Euro-Mediterranean Partnership.

12 For example, the Cotonou Partnership Agreement concluded with the ACP countries.

13 For example, the framework agreement between the EEC and the Cartagena Agreement and its member countries, namely the Republic of Bolivia, the Republic of Colombia, the Republic of Ecuador, the Republic of Peru and the Republic of Venezuela.

14 Opinion 2/91 of 19 March 1993, Opinion 1/03 of 7 February 2006.

15 *AETR* case, par. 16; Opinions 2/91 and 1/03.

16 Opinion 2/91.

17 Opinion 1/00.

18 *Commission v Ireland*, Case C-459/03.

19 ERTA Judgment and Opinions 2/92, 1/94 and 2/94.

20 Opinion 1/75.

21 CJ, Judgment of 6 May 1981, *Commission v United Kingdom*, case 804/79.

22 Opinion 2/92.

23 However, it must be noted that the 10th declaration joined to the Maastricht Treaty specified that those provisions did "*not affect the principles esulting from the judgement handed down by the Court of Justice in the AETR case.*" On the AETR case, see note 6 above.

24 Opinion 2/91.

25 Opinion 2/00.

26 They are regulated by Article 218 FEU that reproduces Article 111 of the EC Treaty.

27 It is interesting to note that the English version of the EU Treaty uses the term 'consistency' whereas all the other official languages refer to the term 'coherence'.

28 Common commercial policy, development cooperation, economic, financial and technical cooperation, humanitarian aid, restrictive measures, agreements, and relations with international organisations.

Bibliography

Azoulai, Loïc (2005), 'The *acquis* of the European Union and international organisations', *European Law Journal*, 11: 196–231.

Cremona, Marise (2006), 'External relations of the EU and the member states: competence, mixed agreements, international responsibility, and effects of international law', *EUI Working Papers, Law*, No. 2006/22 (available at http://ssrn.com/abstract=963316).

Eeckhout, Piet (2005), *External Relations of the European Union, Legal and Constitutional Foundations*, London: Oxford EC Law Library.

Hable, Angelika (2006), 'The European Constitution and the reform of external competences', in Lenka Rovná and Wolfgang Wessels (eds), *EU Constitutionalisation: From the Convention to the Constitutional Treaty 2002–2005 – Anatomy, Analysis, Assessment*, Prague: Institute for European Policy.

Koutrakos, Panos (2006), *EU International Relations Law*, Oxford and Portland: Hart Publishing.

de Schoutheete, Philippe and Sami Andoura (2007), 'The legal personality of the European Union', *Studia Diplomatica*, LX: 1.

7 The EU's common commercial policy and regional/global regulation

Paola Conconi

Summary

The EU constitutes the largest trading bloc in the world. It is the world largest exporter and the second largest importer of goods, and it is the first trader of commercial services. Though its members represent just over 7 per cent of the world's population, they account for more than a fifth of global imports and exports.

At the basis of this leading role lies the common commercial policy (CCP) which, together with agricultural policy and competition policy, is the only truly centralised policy of the Union. Since the Treaty of Rome in 1957, EU member countries accepted to speak with one voice in trade, transferring their sovereignty in this policy area to the supranational level.[1]

In 1968, the Customs Union entered into force among the six original EU member countries, remaining duties were eliminated among them, and a Common External Tariff (CET) was introduced to replace national tariffs *vis-à-vis* non-member countries. Since then, the scope of the CCP has expanded in two important dimensions: first, the members of the Customs Union have increased to twenty-seven; second, commercial policy has broadened to include not only border measures restricting trade in goods, but also policies affecting trade in services and a vast range of trade-related regulatory measures (e.g., intellectual property, technical standards).

In terms of the decision-making process, the European Commission is responsible for the implementation of the CCP, proposing new trade initiatives to the Council, managing tariffs and other trade policy instruments, and conducting trade negotiations. Contrary to other policy areas in which member states decide by unanimity, trade policy decisions by the Council are taken by qualified majority.

Trade policy thus lies at the heart of the identity of the EU and of its presence in the world. This is also reflected in the World Trade Organization, one of the only international organisations in which the Union is itself a member and in which EU member countries are represented by the European Commission. Reaching a 'single voice' in trade policy is often a complicated process, since EU members have different trade policy interests and agreeing on a collective policy and bargaining position requires compromises among them.

This chapter covers various aspects of EU trade policy. We describe the patterns of EU trade with the rest of the world, then the instruments of the CCP and the process through which EU member countries manage to reconcile their differences to reach a common position on trade. Next, we look at the complex system of trade preferences of the EU, and examine the role of the EU within the multilateral trade system. Then we discuss the tensions between EU regionalism and multilateralism, before offering some concluding remarks.

The EU and world trade

The EU is the largest trading actor in the world. As it can be seen in Table 7.1, the Union is the world's leading exporter and second-leading importer of goods and is the biggest exporter and importer of commercial services. In 2006, it accounted for 16.4 per cent of world exports and 18.1 per cent of world imports in goods. The shares of EU external trade in total world trade are even higher for trade in services, with the EU-25 representing 27.3 per cent of world exports and 24 per cent of world imports (WTO 2007a).

The trade shares reported in Table 7.1 do not take into account intra-EU trade, which has increased over the years as a result of trade with the acceding countries now having become internal. If we include trade among the member states, in 2006 the EU was responsible for almost 40 per cent of world merchandise imports and

Table 7.1 Leading countries in world merchandise and service trade (2006)

Merchandise trade

	Exports		Imports	
	Value (billion US$)	*Share of world trade*	*Value (billion US$)*	*Share of world trade*
EU 25*	1481.7	16.4	1697	18.1
USA	1038.3	11.5	1919.4	20.5
Japan	968.9	10.7	791.5	8.5
China	649.9	7.2	579.6	6.2

Service trade

	Exports		Imports	
	Value (billion US$)	*Share of world trade*	*Value (billion US$)*	*Share of world trade*
EU 25*	554.4	27.3	471.7	24.0
USA	388.8	19.1	307.8	15.7
Japan	122.5	6.0	144.0	7.3
China	91.4	4.5	100.3	5.1

Source: WTO (2007a).

Note
* Excludes intra-EU trade.

Table 7.2 EU merchandise trade by country (2006)

	Exports			Imports	
	Value (billion US$)	Share of world trade		Value (billion US$)	Share of world trade
EU 25*	3050.8	67.3	EU 25*	3050.8	67.3
USA	332.8	7.3	China	240.5	5.1
Switzerland	106.8	2.4	USA	220.6	4.6
Russian Federation	89.3	2.0	Russian Federation	148.7	3.1

Source: WTO (2007a).

Note
* Excludes intra-EU trade.

exports. The importance of intra-EU trade can also be seen from Table 7.2, which looks at the major EU trading partners: the overwhelming majority of trade occurs between member countries; outside the EU, the main trading partners are the USA, Russia, Switzerland and China.

In terms of trade composition, EU merchandise trade consists predominantly of trade in manufactured goods, while trade in services is mainly in travel and transportation (see Table 7.3). It should be pointed out that the commodity structure of EU trade varies greatly across trading partners. In particular, manufacture goods dominate EU merchandise trade with other developed countries, while primary products figure more prominently in trade patterns with developing countries.[2]

Looking at the relations between the EU and its trading partners reveals that many neighbouring countries are largely 'dependent' on the EU market. For example, in 2006 the EU accounted for a large share of trade of the Russian Federation (56.7 per cent of its exports and 43.9 per cent of its imports) and of Turkey (52.5 per cent of its exports and 39.5 per cent of its imports). In contrast, trade with these countries accounted for much smaller shares of EU trade (WTO 2007a).[3]

The EU has often exploited this commercial hegemony as a diplomatic tool.

Table 7.3 Composition of EU trade as a percentage of world trade (2006)

Merchandise trade			Trade in services		
Commodity groups	Exports	Imports	Service categories	Exports	Imports
Manufactures	83.3	60.4	Travel	63.3	15.2
Fuel and mining products	7.0	3	Transportation	16.1	47.7
Agriculture	6.4	7.3	Other commercial services	20.6	37.1

Source: WTO (2007a).

Indeed, it has been argued that 'trade policy has always been the principal instrument of foreign policy for the EU' (Sapir 1998). Access to the EU market, combined with financial aid, economic cooperation and infrastructural links have been used to foster the Union's geopolitical interests. An example is the European neighbourhood policy (ENP), launched by the European Commission in 2003. This offers to the EU's immediately neighbouring countries by land or sea a privileged trade relationship in the form of association or cooperation agreements (see below) in exchange for their commitments to some values (e.g., respect for the rule of law, good governance, respect of human rights), with the explicit goal of extending stability, security and economic development.

The common commercial policy

In this section, we review the main instruments of the EU common commercial policy (CCP) and describe the institutional process through which member countries manage to reconcile their differences to reach a common position on trade.

The key provisions of the CCP are contained in Articles 131–4 (ex Articles 110–16) of the Treaty of Rome. The cornerstone of the CCP is Article 133, according to which the CCP establishes uniform principles between all member states governing EU trade policy including changes in tariff rates, the conclusion of tariff and trade agreements with non-member countries, uniformity in trade liberalisation measures, export policy and instruments to protect trade such as anti-dumping measures and subsidies.

Main instruments of the CCP

Article 133 does not exhaustively specify the instruments of EU trade policy. Indeed, as discussed below, EU trade policies and the environment in which they are applied have substantially changed over the years. While in the 1960s and 1970s the CCP consisted mainly of the Common External Tariff (CET) and other border measures, it now comprises various measures which are only indirectly trade-related (e.g., domestic regulatory barriers and the protection of intellectual property rights).

When the Treaty of Rome was signed in 1957, the liberalisation of merchandise trade between industrialised countries still had a long way to go and *tariffs* were the main instrument of trade protection. Since then, tariffs have been drastically reduced and their levels have been bound through successive rounds of multilateral trade negotiations.

EU tariffs combine *ad valorem* duties and specific duties and vary substantially across sectors and individual products. Although the average EU applied Most Favoured Nation (MFN) tariff is relatively low (6.9 per cent in 2006), a significant proportion of imports enter the EU at very high tariff rates. In particular, higher tariffs are imposed on many agricultural products and other 'sensitive sectors' (e.g., food, textiles and clothing, footwear, trucks, cars), with rates ranging up to 427.9 per cent on certain processed food products (WTO 2007b).

In addition to tariffs, the EU has made wide use of various *non-tariff barriers* (NTBs). The main types of NTBs imposed by the EU in the past have been import quotas and voluntary export restraints (VERs). The 1990s saw a clear tendency towards the decreasing use of quantitative trade measures. This was mostly due to the fact that the Uruguay Round agreements prohibited VERs and led to the 'tariffication' of many import quotas. As a result of the Uruguay Round Agreement on Textiles and Clothing, the EU eliminated in 2005 the quotas it had imposed on imports of clothing and textiles under successive Multifibre Agreements (MFAs).

As traditional trade barriers are dismantled, other ways of restricting imports on 'sensitive' sectors are often resorted to. Frequent use of *anti-dumping duties* is an example of such practice. Dumping is a form of price discrimination, in the sense of charging different prices in separate geographical markets. Article VI of the General Agreement on Tariffs and Trade (GATT) refers to 'export prices being lower than prices in the domestic market of the exporter'. In the EU, anti-dumping duties are generally triggered by a claim from EU manufacturers that an export has caused them damage. The Commission then has to establish, consulting with member countries, if dumping has occurred, if the industry concerned has been injured, and where the 'Community interest' lies, based on an assessment of the costs and benefits of imposing anti-dumping duties. The Commission can impose preliminary duties, while the Council considers whether to impose definite duties, which can last up to five years.

Although anti-dumping duties were originally devised to combat unfair trade, their broad and arbitrary use has led economists to conclude that anti-dumping 'has nothing to do with keeping trade "fair" [...] It is simply another form of protection' (Blonigen and Prusa 2003). The EU has been a heavy user of anti-dumping measures,[4] particularly on mineral products and chemicals, textile products and machinery equipment. Since the mid-1990s, more countries became frequent users of anti-dumping measures (e.g., India, Brazil, China and South Africa) and the EU now finds itself increasingly on the receiving end of anti-dumping investigations (see Vandenbussche and Zanardi 2008).

Trade policy instruments further include *export subsidies*, which are mostly used on agricultural products (e.g., dairy products, sugar). Although their use is on the decline, 'in value, export subsidies notified by the EC represent approximately 90 per cent of all the WTO Members' notified export subsidies' (WTO 2007b).

Protectionist measures also include *technical barriers* that products imported into the EU must comply with. This type of barrier arises whenever foreign producers have to alter their products in order to comply with EU regulations, which are usually justified in terms of health, safety, environmental or consumer protection and can be imposed by governments or by non-governmental organisations. The use of these measures is restricted by the WTO agreement on Technical Barriers to Trade (TBT Agreement).

As mentioned above, the EU is the first exporter and importer of commercial services in the world. EU external *policy on trade in services* must comply with the WTO General Agreement on Trade in Services (GATS). This was the first multilateral agreement aimed at liberalising trade in crucial sectors such as telecommunications and financial services. The issue of service liberalisation arises, too, in preferential trade agreements, although the coverage and the extent of l.. vary widely across the different agreements. Similarly to the rules governing preferential trade in goods in the GATT (see discussion below), the GATS requires that overall barriers to service trade faced by non-member countries should not rise, that bilateral trade agreements must have 'substantial sectoral coverage' and eliminate 'substantially all discrimination'.

The protection of *intellectual property rights* has become a trade policy issue, given the increased importance of trade in 'knowledge goods' – for which most of the value of new products arises from initial efforts in research and development (e.g., pharmaceuticals or high technology products) – and 'brand goods' – for which most of the value comes reputation effects (e.g., trademarks, appellations of origin). With respect to these types of goods, trade policy consists of measures aimed at protecting owners' property rights. The Uruguay Round negotiations led to the Agreement on Trade Related Intellectual Property Rights (TRIPs), under which signatories have to establish minimum standards of intellectual property rights protection and extend the traditional GATT principles of non-discrimination to intellectual property.

The common agricultural policy

We must stress the fundamental link between the EU's commercial policy and its common agricultural policy (CAP). This has been a controversial policy, which has even been referred to as 'the single most idiotic system of economic mismanagement of all times' (*The Economist*, 29 September 1990). As discussed later in this chapter, the CAP has also constituted a major obstacle in all rounds of GATT/WTO trade negotiations.

The objectives of the CAP as stated in Article 39 of the Treaty of Rome were: to increase agricultural productivity, to ensure a fair standard of living for the agricultural community, to stabilise markets, to provide certainty of food supplies and to ensure that those supplies reached consumers at reasonable prices. In an attempt to achieve these sometimes conflicting objectives, two main mechanisms were used. First, a generous EU-wide common 'target price' was set for each of the major farm products. Agricultural products entering the EU from non-member countries were subject to 'variable levies' (tariffs), which prevented target prices from being undercut by cheaper imports. Second, if a commodity's market price within the Union fell to an appointed 'intervention price', then national agencies would purchase all produce that could not otherwise be sold at that price, artificially removing supply and thereby preventing a further fall in price.

The establishment of the CAP helped to reduce Europe's reliance on imported food. However, when prices were set above what the market could bear, government agencies had to take stocks off the market in order to sustain the price. The result was overproduction of butter, wine, beef and other products. Some of the product surpluses were held in storage or destroyed, while others were exported at prices far below the costs of production with the help of export subsidies. These measures had a high budgetary cost and led to an increase in agricultural prices within the EU, becoming unpopular with European taxpayers and consumers. They also distorted agricultural world markets and angered producers in developing countries, making it harder for the EU to be perceived as a leading actor in multilateral trade negotiations and to campaign for the liberalisation of world trade in other goods and services.

CAP reform began in the early 1990s, with the goal of reducing support prices and compensating farmers by paying them direct aid. Several rural development measures were introduced, notably to encourage environmentally sound farming. Production limits helped to reduce surpluses. The so-called Agenda 2000 reforms reinforced the move to make farmers more reliant on the market and improved incentives to farm in an environmentally sensitive way, adding a comprehensive rural development policy that encouraged many rural initiatives and helped farmers to diversify and restructure. The budget available to agricultural policy was capped to reassure taxpayers that CAP costs would not escalate, and export subsidies were reduced on various goods.

The institutional process

As discussed in Chapter 6, the Commission has sole competence over the implementation of the CCP, proposing eventual new initiatives to the Council and managing trade tariffs. When the EU is engaged in trade negotiations with third countries, its members act as a 'single voice'. This is reflected by the fact that the EU is a member in its own right of the World Trade Organization (WTO). Although every member state has the right to attend WTO meetings, it is only the European Commission that represents the entire EU.

In negotiating trade agreements at the bilateral, regional or multilateral level, all member states must thus coordinate in order to present a cohesive EU external policy. Under Article 133(2), the Commission has the right of initiative as far as trade negotiations are concerned, but must seek and obtain a mandate from the Council of Ministers. Commission officials must conduct international trade negotiations within the limits set by the Council's mandate.

When the European Commission negotiates trade agreements on behalf of the member states, it acts in consultation with a special committee, the Article 133 Committee. This is composed of representatives from the twenty-seven member states and the European Commission and its main function is to coordinate EU trade policy. The Committee meets on a weekly basis, discussing various trade policy issues affecting the EU (e.g., strategic issues linked to multilateral, regional or bilateral negotiations, difficulties encountered in particular export or import-competing sectors).

At the conclusion of negotiations, the Council approves or rejects the negotiated trade agreement. Article 300 of the amended Treaty describes the intra-EU procedures governing ratification. With the exception of a few sensitive areas, the Council decides according to qualified majority voting (QMV). Member states are assigned different voting weights, which reflect the size of their populations, and ratification requires approval by two-thirds of the votes. However, on most occasions member countries try to reach a general consensus, without resorting to a formal vote.

Unanimity applies to agreements involving non-traditional trade sectors, in which the Community and the member states have shared competence. The Treaty of Nice, which entered into force in 2003, has broadened EU trade competences on non-traditional trade issues, enabling the EU to conclude international agreements covering trade in services and intellectual property rights by QMV and without ratification by the member states.[5]

The Treaty of Rome provided no role in trade policy for the then European Assembly. The European Parliament has acquired some trade policy powers under Article 310, according to which ratification of the Parliament by simple majority voting may be required for association agreements.

The EU policy process has also allowed lobby groups to voice their interests. In particular, the Commission has established a consultative process with various civil society organisations, including business groups, sectoral interests and consumer groups. EU consultations with interest groups are not based on any formal rules, and have been criticised for not being transparent enough.

It is often argued that the EU is 'handicapped' internationally by the complexity of its institutions and the constraints imposed on its negotiators. For example, ratification of a trade deal negotiated between the USA and the EU may only require a vote by simple majority in the US Congress, but requires the approval of at least a qualified majority of the European Council. However, it could be argued that the institutional limitations faced by EU negotiators might actually help to strengthen its bargaining position and extract concessions from its trading partners. As first argued by Schelling (1956), 'the power of a negotiator often rests on a manifest inability to make concessions and to meet demands'.[6]

The system of EU trade preferences

A key feature of EU commercial policy is the combination of regionalism and multilateralism: on the one hand, the Union has been a strong supporter of multilateral trade rules; on the other, it has developed the most extensive network of preferential trade agreements (PTAs) of any GATT/WTO member.

The fundamental principle of multilateral trading rules is that of non-discrimination. The goal is to eliminate any form of preferential treatment in international trade. In particular, Article I of the WTO establishes the MFN principle, according to which all WTO members should receive from any given member country the same trade preferences accorded to the partner that receives the best (most favoured) treatment. If enforced, the MFN treatment would guarantee that the tariff rate on any given product would be uniform across trading partners.

The creation and expansion of the EU, as well as the various agreements negotiated between the EU and some of its trading partners, violate the MFN principle. Article XXIV of the WTO allows for an exception to the MFN rule for countries that sign regional trade agreements in the form of customs unions (CUs) or free trade area (FTAs). To be WTO-compatible, regional trade agreements should fulfill two criteria: they should not lead to an increase in average trade barriers against third parties, and they should lead to the elimination of tariffs and non-tariff barriers on 'substantially all' trade between member countries.

WTO members are bound to notify of the preferential trade agreements (PTAs) in which they participate. Nearly all of the WTO's members have notified participation in one or more PTAs (some members are party to twenty or more). Notifications may also refer to the accession of new parties to an agreement that already exists, e.g., the notification of the accession of Bulgaria and Romania to the EU Customs Union. In the period 1948–94, the GATT received 124 notifications of PTAs (relating to trade in goods); in the period 1995–2007, over 240 additional arrangements covering trade in goods or services have been notified.

Figure 7.1 describes the so-called EU 'pyramid of trade preferences'. The top of the pyramid captures the maximum preferential treatment that the EU can grant to another country, i.e., membership to the Union. Intra-member relations are characterised by the deepest integration, involving not only common commercial policy, but also common agricultural policy and competition policy, and common basic rules governing the movement of goods, services, capital and persons.

One level below, we find *association agreements*, which involve the creation of a CU or an FTA between the EU and the trading partner, as well as common rules

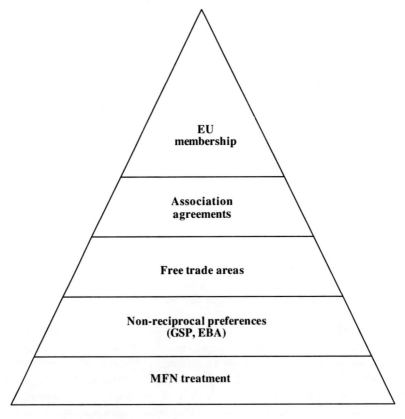

Figure 7.1 The EU pyramid of trade preferences.

on non-trade issues (e.g., mobility of citizens, industrial standards, financial aid and development). An example of this type of preference is the European Economic Association between the EU, Iceland, Liechtenstein and Norway.

One step below are the *free trade areas* between the EU and various trading partners, such as Mexico, Chile, South Africa and Israel. Examples also include the Economic Partnership Agreements (EPAs) negotiated between the EU and its former colonies from African, Caribbean and Pacific (ACP) regions. With respect to the relations between the EU and its former colonies, it should be stressed that the EU's system of preferences has been greatly simplified as a result of the expiration of the WTO waiver for discriminatory and non-reciprocal contractual preferences (Lomé/ Cotonou Agreements). This has led to the EU's promotion of regional grouping among ACP countries, with the goal of negotiating reciprocal trade agreements with them. For example, in January 2008 a trade and aid EPA entered into force between the EU and fifteen Caribbean nations.

Next we find *non-reciprocal preferences* granted by the EU to developing countries under the Generalised System of Preferences (GSP). This is legitimised under the 1979 Enabling Clause, which allows GATT/WTO members to offer lower-than-MFN tariffs to developing countries. Under its GSP scheme, the EU offers tariff-free access, without demanding reciprocity,[7] to some industrial and agricultural products from developing countries. GSP preferences are lost upon 'graduation', i.e., when a beneficiary country is deemed by the granting country to have attained a sufficient level of progress. For example, in 1998 the EU graduated three countries (Hong Kong, the Republic of Korea and Singapore) from its GSP scheme, and their exports now face MFN duties. Under the so-called Everything But Arms (EBA) initiative, the EU grants duty-free access in all sectors, with the exceptions of arms and munitions, to all least developed countries (LDCs).[8] The EU has also established special preferential GSP schemes for countries that have programs to combat drug trafficking and to protect labour rights and the environment.[9]

Finally, at the bottom of the EU pyramid of trade preferences are countries that do not enjoy any trade preferences, which only export to the EU under MFN treatment. It should be stressed that, although there are only nine such countries (Australia, Canada, Chinese Taipei, Hong Kong, Japan, Republic of Korea, New Zealand, Singapore and the USA), the importance of trade preferences should not be exaggerated, since approximately three-quarters of imports by the EU enter on non-preferential (MFN) terms (see WTO 2007a).[10]

The EU and multilateralism

The EU in the world trading system

In the post-World War Two period, the USA and the EU have been strong supporters of multilateral trade rules, recognising the economic benefits of trade cooperation. Economic theory has stressed two main economic arguments for trade cooperation (see Bagwell and Staiger (2002) for a discussion). According to the so-called 'terms of trade argument', a country seeking to improve its terms of trade (relative price of exports in terms of imports) by unilaterally increasing its import tariffs may provoke retaliatory behavior from other trading partners, making all parties concerned worse off. According to the 'commitment argument', if governments lack credibility *vis-à-vis* domestic economic agents, they may wish to 'tie their hands' by signing an international agreement. For example, if the decision of a government to liberalise trade in a particular sector at a certain future date is not deemed credible by the industry concerned, the latter may fail to undertake the required restructuring during the transition period. This implies that, when the due date comes, trade liberalisation will not be optimal because the sector will not be ready for international competition. An international trade agreement can be a way to solve this time inconsistency problem.

In what follows, we briefly describe the GATT and the WTO, outlining the role played by the EU in shaping the evolution of the multilateral trading system.

The GATT

The multilateral trading system was originally set up under the GATT in the aftermath of World War Two. The Bretton Woods Conference of 1944 recognised the need for an international trade institution to complement the International Monetary Fund (IMF) and the World Bank. In particular, the USA – the leading political and economic power in the postwar period, which took over a large share of responsibility for building a new international economic system – wanted at all costs to avoid a return to the protectionist battles of the 1930s.[11]

The GATT agreement was signed in Geneva in 1947 by twenty-three countries. Originally, the GATT was intended to serve as a temporarily until the ratification of the Charter of the International Trade Organization (ITO). This was signed in 1948 by fifty-three nations, but never entered into force, since it was not ratified by the US Congress.[12]

The GATT consisted mainly of the commercial policy provisions of the ITO Charter, with minor formal adjustments. The overall objective of the GATT was to reduce barriers to trade, especially tariffs, and to limit the use of certain trade barriers, such as quotas. The negotiating parties agreed that substantial tariff cuts could only be achieved if certain exceptions were included in the structure of trade rules. The GATT therefore contains several escape clauses and contingent provisions.

The system was developed through a series of trade negotiations, or rounds, held under GATT. Early negotiation rounds dealt mainly with tariff reductions, while later negotiations included other areas such as anti-dumping and non-tariff measures. Since the Treaty of Rome was signed in 1957, the process of European integration has had a critical impact on GATT trade rounds. The creation of the European Economic Community (EEC) raised the question of how to manage trade relations between the members of this upcoming customs union and the other GATT members. The fear was that an unsatisfactory adjustment would undermine the multilateral trading system. This concern was one of the main driving forces behind the Dillon Round 1960–61, which was meant to transform the tariffs of the six EEC members into a common schedule applied by all six towards non-member countries. In accordance with Article XXIV of GATT, the new common external tariff could be no higher on average than the separate tariffs of the six countries. Whenever the EEC members wanted to deviate from this rule, they had to offer tariff concessions on other items as compensation. The negotiations made satisfactory progress, except in the field of agriculture.

The Kennedy Round (1964–67) was to a large extent motivated by the growth and steady integration of the European Common Market, which was perceived as a threat to US trade interests.[13] In the field of tariff reductions on industrial goods, the Kennedy Round achieved an average cut of 38 per cent, covering two-thirds of developed countries' tariff-bound industrial imports. Tariff reductions for textile products, however, remained much below the average cut for industrial products. This was the first round that went beyond tariffs (anti-dumping duties in particular) and in which the negotiating parties agreed to include agricultural products as a major negotiating topic, acknowledging that trade in agriculture was distorted by highly interventionist policies. However, the outcome on agriculture was very limited, mainly due to fact that the EU struggled to reconcile the objectives of elaborating and putting into force its CAP and participating in international trade negotiations on agriculture.

The enlargement of the EU to the UK, Denmark and Ireland was a major motivation for the launch of the Tokyo Round (1973–79). In particular, the USA perceived the membership of the UK, which accounted for the vast majority of US investment in the EU, as a threat to its interests. Tokyo was chosen strategically as the location to initiate a new multilateral round of trade negotiations because Japan had become one of the biggest world exporters and several other Asian economies were gaining expanding shares of world trade. The main protagonists of the round were again developed countries, in particular the USA, the EU and Japan. However, since the agenda also included a variety of development issues, non-member countries were invited to participate in the negotiations. Nearly thirty developing countries took up this invitation, increasing the number of participants to over 100 countries. During the Tokyo Round, agriculture, once again, proved intractable: attempts to reconcile the positions of the USA and the EEC on agriculture failed during 1975 and 1976 and held up progress in almost every other area of the negotiations. In July 1977, both parties agreed to drop most substantive questions dividing them, such as market access and subsidies. This at least allowed the negotiations to go forward (UNCTAD 1982).

The WTO

The agenda of the Uruguay Round (1986–94) was the broadest ever agreed to in multilateral negotiations: the talks extended the trading system into several new areas, notably trade in services and intellectual property, and to reform trade in the sensitive sectors of agriculture and textiles; all the original GATT articles were up for review.

The round was supposed to end in December 1990, but the USA and EU disagreed on how to reform agricultural trade and decided to extend the talks. Finally, in

November 1992, the USA and EU settled most of their differences in a deal known informally as 'the Blair House accord' and, in April 1994, a deal was signed by ministers from the 123 participating governments. The agreement established the WTO, which came into being upon its entry into force in January 1995, to replace the GATT system. This is widely regarded as the most profound institutional reform of the world trading system since the GATT's establishment.

The WTO is composed of governments and political entities (such as the EU) and is a member-driven organisation, with decisions mainly taken on a consensus basis. Between 1995 and 2008, the number of its members expanded from 123 to 151, the vast majority of which are developing countries. The EU is the largest and most comprehensive entity is the WTO. As mentioned above, its member states coordinate their positions in Brussels, while the European Commission alone speaks for the EU at WTO meetings in Geneva.

The top-level decision-making body of the WTO is the Ministerial Conference, which meets at least once every two years. The latest conferences were in Seattle (1999), Doha (2001), Cancun (2003) and Hong Kong (2005). Below this, the General Council meets several times a year in the Geneva headquarters. Both are composed of representatives of all member states.

The dispute settlement mechanism, which came into being with the WTO in 1995, is one of the cornerstones of the world trading system. It gives all WTO members the confidence that the agreements negotiated will be respected. The rationale behind the Dispute Settlement Understanding (DSU) is to provide members with a clear legal framework for solving disputes which may arise in the course of implementing WTO agreements.

During the Uruguay Round, dispute settlement procedures were strengthened in an unprecedented manner, with the introduction of the quasi-automatic adoption of reports and the establishment of the Appellate Body as a standing organ for legal review. Clearly, agreed solutions between members are the most desirable way of solving disputes. However, if this is not possible, members can ask for WTO panels and appeal procedures to solve the dispute.

The Panels and the Appellate Body are limited to making recommendations; decisions based on these recommendations are taken by the Dispute Settlement Body (DSB), which consists of a session of the General Council. The DSB uses a special decision procedure known as 'reverse consensus', which makes it almost certain that the recommendations of the Panel (possibly amended by the Appellate Body) will be accepted. The process requires that the recommendations should be adopted, unless there is a consensus of the members against adoption. Once it has decided on the case, the DSB may direct the losing member to take action to bring its laws, regulations or policies into conformity with the WTO rules. If the losing party fails to do so within a 'reasonable period of time', the DSB may authorise a successful complainant to take retaliatory measures to induce action on the part of the losing party.

Since the establishment of the WTO, the EU has been involved in many disputes, being on the offensive more than on the defensive: between 1995 and 2008, it has acted as a complainant in seventy-seven cases and as a respondent in fifty-nine cases. Some of these cases have been widely publicised, such as the long-running disputes between the EU and the USA over the EU tariff system for banana imports or over the US subsidies to foreign sales corporations.

Regionalism versus multilateralism?

Since the early 1990s, the proliferation of PTAs has generated a heated debate on whether such agreements represent a threat to the multilateral trading system. In the words of Bhagwati (1991), the question is whether the PTAs are 'stumbling blocks' or 'building blocks' towards multilateral free trade. In what follows, we summarise the arguments of two opposite views on regionalism; in light of these arguments, we then try to evaluate the impact of EU regionalism on the multilateral trading system.

PTAs as 'stumbling blocks'

This view highlights the discriminatory nature of PTAs and provides a pessimistic prognosis on the effects of regionalism on multilateral liberalisation. Below, we outline four of the main arguments put forward by the proponents of this view.

First, PTAs may promote *trade diversion* rather than trade creation, thus reinforcing vested interests and increasing opposition to multilateral trade liberalisation.[14] The argument is that, if there is trade diversion, a firm located in a member country, although inefficient, may be able to overcome competition from a more efficient firm located in a non-member state, because it benefits from preferential tariff rates. This inefficient firm will then lobby against future global liberalisation, in order to retain its privileged access to the regional market. Consequently, trade-diverting PTAs are not only welfare reducing, but might also have negative effects on further liberalisation of the multilateral trading system (see Grossman and Helpman 1995).

Second, the market power effect that accompanies the formation or enlargement of customs union can lead to *increased protection* against outside countries. The increase in trade barriers may take the form of higher tariffs or of anti-dumping duties, when tariffs are bound by WTO commitments.

Third, large countries may benefit from signing preferential agreements with small countries, in which they can use their market power to extract concessions on non-tariff issues, such as labour market or environmental standards, migration or intellectual property protection. This implies that large countries may have an incentive to *slow down multilateral liberalisation*, in order to maintain their bargaining power *vis-à-vis* that of their partners (see Limão 2007).

Finally, it is often argued that being engaged in regional negotiations may *crowd out resources from multilateral negotiations*, stalling the process of MFN liberalisation.

PTAs as 'building blocks'

The alternative view on the relationship between regionalism and multilateralism predicts a benign effect of PTAs. Several arguments have been put forward as to why regionalism can complement the multilateral trading system and be a driving force for multilateral trade liberalisation.

One argument is that PTAs increase the pressure to act in the direction of further multilateral liberalisation. The idea is that the proliferation and expansion of PTAs leads to the *erosion of existing preferences*, thus reducing the opposition to multilateral liberalisation.

It is also argued that by reducing the margin of competitiveness of countries that remain outside the agreement relative to partner countries, the formation of PTAs may prompt non-member countries to *pursue more multilateral trade liberalisation* to avoid the negative effects of trade diversion. Furthermore, the anticipation of a strengthening of regionalism may offer a boost to multilateralism, as it may increase the penalty associated with retaliation in case of a defection from multilateral rules (see Bagwell and Staiger 1999).

Another argument in support of the complementarity between regionalism and multilateralism is that PTAs act as *laboratories of international cooperation*, whereby cooperation can be tested among a small number of countries before being extended multilaterally. This can help to build up the political consensus for further liberalisation, thus making multilateral liberalisation politically viable.

The case of EU regionalism

In line with the negative view of regionalism, some evidence suggests that the creation and expansion of the EU may pose a threat to multilateral trade liberalisation. In particular, it could be argued that the process of EU integration may have stalled multilateral liberalisation by absorbing resources away from multilateral negotiations. For example, during the Kennedy Round, the chairman to the Meeting of the Trade Negotiations Committee pointed out to the EU representatives that, with respect to agriculture negotiations, 'all delegations were aware that in many respects there was a real dilemma for them because they were really engaged in two operations at the same time',[15] i.e., elaborating and puting into force a common agricultural policy for the Community, and participating in international negotiations covering the same field.

However, other considerations suggest that EU regionalism may instead be compatible with multilateral trade liberalisation. In particular, there are at least three reasons to believe that the EU system of preferences promotes more trade creation than trade diversion: first, as mentioned above, although very few countries conduct their trade with the EU on a purely MFN basis, with approximately three-quarters of imports by the EU entering on non-preferential terms; second, the expansion of the EU web of PTAs – from agreements with neighboring countries and former colonies to transcontinental agreements that are not driven by geographical or historical links – implies that trade-diverting effects are less likely to occur; third, the progressive reduction in MFN tariffs has 'eroded' the preferences of beneficiary countries, reducing the risk of trade diversion.

It should also be noted that the EU has on various occasions complied with WTO restrictions aimed at reducing the discriminatory effects of its trade policies. For example, since the WTO did not allow for the continuation of the discriminatory and non-reciprocal trade provisions of the Lomé/Cotonou Agreements, the EU has replaced them with reciprocal trade agreements (see discussed above). Similarly, following the Appellate Body ruling in the dispute between the EU and India (see Note 9), the EU has made changes to its GSP program, with the objective of making it non-discriminatory and more transparent.

Concerning the risk of an increase in external tariffs as a result of EU enlargement, there is evidence that the alarming predictions about 'fortress Europe' have not been realised. On the contrary, it has been argued that European integration has played a considerable role in the liberalisation of European external trade policy by changing the institutional context in which trade policy is made. In particular, the implementation of the *Single European Act* has undermined the effectiveness of national trade barriers: before this Act, member states could limit imports by a variety of national regulations to protect their economies (e.g., health, safety and technical standards); with the completion of the single market, states lost the tools they needed to maintain national non-tariff barriers against non-EU imports (see Hanson 1998).

Finally, different waves of EU regionalism have triggered fears of trade diversion in the USA and other non-member countries. As discussed above, these fears have been an important driving force behind different rounds of GATT/WTO negotiations. First, the period 1958–65 saw the formation of the EEC, together with the launch of the Dillon Round and the Kennedy Round. Second, the period 1973–79 saw the enlargement of the EEC and the signing of the EEC–EFTA FTAs, where almost all tariffs in Western Europe were eliminated and, on the multilateral side, the launch of the Tokyo Round. Third, the Uruguay Round was launched in 1986, the same year in which the *Single European Act* was signed.

Conclusions

We conclude by discussing the challenges faced by the multilateral trading system after the creation of the WTO and the crucial role played by the EU in the controversial Doha Development Round (DDR), launched in December 2001 at a WTO Ministerial Conference in Doha, Qatar.[16]

The Ministerial Declarations agreed in Doha set a detailed work program, with the goal of completing it by 2005. The main objective of the Doha Development Agenda was to put development at the heart of the world trade system, so as to help combat poverty. Negotiations involve commitments to take measures necessary to integrate developing countries into the world trading system, notably by strengthening assistance to build capacity.

As in previous rounds, the limited scope for concessions on agriculture on the part of the EU, due to the continuing resistance of France and other member countries to the dismantling of the CAP,[17] has meant that the EU's trading partners (especially the large developing countries) have refused to make more ambitious offers to liberalise their service sectors and tariffs on industrial products, which are of direct concern to EU's commercial interests.

EU enlargement also has the potential to crucially affect the outcome of the DDR. New member states may aggressively assert their commercial policy interests, being less supportive of new trade policy issues (e.g., strengthening of intellectual property rights regimes abroad and opening foreign financial markets), preferring instead measures that promote more traditional trade policy objectives (e.g., better access to the product markets of middle-income developing countries and promotion of foreign direct investments). Given the use of qualified majority voting in trade policy decisions within the Council, this could lead to fundamental changes in the EU's position in multilateral negotiations.

Looking at the history of past multilateral negotiations suggests that the initial deadline for the completion of the Doha Round by 2005 was far too optimistic. Since the creation of the GATT in 1947, the number of its member countries has increased from twenty-three to more than 150 and the multilateral trading system has moved from being bipolar – dominated by the USA and the EU – to being multipolar – with Brazil, India and China playing an increasingly important role in the WTO. As a result, multilateral negotiations have become more complex and have taken longer to conclude.[18]

Multilateral negotiations have also become more complex with respect to the number of issues covered. While in early rounds the negotiating agenda included mostly tariff reductions in product markets, over the years it has expanded to include non-tariff barriers and new issues such as the liberalisation of trade in services and the protection of intellectual property rights. The text of the Uruguay Round Agreements (26,000 pages) reflects this increased complexity.

Since the end of the Uruguay Round, there has been an intense debate over the potential overlaps between trade and non-trade objectives, especially with respect to environmental protection and workers' rights. Should trade sanctions be used to buttress environmental policy cooperation or promote more stringent labour standards? Or should the WTO forbid the use of trade sanctions to enforce non-trade agreements? Economic analysis suggests that the answer to these questions is far from obvious: on the one hand, linking different policy dimensions may allow negotiating parties to arrive at a mutually advantageous (and economically efficient) exchange of concessions across different issues; on the other hand, making trade cooperation conditional on cooperation on other policy issues such as environmental protection may hinder the viability of multilateral cooperation in both areas (see Conconi and Perroni 2002).

The demand that trade liberalisation be linked to labour and environmental standards has received some backing in developed countries. However, labour and environmental standards are unlikely to be included in the Doha Round of multilateral negotiations, since the vast majority of developing countries regard them with scepticism and hostility, considering them as hidden forms of protectionism.[19] It remains unclear whether other trade-related policy issues will be included in the Doha Development Agenda, such as competition policy issues arising in connection with cross-border mergers and acquisitions (see Chapter 3 for a discussion).

Notes

1 Legally, responsibility for external trade policy remains with the European Communities. However, to simplify the exposition, throughout most of the chapter we will refer to the EU.

2 For example, if we look at the relations between the EU and North America, manufactured goods comprise 80.4 per cent of EU imports and 83.8 per cent of exports in 2006, while agricultural goods make only 6 per cent of imports and 5.3 per cent of exports. In comparison, manufactured goods represent 24.6 per cent of imports and 79.2 per cent of exports to African countries, while agricultural goods comprise 12.0 per cent of imports and 10.1 per cent of exports (WTO 2007a).

3 In the same year, Russia accounted only for 2 per cent of EU exports and 3.1 per cent of EU imports, while the shares of EU exports and imports from Turkey were 1.3 per cent and 1.9 per cent, respectively.

4 However, the EU has seemingly become less aggressive in its use of anti-dumping since the turn of the century: the annual average number of initiated anti-dumping proceedings was thirty-one in 1991–95, forty-four in 1995–99, and fifteen in 2004–06 (WTO 2007b).

5 As a result of pressures by France, a cultural exception on goods and services was included in Article 133(5) and Article 133(6). This concerns international negotiations related to audio visual services, educational services, and social and human health services, for which unanimity is still required.

6 See Meunier (2000) for an analysis of the impact of EU institutional complexities on trade negotiations and Conconi, *et al.* (2008) on trade negotiation procedures in the USA.

7 However, explicit or implicit elements of conditionality are often included in GSP programs (see Conconi and Perroni 2005).

8 These are designated by the United Nations and the World Bank on the basis of various criteria: national income below a certain threshold, weak human assets (based on health, nutrition and education indicators) and high economic vulnerability (based on indicators of instability of agricultural production and exports, inadequate diversification and economic smallness).

9 In a case brought before the WTO, India has targeted the EU for granting preferential GSP treatment to some countries because of their efforts to combat illegal drugs. In 2004, the WTO Appellate Body ruled that developed countries are allowed to grant different GSP treatment to different developing countries, provided this is done in a non-discriminatory and transparent manner.

10 The limited importance of trade preferences in terms of trade volumes is partly due to the administrative rules restricting their use. In particular, to take advantage of EU tariff preferences, an exporting country must satisfy cumbersome 'rules of origin' to substantiate the claim that it indeed produced the good, rather than import it from another country excluded from the preferences.

11 In the 1930s, the adoption of the infamous *Smoot-Hawley Act* in the USA raised import duties to record levels and was widely blamed at the time for sharply reducing trade, triggering retaliatory moves by many other countries, and exacerbating the Great Depression (see Irwin 1998).

12 A majority in the US Congress opposed the ITO Charter, considering that it was overloaded with topics only indirectly related to trade (e.g., employment and anti-trust measures). At the end of 1950, President Truman decided not to submit the ITO for congressional approval.

13 Although the USA was concerned about a European 'tariff wall', it was keen to support the expansion and further integration of the EU to enhance economic and political cooperation among European countries, thus reducing the risk of war between them, and to oppose communist expansion.

14 Trade creation implies a shift from costly domestic producers to lower cost PTA partners; trade diversion refers to the fact that PTAs may shift imports from more efficient non-member countries to less efficient member countries.

15 See the summary of the Progress Report by the Chairman to the Meeting of the Trade Negotiations Committee, WTO document TN 64/28: 3.

16 The terrorist attacks in the USA on 11 September 2001 were arguably an important contributing factor to the launch of the Doha Round, generating the geopolitical imperative to demonstrate that the world's governments could cooperate at a time of heightened uncertainty.

17 For example, proposals in 2002 by the EU Agriculture Commissioner Fischler for a modest reform in the CAP were blocked by a bilateral agreement between French President Jacques Chirac and German Chancellor Gerhard Schröder with the objective of freezing CAP spending until 2013. In February 2008, France argued that 'twenty European Union countries are opposed to compromise proposals on agriculture floated by a World Trade Organisation mediator as part of a bid to rescue global trade talks', though the EU Trade Commissioner Peter Mandelson shrugged off the criticism and said he still had the backing of the bloc (Reuters, 18 February 2008).

18 Based on the relationship between the number of participants and the duration of the negotiations in earlier rounds, the Doha Round should end in 2010 (see Neary 2004).

19 The official position of the WTO is to leave the responsibility for the protection of labour and environmental standards to the ILO and to international environmental agreements such as the Kyoto Protocol. In particular, during the 1996 Singapore ministerial meeting, WTO members agreed that core labour rights should be globally recognised and protected; however, its fundamental legal mandate is to regulate trade and international protection of labour rights should be primarily the task of the ILO.

Bibliography

Bagwell, K. and R. Staiger (1999), 'An economic theory of GATT', *American Economic Review*, 89: 215–48.

Bagwell, K. and R.W. Staiger (2002), *The Economics of the World Trading System*, Cambridge, MA: MIT Press.

Bhagwati, J. (1991), *The World Trading System at Risk*, Cambridge, MA: MIT Press.

Blonigen B. and T.J. Prusa (2003), 'Antidumping', in E.K. Choi and J. Harrigan (eds), *Handbook of International Trade*, Oxford, UK and Cambridge, MA: Blackwell Publishers.

Conconi, P., G. Facchini and M. Zanardi (2008), 'Fast track authority and international trade negotiations', mimeo, Université Libre de Bruxelles.

Conconi, P. and C. Perroni (2002), 'Issue linkage and issue tie-in in international negotiations', *Journal of International Economics*, 57: 423–7.

Conconi, P. and C. Perroni (2005), 'Special and differential trade regimes', CEPR Discussion Paper No. 4508.

Grossman, G.N. and A.O. Sykes (2005), 'A preference for development: the law and economics of GSP', *World Trade Review* 4, No. 1.

Grossman, G.M. and Helpman, E. (1995), 'The politics of free trade agreements', *American Economic Review*, 85: 667–90.

Hanson, B.T. (1998), 'What happened to fortress Europe? External trade policy liberalization in the European Union', *International Organization*, 52: 55–85.

Irwin, D.A. (1998), 'The Smoot-Hawley tariff: a quantitative assessment', *Review of Economics and Statistics*, 80: 326–4.

Limão, N. (2007), 'Are preferential trade agreements with non-trade objectives a stumbling block for multilateral liberalization?', *Review of Economic Studies*, 74: 821–55.

Meunier, S. (2000), 'What a single voice? European institutions and EU–US trade negotiations', *International Organization*, 54: 103–35.

Neary, P. (2004), 'Europe on the road to Doha: towards a new global trade round', *CESifo Economic Studies*, 50: 319–12.

Sapir, A. (1998), 'The political economy of EC regionalism', *European Economic Review*, 42: 717–32.

Schelling, T.C. (1956), 'An essay on bargaining', *American Economic Review*, 46: 281–306.

United Nations Conference on Trade and Development (UNCTAD) (1982), *Assessment of the Results of the Multilateral Trade Negotiations*, Geneva: UNCTAD.

Vandenbussche, H. and M. Zanardi (2008), 'What explains the proliferation of antidumping laws?', *Economic Policy*, 23 (53): 93–138.

WTO (2007a), *International Trade Statistics 2007*.

WTO (2007b), Trade Policy Review of the European Communities (WT/TPR/S/177).

8 The EU's common development cooperation policy

Nico Schrijver

Summary

During its fifty years of existence, the EU has emerged as a major actor in international development cooperation, both in terms of granting development aid and as a trading bloc. In addition, the development policy of the EU gradually expanded beyond aid and trade and now addresses virtually every dimension of the development process of developing countries, including the promotion of poverty eradication, sustainable development, good governance, respect for human rights and peace and security. For a long time development cooperation was practised without a clear legal basis. It was the Maastricht Treaty (1992) which at last filled the legal gap with a new section on development cooperation. Subsequently, the Lisbon Reform Treaty proposed to integrate the principles and objectives of development cooperation into the general articles on the Union's external action. Meanwhile, special development cooperation relationships had evolved with countries in Africa, the Caribbean and the Pacific (ACP) through the successive Lomé Conventions and the subsequent Cotonou Partnership Agreement. Currently, the preferential nature of the ACP–EU relationship is under stress resulting from EU outreach to non-ACP countries (Latin America, Asia and China) and the pressure to conclude new trading arrangements with the ACP countries which are compatible with the requirements of the World Trade Organization. While the EU's development aid performance has improved considerably in recent years, the Union still faces huge challenges in its development policy. A primary challenge is to ensure its coherence with other fields of policy, such as agriculture, fisheries and trade.

The legal basis: from the Treaty of Rome through Maastricht to Lisbon

The issue of relations between the future European Economic Community (EEC) and the colonies of its member states was addressed only at the very last stage of the negotiations on the draft EEC Treaty (Grilli 1993; McMahon 1998). Up to this point, all attention was focused on the internal dimensions of the envisaged EEC; furthermore, development problems enjoyed little attention at the time. However, under strong pressure by France, supported by Belgium, an association arrangement was included for colonies of EEC member states with the future EEC. This was laid down in Part IV of the Treaty of Rome (Articles 131–6). Further cursory references were made to overseas countries, confirming the solidarity that binds Europe and the overseas countries and expressing the intention to jointly promote economic and social development.[1]

Part IV of the Treaty of Rome, which still appears in the Lisbon Reform Treaty in an unmodified form (Articles 198–204), is clearly rooted in colonial relations. Association of the overseas countries and territories only related to the non-European (predominantly African) countries and territories that had colonial relationships with Belgium, France, Italy and the Netherlands. Association was imposed upon them without consultation, let alone third country consent. The stated purpose of association was to promote the economic and social development of the overseas countries and territories and to establish close economic relations between them and the Community as a whole. It was primarily intended to further the interests and prosperity of the inhabitants of the associated countries 'in order to lead them to the economic, social and cultural development to which they aspire'. Part IV is almost exclusively economically oriented. It provides for most favoured nation (MFN) treatment, abolishment of customs duties, right of establishment of enterprises, freedom of movement for workers and development assistance. From the early days, the association regime was supported by the establishment of the European Development Fund (EDF). Initially, EDF money was spent mostly on economic and social infrastructure projects.

There can be little doubt that the entire association regime was meant to maintain colonial linkages and the economic advantages that resulted from them and to spread the costs over all EEC members. Part IV had hardly any relevance with the other parts of the Treaty of Rome.[2] The rapid decolonisation process and the start of the international development debate made Part IV largely outdated nearly from the outset. Obviously, the association regime as it stood could not be applied to newly independent states. New multilateral development agencies, funds and programmes were established, including the World Bank's International Finance Corporation (IFC, 1956) and International Development Association (IDA, 1960), the First United Nations (UN) Development Decade (1961–70), the UN Conference on Trade and Development (UNCTAD, 1964), the United Nations Development Programme (UNDP) and the United Nations Industrial Development Organization (UNIDO). Naturally, this had an effect on European policies towards overseas countries.

A legal gap until 1992

On various occasions, Community competence in development cooperation was underscored in declarations, resolutions and memoranda. Highlights included the Paris Summit Declaration (1972), the Hunger Resolution adopted by the European Parliament (1979) and the Pisani Memorandum (1982) (see Arts 2000). Yet, they all fell squarely short of providing a firm legal basis for coherent European Community (EC) development policies. The momentum of the drafting of the *Single European Act* (*SEA*), adopted in February 1986, could also not be used for this purpose, as other priorities prevailed.

Table 8.1 Key policy documents in the evolution of EU development cooperation

Paris Summit Declaration of the Council of Ministers (1972)
Hunger Resolution adopted by the European Parliament (1979)
Pisani Memorandum of the European Commission (1982)
Commission Memorandum on Development Policy of the European Community (2000)
Joint Declaration of European Consensus on Development (2006)
EU Code of Conduct on Complementarity and Division of Labour in Development Policy (2007)

This Act merely introduced some changes in the procedures for concluding association agreements, including the required consent of the European Parliament acting by absolute majority. However, the *SEA* failed to fill the legal gap as regards the substantive basis for development cooperation.

It is therefore notable that the evolution of special development cooperation treaties with former colonies in Africa, the Caribbean and the Pacific (ACP) and other forms of cooperation with non-ACP developing countries (all to be discussed presently) took place without a clear embedding in, or interaction with EC law. After the independence of the overseas countries and territories, Part IV of the Rome Treaty could no longer serve as the legal basis for development association because it did not envisage a relationship between (equally) sovereign states. Since the Rome Treaty did not specify any other competence or instruments in the field of development cooperation, guidance was found in the section on 'General and final provisions'. Article 238 of the Treaty of the EC allowed the conclusion of agreements between the Community and third states or international organisations 'establishing an association involving reciprocal rights and obligations, common action and special procedures'. This did not occur without (legal) argument, since, among other things, reciprocity was considerably lacking in development cooperation arrangements. Partly for this reason, the successive Lomé Conventions between the EC and the ACP countries have always been concluded as 'mixed agreements'. This means that on the European side, these conventions were signed and ratified by both the EC (since 1985 represented by the Council and the Commission, earlier by the Council only) and all individual member states.

In addition to Article 238, Article 113 of the Section on the common commercial policy was interpreted to grant the EC competence to pursue common commercial and agricultural policies with development policy aspects at the international level, even though the words 'development' or 'developing countries' do not feature in this article. Such policies included generalised trade preferences, participation in international commodity agreements and food aid.

At long last, the Maastricht Treaty of 1992 would provide a firm legal basis for development cooperation.

Filling the legal gap

The Maastricht, Amsterdam and Lisbon treaties sought to amend the Treaty of Rome a number of ways as regards development cooperation. Maastricht Article 3 (subsection (r)), in listing the activities of the Community included 'a policy in the sphere of development co-operation'. In the spirit of the World Commission on Environment and Development (also known after its chair as the Brundtland Commission) report, *Our Common Future*, Article 6 (now Article 11 of the Lisbon Reform Treaty) refers to the aim of 'sustainable development' in stipulating the integration of environmental protection requirements in all Community policies and activities 'with a view to promoting sustainable development'. The latter was also elevated as a general objective of the EU in Article 2 of both the EU Treaty and EC Treaty, albeit in unidentical terms.

The most important innovation of the Maastricht Treaty was the insertion of a completely new Section XVII on Development Co-operation (later Section XX and currently Section III of Part V), just following the pre-existing Part IV on Association of the Overseas Countries and Territories.[3] The new section first set out the objectives of Community development cooperation. These included promoting sustainable development, integration of the developing countries into the world economy, poverty eradication, democracy and the rule of law and respect for human rights. This list appears to reflect the main trends in contemporary international development cooperation. No other multilateral or regional treaty in the entire world does so, apart from the ACP–EU Cotonou Convention. Even in the context of the United Nations, one can only refer to UN General Assembly Declarations,[4] the final documents of the world summits,[5] the Millennium Development Goals and reports of the UN Secretary-General, such as Boutros Boutros-Ghali's *Agenda for Development* (1995) and *Agenda for Democratization* (1996) and Kofi Annan's *Millennium* Report (2000) and *In Larger Freedom* (2005).

During the early years of the twenty-first century, intensive discussions focused on a more coherent and firm legal footing for the EU, resulting in the Constitutional Treaty signed in 2004.[6] Following referenda with negative results in France and the Netherlands, the EU member states decided to embark on the Lisbon Reform Treaty or the Treaty on the Functioning of the European Union (TFEU).[7] For purposes of this chapter it is important to note that the Draft Constitution effort to integrate development policy objectives into the general goals of EU policies was consolidated in the FEU Treaty. Thus, the Lisbon Treaty contains several new general and specific objectives of development cooperation. Table 8.2 lists the general development-related objectives that the EU pursues in its relations with the wider world (Article 3, TFEU).

Table 8.2 Renewing EU goals and objectives relevant to development policy in the Lisbon Treaty

peace and security
sustainable development of the earth
solidarity and mutual respect among peoples
free and fair trade
eradication of poverty
protection of human rights

These general goals of external action that the Union seeks to pursue in the wider world are based upon the following principles: democracy, the rule of law, the universality and indivisibility of human rights and fundamental freedoms, respect for human dignity, equality and solidarity, and respect for the principles of the United Nations Charter and international law. Moreover, the Union's mission is to promote multilateral solutions to common problems, in particular in the framework of the UN (Article 21, TFEU). Based on these principles, the Union pursues common policies and actions in order to:

- consolidate and support democracy, the rule of law, human rights and the principles of international law
- preserve peace, prevent conflicts and strengthen international security
- foster the sustainable economic, social and environmental development of developing countries, with the primary aim of eradicating poverty
- encourage the integration of all countries into the world economy, including through the progressive abolition of restrictions on international trade
- help develop measures to preserve and improve the quality of the environment and the sustainable management of global natural resources, in order to ensure sustainable development
- assist populations, countries and regions confronting natural or man-made disasters
- and promote an international system based on stronger multilateral cooperation and global good governance.

Examining the Lisbon Treaty of 2007 on development cooperation

With the principles and objectives of the EU, including those on development cooperation, spelled out in the general part, the specific section on development cooperation of the Treaty of FEU is short and consists of four articles only. The opening Article 208 of Section III of Part V of the FEU Treaty expresses the principle of 'complementarity', providing that Community development cooperation policy shall be complementary to the policies pursued by the member states. In Lisbon, the words 'and reinforce each other' have been added. This article indicates that development cooperation is still a shared competence between the Union and the member states. A literal interpretation of the wording in Article 208 of the FEU Treaty could argue that Community policy is subordinate to member states' policies. While this would be in line with the principle of subsidiarity as endorsed by Article 5 of the FEU Treaty, perhaps a more correct interpretation is that member states and the Union share competencies in this field which can be exercised alongside each other. This was also the finding of the European Court of Justice in the Case C-268/94 *Portuguese Republic v Council of the European Union* concerning the (admittedly somewhat specific) context of cooperation agreement between the EC and India.[8]

It is notable that only one of the series of objectives to be pursued through development cooperation, as listed in the above-mentioned Article 21, is singled out and specifically mentioned in Article 208, i.e. 'the reduction and, in the long term, the eradication of poverty'. This redundancy sends a clear political signal that the campaign against poverty features as the top priority of EU development cooperation. Article 208 also reflects the fundamental principle of coherence, stipulating that the Union 'shall take account of the objectives of development co-operation in the policies that it implements which are likely to affect developing countries'. This provision warrants two comments. First, the wording is rather weak and the soft nature of the coherence obligation is only partly compensated by the preceding mandatory word 'shall'. Second, comparing this Article 204 with Article 11 of the FEU Treaty on integration of environmental protection ('Environmental protection requirements must be integrated into [...]') leads to the conclusion that coherence of development policies is not of equal weight as integration of environmental protection, for two reasons. First, Article 11 is positioned in the opening part of the EU Treaty on Principles, and thus embraces all activities and policies of the Community; by contrast, Article 208 is placed in Part V, on external action of the Union. Second, the wording of the two articles differs significantly. Whereas Article 11 contains formulations such as 'requirements', 'must' and a reference to the nearly twenty fields of activities and policies of the Union, Article 208 uses the phrases 'take account', 'objectives' and 'likely to affect developing countries', thus leaving considerable discretion to the EU and its member states.

Article 208 of the Lisbon Treaty also stipulates that the Union and the member states comply with the commitments and take account of the objectives they have approved in the context of the UN and other competent international organisations. This may, for example, refer to the UN's Millennium Development Goals. This article also warrants further discussion. It could be understood as an additional coordination and coherence instruction. However, there are only a few areas where the Union and the member states share competencies in the sphere of international development cooperation in the context of the UN and its specialised agencies, including: international commodity agreements in the context of UNCTAD; multilateral environmental agreements concluded under UN auspices, such as the Climate Change Convention and the Kyoto Protocol; and the development-related policies of specialised agencies of which the EU itself is a member, such as the Food and Agriculture Organisation (FAO) of the UN and the World Trade Organization (WTO). However, in most areas of activities of the UN and its specialised agencies the EU has no formal powers and performs merely a coordinating role. This also applies to the IMF and the World Bank. Lastly, in terms of overall coherence it is rather striking that objectives 'approved in the context of the United Nations and other competent international organisations' are merely to be 'taken into account' by the Union and the member states (Article 208, para. 2).

Article 209 relates to the division of competences. It reminds members that it is the prerogative of the European Parliament and the Council of Ministers to adopt the budget for the multi-annual and thematic programmes for cooperation with developing countries. This may involve contributions from the European Investment Bank. Article 209 also provides that the EU may conclude agreements in the field of development cooperation with developing countries and competent international organisations, without prejudice to member states' own competence to negotiate in international bodies and to conclude agreements.

Lastly, next to the 'complementarity' and 'coherence' provisions of Article 208, there is also a separate 'co-ordination' article. Despite its mandatory wording, the duty to coordinate is cast in rather general terms in Article 210 of the FEU Treaty. Consultation is specifically required for aid programmes, including in international organisations and during international conferences. The term 'international organisations' should likely be interpreted to include UN organs such as UNDP, as well as specialised agencies such as the World Bank group.[9] 'International conferences' probably refers to pledging conferences. The final sentence of Article 210, paragraph 1, relates in fact more to the principle of complementarity than to that of coordination: 'Member States shall contribute if necessary to the implementation of Union aid programmes.' Lastly, Article 210 vests the Commission with a right of initiative to promote coordination. This is merely meant to emphasise and perhaps even expressly welcome such initiative, although it is somewhat odd that the adjective 'useful' has been added, thus suggesting that the Commission might sometimes also embark on non-useful initiatives in this field. On balance, this provision of Article 210, paragraph 2, is not wholly necessary. The final article of the section on development cooperation, Article 211, recalls that the Union and the member states shall cooperate with third countries and with the competent international organisations, within their respective spheres of influence.

In sum, the Maastricht and Lisbon treaties have in the end created a rather strong treaty basis for development cooperation policies. This is a very positive development. However, as discussed above, the articles are not always very clear and nor are they free from ambiguities. Furthermore, there is bound to be some overlap with the common foreign and security policy (CFSP), which is within the competence of the Council of Ministers and its High Representative for Foreign Affairs and Security rather than of the European Commission, which has the primary resposibility for the common development cooperation policy only. In practice, this may well give rise to duplication and controversy.

From Yaoundé through Lomé to Cotonou and beyond: special development cooperation arrangements

Yaoundé: a prototype for modern development cooperation?

An early response to the decolonisation process was the conclusion of the Yaoundé Agreement in 1963, between the EEC and eighteen independent African states, nearly all former associates. 'Wishing to demonstrate their common desire for co-operation on the basis of complete equality and friendly relations, observing the principles of the United Nations Charter' (Preamble), the 18 African and six EEC contracting parties concluded an agreement. Its contents were much more elaborate than Part IV of the Treaty of Rome, but still of a predominantly economic nature.[10] Its sections address: trade; financial and technical cooperation; the right of establishment, services, payments and capital; institutions of the association; and general and final provisions. Yaoundé was an interesting agreement in several respects. For example, it instructed the Community to take the interests of the associated states into consideration when drawing up its common agricultural policy, and required consultation for this purpose (Article 11). This could well be viewed as an early example of a coherence article. Low-key coordination can be identified in the provisions concerning commercial policy, where the parties agreed to keep each other informed and to consult upon request by one party. In 1969 a similar Yaoundé II Agreement was concluded with an expanded number (now twenty-seven) of Francophone African countries, while in 1968 the Arusha Convention also came into being with the three Anglophone member states of the then East African Community, namely Kenya, Tanzania and Uganda.

The Lomé era

In 1975, the nine member states of the enlarged EEC and as many as forty-six developing states in the ACP concluded the first Lomé Convention which replaced both the Yaoundé Convention and the Arusha Convention. The Lomé Convention differed considerably from the previous association-type conventions and reflected new trends in international development cooperation, such as the non-reciprocity principle incorporated in Part IV of the GATT and the UNCTAD–GATT scheme for a Generalised System of Trade Preferences (GSP). This GSP enabled the EC to grant developing countries access to its common market at reduced tariff rates on a non-reciprocal basis. Furthermore, the Lomé Convention introduced a system for the Stabilisation of Export Earnings (STABEX), which guaranteed ACP states a certain level of income from the production and export of originally twelve (mainly agricultural) primary commodities, by protecting them from severe price fluctuations and interruptions in production due to natural disasters and the like. The Lomé Convention included further preferential treatment for certain sub-categories of ACP states, including those which were the least developed, or so situated as to be landlocked or islands. The Convention also stressed the need to strengthen the economies of ACP states through diversification of their economies, by means of industrialisation, the strengthening of economic and social infrastructures, rural development and (inter)regional cooperation with other ACP states.

There can be little doubt that the 1975 Lomé Convention was the product of a particular period in the 1970s during which developing countries, associated in the Group of 77, campaigned for a New International Economic Order (NIEO). The NIEO debate was one of the most important political issues at the time. Europe and the West in general were confronted with high inflation, rising unemployment and international monetary instability. The oil crisis, due in part to the assertive cartel policy of the Organization of Petroleum Exporting Countries (OPEC), the Yom Kippur War and the publication of the Club of Rome's report *Limits to Growth*,[11] highlighted the need for consultations at an international level and the coordination of policies. The NIEO resolutions as adopted by the UN General Assembly in 1974 addressed a wide variety of structural issues, including commodity prices, industrialisation, preferential treatment in trade, debt rescheduling and the participation of developing countries in international economic consultation and decision-making.[12] In certain respects, these resolutions amounted to a new call for coordinated and coherent international development policies. The Lomé Convention was a unique and elaborate response to that. Its uniqueness lies especially in three features: its form, i.e., a binding treaty; its comprehensive scope; and the financial commitments made by the EU to the ACP states.

Successive Lomé conventions were adapted to changed circumstances and each renewal incorporated new elements. The last Lomé Convention, Lomé IV *bis* (B) as concluded in Mauritius on 4 November 1995, consisted of as many as 370 articles and ten protocols and addressed twelve main areas of ACP–EC cooperation, ranging from environment through industrial and enterprise development to cultural and social cooperation.[13]

Cotonou, the new ACP–EU Partnership Agreement for 2000–20

The next main development in the evolution of EU law and policy on development cooperation was the conclusion of the new ACP–EU Partnership Agreement, signed on 23 June 2000 in Cotonou, Benin.[14] It is the successor to the Lomé IV *bis* Convention. In a number of respects the new agreement represents a significant change, as compared with the previous Lomé conventions (Arts 2003). The objectives of the Cotonou Agreement are formulated more specifically and in more detail than in the Lomé conventions. The most important innovation compared to the Lomé conventions is the explicit central objective of the ACP–EC Partnership: 'reducing and eventually eradicating poverty consistent with the objectives of sustainable development and the gradual integration of the ACP countries into the world economy' (Article 1). This is fully in line with what was Article 177 of the Maastricht Treaty, and what is now Article 21 of the FEU Treaty. As a part of this strategy, the EU seeks to foster regional cooperation among ACP countries, both intra- and interregional cooperation, which may also involve non-ACP developing countries. In addition, development of the ACP states shall be pursued 'with a view to contributing to peace and security and to promoting a stable and democratic political environment'.[15] This clause postdated the 1992 Treaty of Maastricht. Its insertion reflects an increased awareness during the 1990s of the close relationship between development and peace. A further major change is the second fundamental principle spelled out in Article 2 of the Cotonou Agreement, specifically that of public participation. This includes opening up the partnership to non-central government actors, such as civil society organisations.

In addition to the pre-existing 'essential elements' of ACP–EC cooperation, i.e., 'respect for human rights, democratic principles and the rule of law'[16] (see Arts 2000), the Cotonou Convention introduces a new legal category of important principles underlying the partnership. It is the so-called 'fundamental element' of good governance, defined as 'the transparent and accountable management of human, natural, economic and financial resources for the purposes of equitable and sustainable development' (Article 9, para. 3). Good governance here entails clear decision-making procedures at the level of public authorities, transparent and accountable institutions, the primacy of law in the management and distribution of resources, and capacity-building for elaborating and implementing measures aimed in particular at preventing and combating corruption. Serious cases of corruption, including acts of bribery leading to corruption, may give rise to 'appropriate measures' such as punitive actions, which may – depending on the seriousness of the situation – amount to partial or full suspension of the Partnership Agreement.[17] In Cotonou, stronger than in the Lomé conventions, political conditionality has now entered into the ACP–EU partnership in the areas of democracy, human rights, rule of law and good governance.

Besides its strong focus on poverty alleviation, its emphasis on participation of non-state actors and the increased scope of political conditionality, the major new contribution of the Cotonou Agreement is its identification of cross-cutting issues – gender, environmental protection, the sustainable utilisation and management of natural resources, and institutional development and capacity-building – for all development cooperation strategies elaborated within the ACP–EU Partnership Agreement.[18] Yet the modes of implementing these articles remain alarmingly vague.

As envisaged, the Cotonou Partnership Agreement was submitted to a review after five years. This review resulted in various amendments in 2005 and a new financial protocol; new provisions were added in the areas of political dialogue, transparency, increased social responsibility and security. The new provisions on security again reflect an increased awareness of the linkage between development and peace and security, building on commonsense notions such as 'no peace without development' and 'no development without peace'. The new provisions added to Article 11 – dealing with peace-building policies and with conflict prevention and resolution – relate to the prevention of mercenary activities, child soldiers, military expenditure, the arms trade and anti-personnel mines. Furthermore, parties are called upon to ratify and implement the Rome Statute of the International Criminal Court and to actively combat terrorism, including 'to prevent terrorism from growing in fertile environments'. Lastly, the parties agree to cooperate in countering the proliferation of weapons of mass destruction (Hadfield 2007).

Beyond Cotonou: increased cooperation with non-ACP states and erosion of the Lomé/Cotonou acquis

From the 1980s onwards, the EU sought to expand its development cooperation policy more explicitly to Latin America and Asia. Many Latin American countries had managed to shake off the yoke of dictatorial regimes. In addition, the accession of Spain and Portugal to the EU in 1986 provided a strong impetus for establishing closer relationships with Latin America. Among other forms of cooperation, this led to the special relationship between the EU and the trade area of Argentina, Brazil, Paraguay and Uruguay (MERCOSUR), established in 1995. Similarly, the EU reached out to Asia and established cooperation with China as well as the Association of South East Asian Nations (ASEAN). Furthermore, it engaged in an institutionalised dialogue with nearly all Asian countries in the Asia–Europe Meeting (ASEM).

Table 8.3 ACP–EU Development Cooperation Agreements

Yaoundé Treaty I and II (1963–74)
Arusha Treaty (1968–74)
Lomé Convention I – IV *bis* (1975–2000)
Cotonou Partnership Agreement (2000–20)

Meanwhile, in response to the establishment of the WTO in 1995, severe criticism of other industrial countries such as the USA and Japan as well as non-ACP developing countries such as India and a highly critical evaluation by the EU itself of the effectiveness of the Lomé trade preferences (European Commission 1997), the EU decided to gradually dismantle the special preferential and non-reciprocal treatment in international trade for all ACP countries as a whole. It was decided that new Economic Partnership Agreements (EPAs) were to be concluded with specific regions, to be in place by 1 January 2008.[19] For the least developed countries, many of which (forty-four out of a total of fifty) belong to the ACP group, a special Everything But Arms initiative (EBA) was put into place to provide this particular category of countries with duty-free access for all exports into the EU except arms and ammunition (temporary exceptions were also added for fresh bananas, rice and sugar). The negotiation and conclusion of various EPAs has given rise to bitter feelings among many ACP countries as regards their special relationship with the EU.[20] It may well be that the advent of EPAs marks the erosion not only of the traditional position of the ACP countries as preferred partners but also of the special ACP–EU bond, if not of the existence of the ACP group as such.

Opportunities and challenges in EU international development cooperation

It is common knowledge that the integration process of the EU, its common development policy and its foreign and security policy are all still facing considerable difficulties. Many member states, not least the three largest among them and some of the new members, are simply unwilling to allocate more competence and power to central EU organs. Furthermore, the expansion of the EU has complicated the attainment of a clear profile in the Union's foreign, security and development policy. This cannot but reflect negatively on the world's perception of the content and status of EU common development cooperation policy.

At the same time, the EU is a powerful player in the world economy. No other economic entity has so large a gross domestic product (GDP). Furthermore, it is the largest exporter and the second largest importer (behind the USA) of goods and the largest exporter and importer of services.[21] The EU and its member states collectively are also the largest donor of development assistance. As a major player in world economic relations and a large donor, the EU is in a prominent position to play a leading role in international development cooperation and humanitarian assistance. However, in taking up such a role the EU faces a number of important challenges, which have to be addressed. These are considered below.

The myriad of competences, organs, funds and programmes in European development cooperation

Development cooperation is a shared competence between the member states and the EU. The development policy of most member states has a particular background and profile and there appears to be little inclination to fully 'communitarise' it. Furthermore, in the sector of development cooperation a host of institutions, organs, funds and programmes operate within the general institutional framework of the EU itself. Various EU Commissioners have principal competences in this field, including those responsible for Development; International Trade; Expansion of the EU (the Balkans and Turkey); and External Relations. The fragmented nature of Commissioners' competences is reflected in the Commission's bureaucratic structure, with Directorates General (DG) each for Development (DEV); External Relations (RELEX); Humanitarian Aid (ECHO); the new Europe Aid Cooperation Office (EuropeAid); Expansion (the Balkans and Turkey); International Trade; and Economic and Financial Affairs, including macro-financial assistance to Balkan countries and newly independent states.

Development financing and humanitarian assistance takes place through ten financial instruments, most notably the European Development Fund, the Development Cooperation Instrument and other instruments in the fields of humanitarian assistance, neighbourhood and partnership policy, democracy and human rights, stability in peace and security, and pre-accession.

Multilateral and bilateral development assistance: complementary?

The EU conducts a very extensive development assistance programme and is the only donor agency in the world that operates in as many as 145 countries, with delegations in approximately 125 countries.[22] The total Community aid budget in 2006 amounted to 12.1 billion euros, including 9.8 billion euros as official development assistance (ODA), according to the grant criteria of the OECD.[23] Together with bilateral assistance, the EU contribution in 2006 amounted to nearly 50 billion euros, representing 57 per cent of the total ODA flows. In view of recent commitments in the context of the Monterrey Consensus on development financing (2002) and endorsements in the 2005 European Consensus on Development, this contribution is scheduled to increase to 79 billion euros in 2010 and 116 billion euros in 2015. Apart from the development assistance provided by the EU, most member states are determined to continue their individual development assistance programmes, with a notable increase scheduled by the new member states (from an average 0.1 per cent of gross national income now to 0.33 per cent in 2015).

Performance: is European aid spent effectively?

For a long time, development assistance spent through EU channels has been considered far from effective and has often been the subject of severe criticism. One response to this criticism was the establishment of the EuropeAid Cooperation

Office, now charged with the implementation of the EU's aid policy. Another was the adoption of the EU Code of Conduct on Complementarity and Division of Labour in Development Policy, in 2007. It must be noted that in the 2007 DAC Peer Review of European Aid considerable progress was recorded (OECD 2007). Furthermore, increasing cooperation among the EU states and the integration of policies requires greater common efforts. In addition, the EU cooperates increasingly with non-governmental organisations, both in Europe and in the developing world. This facilitates policy dialogue, renewed outreach to the poor and implementation of projects and programmes.

The traditional focus on ACP states

As a result of the former colonial relationships and the subsequent Lomé/Cotonou Conventions, for a long time development cooperation has been principally directed to the ACP states, now numbering seventy-eight. In recent years, the EU has begun globalising its development policies but the average aid received per capita in ACP states is still considerably higher than in Latin America and Asia. Nevertheless, development cooperation is increasingly embedded in wider forms of international cooperation, for example in bilateral agreements between the EU and China or India and in interregional agreements with MERCOSUR and ASEAN.[24]

More than aid and trade: increased conditionality on all scores

Assisting developing countries and with development as such is now widely viewed as a complex, multifaceted process. With this understanding, development cooperation nowadays touches on many fields of policy, ranging from classical aid and trade issues through human rights and environmental policies to good governance, migration, combating international terrorism, and peace and security policies. This expanding scope of development policies has also resulted in a proliferation of conditions which are all too often at odds with traditional notions such as respect for sovereignty, self-determination and partnership. Furthermore, for the EU, traditional sovereignty has often proved to be in sharp contrast with, if not contradictory to, the proclaimed goals – such as transparency, accountability and good governance. The question arises whether EU development assistance policy is too readily attuned to the conditionality inherent in the structural adjustment policies of the World Bank and IMF and therefore also the Washington Consensus. These policies often link loans and access to international credits to establishing a policy more friendly to the private sector and to cuts in government expenditure, including that on education and food subsidies. In principle, the EU could well, and therefore should, have a distinctly individual development policy with a human face, given both its own long-standing experience and record in development cooperation and the potentially integrated nature of its policies in the field of international trade, agriculture, peace and security, environmental conservation and development cooperation.

The coherence of EU development cooperation policy

Despite this potential for integration, development policy often still operates in isolation from other policies which affect developing countries and the development processes of their people. The common agricultural policy, the EU fisheries policy, the external trade policy as well as the transportation, energy and migration policies all have a significant bearing on development policy and development cooperation. Yet, at the level of the EU and other international institutions, these policies are more often than not framed separately, and are insufficiently or not at all coordinated, let alone coherent and integrated. True coherence would require both a more prominent place for development cooperation than the one detailed in the Lisbon Reform Treaty, and enhanced status for the relevant Commissioners. However, political will and ambition for such enhancements currently appear to be lacking.

Conclusion

With fifty years of experience as well as an elaborate set of values, principles and objectives, and a host of instruments, the EU is uniquely placed to serve as a key global actor in international development cooperation. Poverty eradication has evolved as the primary objective of development cooperation, accompanied by objectives such as sustainable development, the integration of developing countries into the world economy, promoting respect for human rights, democracy and the rule of law, and peace and security. It is now widely realised that development is a multi-dimensional process, involving economic, human, political and social-cultural factors. The Lisbon Reform Treaty, the ACP–EU Cotonou Partnership Agreement and the European Consensus on Development all reflect and contribute to this realisation. As discussed above, the EU faces considerable challenges in formulating and implementing an effective and coherent development policy. At the same time, opportunities abound. It is to be hoped that the EU continues to seize these opportunities, reinforced by the efforts of individual member states and civil society.

Notes

1 See the Preamble and Article 3 (k) of the EEC Treaty of Rome.
2 Further on this, see J. Ravenhill (1985), *Collective Clientelism: The Lomé Convention and North–South Relations*, New York: Columbia University Press.
3 Section XVII on Development Co-operation in the 1992 Maastricht Treaty, later Section XX and currently Section III of Part V of FEU Treaty of Lisbon, 2007.
4 For example, the Declaration on International Economic Co-operation, in particular the Revitalization of Economic Growth and Development of the Developing Countries, UN Doc. A/RES/45/99, 21 December 1990; the Millennium Declaration, UN Doc. A/RES/55/2, 8 September 2000; and the World Summit Outcome, UN Doc. A/RES/60/1, 24 October 2005.
5 These include the Children Summit (1990), the Earth Summit (1992), the World Conference on Human Rights (1993), the Population and Development Conference (1994), the Beijing Conference on Women (1995), the Social Summit (1995), the

Millennium Summit (2000), the Monterrey UN Conference on Financing for Development (2002), the World Summit on Sustainable Development (2002) and the World Reform Summit (2005).

6 Treaty Establishing a Constitution for Europe (Constitutional Treaty), Rome, 29 October 2004, not in force; 2004 O.J. (C 310) 1.

7 Treaty of Lisbon amending the Treaty on European Union and the Treaty establishing the European Community, Lisbon, 13 December 2007, not yet in force; CIG 14/07 (3 December 2007); 2007 OJ (C 306) 1. See, for an analysis of the debate and reform efforts relating to the Draft Constitution and the final Lisbon Reform Treaty, Chapter 6 by Marianne Dony, in this volume.

8 ECJ Judgment of 3 December 1996, Case C-268/94. The Court concluded that it is apparent from Section XVII (now Part Five, Section III) that:
    'on the one hand, the Community has specific competence to conclude agreements with non-member countries in the sphere of development co-operation and, on the other hand, that competence is not exclusive but complementary between the Community's development co-operation policy and the policies of the member states.'

9 This raises the question whether it is synonymous to the phrase 'United Nations and other competent international organizations' in Articles 208 and 209.

10 Text in *Official Journal of the European Communities*, 11 June 1964, 1431/64.

11 D. H. Meadows, *et al.* (1972), *The Limits to Growth: A Report for the Club of Rome's Project on the Predicament of Mankind*, New York: Universe Books.

12 See, among many publications, R. F. Meagher (1979), *An International Redistribution of Wealth and Power: A Study of the Charter of Economic Rights and Duties of States*, New York: Pergamon.

13 On Lomé IV *bis* (B) see K. Arts and J. Byron (1997), 'The mid-term review of the Lomé IV Convention: heralding the future?', *Third World Quarterly* 18 (1997), No. 1, 73–91.

14 For its complete text, see the Special Issue of *The Courier*, September 2000. Also available through http://Europa.eu.int/comm/development/Cotonou

15 See also Article 11 on Peace-building policies, conflict prevention and resolution.

16 Articles 2 and 9(2) of Lomé IV B. On the human rights-related provisions and concrete supportive and punitive human rights policies within the Lomé framework during the period 1975–99.

17 Articles 9(3) and 97 of the Cotonou Partnership Agreement.

18 Ibid., Articles 31–3.

19 See Article 37 of the Cotonou Convention.

20 K. Arts (2009), 'A human rights-based approach to the ACP–EU Economic Partnership Agreements: issues and implications', in G. Faber and J. Orbie (eds), *Beyond Market Access for Economic Development: EU–Africa Relations in Transition*, London/New York: Routledge; G. Thallinger (2007), 'From apology to utopia: EU–ACP Economic Partnership Agreements oscillating between WTO conformity and sustainability', in *European Foreign Affairs Review* 12: 499–516.

21 A. Sapir (2007), 'Europe and the global economy', in A. Sapir (ed.), *Fragmented Power: Europe and the Global Economy*, Brussels: Brueghel Books, 1.

22 See European Commission (2004), *EU Donor Atlas Mapping*, Official Development Assistance, Brussels.

23 Official Development Assistance (ODA) means grants or loans to developing countries which are: (a) undertaken by the official sector; (b) with promotion of economic

development and welfare as the main objective; (c) at concessional financial terms. In addition to financial flows, technical cooperation is included in aid. Grants, loans and credits for military purposes are excluded. See www.oecd.org/glossary
24 See Chapter 13 by Santander and Ponjaert in this volume.

Bibliography

Arts, Karin (2000), *Integrating Human Rights into Development Co-operation: The Case of the Lomé Convention*, The Hague: Martinus Nijhoff.

Arts, Karin (2003), 'ACP–EU relations in a new era: the Cotonou Agreement', in *Common Market Law Review* 40: 95–116.

Arts, Karin and Anna K. Dickson (eds) (2004), *EU Development Cooperation: From Model to Symbol*, Manchester: Manchester University Press.

Babarinde, Olufemi and Gerrit Faber (eds) (2005), *The European Union and the Developing Countries: the Cotonou Agreement*, Leiden: Nijhoff.

Dutch Advisory Council International Affairs (2008), *The Netherlands and the European Development Cooperation*, The Hague: Ministry of Foreign Affairs, Report No. 60 (also available at www.aiv-advice.nl).

Frish, Dieter (2008), *The EU's Development Policy. A Personal View of 50 Years of International Cooperation*, Brussels: ECDPM.

European Commission, Council of Ministers and European Parliament (2006); 'European Consensus on Development', *Official Journal of the European Union*, C 46/1-C 46/19.

European Commission (1997), 'Green Paper on relations between the European Union and the ACP countries on the eve of the 21st century: challenges and options for a new partnership', Brussels: European Communities.

Grilli, Enzo R. (1993), *The European Community and the Developing Countries*, Cambridge: Cambridge University Press.

Hadfield, Amelia (2007), 'Janus advances? An analysis of EC development policy and the 2005 Amended Cotonou Partnership Agreements', *European Foreign Affairs Review* 12: 39–66.

Lister, Marjorie (1997), *The European Union and the South*, London: Routledge.

McMahon, Joe A. (1998), *The Development Co-operation Policy of the EC*, London and The Hague: Kluwer Law International.

Mold, Andrew (ed.) (2007), *EU Development Policy in a Changing World. Challenges for the 21st Century*, Amsterdam: Amsterdam University Press.

OECD, Development Assistance Committee (2007), *DAC Peer Review European Community*, OECD: Paris.

9 The role of the EU in global environmental and climate governance

Sebastian Oberthür[1]

Summary

Global environmental problems have taken centre stage in European and international politics. Since the second half of the 1980s, the EU has assumed a clear leadership role in international environmental and climate governance and has, over the years, considerably improved its leadership record and its recognition as a global actor. The Union has enhanced the organisation and coordination of its foreign environmental policy, which has contributed to greater EU unity and enhanced capacity for outreach to other parties. Progress in the development and implementation of internal climate and energy policies helped to reduce the credibility gap between international positions and domestic action of the EU. However, a number of challenges remain. Internally, far-reaching legislative proposals presented by the European Commission in 2007 and 2008 need to be enacted and further measures are required to improve policy coherence across policy domains. Externally, an enhanced coordination of EU environmental diplomacy holds significant promise. Also, the EU needs to adapt to a changing and expanding international environmental and climate agenda, and preserving a still precarious EU unity constitutes a constant challenge. Finally, the impacts of EU enlargement pose a particular challenge. Despite these challenges, the EU can be expected to remain a progressive force in global environmental governance for some time, given recent overall political developments (energy security, high political salience) and the advances of its domestic climate and energy policies.

Introduction

Global environmental problems have taken centre stage in European and international politics since the beginning of the twenty-first century. Worldwide, climate change is seen as one of the most serious challenges to international security and the well-being of humankind. At the European level, EU action on environmental protection and 'global warming' enjoys high popular support and increasingly provides a major new rationale for advancing European integration. Under these circumstances, it is not surprising that the EU has established itself as the primary international leader in international environmental politics.

   This chapter reviews the phenomenon of EU leadership in global environmental politics and the factors that underpin this leadership, with a particular focus on climate change. It also provides a more detailed account of EU leadership in this policy field. The subsequent discussion focuses on the achievements of the EU with respect, first, to the specific organisation of EU foreign environmental policy and, second, to the implementation of internal EU policies as a basis of the EU's international credibility. Next, several challenges to EU leadership in global environmental and climate governance are explored. Finally, a number of strategic motivations are identified that have come to support and shape EU leadership in global environmental and climate governance.

EU leadership in global environmental and climate governance

Global environmental and climate governance

Environmental governance has matured as a field of global policy since the second half of the 1980s. While the first global UN Conference on the Human Environment was held in Stockholm as early as 1972 and led to the creation of the UN Environment Programme (UNEP), it is since 1985 that ten major global environmental agreements have been concluded (Table 9.1). In addition to the regular conferences of the contracting states to these agreements, a number of extraordinary global conferences have provided focal points for political attention to global environmental problems. Most importantly, the UN Conference on Environment and Development held in Rio de Janeiro in 1992 was heralded as the 'Earth Summit', and followed ten years later by the Johannesburg World Summit for Sustainable Development. Furthermore, the Global Environment Facility (GEF) was established in 1991 as a separate international financial institution to provide funding for combating global environmental problems. In summary, an elaborate infrastructure for the further development and implementation of global environmental policy exists today.

Table 9.1 Major global environmental agreements

1973	Convention on International Trade in Endangered Species of Wild Fauna and Flora (CITES)
1985–87	Vienna Convention for the Protection of the Ozone Layer, and Montreal Protocol on Substances That Deplete the Ozone Layer
1989	Basel Convention on the Control of Transboundary Movements of Hazardous Wastes and Their Disposal
1992	UN Framework Convention on Climate Change (UNFCCC) Convention on Biological Diversity (CBD)
1994	UN Convention to Combat Desertification (UNCCD)
1997	Kyoto Protocol to the UNFCCC
1998	Rotterdam Convention on the Prior Informed Consent Procedure for Certain Hazardous Chemicals and Pesticides in International Trade
2000	Cartagena Protocol on Biosafety to the Convention on Biological Diversity
2001	Stockholm Convention on Persistent Organic Pollutants (POPs)

Climate change constitutes the most prominent and urgent global environmental problem. As elaborated in the fourth assessment report of the Intergovernmental Panel on Climate Change (IPCC) in 2007, the impacts of unabated climate change – including, among other things, rising sea levels, changing precipitation patterns and more frequent extreme weather events – represent a major threat to human and societal development and security.[2] In order to enable the manageable adaptation of societies and ecosystems, major reductions of greenhouse gas (GHG) emissions are required. Based on the best available scientific advice, the EU has set a target of limiting the increase of the global average temperature to below 2 degrees Celsius compared with the pre-industrial level. As agreed by the Council of Environment Ministers in 2007, meeting this objective will require worldwide reductions of GHG emissions of 'up to 50 per cent by 2050 compared to 1990'. Industrialised countries would consequently have to reduce their emissions by 60–80 per cent by 2050. Even with such emission reductions, ongoing climate change and the adaptation to its impacts will constitute a major political challenge, in particular in developing countries.

Against this background, climate change has become an issue of 'high politics'. The 1992 UN Framework Convention on Climate Change (UNFCCC) and its 1997 Kyoto Protocol, as further elaborated in the so-called Marrakech Accords of 2001, provide the major forum for international cooperation. At the annual conferences of parties to the UNFCCC and the Kyoto Protocol there has been increasing involvement of the highest political levels, with the UN Secretary-General addressing the conferences in both 2006 and 2007. In general, political leaders around the globe have increasingly become involved in addressing the daunting challenge of climate change. In this respect, 2007 saw a new record of high-level political engagement. Climate change became a top priority at the G8 Summit in June 2007, and both the UN Security Council and the UN General Assembly placed it high on their agendas. Overall, there is hardly any high-level political encounter anymore where the issue is not discussed.

EU leadership on climate change and the environment

Understood as a targeted and consistent effort to direct other actors towards a collective goal, international leadership has at least two fundamental requirements. First, an actor with leadership aspirations needs to have the capacity to exert significant influence on other actors. Second, the leading actor has to have more progressive positions with regard to the collective goal than those of the followers, rendering leadership a relative concept. For leadership to be characterised as *effective*, finally, a third requirement needs to be met. The leader has to be successful in mobilising available resources (power, legitimacy/credibility, knowledge and skills) to achieve outcomes that help to reach the collective goal.[3]

As global environmental problems climbed the political agenda, the EU has emerged as the major leader in global environmental governance. Given its general weight in international affairs, the EU does have the capacity to exert significant influence on other actors. As regards international positions, the EU took over the lead from the USA during the second half of the 1980s. First, the EU became the frontrunner in negotiations under the Montreal Protocol for the protection of the ozone layer, which the USA had led initially (Oberthür 1999). It then was the major driving force behind the Rio Earth Summit in 1992 and constantly pushed for the most stringent environmental measures in relevant negotiations. In the first decade of the twenty-first century, the EU also became a major supporter for the upgrading of the UN Environment Programme to a UN Environment *Organisation* with more resources and a stronger mandate (Falkner 2007; Vogler and Stephan 2007; Bretherton and Vogler 2006).

Since the negotiations on the Climate Change Convention began in 1991, the EU has also been the prime international leader in the paradigmatic area of climate change policy. Even as early as the Convention negotiations, the EU (unsuccessfully) supported legally binding emission reduction targets for industrialised countries. In the negotiations on the Kyoto Protocol of 1997, the EU proposed the deepest emission cuts and accepted the highest reduction target among the major industrialised countries (minus 8 per cent). The EU has also championed calls for ensuring the 'environmental integrity' of the Protocol by demanding priority for domestic action and limits on the use of forests and other carbon sinks. Furthermore, the EU was instrumental in saving the Kyoto Protocol, after US President Bush expressed opposition against it in 2001, and the Union was also the major driver behind the Protocol's entry into force (Damro 2006; Bretherton and Vogler 2006; Groenleer and van Schaik 2007). Finally, based on the European Council's 'independent commitment' of March 2007 to reduce the GHG emissions of the EU by 20 per cent from the 1990 level by 2020 (see below), the EU was a major driving force behind the launch of negotiations on a global post-2012 climate agreement that was concluded by the parties to the UNFCCC at Bali in December 2007.[4]

EU leadership in global environmental and climate governance has grown more effective in recent years. Despite the EU's leadership efforts, its actual impact on the UNFCCC and the Kyoto Protocol, for example, was rather limited. It appears, in fact, that the overall design of the Kyoto Protocol was heavily influenced by the USA. The achievements of EU leadership have been more impressive in the twenty-first century, when the Union played a vital role in securing agreement on the Cartagena Biosafety Protocol to the Convention on Biological Diversity in 2000, and was instrumental in ensuring the entry into force of the Kyoto Protocol (Falkner 2007; Damro 2006).

Despite these improvements, EU leadership in global environmental and climate governance has fallen short of ensuring the collective goal of environmental sustainability. Several assessments have provided ample evidence that the challenge of global environmental change has by no means diminished.[5] As regards climate change, for example, the Kyoto Protocol has so far only succeeded in slowing down the growth of global GHG emissions. Compared with the requirement to achieve a cut of worldwide GHG emissions of at least 50 per cent by 2050, this achievement can only be considered a first step.

Overall, the EU has to a large extent relied on 'soft' power resources for pursuing its international leadership on climate change and other environmental issues. In addition to relying on its general political and economic weight, the EU has primarily exerted 'directional leadership', which is based on the non-confrontational means of diplomacy, persuasion and argumentation; leadership by example; and the creation of new incentives for other parties. On the one hand, this leadership approach correlates well with the notion of the EU as a civilian power in pursuit of a rule-based global governance. On the other hand, the position of the EU as one non-hegemonic pole in the international system among others constrains its capabilities. The EU neither has the military capabilities nor the economic clout to force others to fight climate change and other environmental problems. Also, its power position in global environmental politics remains limited. The EU share in global GHG emissions is only around 15 per cent. The soft leadership strategy of the EU may thus be as much a matter of necessity as of preference/choice.

Under these circumstances, two factors deserve particular attention in the attempt to account for the phenomenon of EU leadership in global environmental and climate governance. First, the ability of the EU to act as a unitary actor at the international level will be of central importance for its capacity to engage in directional leadership (persuasion, diplomacy, etc.). Second, the credibility of the EU as an international leader will crucially depend on the development of its own domestic measures ('leadership by example'). These two aspects are addressed in turn in the following sections.

Becoming an international actor: the organisation of EU foreign environmental policy

Since the second half of the 1980s, the EU has made significant progress in establishing itself as an actor in global environmental politics. Despite long-lasting scepticism and even opposition, especially from the USA, the EU has been recognised as an international actor in the field. As a sign of formal recognition, the European Community (EC) has become a member of most multilateral environmental agreements mentioned above (Table 9.1). In addition, the EU has *de facto* been accepted as an actor in its own right even within institutions in which it does not enjoy formal membership (such as the UN Commission on Sustainable Development, UNEP, CITES and others).

Beyond formal or informal recognition, the internal coherence of the EU constitutes a particular challenge due to the EU's nature as a multiple actor. As a general rule, EU foreign environmental policy falls within the 'mixed competence' of both the EU/EC and its member states. Consequently, both the EC (represented by the European Commission) and the member states are usually represented in international environmental negotiations. There is therefore an evident need for close coordination between the EC and the member states to ensure they speak with one voice (Delreux 2006).

In response to this challenge, a flexible system of coordination and representation of the EU in global environmental governance has been established. Working groups of the Council in Brussels prepare for international negotiations and agree on negotiating positions that are then usually reflected in Council conclusions. On this basis, the delegations of the member states and the European Commission coordinate their strategy at international negotiations. Except for matters within the exclusive competence of the EC (e.g., international trade aspects), the current EU Presidency usually represents the EU flanked by the European Commission and the incoming Presidency (together forming the so-called 'EU troika').[6]

The flexible adaptation of this system of EU coordination and representation has enabled the EU to respond to changing needs and to enhance its effectiveness. In response to the expanding negotiating agenda in international climate policy, for example, the EU has diversified the system of expert groups supporting the Council working group and has delegated more authority for the development of negotiating positions to them. Furthermore, to enhance the efficient use of expertise existing within the EU and to provide for greater continuity and coherence in negotiations, lead negotiators from various member states and the Commission are assigned to represent the EU in various negotiating groups over longer periods of time (on behalf of the EU Presidency). These negotiators also take a lead in developing the EU position in cooperation with selected 'issue leaders'.

This system of EU coordination and representation has delivered important achievements. First, it has allowed the EU to achieve a remarkable degree of coherence as an actor in international environmental and climate policy. EU member states seem to have learnt from past experiences of political in-fighting that have, at times, undermined the EU's international position (Groenleer and van Schaik 2007). Internal coherence has also benefited from the elaboration of the *acquis communautaire* (fundamental principles of the Community) regarding the environment, especially following the *Single European Act* of 1987. The development of EU legislation has repeatedly been found to support EU environmental leadership (Oberthür 1999; Falkner 2007). By focusing preparatory work on establishing robust general EU positions and delegating negotiating authority to lead negotiators and the Presidency, the EU has also been able to streamline EU coordination to help gain capacity for outreach to other countries at international negotiations. Finally, internal EU discussions have served as a laboratory of and effective preparation for broader international debates. They have also served to 'Europeanise' participants.

Nevertheless, EU actorness in international environmental politics still faces significant limitations. To start with, coordination within the EU, even if streamlined, takes significant time and effort, which limits the capacities of the EU for outreach. Under these circumstances, constraints on the full mobilisation of the EU's diplomatic potential in support of EU leadership on environmental matters weigh particularly heavily. Furthermore, the differentiating system of EU expert groups is particularly taxing on smaller member states with limited resources, which threatens to weaken the integrative force that has traditionally emanated from internal EU discussions. Finally, internal EU coherence remains fragile especially with respect to several areas of energy policy (see also later in this chapter).

Addressing the credibility gap: the progress of EU domestic climate policy

Domestic EU environmental policy has twofold significance for the EU's international leadership aspirations. First, it supports EU coherence and unity by establishing an effective least common denominator for the EU's foreign environmental policies. Second, it affects the international credibility of the EU, which is central to the EU's 'soft' leadership aspirations ('leadership by example').

The following discussion of the evolution of EU climate and energy policy over three phases suggests that the EU may be on its way towards closing the credibility gap that has hampered its international leadership aspirations. The gap between promises at the international level and domestic implementation has long been the Achilles' heel of EU leadership in international environmental policy in general and international climate policy in particular (Sbragia 2002; Grubb and Gupta 2000). Since the 1990s, however, the EU has made significant progress in developing domestic climate and energy policies and may experience a similar learning curve in this policy area, as it did earlier with respect to the protection of the ozone layer (Oberthür 1999).

Rhetorical leadership (1990s)

In the 1990s, a considerable credibility gap between international EU leadership aspirations and domestic EU climate policies existed. EU discussions focused on the introduction of a combined European CO_2/energy tax. The related proposal of the European Commission, however, failed to receive sufficient support from the EU-12 (until 1995) and then EU-15 member states. In addition, voluntary agreements with European, Korean and Japanese car manufacturers regarding reduced CO_2 emissions from cars were concluded in 1998 and 1999, but failed to deliver the agreed emission cuts. A limited number of other measures with a positive effect on GHG emissions were in most cases motivated by other considerations. Most important among these measures was the Landfill Directive (Directive 1999/31/EC) that requires recovery of methane from biodegradable waste in landfills (Table 9.2).

GHG emissions and projections confirm that there was insufficient progress in the implementation of EU climate policies in the 1990s. That GHG emissions in the EU-15 decreased slightly in the 1990s was largely the result of political developments in certain member states in the early 1990s that were unrelated to climate change (the dash from coal to gas in the UK and German reunification). Consequently, progress in reducing emissions stagnated, and emissions even increased slightly after 1994. More importantly, projections at the turn of the century showed that with existing measures only, GHG emissions in the EU would increase to 1 per cent above base year levels (1990) by 2010.[7]

Initiating climate policies (2000–06)

The development of EU climate and energy policy gained momentum in the aftermath of the adoption of the Kyoto Protocol in 1997 and the Marrakech Accords in 2001. In 2000, the European Commission launched the European Climate Change Programme (ECCP) that serves to elaborate and prepare additional climate policies and measures. While a comprehensive overview and assessment of existing EU climate policies is beyond the scope of this chapter, major relevant legislative Acts enacted since 2000 are listed in Table 9.2.

Table 9.2 Major EU climate policies and measures and their reduction potential in the EU-15 by 2010 (selection, end of 2007)

Year (Adoption)	Policy	Reduction potential by 2010 (Mt CO₂eq.)
1998–99	Voluntary agreements with car manufacturers	75–80
1999	Landfill Directive 1999/31/EC	ca. 40
2001	Renewable Energy Directive 2001/77/EC	100–125
2003	Directive 2003/30/EC on Promotion of Biofuels	35–40
2003–04	Emissions Trading Directive 2003/87/EC and Linking Directive 2004/101/EC	ca. 70*
2006	Directive 2006/32/EC on Energy End Use Efficiency and Energy Services	40–55
Until 2007	Other policies and measures	160–200**
Total	*All existing EU policies and measures*	*515–615*

Source: European Commission, 'Progress towards achieving the Kyoto Objectives', 2007, Brussels: Commission of the European Communities; figures partially rounded.

Notes
* Combined for both the Emissions Trading and the Linking Directives; own calculation on basis of source (2005–06 verified emissions minus annual allocation 2008–12).
** Policies and measures already existing, including Directive 2002/91/EC on the Energy Performance of Buildings, Directive 2003/96/EC on Energy Taxation, Directive 2004/8/EC on the Promotion of Cogeneration, and Regulation EC 842/2006 and Directive 2006/40/EC on Fluorinated GHGs (among others); own estimate on basis of source.

As the centrepiece of the EU's new climate policy, the EU Emissions Trading Directive (2003/87/EC) was adopted in 2003 and deserves special mention. The Emissions Trading Scheme (ETS) sets limits for the CO_2 emissions of large installations accounting for about 40 per cent of the EU's CO_2 emissions. An apparent over-allocation of emission allowances for the pilot phase 2005–07 has led to more stringent review arrangements for national allocations for 2008–12.[8] The Emissions Trading Directive was complemented with Directive 2004/101/EC linking the ETS to the Kyoto Protocol project mechanisms, namely the Clean Development Mechanism (CDM) and Joint Implementation (JI). Both mechanisms allow investors to gain emission credits from emission-reduction projects financed in developing countries (CDM) and Eastern European countries with 'economies in transition' (JI).

In addition to common and coordinated climate policies, the EU relies on a burden-sharing agreement for its implementation of the Kyoto Protocol. This agreement shares the effort required to implement the EU's joint emission reduction target of

8 per cent under the Kyoto Protocol among the EU member states. The resulting reduction targets, codified into supranational EU law by means of Council Decision 2002/358/EC, range from minus 28 per cent for Luxembourg to plus 27 per cent for Portugal. Each member state is thus responsible for taking any additional domestic measures needed to ensure compliance with its national emission target.

The EU made significant progress towards closing the credibility gap in this period. The increasing number of common and coordinated policies and measures enacted by the EU added a considerable potential for the reduction of GHG emissions (Table 9.2). The maximum combined emission reduction *potential* of the EU measures passed until 2007 of about 600 Mt CO_2 equivalent nearly closes the gap of 680 Mt CO_2 equivalent between projected business-as-usual emissions in 2010 and the Kyoto target (Table 9.3). While by 2005 GHG emissions of the EU-15 were stagnating at 2 per cent below base year levels, emissions were projected to fall to 4 per cent below base year levels by 2010 with existing measures of the EU and its member states (Table 9.3) – a considerable improvement on the situation at the turn of the millennium when an increase was projected for 2010.

However, the EU nevertheless remained vulnerable to challenges. First of all, the great majority of the EU measures taken (with the notable exception of the EU ETS) depend on member states or even private actors (car industry) for their implementation. As a result, several of the measures have been under-performing (including the Renewable Energies Directive and the voluntary agreements with car manufacturers). Accordingly, 2007 projections of EU GHG emissions in 2010 showed that the EU's common and coordinated policies and measures would fall short of delivering the lower end of their emission reduction potential given in Table 9.2: existing measures by the EU *and the member states* still fell about 170 Mt CO_2 equivalent short of achieving the Kyoto target (Table 9.3). Even when taking into account planned enhancement of carbon sinks (such as forests) and use of the Kyoto mechanisms, additional measures were required for the EU-15 to achieve its Kyoto target.[9]

Table 9.3 GHG emissions and emission projections in the EU-15 (2007)

	Base year	Business as usual in 2010	Kyoto target	With existing measures*	With sinks and Kyoto mechanisms
			Projection for 2010		
Mt CO_2 eq	4,270	4,610	3,930	4,100	3,955
%	100	108	92	96	92.6

Source: European Commission, 'Progress towards achieving the Kyoto Objectives', 2007, Brussels: Commission of the European Communities; figures rounded.

Note
* Common and coordinated policies and measures of the EU as well as domestic measures of EU member states.

Closing the credibility gap? (2007 onwards)

The year 2007 marked the initiation of EU climate policies that could redress this credibility gap. First of all, in March 2007, the European Council adopted far-reaching conclusions on climate change. In particular, EU heads of state and government made an 'independent commitment' for the EU to reduce its GHG emissions by 20 per cent from the 1990 level by 2020. It also declared its intention to commit to a 30 per cent reduction in the case of comparable commitments by other industrialised countries and adequate contributions by advanced developing countries. In addition, the European Council agreed to increase the share of renewable energy in EU energy supply to 20 per cent and the contribution of biofuels in transport to 10 per cent in 2020.

Following the guidance provided by the European Council, the European Commission presented a number of proposals for implementing legislation. Most importantly, the Commission presented its climate and energy package in January 2008 containing three legislative proposals: a revised emissions trading directive to strengthen and extend the EU ETS; a new decision on the burden-sharing among EU member states of the 20 per cent reduction target by 2020 with respect to the sectors not covered by the EU ETS; and a directive on the promotion of renewable energy including a proposed translation of the overall target of 20 per cent by 2020 into national binding targets. In addition, a Regulation proposed in December 2007 aims to achieve a reduction of CO_2 emissions of new cars, of nearly 20 per cent by 2012. Finally, the Commission also proposed to include aviation fully in the ETS by 2012.[10]

The adoption of the proposed measures would go a long way to providing credibility for the EU's international leadership in elaborating a new global agreement on combating climate change by 2009. The proposed legislative measures would together account for up to three-quarters of the EU's 20 per cent emission reduction commitment by 2020. The proposal for an improved and extended ETS would alone result in a reduction of around 450 Mt CO_2 equivalent compared with 2005. The proposals regarding CO_2 and cars and renewable energy could, together with other EU measures, make additional contributions exceeding 300 Mt. The proposed burden-sharing decision would furthermore subject EU member states to binding supranational obligations with respect to reductions in non-EU ETS sectors. Perhaps more importantly, the implementation of the proposed measures would, once adopted, depend far less on EU member states than the mix of EU climate policies so far. The measures would also put in place a credible infrastructure for implementing a further strengthened commitment that could result from international negotiations. Such a strengthened commitment could, to a large extent, be implemented by stepping up the numbers included in the current proposals for a revised ETS and a burden-sharing decision. However, at the time of writing (early 2008), the legislative process had only just started so that it was uncertain whether the leadership potential inherent in the new legislative proposals could be realised.

Implications

The trend towards an increasing body of EU legislation on climate change and the environment has at least three implications for the future of the EU as an actor in global environmental and climate governance. First, progressive domestic policies and measures constitute a most effective support for EU unity at the international level. With these measures, all EU member states acquire an interest in international regulation that provides for a global level-playing field. Since existing and proposed EU climate policies go significantly beyond existing international standards, they provide an effective basis for continued international leadership of the EU.

Second, the progress in the elaboration and implementation of common and coordinated EU climate and energy policies implies a major shift of emphasis and competence in this policy field from the member states to the European level. While EU member states will still have a major role to play, a new 'communitarised' policy field, including a significant part of energy policy, is emerging that has a considerable impact on member states and on the daily life of European citizens. In line with the rulings of the European Court of Justice, this expansion of the internal competence of the Community will also likely affect the external EU competence.

Third, the emerging policy framework establishes a firm structure and sets EU climate and energy policies on a clear path for medium- and long-term evolution. Once this structure, with the EU ETS as its core, is in place, its cornerstones may not be easily removed. Given the experience gained in the operation of the EU ETS, it is to be hoped that fundamental changes will not be required. Within the agreed parameters, however, the new structure provides stability, certainty and a firm basis for the further evolution and strengthening of EU climate and energy policies.

Challenges ahead

Despite the progress in the organisation of its foreign environmental policy and the development of domestic policies, the EU faces a number of challenges and opportunities in its aspirations for international leadership on climate change and the environment. On the basis of the preceding analysis, five areas deserve particular attention: the further development and implementation of domestic policies; the further coordination of the EU's environmental diplomacy; the implications of the enlargement from fifteen to twenty-seven member states; the further development of EU policies beyond GHG emission mitigation; and ensuring and enhancing EU unity and coherence.

Advancing the EU policy framework

Even though the EU has made important progress in its domestic climate and energy policies, enormous scope for further improvements exists. First of all, realising the potential of the legislative proposals presented by the European Commission in 2007 and early 2008 (relating in particular to the EU ETS, the expansion of renewable energies and CO_2 emissions of cars) depends on their early implementation. The new legislation would need to be adopted before the election of a new European Parliament in mid-2009 in order to support EU leadership in the international negotiations on a future climate agreement that are to be concluded by the end of 2009. Beyond these legislative proposals, further scope for advancing domestic action on climate change exists in two respects. First, improving energy efficiency holds much potential and promises multiple dividends (e.g., reducing costs, protecting the climate, enhancing energy security). However, progress in increasing energy efficiency has so far been dismal. Second, the need for enhanced policy coherence persists. Efforts to liberalise energy markets in Europe, for example, have failed to exploit the potential for synergy with the climate policy agenda. With regard to the EU's external policies, both trade policies and EU development assistance have been slow to integrate climate and environmental concerns (Vogler 2005).

Advancing the EU's environmental diplomacy

The EU's international performance can be further improved, in particular by leveraging the diplomatic potential of the EU. Since other resources available to the EU are limited, the Union has to focus its efforts on developing its 'soft' power capabilities. Diplomacy constitutes a prime tool of 'soft' power and of foreign policy in general, and the EU possesses particular diplomatic potential because of the diverse contacts of various member states with a multitude of actors internationally. However, this potential remains to be exploited more fully. Diplomacy is still the prerogative of the foreign ministries of individual member states. Apart from the establishment of a loose 'green diplomacy network', coordination of the EU's diplomatic efforts has been piecemeal so far (Vogler 2005). The establishment of an EU diplomatic service ('External Action Service') as detailed in the Lisbon Treaty may make a contribution to improving the situation.[11] However, national foreign services are likely to remain at the centre of EU diplomacy, so major benefits may especially be reaped from an improved coordination of the diplomatic efforts of member states.

Coping with enlargement

The challenges arising from the enlargement of the EU to twenty-seven member states are continuing to unfold. This enlargement has widened internal diversity. Pending the entry into force of the Lisbon Treaty and further institutional reform, it is set to complicate decision-making on internal and external environmental and climate policies. The sheer increase in the number of countries makes reaching agreement more difficult, even in the case of qualified majority voting because the options for forming blocking minorities increase. The new member states have also so far been less enthusiastic and pro-active in supporting stringent climate policies at both the international and European levels. Under these circumstances, intensified efforts to broaden and deepen a joint European vision of global environmental and climate governance might be needed to enhance the 'Europeanisation' of this policy area and to foster internal coherence. If done successfully, enlargement may turn from a challenge to an opportunity for EU leadership because it increases the weight of the EU and its diplomatic potential.

Dealing with a broadening international agenda

International leadership by the EU faces the challenge of keeping step with the evolution of the international environmental and climate agenda. Effective long-term EU leadership will require actively developing this agenda and responding to its changing shape. Most importantly, the international climate agenda has evolved in the twenty-first century to give much more weight to building the capacity of developing countries to respond effectively to the challenge of global warming and sustainable development. Consequently, the international climate policy agenda has broadened beyond GHG emission mitigation to include financial assistance, technology transfer, adaptation and equity as equally central elements. This broadening agenda requires the EU to develop its leadership beyond a 'leadership by example' of domestic climate and environmental policies. Logically, climate change and other environmental challenges cannot be countered effectively without major contributions from developing countries and, in particular, from the larger and more advanced ones among them (including China, India, Brazil, South Korea, South Africa and others). To this end, it seems necessary to develop policies that respond to the particular needs of developing countries and enable them to make the required contributions. As a consequence, keeping its leadership position will require the EU to intensify its efforts to develop effective internal and external policies addressing the broadening agenda. By implication, this broadening agenda also poses additional demands on the EU to enhance the coherence of related policies, including international trade and investment and development assistance.

Preserving and expanding EU unity

Finally, EU unity in foreign environmental policy remains precarious. With the rise of EU leadership in global environmental governance since the turn of the century, keeping EU ranks closed has been facilitated by favourable external circumstances. In particular, the relative disinterest and even refusal of the Bush Administration to engage in global environmental affairs has helped to unite Europe. Also, EU leadership in global environmental governance has not yet been seriously challenged by developing countries. However, developing countries increasingly engage actively in global environmental governance, and internal US politics suggest an imminent re-engagement of the USA in global environmental cooperation (Oberthür 2007). These international dynamics are likely to reinforce the challenge of securing EU unity in at least two interrelated respects. First, judging from past experience, the international partners of the EU, once they become more assertive, are likely to try to weaken the EU by dividing it. Second, and as a result, the need for the EU to address potentially divisive issues will intensify. Two noteworthy policy areas displaying limited coordination and coherence of policy approaches within the EU relate to the use of nuclear energy and to external energy policy (e.g., the conflict between

Germany and Poland regarding the planned Northstream gas pipeline through the Baltic Sea). The challenge of securing EU unity may thus grow in the future.

Driving forces and strategic motivations underpinning EU leadership

Three broader strategic motivations can be identified that support and reinforce the EU's aspirations for international leadership in global environmental and climate governance in the twenty-first century. While there is no space to delve into a detailed assessment of the driving forces, both domestic politics (relative strength of societal support for environmental objectives; relative favourable economic interests, e.g., limited domestic fossil fuel resources) and institutional underpinnings (strength of Green parties and favourable conditions for articulation of environmental interests) have supported EU leadership in global environmental and climate governance (Oberthür 2007). These conditions have remained relatively stable during the history of international environmental/climate policy. The following discussion focuses on three strategic motivations that have grown stronger with the rise of climate change on international and European political agendas.

First, environmental protection, and climate change particularly, has become an important driver of European integration in general. Environmental protection had been pushed onto the defensive at the beginning of the twenty-first century in the wake of the Lisbon Agenda of 2000 that placed particular emphasis on improving the competitiveness of the European economy. The situation changed with the failure of the Treaty establishing a Constitution for Europe in 2006 and the consequent legitimacy crisis of the EU. Under these circumstances, the broad and strong public support for action on the environment and climate change at the European level, together with the increased urgency and importance of the issue, opened a window of opportunity for advancing both internal and external EU environmental and climate/energy policy. Both the scientific community and environmental groups helped to amplify this driving force. The European institutions grasped this opportunity for enhancing their legitimacy, and the legitimacy of the European integration process by moving climate change and the environment – policy areas that do not belong to the core of the Common Market project – into the centre of the European integration process.

Second, intensifying discussions about the security of future energy supplies to Europe have lent strong support for the development of stringent climate policies. Soaring oil and gas prices since 2005 have particularly highlighted the dependence of the EU on energy imports. In 2005, the EU imported more than 50 per cent of the energy it used. Without targeted counter-measures, dwindling domestic energy reserves are set to increase this dependence even further in the future; energy imports are projected to account for about 70 per cent of European energy needs by 2030.[12] At the same time as oil and gas prices increased, political developments in regions with major reserves, including the Middle East and Russia, have fuelled concern about the security of Europe's energy supplies. The growing dependence on an increasingly autocratic Russia has generated particular political disquiet. The resulting energy security agenda has significantly reinforced the climate agenda, especially regarding policies aimed at increasing energy efficiency and the use of alternative sources of energy. Under these circumstances, discussions about energy market reforms that might support a long-term climate-friendly restructuring of the energy sector have also progressed.

Third, the position of the EU in the international system and its strategic orientation in international relations – specifically including its strong support for multilateralism – also support EU leadership in global environmental and climate governance. The EU has for some time pursued the objective of enhancing its role as a global actor. It has also been one of the most fervent supporters of multilateralism and international law as the backbone of global governance. This strategic orientation for realising the EU's global aspirations is in line with its limited military and economic power resources – both in absolute terms and in relation to other world actors – and seems to be deeply ingrained in the 'genes' of the EU – which forms a multilateral microcosm of the international system itself. Under these circumstances, the environment and climate change have been particularly well-suited areas for the EU to pursue international leadership. Climate change and the Kyoto Protocol enjoy a particularly high international profile. Also, leadership in this area can build upon 'soft' power resources that the EU may mobilise more easily than other resources. The EU's progressive role has also made it the natural ally of the international scientific community and environmental groups, which has reinforced the EU claim for leadership. Furthermore, existing international environmental agreements and international institutions provide a proven multilateral framework for pursuing EU leadership.

Having grown in importance during the first decade of the twenty-first century, these strategic factors can, on balance, also be expected to continue to support EU leadership in international environmental and climate policy for some time. Since high public concern about the environment and climate change has been relatively stable for decades, we may expect public support for related European-level action to remain relatively stable as well. Bound by their past commitments, European heads of state or government are furthermore likely to continue to use this source of legitimacy. There are also no far-reaching changes expected in the factors underlying the energy security agenda (high/increasing energy prices, limited/falling European energy reserves, problematic political situation in supplier countries). Climate governance, finally, can be expected to remain a primary and most suitable forum for the EU's pursuit of a role as a global actor in the context of multilateralism. While growing concern about food security may limit use of first-generation biofuels, alternative options for reducing GHG emissions from the transport sector already exist and are under development (including so-called second-generation biofuels). Overall, these factors should thus continue to support the development of both strong external and internal climate policies.

Conclusion

Since the second half of the 1980s, the EU has assumed a clear leadership position in international environmental and climate governance. It has consistently been the force, among the major international actors, pushing for the most far-reaching measures to protect the environment. While the EU's leadership role has extended to many items on the agenda of global environmental governance (including the protection of the ozone layer, biodiversity, the management of genetically modified organisms and chemicals), it has been particularly pronounced with respect to the most prominent issue on this agenda, namely climate change. In 2007, the EU renewed this leadership by unilaterally committing to cutting its GHG emissions by 20 per cent by 2020 and calling upon other countries to join it in the global fight against climate change.

Over the years, the EU has been able to improve considerably its leadership record. First of all, the Union has enhanced the organisation and coordination of its foreign environmental policy. Internal reforms have enhanced the capacity of the EU for outreach to other parties and have contributed to a greater unity of the EU, which has in turn improved the recognition of the EU as a global actor. Furthermore, progress in the development and implementation of internal climate and energy policies has helped to reduce the credibility gap between international promises and domestic action. The EU Emissions Trading Scheme that started operation in 2005 constitutes the flagship activity in this respect, but has been complemented with a number of common and coordinated policies and measures. In addition, the European Commission presented a set of legislative proposals in 2007 and early 2008, which, if implemented, would greatly enhance the effectiveness of EU climate policy. The implementation of these legislative proposals would also result in the communitarisation of a large and important policy area, including a significant part of energy policy.

Despite this progress, a number of challenges remain to be addressed. The legislative proposals need to be enacted and further measures need to be initiated in order to enhance policy coherence and effectiveness across policy domains (including trade, agriculture and development assistance). Internationally, the role of the EU can be considerably strengthened by an improved coordination of EU environmental diplomacy. The enlarged Union represents a challenge for ensuring and improving EU unity and environmental leadership. The EU needs to come to grips with a changing and expanding international environmental and climate agenda. On this agenda, capacity-building, adaptation, technology transfer, and finance and investment have gained in importance, which requires the Union to elaborate concepts and approaches that integrate these new elements in order to ensure effective global action on climate change and the environment. Finally, ensuring and enhancing EU unity in the face of increasing external challenges and persistent internal policy divergences (e.g., nuclear energy, external energy policy) remains a constant and probably intensifying challenge.

A number of factors have come to support EU leadership in global environmental and climate governance in the twenty-first century. EU leadership, especially on climate change, has increasingly been driven by the aspirations of the EU as a global actor and its pursuit of multilateralism. High levels of public support for European-level action on the environment and climate change have had a particular impact in the aftermath of the failure of the EU Constitutional Treaty in 2005 and the ensuing search for legitimacy within the European Institutions. As a result, the environment and climate change have become important drivers of the European integration process and the European Council has committed to taking action in this field. Finally, the heightened energy security agenda and concern about rising energy prices support effective EU climate policies. These factors can also be expected to support EU leadership on the environment and climate change for some time into the future.

Overall, the EU can be expected to remain a progressive force in global environmental governance. Whether the EU remains an international leader will depend not only on its own actions but also on the evolution of the policies of other actors. The policy changes initiated, if carried through, provide a sound basis for the EU to work credibly towards long-term GHG emission reductions, as recommended by scientists, and towards the fundamental changes in our energy systems that are required. If the EU also manages to address effectively the aforementioned challenges, it will, without doubt, be one of the favourites in the competition for international leadership in global environmental governance. If the leadership of such a strengthened EU turned out to be contested by other world players (Oberthür 2007), this may not only provide evidence of the success of EU leadership, but it would also be excellent news for the global environment.

Notes

1 With contributions by Claire Roche Kelly.
2 Intergovernmental Panel on Climate Change (IPCC) 'Fourth Assessment Report: Synthesis Report', 2007, Geneva: IPCC.
3 For a discussion of leadership in global environmental governance, see T. Skodvin and S. Andresen 'Leadership revisited', *Global Environmental Politics*, 2008, 6: 3, 13–27; references regarding EU leadership in global environmental and climate governance can be found at the end of the chapter; see there for further references on this section and the overall chapter.
4 H. E. Ott, W. Sterk and R. Watanabe, 'The Bali roadmap: new horizons for global climate change', *Climate Policy*, 2008, 8: 1, 91–5.
5 Global Environment Outlook, GEO-4, Environment for Development, 2007, UNEP; World Resources Institute, Millennium Ecosystem Assessment, 2005. Ecosystems and Human Well-Being: Synthesis, Washington, 2005.
6 L. G. van Schaik and C. Egenhofer, 'Improving the climate: will the new constitution strengthen the EU's performance in international climate negotiations?', *CEPS Policy Brief*, No. 63 (February 2005); N. S. Lacasta, S. Desai, E. Kracht and K. Vincent, 'Articulating a consensus: the EU's position on climate change', in P.G. Harris (ed.), *Europe and Global Climate Change: Politics, Foreign Policy and Regional Cooperation*, 2007, Cheltenham: Edward Elgar, 211–31.
7 European Commission, 'Third National Communication from the European Community under the UN Framework Convention on Climate Change', 2001, Brussels: Commission of the European Communities.
8 J. Delbeke (ed.), *EU Environmental Law: The EU Greenhouse Gas Emissions Trading Scheme; EU Energy Law, Volume IV*, 2006, Leuven: Claeys & Casteels; J.B. Skjærseth and

J. Wettestad, *EU Emissions Trading: Initiation, Decision-making and Implementation*, 2008, Hampshire: Ashgate.
9 Table 9.3 and European Environment Agency (EEA), 'Greenhouse gas emission trends and projections in Europe 2007: tracking progress towards Kyoto targets', EEA Report No. 5/2007, Copenhagen.
10 European Commission, '20 20 by 2020: Europe's climate change opportunity', 2008a, Brussels: Commission of the European Communities.
11 L. G. van Schaik and C. Egenhofer, op. cit.
12 European Commission, 'Green Paper: A European strategy for sustainable, competitive and secure energy', 2006, Brussels: Commission of the European Communities.

Bibliography

Bretherton, C. and J. Vogler (2006), *The European Union as a Global Actor*, second edition, London: Routledge.

Damro, C. (2006), 'EU–UN environmental relations: shared competence and effective multilateralism', in K.V. Laatikainen and K.E. Smith (eds), *The European Union at the United Nations: Intersecting Multilateralisms*, Basingstoke: Palgrave Macmillan, 175–92.

Delreux, T. (2006), 'The European Union in international negotiations: a legal perspective on the internal decision-making process', *International Environmental Agreements*, 6, 231–48.

Falkner, R. (2007), 'The political economy of "normative power" Europe: EU environmental leadership in international biotechnology regulation', *Journal of European Public Policy*, 20, 507–26.

Grubb, M. and J. Gupta (eds) (2000), *Climate Change and European Leadership*, Dordrecht, NL: Kluwer Academic Publishers.

Groenleer, M.L.P. and L.G. van Schaik (2007), 'United we stand? The European Union's international actorness in the cases of the International Criminal Court and the Kyoto Protocol', *Journal of Common Market Studies*, 45: 5, 969–8.

Harris, P.G. (ed.) (2007), *Europe and Global Climate Change: Politics, Foreign Policy and Regional Cooperation*, Cheltenham: Edward Elgar.

Oberthür S. (1999), 'The EU as an international actor: the protection of the ozone layer', *Journal of Common Market Studies*, 37: 4, 641–59.

Oberthür, S. (2007), 'The European Union in international climate policy: the prospect for leadership', *Intereconomics – Review of European Economic Policy*, 42: 2, 77–83.

Oberthür, S. and H.E. Ott (1999), *The Kyoto Protocol: International Climate Policy for the 21st Century*, Berlin: Springer.

Sbragia, A. (2002), 'Institution-building from below and above: the European Community in global environmental politics', in A. Jordan (ed.), *Environmental Policy in the European Union: Actors, Institutions and Processes*, London: Earthscan, 275–98.

Vogler, J. and H.R. Stephan (2007), 'The European Union in global environmental governance: leadership in the making?' *International Environmental Agreements*, 7: 389–413.

Vogler, J. (2005), 'The European contribution to global environmental governance', *International Affairs*, 81: 4, 835–49.

Zito, A.R. (2005), 'The European Union as an environmental leader in a global environment', *Globalizations*, 2: 3, 363–75.

10 The external dimension of the European Area of Freedom, Security and Justice[1]

Philippe De Bruycker and Anne Weyembergh

Summary

The external dimension of the EU's Area of Freedom, Security and Justice became progressively more important as it became evident that the EU could not build the said area unless it cooperated with third countries. In the field of immigration, the EU defined a 'global approach to migration' aimed at linking migration and development, although progress was hindered by attempts to impose upon third countries the priority to fight against illegal immigration. It remains to be seen if this policy as defined on paper will be implemented effectively and whether it will allow the EU to meet the challenges linked to the definition of a policy for legal immigration and a more coherent management of the labour market. In the field of criminal judicial and police cooperation, external relations have developed but have been hindered by several factors, especially institutional and decisional ones. One of the main challenges with which the EU is confronted when developing the external dimension of its penal area is the need to safeguard some of its own values and standards when cooperating with its partners, namely to find the right balance between the 'sword and shield functions' of penal law.

Introduction

Cooperation in the field of Justice and Home Affairs (JHA) has developed since the 1970s but for a long period work focused on its internal dimension, namely cooperation within the EU. Although some first steps were made under the Maastricht Treaty, relations between the EU and third countries, or third organisations, within the JHA field have only significantly developed and multiplied since the entry into force of the Amsterdam Treaty. The external dimension of the Area of Freedom, Security and Justice (AFSJ) is thus quite recent. Its development is the logical consequence of the cross-border nature of the issues at stake. It mainly aims at serving the internal policy by creating a secure external environment. The EU cannot act alone to achieve an internal AFSJ: in order to combat illegal immigration, terrorism and organised crime, the EU must foster cooperation with its neighbours and other partners throughout the world.

Common global political guidelines were established with regard to some horizontal programmes related to the AFSJ. Three have been of particular importance:

- the Tampere Programme of October 1999, in which the European Council called the Union to develop its capacity to act and be regarded as a significant partner on the international scene, by developing stronger external actions in this field. It underlined that all competences and instruments at the disposal of the Union, and in particular in external relations, must be used in an integrated and consistent way to build the AFSJ.
- the conclusions of the Santa Maria de Feira European Council of June 2000, which established the EU geographical and substantive priorities and objectives for external relations in the field of JHA.
- the Hague Programme of November 2004 together with its Action Plan of June 2005, which presented the external dimension in the field as 'a growing priority', stressing the need for coherence and identifying five criteria for external action (i.e., the existence of internal policies as the key parameter justifying the need for external action; the need for value-adding in relation to projects carried out by the member states; the contribution to the general political objectives of the Union's external policy; the possibility of achieving the goals within a reasonable period of time; and the possibility of long-term action).

These first broad orientations were further detailed by the Strategy for the External Dimension of JHA: Global Freedom, Security and Justice, adopted by JHA Council in December 2005.[2] This strategy clearly aims at improving coherence and continuity in this field. Successive JHA External Relations Multi-Presidency Programmes share the same purpose. The quest for coherence is one of the main challenges that the EU has had to face when developing the external dimension of the AFSJ. Coherence should be guaranteed between the internal and external dimensions of the area, but also between the external aspects of the AFSJ and the rest of the EU's external objectives in the field of stability, development and so on.

For reasons of clarity, this chapter will deal separately with the EU external relations in the field of immigration (but not asylum) on the one hand, and police cooperation and judicial cooperation in criminal matters on the other hand. Questions related to the enlargement are excluded as well as judicial cooperation in civil matters. Each sector presents its own specific issues and challenges. Besides clear differences regarding their respective purpose, the identity of their privileged partners, and their key challenges, these two fields also differ in light of their specific institutional framework. Following the progressive 'communitarisation'[3] of immigration initiated by the Treaty of Amsterdam, the EU external relations in this field have been submitted to EC law. In early 2008, such 'communitarisation' of police cooperation and judicial cooperation in criminal matters had yet to be realised. Consequently, the core activities related to the external dimension of the European penal area are still undertaken within the so-called third pillar of the Treaty, namely within Title VI of the TEU. However, according to the Treaty of Lisbon, matters are to change radically. As a consequence of the abolition of the third pillar, both the internal and external aspects of police cooperation and judicial cooperation in criminal matters are transferred to the Treaty on the Functioning of the European Union (TFEU) and submitted to the community method. External relations in the field of immigration and in penal matters are thus 'reunited' and governed by the same institutional framework.[4]

The external dimension of the immigration policy

Sources

The European immigration policy was launched by the Amsterdam Treaty, and started with its entry into force on 1 May 1999.[5] In October 1999, a European Council was convened in Tampere under the Finnish Presidency, to indicate how the new competences of the European Community (EC) would be implemented. The first of the four principles of the Tampere conclusions to be applied to the development of a European immigration policy was a partnership with countries of origin:

> The European Union needs a comprehensive approach to migration addressing political, human rights and development issues in countries and regions of origin and transit. This requires combating poverty, improving living conditions and job opportunities, preventing conflicts and consolidating democratic states and ensuring respect for human rights, in particular rights of minorities, women and children. To that end, the Union as well as Member States are invited to contribute, within their respective competence under the Treaties, to a greater coherence of internal and external policies of the Union. Partnership with third countries concerned will also be a key element for the success of such a policy, with a view to promoting co-development.

The idea of developing a partnership with third countries is obvious for the success of a policy on immigration, as it is concerned with individuals coming from countries of origin, who might pass through countries of transit on their way to the EU. One cannot imagine effectively managing migratory flows without taking into consideration the situation in the countries where the migrants are coming from. This led to the idea of integrating the immigration policy into the Union's relations with third countries. The question dominated the agenda at the Seville Summit, in June 2002, where the following conclusions were adopted:

> 33 The European Council considers that combating illegal immigration requires a greater effort on the part of the EU and a targeted approach to the problem, with the use of all appropriate instruments in the context of the EU's external relations. To that end, in accordance with the Tampere conclusions, an integrated, comprehensive and balanced approach to tackling the root causes of illegal immigration must remain the EU's constant long-term objective. With this in mind, the EU points out that closer economic cooperation, trade expansion, development assistance and conflict prevention are all means of promoting economic prosperity in the countries concerned and thereby reducing the underlying causes of migration flows. The European Council urges that any future cooperation, association or equivalent agreement which

the EU or the EC concludes with any country should include a clause on joint management of migration flows and on compulsory readmission in the event of illegal immigration.

34 The European Council stresses the importance of ensuring the cooperation of countries of origin and transit in joint management and in border control as well as on readmission. Such readmission by third countries should include that of their own nationals unlawfully present in a Member State and, under the same conditions, that of other countries' nationals who can be shown to have passed through the country in question. Cooperation should bring results in the short and medium term. The Union is prepared to provide the necessary technical and financial assistance for the purpose, in which case the EC will have to be allocated the appropriate resources, within the limits of the financial perspective.

The most controversial question, raised by the UK, concerned the idea of sanctioning third countries if they did not cooperate with the EU in the fight against illegal immigration, which had been identified as a top priority of Union.[6] The European Council considered, under points 35 and 36 of the conclusions, that it was:

> necessary to carry out a systematic assessment of relations with third countries which do not cooperate in combating illegal immigration. That assessment will be taken into account in relations between the EU and its Member States and the countries concerned, in all relevant areas. Insufficient cooperation by a country could hamper the establishment of closer relations between that country and the Union. If full use has been made of existing Community mechanisms but without success, the Council may unanimously find that a third country has shown an unjustified lack of cooperation in the joint management of migration flows. In that event the Council may, in accordance with the rules laid down in the treaties, adopt measures or positions under the Common Foreign and Security Policy and other EU policies, while honouring the Union's contractual commitments but not jeopardising development cooperation objectives.

If the idea of sanctioning third countries unwilling to cooperate in the fight against illegal immigration had thus almost been rejected, the link between migration and development rapidly attracted more and more attention, not only from the EU, but also at the international level. The United Nations thus launched in 2006 a High-Level Dialogue on International Migration and Development, which led to the establishment of a Global Forum on Migration and Development. On the basis of a communication of the Commission entitled 'Integrating migration issues in the EU's relations with third countries',[7] the Council considered in its own conclusions on migration and development, adopted on 5 May 2003,[8] that an 'integrated, comprehensive and balanced approach to manage migration flows more effectively, to tackle the root causes of illegal immigration and to combat smuggling and trafficking in human beings should remain one of the European Union's constant long-term objectives'. The idea that it is possible to use migration as a tool for development slowly came to gain ground. In the conclusions dated 21 and 22 November 2005, the Council underlined that 'migration can be an essential part of the development agenda and development policy and when managed effectively can have a substantial positive impact both for the host country and for the country of origin'. It invited 'the Commission to play an active role in promoting an integrated and coherent approach to migration and development, including encouraging the involvement of migrants themselves'. In its communication dated 1 September 2005,[9] the Commission subsequently proposed concrete orientations: the fostering of cheap, fast and secure ways of sending remittances of migrants back to their country of origin and facilitating the contribution of remittances to the development of migrants' countries of origin; helping developing countries to map their diasporas and build links with them; facilitating circular migration and brain circulation; and mitigating the adverse effects of the brain drain so detrimental to the migrants' countries of origin.

Assaults on Ceuta and Melilla, the Spanish city-enclaves within Moroccan terri-tory, by migrants trying to illegally enter the EU, led to the adoption by the European Council of a Global Approach to Migration in December 2005. This approach is a large catalogue of various measures aimed at increasing the operational coordination between member states, with an eye to better controlling the EU's external borders. A deepening of the dialogue and cooperation with Africa, as well as work with neighbouring countries in the field of migration were further identified objectives. The year 2006 was marked by the organisation of two important international conferences. The first one, the Euro-African Ministerial Conference on Migration and Development, held following the initiative of Morocco and Spain in Rabat in July 2006, led to the adoption of the Euro-African partnership on migration and development (the so-called Rabat Declaration) which was further accompanied by a specific action plan. The second one, the EU–Africa Ministerial Conference on Migration and Development, which took place in Tripoli in November 2006, led to the adoption of the Joint Africa–EU Declaration on Migration and Development, which was endorsed at the second EU–Africa Summit in December 2007 alongside a formal action plan for the period 2008–10 which included eight partnerships, among which was one on migration, mobility and employment. Furthermore, the first Euro-Mediterranean ministerial meeting on migration was organised in Portugal in November 2007 within the framework of the Euro-Med dialogue. It also led to the adoption of specific conclusions on migratory issues. Apart from the differences regarding their geographical area (the Rabat Conference covers West and North Africa; the Tripoli Conference, the entire African continent; and the Euro-Med process, ten Mediterranean third states), all declarations and actions plans[10] focus on identical issues:

- *migration and development*: facilitating the role of diasporas in contributing to the sustainable development of their countries of origin; implementing cooperation projects in particular fields which generate employment in areas with high levels of migration; granting technical assistance to migrants wishing to develop entrepreneurial projects in their countries of origin; reducing, by working with banks, the costs of savings transfers for migrants to their countries of origin

- *legal migration*: reinforcing the administrative services responsible for migration, so as to enable them, among other things, to provide information to potential migrants on available channels for legal migration; to facilitate and simplify, on a bilateral and voluntary basis and taking into account the needs of labour markets, legal migration procedures for skilled and unskilled workers, in order to improve legal channels for migration; to promote means of facilitating circular and temporary migration between countries of origin and destination, taking into account the needs of the labour markets
- *illegal immigration*: setting up efficient readmission systems between all concerned countries; providing technical and logistical support for the identification of the illegal migrants' nationality; facilitating the reintegration of irregular migrants who have returned to their home country; promoting better security standards in third countries' travel documents, such as biometry.

In December 2006, the European Council insisted once more on the fact that 'migration needs to be addressed in a comprehensive manner and that future work should broaden the scope of action to other policy areas' and required consideration to be given 'to how legal migration opportunities can be incorporated into the Union's external policies in order to develop a balanced partnership with third countries adapted to specific EU member states' labour market needs'. On 16 May 2007, the Commission published a communication on circular migration and mobility partnerships between the EU and third countries.[11] This interesting policy initiative broached the question of legal migration, formally introducing it into the debate on a European immigration policy from two angles.

- *Circular migration* gives to migrants already admitted into the EU, and considered as *bona fide* because they have respected the rules on the length of stay, certain facilities enabling them to go back and forth legally between the EU and their country of origin. It concerns third-country nationals already established in the EU towards their country of origin, as well as the mobility of third-country nationals living abroad towards the EU. Examples quoted are seasonal workers, students, vocational trainees, researchers, persons participating in intercultural exchanges and volunteers. Tools used are: multi-annual permits for seasonal workers; the extension of the period of authorised absence without losing the right to stay; improvement of the rules on mutual recognition of qualifications; retention of student grants for a certain number of years after the return to the country of origin; assistance provided to researchers in order to allow them to continue their work upon having returned; and measures to ensure ethical recruitment in order to mitigate the effects of the brain drain in sectors suffering from a lack of human resources in developing third countries.
- *Mobility partnership* is an agreement based on mutual commitments. Third countries would commit themselves to action such as: readmitting their own nationals and third-country nationals having transited illegally to the EU through their territory; organising preventive information campaigns against illegal immigration; improving their border controls; securing their travel documents;

and seriously fighting smuggling and trafficking. The EU and its member states would commit themselves to opening more channels of legal migration to the nationals of the concerned third countries, under the form of: reserved quotas or privileged admission of certain categories of immigrants; technical and financial assistance to help third states to better manage migration flows through, for instance, providing information on work in the EU; reintegration programmes for return migrants as well as facilitation of short-term visas already offered to Eastern countries with which the EU has concluded several external agreements (see policy developments below).

Since the adoption of these measures, two further developments have occurred. On the one hand, the Council decided[12] in June 2007 to extend the scope of this global approach to the Eastern and South-Eastern regions (Turkey, Ukraine, Moldova, Belarus, the Western Balkans, Southern Caucasus and Russia) neighbouring the EU. On the other hand, the Commission has published two reports – one in 2006[13] and one in 2007[14] – on the progress made in the implementation of the said global approach, which offers a detailed analysis of the relevant policy developments.

Policy developments

From the outset, the EU professed to develop its immigration policy in partnership with third countries, as underlined in the first principle of the Tampere conclusions. However, problems arose from the fact that the main political option favoured by the EU is to fight illegal immigration, as underlined in the strategy for the external dimension of JHA adopted by the Council on 6 December 2005,[15] and that it wanted to impose this priority to third countries. The conclusion of readmission agreements, aimed at facilitating the return of illegal immigrants residing in the EU, therefore appeared on the top of the EU's political agenda. Even the partnership agreement between the African, Caribbean and Pacific (ACP) group of states and the EC, signed in Cotonou on 23 June 2000, followed this political orientation.[16] The idea of imposing sanctions on third countries by cutting development aid to those unwilling to collaborate in the fight against illegal immigration was even debated in 2002 at the Seville EU summit but was ultimately implicitly rejected (see above).

Third countries rejected the political orientation championed by the EU. It quickly became patent that fighting illegal immigration was not a priority for them, for differing reasons yet mainly because it was not in their interest and could result in an important financial burden. Emigration is often an alternative to unemployment, alleviating the social and economic problems of third governments, in particular because emigrants send back remittances (independently of their legal or illegal status in the country of destination) which are, in some cases, as important as public development aid. Moreover, the EU's request to include in the scope of readmission agreements not only nationals from the party states, but also third-country nationals who transited towards the EU through their territory, is difficult to accept for third states. This would oblige them to take back and send those aliens to their country of origin, yet they often do not have the means to control their borders and even less to organise return procedures. It is easy to understand how third countries have come to consider the issue of readmission of third-country nationals willing to emigrate as an EU problem which is not theirs.

This situation led to a political conflict not only between the EU and third countries, but also internally within the EU between officials in charge of immigration policies and those concerned with development policies. Immigration policy-makers may want to steer development aid towards the reduction of migration flows in order to produce results in the short term, while development specialists want to allocate aid to the eradication of poverty in the context of sustainable development and consider that it will contribute to the reduction of migration flows in the long term. The agreement upon the idea to link immigration and development policies – by using migrants as a vector for development and taking measures with regard to migration management, mobility, brain drain, remittances and diasporas – appears to be a compromise between the two aforementioned options. Migration became one of the twelve policy areas for which the EU committed itself to pursue Policy Coherence for Development (PCD) objectives, setting priorities for action as a means of contributing to poverty reduction and to achieving the Millennium Development Goals (MDGs).[17] A new set of policy instruments is therefore progressively being developed by the EU and its member states. Among these instruments are:

- *mobility partnerships*, which have already been defined (see above). On the basis of the results of preliminary discussions about its May 2007 communication on circular migration and mobility partnerships, the Council, in December 2007, invited the Commission, in close liaison with member states, to open dialogue with Cape Verde and Moldova, with a view to launching pilot mobility partnerships with those two countries.[18]
- *cooperation platforms*, which are local working-level instruments, initially promoted by the UK, bringing together representatives of the concerned third countries, the EU member states, the Commission and international organisations. They strive to facilitate the exchange of information on migration and migration-related issues of common interest, and the coordination of projects in the area of migration and development, with a country-specific approach. Following a concept paper published on 4 February 2008, Cape Verde and Ethiopia were identified as the first countries with which such cooperation platforms were to be organised.
- *migration profiles*, which are documents containing any information relevant to the design and management of a joint migration and development policy, such as data on migratory flows, skills available within the diasporas, and remittances to the country. They have been prepared for many third countries and are annexed to the regional or country strategy papers used to lay down the bilateral cooperation strategy between the EU and third states on the basis of a political and socio-economic analysis of their specific situation.
- *a Migration Information and Management Centre*, which was to be created in Mali, with the financial support of the EU. In 2007 it was decided that such a centre was needed, for a variety of reasons: to provide information about work

opportunities at the national, regional and European levels; to warn potential victims of the risks of illegal migration; to provide services for the return
of migrants with regard to their socio-economic reintegration; to facilitate
remittances and the use of the competences of the various diasporas; and to
undertake research on migration flows and prospective labour market analysis.

During the transitional period between May 1999 and May 2004 regarding the
establishment of the Area of Freedom, Security and Justice, the difficulties born from
engaging third countries in a dialogue on migration based on the EU's preferred focus
on the fight against illegal immigration produced few results, as only five readmission
agreements were concluded: with Macao, Hong Kong, Sri Lanka, Albania, and a
special agreement with China. This has led the EU to broaden the political agenda
concerned with migration.

First, the EU searched for elements allowing it to strengthen its bargaining position
on migration *vis-à-vis* third countries. It opted to offer cooperative third countries
easier provisions regarding the delivery of short-term visas. After the conclusion of
a readmission agreement, in parallel with a visa facilitation agreement, with Russia
in 2007, this model produced quick results with other Eastern (Ukraine, Moldova)
and Balkan countries (Montenegro, Macedonia, Bosnia-Herzegovina and Serbia).
The EU also realised that third countries actually needed help to manage migration.
As a result it offered, through a thematic programme for cooperation in the areas of
migration and asylum, some financial support aimed at capacity-building. This new
policy avenue is indeed the opposite of the initially contemplated idea of imposing
financial sanctions as examined by the European Council at its 2002 meeting in Seville
(see above). This new programme, with a budget of 205 million euros for 2007–10,
has five strategic objectives: to foster links between migration and development; to
promote well-managed labour migration; to fight illegal migration and facilitate
the readmission of illegal immigrants; to protect migrants against exploitation and
exclusion; to promote asylum and the international protection of refugees.

The most significant evolution is certainly the enlargement of the scope and
the concretisation of the political dialogue with third countries through the Euro-
African conferences that took place in 2006 and 2007 (see above). The idea of linking
migration and development concerns might be the beginning of a policy that takes
into consideration the interests of sending countries as well as those of receiving
countries. In particular, the extension of the discussions with the migrants' countries
of origin – which the EU had wanted initially to limit to the matter of the fight
against illegal immigration – to the question of legal migration, through for instance
mobility partnerships (see above), shows that the EU and its member states have,
after some years, understood that a much more balanced policy is necessary.

Main issues at stake

The first challenge that the EU will have to face in the future is determining the
degree to which its member states might open up to a certain level of immigration in
a global world characterised by strong imbalances in the distribution of wealth and

population. The rhetoric option of zero immigration, which was never implemented, has been progressively replaced by a positive approach that can be found in The Hague Programme linking economic growth and the Lisbon Strategy.[19] In the same vein, the Council of Economy and Finance Ministers adopted, on 4 December 2007, conclusions insisting upon the positive impact of immigration on European economies. As the European immigration policy has been clearly oriented towards the fight against illegal immigration, the main question rests on the re-opening of legal channels of migration beyond family reunification, which has remained feasible even if the member states have tended to implement more restrictive conditions for the admission of family members. Such a debate is clearly concerned with striking the right balance between the different components of an immigration policy which has historically favoured the fight against illegal immigration while not paying enough attention to the opportunities arising from legal migration.

The EU has already concluded agreements on short-term visa provisions with Eastern and Western Balkan countries (see above). Subsequently, it must bargain with African countries on this point, assuming there is no reason why those countries should not get what others have obtained. However, the debate is actually much larger, and concerns not only the freedom to travel for a maximum period of three months, but real immigration for work purposes. The Commission communication about circular migration (see above) fosters more questions than answers, due to a lack of definition of what this new concept entails precisely and to what extent it differs from traditional temporary migration. For some states, there is also the memory of post-war temporary migration, and the subsequent difficulties when the immigration in fact became permanent. Moreover, the need for permanent immigration as a solution to the problems associated with the demographic downturn should not been ignored, even if it is extremely sensitive politically. Its external dimension will to a certain extent play the role of a catalyst with regard to the definition of an internal immigration policy. The desire of the member states to secure the collaboration of third countries in the fight against illegal immigration has led them to think of using legal migration as a bargaining tool, in particular in exchange for the signing of readmission agreements. The problem remains nevertheless that the immigration policy, in the strict sense understood as the admission of third-country nationals for work purposes and possibly settlement, still needs to be more clearly defined by the EU and its member states.

Moreover, the negotiations with third countries regarding immigration issues will certainly be handicapped by the distribution of competences between the EU and its member states. If the EU enjoys an external competence in the field of illegal immigration and with regard to short-term visa policy, the situation is much more complicated regarding legal immigration. The Lisbon Treaty stipulates that the Community competence in immigration shall 'not affect the right of member states to determine volumes of admission of third-country nationals coming from third countries to their territory in order to seek work, whether employed or self-employed' (see the new paragraph 5 of Article 79, TFEU). This means that the conclusion of new tools, such as mobility partnerships, might be quite complicated as they could involve mixed external agreements, with some provisions belonging to the competence of the EU, while others remain within the scope of its member states.[20] The Council of Ministers has stressed 'the fact that mobility partnerships will need to strictly respect the division of competences between the EU and the Member States' in its conclusions on mobility partnerships and circular migration.[21] These elements of legal complexity could make negotiations with third countries more difficult, as the division of competences between the EU and its member states coincides with the interests of the Treaty parties. The EU level is indeed competent for what is in its own interest (readmission agreements) and the member states retain the competence for what it is in the interest of third states (the volume of legal labour immigration). One can imagine that third states will be quite mistrusting in such a political and legal context. This also explains why bilateral relations between third countries and individual member states, instead of the EU, will remain relatively important, as shown by the agreements signed by Spain and France on migration with several African countries.

The second challenge is related to the management of the labour market within the EU in connection with third countries. After the failure of its general proposal on economic migration of 2001, the Commission has adopted in its policy plan on legal migration[22] a new strategy distinguishing between several categories of workers (highly skilled, seasonal, intra-corporate transferees and remunerated trainees). One may wonder whether there exists a risk that channels of legal migration towards the EU will be limited mainly to (highly) skilled workers, while a substantial part of non- or low-skilled migration would be abandoned to smugglers and exploiters on the black labour market. In 2007, the Commission fortunately proposed a directive providing for sanctions against employers of illegally residing third-country nationals.[23] This text is essential for the overall coherence of the immigration policy, as the EU affected until then to prioritise the fight against illegal immigration while ignoring pull factors such as the informal labour market which obviously attracts illegal migrants.

Questions of labour market management are also a key variable with regard to the relations the EU entertains with third countries in the field of immigration. The possibility of finding local employment in one's own country is one of the elements determining emigration towards countries offering more opportunities. This explains why one of the first actions supported by the EU in its new policy aimed at linking migration and development was the creation in Mali of a Migration Information and Management Centre which, among other tasks, will have to provide information on work opportunities at the national, regional and European levels (see above). Managing the labour markets will not only be necessary to prevent migration; the mismatch of demand and supply will obviously be a key element for the conception and implementation of mobility partnerships, as in any labour immigration policy.

The third challenge is maintaining the coherence of EU policies, particularly between its immigration and development policies. Will migration effectively become a new tool used to enhance the results of the development policy and benefit the countries of origin? The assessment on migration, made by the Commission in its 2007 Report on policy coherence for development, is interesting:

There is now a clear understanding that migration can be good for development and vice versa. Progress in the field of migration and development has so far been good as regards establishing the policy framework and launching the political dialogue at regional and country levels, particularly with Africa. With a solid framework in place, progress is now needed on translating policy orientations, agreements and action plans into concrete actions that have a genuine impact. So far, only a few actions have been taken to make remittances cheaper, faster and safer, to support cooperation with diaspora communities and to turn brain drain into brain circulation, areas where most member states are just beginning to develop adequate measures.[24]

One can indeed note some delays in the implementation of the Council's 2003 conclusions on migration and development,[25] as well as of the 21 and 22 November 2005 conclusions on migration and external relations.[26]

Apart from the political will of the EU to implement the part of the measures which is primarily in the interest of third countries, the question of the means devoted to the new policy linking migration and development will become essential to its implementation. The financing of the initiatives envisaged by the action plans and conclusions on migration and development adopted at the Rabat and Tripoli conferences, as well as the EU–Africa Summit in Lisbon, remains an open question. The most important part of the credits which can be mobilised to fund migration and development issues is available under the geographical programmes, which are much more important than the thematic programme for the cooperation with third countries in the field of migration and asylum. It remains to be seen if the different Directorates General of the Commission (Justice, Liberty and Security, Aidco, Development) and the different competent ministries of the member states will act in unison, with sufficient coherence to ensure real and significant progress in the implementation of this new policy.

The fourth and last challenge is more general and concerns the global dimension of immigration, which has risen to the top of international concerns – as shown by the decision of a group of thirty-two states to set up a Global Commission on International Migration. In 2006 this commission produced a report entitled *Migration in an Interconnected World: New Directions for Actions*. Migration has increasingly become a relevant policy field for a growing number of countries progressively encouraged by the EU to develop a public policy on the issue – and notably one that reproduces to a certain extent European policies. These include in particular: controlling their own borders, developing a visa policy towards other countries and securing their travel documents. The strategy of the EU is clearly to prevent people from continuing to emigrate illegally from their country of origin, and also to encourage transit countries (in particular the ones neighbouring the EU) to better manage migration so as to prevent people from even reaching the EU. The question of policy balance must be taken into consideration if one wants to avoid a world where migration will become more and more difficult. Such an evolution could feed policies favouring the fight against illegal immigration and finally hamper the international mobility of persons, which must nonetheless be considered a normal phenomenon in a global world and should therefore not be subject to excessive state controls. This question also challenges the moral dimension for the EU. Even if its current efforts of externalisation hardly seem to engage the EU's legal responsibility – except in the case of interception at sea, which is difficult to combine with the respect of the right to seek asylum – it is nevertheless clear that the way in which, under external pressure, third countries start to manage the immigration phenomenon appeals to the EU's own sense of responsibility. It challenges the values concerned with the respect of human dignity and solidarity, which the EU wishes to promote. One might recall for instance the way in which, in 2005, the Moroccan authorities dealt with black African emigrants blocked on their way to the EU because of increasing European controls. According to different testimonies, these emigrants at times faced violent arrests and, occasionally, abandonment in the desert. The EU and its member states should consider carefully which migratory model they want to represent, not forgetting that the new common policy on immigration which is being elaborated, and which the Union wishes to externalise, will also be judged on the basis of its implications for third countries.

The external dimension of the European penal area

Sources

The European penal area covers police and judicial cooperation in criminal matters. Most of the EU's activities in this field concern 'internal cooperation' between its own member states. In this regard, three main aspects can be distinguished: improvement of cooperation mechanisms (in the field of police cooperation, see for example the improvement of the exchange of information, and in the field of judicial cooperation see the principle of mutual recognition of judicial decisions and the so-called European arrest warrant or EAW); the establishment of European actors (such as Europol or Eurojust); and the approximation of penal legislations. The external dimension of the European penal area has also developed, mainly because of the cross-border nature of the issues at stake.

The heterogeneity of sources developing the external dimension of the European penal area is striking. They are especially plural through their nature, spanning from political to legal, as well as through the institutional frame in which they are adopted. Sources linked to penal matters can be found in each of the pillars of the TEU. Even if the core of external activities in penal matters has been undertaken within the third pillar of the Treaty, namely within Title VI of the TEU, some general and limited provisions related to penal matters have also been included in certain EC external agreements concluded with third partners, and yet other initiatives have been adopted within Title V of the TEU related to a common foreign and security policy (CFSP). Furthermore, some political tools are of a cross-pillar nature, such as those instruments related to the European neighbourhood policy (ENP).

The external dimension of the European penal has developed rather slowly.

At the time of the Treaty of Maastricht, few measures had been adopted in penal matters, especially common positions, through which member states coordinated

their action in penal matters in international organisations and at international conferences. Such rare occurrences included two Common Positions, dated 6 October
and 13 November 1997, on negotiations in the Council of Europe and in the OECD
relating to corruption, and a Joint Position on 29 March 1999 on the draft United
Nations convention against organised crime.

Since the entry into force of the Treaty of Amsterdam, developments have
multiplied. This was the result of various causes. Such multiplication resulted of
course from the political context and will to move forward. This became apparent
through the growing attention granted to the need to strengthen close cooperation
with partner countries and international organisations by means of both horizontal
EU programmes – e.g., the 1999 Tampere conclusions, the 2000 Santa Maria de
Feira conclusions and the 2004 The Hague programme – and especially sector-
specific programmatic texts –e.g., the action plans in the fields of organised crime,
terrorism, drugs, and human trafficking (see below). The multiplication of initiatives
also resulted from the creation by the Amsterdam Treaty of new tools to develop
the external dimension of the European area: it introduced two new specific
provisions related to the external aspects of the third pillar, namely Articles 37 and
38, which refer to Articles 18, 19 and 24 of the second pillar, related to a CFSP. From
these references, it mainly follows that the Union is externally represented by the
Presidency in penal matters, and that the Union may conclude agreements with
non-Union states and international organisations in accordance with the procedure
organised by the Treaty.

As a consequence, there was an increase in the number of legally binding texts
adopted by the EU that were aimed at developing the external dimension of the
European penal area. Besides the adoption of new common positions – such as that
of 27 May 1999, on negotiations relating to the draft convention on cyber crime,
held in the Council of Europe – some EU external agreements, like the so-called
'Article 24–38 agreements', have been concluded. Three concern the USA, namely
two agreements dated June 2003 on extradition and on mutual legal assistance in
criminal matters, and a third one of July 2007 on the processing and transfer of
passenger name records data (EU–US 2007, PNR). They are all narrowly linked to
counter-terrorism. The first two were negotiated and concluded in the immediate
aftermath of 11 September 2001 terrorist attacks. However, their scope is not limited
to terrorist offences as their broad aim is to strengthen transatlantic penal cooperation
concerning a variety of crimes. They complement general bilateral cooperation
agreements concluded by some member states with the USA, and replace some
of their specific provisions. The EU–US 2007 PNR agreement resulted directly
from the need for the EU to respond to domestic US legislation adopted after
11 September 2001, which required all air carriers operating flights to, from or through
the USA to provide US Customs with electronic access to data contained in their
automatic reservation and departure control systems. Such law involved a wide range
of passenger data, and was obviously also addressed to EU carriers. This presented
the latter with a dilemma: in the case of non-compliance with the US obligations,
EU carriers had to face heavy financial sanctions, including the loss of landing rights
at US airports, but in the case of compliance with US law, they could breach their

own national or EU legislation, especially their duties related to the protection of sensitive personal data. Negotiations started in order to reconcile US and EU demands (Mitsilegas 2007). Four other external agreements have been concluded with associate Schengen partners. Two concern Iceland and Norway. They aim at extending to these specific Nordic partners some rules related either to mutual legal assistance (December 2003) or surrender procedure (June 2006). When EU rules are considered as developing the Schengen *acquis*,[27] they are applicable in principle to the Schengen associates.[28] When they are not considered as such, the only way to extend their scope to the Schengen associates is by recourse to Article 24–38 agreements. The remaining two external agreements are association agreements to Schengen signed by the EC and the EU with Switzerland (October 2004) and with Liechtenstein (February 2008).[29]

Besides the Acts adopted or concluded by the EU itself, several agreements have been concluded by European agencies acting in the penal field (Nilsson 2003). On the basis of the Europol Convention and other Council Acts or decisions detailing the rules to apply, Europol signed various agreements with non-EU states and third organisations, such as Interpol.[30] They are intended to enhance cooperation in combating serious forms of transnational crime, especially through the exchange of information. Various types of agreements exist, ranging from operational cooperation – including the exchange of personal data – to technical or strategic cooperation. The so-called 'operational agreements' are the most sensitive ones because they may cover transmission of data related to identified or identifiable individuals. They have mainly been concluded with Northern American countries (Canada and the USA) and the Schengen associates (Iceland, Norway and Switzerland). 'Strategic agreements' have been concluded with non-EU countries such as Moldova, Turkey, Russia and Colombia. On the basis of its 2002 founding Decision, Eurojust also signed agreements with third states, mainly Iceland, Norway and the USA.[31] Their purpose is to foster cooperation in combating serious forms of transnational crime, for instance by providing the secondment of a liaison prosecutor to Eurojust.

Besides such legally binding texts, there are numerous instruments of a more political nature. Without aspiring to be exhaustive in this regard, the cross-pillar texts belonging to the ENP – and especially the various individual action plans with the new neighbours – are worth mentioning. They all focus on security issues and give special attention to criminal matters. The EU–Russia relations deserve some brief comment. Besides a 2001 EU action plan on common action with the Russian Federation on combating organised crime, the common space of freedom, security and justice launched in 2003 with Russia and developed since then includes police and judicial cooperation aspects, as well as action against crime such as organised crime, money-laundering and human trafficking.

Policy developments

Developments of the external dimension of the European penal area follow both geographical and substantive priorities.

Among the favoured partners are third countries directly or indirectly bordering the EU, namely the associate Schengen partners (Iceland, Norway and Switzerland) and the new neighbours, as well as some other third countries such as the USA or Russia. The nature and contents of the cooperation differ very much from one third country to another. The EU concluded Article 24–38 agreements with only a few of them, namely the Schengen associate partners on the one hand, and the USA on the other. The objectives of both groups of agreements are different. Whereas agreements with Schengen associates organise the association itself or intimately linked aspects of it which are very much influenced by EU internal cooperation,[32] the 'transatlantic agreements' are narrowly linked to counter-terrorism and are not as similar to EU internal cooperation as those concluded with the Schengen associates.[33] Such differentiation exists even between third countries belonging to a common geographical area, or to a common group of states. In this regard the differences existing in the collaboration established with the new neighbours is worth mentioning. Besides the differences between the existing provisions related to penal matters in the EC agreements concluded with them,[34] variations also appear in the individual ENP action plans. They all share some common concerns, and most of them refer to the importance of combating similar types of crime, such as counter-terrorism or organised crime, but they also contain clear elements of differentiation which are representative of the various challenges and problems facing the new neighbours. Priorities are different; for instance, some action plans such as the ones with Jordan and Morocco emphasise anti-money-laundering action, whereas others such as the one with Ukraine emphasise aspects such as human trafficking. The level of cooperation pursued may differ as well: cooperation in criminal matters is especially developed with one new neighbour, namely Ukraine.[35]

Among the main substantive priorities, the fight against specific kinds of crime should be underlined. In this regard, reference can be made to some sector-related programmatic texts such as the specific action plans or strategies in the field of terrorism, organised crime, and trafficking in human beings or drugs. Concerning terrorism, various action plans and strategies have been adopted to strengthen international solidarity and cooperation in countering the problem. It is hoped that by promoting international partnership, cooperation will accordingly be fostered with key third countries beyond the EU, particularly within the UN and other international organisations, so as to deepen the international consensus. The partnerships also strive to develop technical assistance strategies, in order to help third countries in enhancing their counter-terrorism capacities. In this regard, one of the basic texts is the EU's counter-terrorism strategy, which rests upon four pillars, namely: 'Prevent, Protect, Pursue and Respond'.[36] Each of these pillars presents essential international aspects, with 'Pursue' especially needing a global dimension, because much of the terrorist threat to Europe originates outside the Union. The EU works to reinforce the international consensus through UN and other international bodies and through dialogue and agreements which include counter-terrorism clauses with key partners. It supports and promotes the UN counter-terrorism strategy and has laboured intensely in favour of an agreement on a UN Comprehensive Convention against terrorism. The EU also works to provide assistance through financing and expertise to priority countries, such as Morocco or

Algeria, so as to help them introduce and implement the necessary mechanisms to head off terrorism. However, as is illustrated by the counter-terrorism coordinator's 2007 implementation reports, this last task aimed at providing technical assistance has encountered various difficulties.[37] Regarding organised crime, one of the eleven basic objectives of the so-called *Prevention and Control of Organized Crime: A Strategy for the Beginning of the New Millennium* (2000) is precisely to strengthen cooperation with third countries and other international organisations. Concerning human trafficking, one of the basic ideas of the *EU Plan on Best Practices, Standards and Procedures for Combating and Preventing Trafficking in Human Beings* (2005) is to develop an integrated approach to tackling the problem, marked by an improvement in understanding the issues involved in human trafficking. Among other things, the plan calls for a better understanding of the root causes in the countries of origin, which in turn implies the development of international cooperation. Regarding drugs, the EU's specific strategy (2005–12) also covers important external cooperation aspects. It aims especially at developing a coordinated, effective and more visible action by the EU in international organisations that enhance and promote a balanced approach to drugs, as well as assisting third countries – including new neighbours and key drug-producing and transit countries – to be more effective in tackling the drugs problem.[38]

Main issues at stake

The main priority for the EU remains that of appearing as an international security actor, strengthening its cooperation in these fields with external partners and thus exporting its values. However, this is quite challenging in the light of the various difficulties facing the EU. Two of these difficulties deserve some explanation: they concern the current EU institutional framework and 'pillarisation' of the Treaty on the one hand, and the quest for striking an appropriate balance between the sword and shield functions of penal law on the other hand.

As seen previously, for the time being the majority of external activities in penal matters are currently undertaken within the third pillar of the TEU, namely within its Title VI. The intergovernmental specificities of the third pillar have of course influenced these aspects of the EU's work and have handicapped them at the same time.

The adoption of new instruments has been difficult, since it is still submitted to a unanimous voting procedure within the Council. This explains at least partly the rather limited number of common positions and Article 24–38 agreements. In addition, the development of the external dimension of the European penal area has been considerably hampered by problems linked to the controversial debate on the legal personality of the EU (Neuwahl 1998; Wessel 2000). Consequently, Article 24 has been variously interpreted depending on whether external agreements of a penal nature have been concluded and signed by the EU in its own name, or rather in the name of the member states. Whereas numerous elements confirm such EU capacity, this point is still not accepted by some member states. Such ambiguity puts the EU in a rather awkward position *vis-à-vis* its partners and also considerably delays the entry into force of Article 24–38 agreements, since they must pass through ratification in the member states.

Moreover, the external dimension of the European penal area suffers from severe democratic and jurisdictional deficits.[39] The European Parliament's involvement is even weaker than in the case of the internal dimension of the European penal area: neither common positions nor Article 24–38 agreements are obliged to seek its input through consultation,[40] and none of these instruments is submitted to the full jurisdiction of the Court of Justice of the EC.

The cross-pillar nature of the external dimension of the European penal area and the heterogeneity of actors jeopardise the EU's visibility and external image. Different legal bases and different interlocutors are difficult to explain to the 'external world' and are understood with difficulty by the third countries and international organisations with which the EU interacts. A particular effort needs to be made by the EU in order to explain its position convincingly to its third partners. Difficulties are exacerbated by the fact that 'pillarisation' results in competition between some of the concerned actors as well as in conflicts of legal bases which handicap the external dimension of the European penal area. In this regard, the abovementioned EU–US 2007 PNR agreement is a good case in point. It is the result of a rather complex evolution, having replaced an interim agreement concluded between the EU and the USA, which had itself replaced the first agreement signed in May 2004 between the USA and the EC within the first pillar of the Treaty, following that agreement's denunciation after an annulment by the Court of Justice of the Commission's adequacy decision and the Council's decision authorising the conclusion of the EC–US agreement[41] (Mitsilegas 2007). This decision was issued on a request introduced by the European Parliament asking for the annulment of the Council decision on the grounds that it breached fundamental rights, the principle of proportionality and European data-protection rules, as well as having been adopted on an erroneous legal basis (i.e., Articles 95 and 300(2), TEC). The Court did not examine the compatibility with fundamental rights and data-protection standards but only the choice of legal basis and concluded that the first pillar legal bases used were wrong. On the grounds that the passenger data are used strictly for the purposes of preventing and combating terrorism and related crimes – other serious crimes, including organised crime, that are transnational in nature – it considered that the transfer of PNR data constitutes processing operations concerning public security and the activities of the state in areas of criminal law. Such annulment for constitutional reasons and the denouncement of the 2004 EU–US PNR international agreement that it implied obviously encroached upon the EU's image as a firm and solid partner on the international stage.

Within the framework of the Treaty of Lisbon, these matters are to be radically changed. The Reform Treaty simplifies the situation since it abolishes the third pillar and transfers penal matters into TFEU. It consequently puts an end to conflicts of legal bases between the first and the third pillars. However, it does not necessarily mean that every conflict concerning legal bases or disputes related to the distribution of competences will disappear. Some conflicts or disputes could remain for instance between TFEU and CFSP and between the EU and member states. As a consequence of the abolition of the previous third pillar and of the transfer of police and judicial cooperation in criminal matters to the TFEU, such matters should be submitted to the EC's ordinary decision-taking methods. This leads to the introduction of qualified majority voting in penal matters and facilitates the adoption of instruments in the field. The innovations set out in the Lisbon Treaty definitely solve the problems related to the legal personality of the EU,[42] reducing the democratic and jurisdictional deficits by leaving more room to the European Parliament and the Court of Justice of the European Community.

Another serious difficulty with which the EU is confronted when developing the external dimension of its penal area is the need to safeguard some of its own values and standards when cooperating with its partners. In this regard, the series of agreements concluded with the USA has been especially heavily contested. The 2003 EU–US agreements on extradition and mutual legal assistance created major concerns. One of the most sensitive issues turned on the extradition by the EU to the USA of individuals who could be subject to capital punishment.[43] Another problem arose with the cooperation granted to US special courts, and notably the military courts established by the US laws after 11 September 2001.[44] The 2003 mutual legal assistance agreement, the above-mentioned PNR agreement and the Europol–US cooperation agreement were also the targets of strong criticisms related to the lack of an extensive and specific data-protection framework in the USA. In this respect, numerous observers raised the question of whether it would be acceptable for the EU to emerge as an external actor by agreeing to standards which might violate its internal legislation and the very values and principles it proclaims to be based upon and tries to export (Mitsilegas 2007). The Union's involvement in the implementation and development of some international rules, such as those defined within the UN related to the terrorist lists, has also created negative reactions and uneasiness. All of this is representative of the difficulties faced by the EU to find an appropriate balance between the sword function (i.e., the protection of individuals against crime) and the shield function (i.e., the protection of individuals against arbitrariness and abuses by repressive authorities) of penal law. However, this challenge is not specific to the external dimension of the European penal area nor even to the EU. The internal aspects of the European penal area, as well as national criminal policies and international organisations themselves face the same difficulties. They are simply the result of the very sensitive nature of penal law and of its complex relation with human rights. As H. Wechsler very clearly stated (Wechsler 1952):

> Whatever view one holds about the penal law, no one will question its importance in society. This is the law on which men place their ultimate reliance for the protection against all the deepest injuries that human conduct can inflict on individuals and institutions. By the same token, penal law governs the strongest force that we permit official agencies to bring to bear on individuals. Its promise as an instrument of safety is matched only by its power to destroy. If penal law is weak or ineffective, basic human interests are in jeopardy. If it is harsh or arbitrary in its impact, it works a gross injustice on those caught within its coils. The law that carries such responsibilities should surely be as rational and just as law can be. Nowhere in the entire legal field is more at stake for the community, for the individual.

However, examples show that the EU does not systematically give way to external pressure exercised by international organisations, or by powerful non-EU states. On the one hand, in spite of requests by third countries to do so, it refuses to extend its most specific penal cooperation achievements. In this regard, it is very interesting to study the debate about extension/non-extension of the mutual recognition process, of mutual trust and especially of the EAW. On the other hand, by exporting some other European achievements, the EU exercises a clear influence on the 'external world' (de Kerchove 2003; Barbe 2003). Indeed its impact on the work achieved within third organisations where it is represented is clear. For instance, through its abovementioned 1999 common position, the EU deeply influenced the negotiations of the 2000 UN Palermo Convention on organised crime; the second protocol to the Convention of the Council of Europe about mutual assistance is nearly identical to the EU 2000 Convention on mutual assistance in criminal matters. Some of the EU's achievements are exported through its bilateral relations: some aspects of the EU–US 2003 agreements about extradition and mutual legal assistance recall aspects of the EU's own internal instruments.[45] Finally, the EU also serves as a source of inspiration for other regional fora. In this regard, it is worth underlining that the European arrest warrant seems to constitute an inspiring model in Latin America.

Conclusion

In light of past developments, it is clear that, since the entry into force of the Amsterdam Treaty, both the external dimension of the immigration policy and the European penal area have undergone important developments. If both topics present important differences, they also present some common features. In this respect, one can highlight:

- the complexity of sources and heterogeneity of tools which resort both to soft and hard law, with a progressive expansion of hard law and a multiplication of legally binding instruments
- the difficulties encountered with regard to implementation, in particular the fact that they both depend on internal factors (distribution of competence between pillars or between the EU and its member states, institutional weaknesses)
- the quest for coherence between internal and external policies but also between external aspects
- the quest to strike the right balance between the different elements of the policies. Regarding immigration, it is about finding an equilibrium between the fight against illegal migration and the opening of legal migration channels; concerning penal aspects, it is about the parallel development of the shield and sword functions of penal law.

Notes

1 The authors did not include the references to the Official Journal of the European Union for the legal instruments which are quoted in this chapter for reasons of space; the reader

can if necessary find them easily on the relevant website http:/eur-lex.europa.eu/JOindex. do?ihmlang=en

2 Doc. 14366/3/05, 30 November 2005 and JHA Council, 1–2 December 2005, 14390/05.
3 This term refers to the submission of policy areas to the 'Community method', characterised mainly by qualified majority voting in Council, co-decision with the European Parliament, the exclusive right of initiative of the Commission and full control by the Court of Justice.
4 http://eur-lex.europa.eu/JOIndex.do?ihmlang=en
5 For a synthesis, see a communication of the Commission, *Towards a Common Immigration Policy*, COM (2007) 780, 5 December 2007.
6 Following estimates, illegal immigrants were about 800,000 persons in 2001 for the EU-25 (see Commission Staff Working Document SEC (2006) 964: 8).
7 COM (2002) 703, 3 December 2002.
8 Council Document 8927/03, 5 May 2003.
9 COM (2005) 390.
10 Which can only be found on the internet, as they are not officially published.
11 COM (2007) 248.
12 Document 10746/07.
13 COM (2006) 735.
14 COM (2007) 1632.
15 Document 15446/05.
16 See Article 13 on migration.
17 See Council and Member States Representatives Conclusions on Coherence Between EU and Development Policies, 20 November 2007 (Document 15116/07).
18 Document 15966/07 (press release of the JHA Council, 6 and 7 December 2007).
19 Document 6054/08.
20 In this volume, see Chapter 6 by Marianne Dony, on the EU's external relations and their evolving legal framework.
21 Document 15966/07 (press release of the JHA Council, 6 and 7 December 2007).
22 COM (2005) 669.
23 COM (2007) 249.
24 Commission working paper COM (2007) 545, 20 September 2007: 8. For more details, see the EU Report on Policy Coherence for Development, SEC (2007) 1202: 106–14.
25 Document 8927/03.
26 Document 14172/05 (press release of the JHA Council, 21 and 22 November 2005).
27 The Schengen *acquis* is the *acquis* resulting from the Schengen cooperation established by the Treaty on the gradual abolition of checks at common borders signed by some Member States of the EU in Schengen on 14 June 1985 and the Convention implementing the Schengen Agreement signed on 19 June 1990. It has been integrated within the European Union by the Treaty of Amsterdam, more precisely by the "Protocol integrating the Schengen acquis into the framework of the European Union". The Schengen acquis is defined in the annex to the above mentioned Protocol and in other official instruments, mainly the Council decision of 20 May 1999 concerning the definition of the Schengen acquis for the purpose of determining the legal basis for each of the provisions or decisions which constitutes the acquis. The so-called Schengen acquis binds the Schengen partners as well as the Schengen associate partners.
28 See the regime established by the Agreement of May 1999, between the Council of the EU and Iceland and Norway, concerning the latter two countries' association with the implementation, application and development of the Schengen *acquis*.

29 Protocol between the EU, the European Community, the Swiss Confederation and the Principality of Liechtenstein on the accession of the Principality of Liechtenstein to the Agreement between the European Union, the European Community and the Swiss Confederation on the Swiss Confederation's association with the implementation, application and development of the Schengen *acquis* (Doc. 16462/06, 13 February 2008).

30 See website of Europol http://www.europol.europa.eu

31 See website of Eurojust http://www.eurojust.europa.eu

32 See the agreement with Iceland and Norway on surrender procedure, which establishes a kind of lightened European arrest warrant procedure.

33 Compare the agreement with Iceland and Norway on surrender procedure and the agreement with the USA on extradition.

34 Among the most developed provisions, see the agreements concluded with Egypt, Algeria and Lebanon.

35 See the 2001 JHA Action Plan with Ukraine, which became the freedom, security and justice part of the 2005 EU–Ukraine Action Plan.

36 Council, Doc. 14469/4/05, Rev. 4, 30 November 2005.

37 See Council, Doc. 15448/07, 23 November 2007.

38 See Council, Doc. 15074/04, not published in the OJ.

39 See Network of Independent Experts on Fundamental Rights, Thematic study, Thematic comment No. 2: 'Fundamental rights in the external activities of the EU in the fields of justice and asylum and immigration in 2003', 4 February 2004.

40 If one considers the 2003 EU–US agreements for instance, there was no involvement of the European Parliament and this was very severely denounced by the European Parliament itself.

41 CJEC, 30 May 2006, C-317/04 and C-318/04, *European Parliament v Council and European Parliament v Commission.*

42 This is a consequence of the transfer of penal matters to the TFEU and of the explicit recognition by the reform treaty of the legal personality to the EU (Article 47, TEU).

43 Article 13 of the EU–US agreement about extradition deals with that problem. Is such provision, and especially the use of the word 'may' in the last sentence, in line with the case law of the European Court on human rights – and the *Soering* case – from which it results that states have to prevent any violation of the European Convention, which forbids them from extraditing persons when there is a real risk of those persons being subjected to torture or to inhumane or degrading treatment or punishment in the requesting country?

44 None of the 2003 EU–US agreements excludes explicitly that such courts might benefit from the cooperation they organise.

45 The US–EU Convention on Extradition contains specific rules related to extradition in case of the concerned person's consent, which evokes the 1995 EU Convention on Extradition. However, they are not comparable to the mechanism of the European arrest warrant. On the other hand, the EU–US Convention on Mutual Legal Assistance provides for joint investigative teams, evoking the Framework Decision on joint investigative teams between member states of the EU.

Bibliography

Barbe, Emmanuel (2003), 'L''influence de l'Union européenne dans les autres enceintes internationales', in G. de Kerchove and A. Weyembergh (eds), *Sécurité et justice: enjeu de la politique extérieure de l'Union européenne*, Bruxelles: éd. de l'Université de Bruxelles: 211–17.

Boswell, C. (2003), 'The external dimension of EU immigration and asylum policy', *International Affairs*, 619–38.

de Kerchove, G (2003), 'Introduction', in G. De Kerchove and A. Weyembergh (eds), *Sécurité et justice: enjeu de la politique extérieure de l'Union européenne, op. cit.*, pp.1–14.

Lavenex, S. and E. Ucarer (2002), *Migration and the Externalities of European Integration*, London: Lexington.

Lavenex, S. (2006), 'Shifting up and out: the foreign policy of European immigration control', *West European Politics*, 329–50.

Mitsilegas, V. (2003), 'The new EU–USA cooperation on extradition, mutual legal assistance and the exchange of police data', *European Foreign Affairs Review*, No. 8: 515–36.

Mitsilegas, V. (2007), 'The external dimension of EU action in criminal matters', *European Foreign Affairs Review*, 477–97.

Neuwahl, N. (1998), 'A partner with a troubled personality: EU treaty-making in matters of CFSP and JHA after the Treaty of Amsterdam', *European Foreign Affairs Review*, 177–95.

Nilsson, H. G. (2003), 'Organs and bodies of the third pillar as instruments of external relations of the Union', in G. de Kerchove and A. Weyembergh (eds), *Sécurité et justice: enjeu de la politique extérieure de l'Union européenne*, Bruxelles: éd. de l'Université de Bruxelles: 200–11.

Rodier, C. (2006), *Analysis of the External Dimension of the EU's Asylum and Immigration Policies*, A study done for the European Parliament, (see http://www.europarl.europa.eu/meetdocs/2004_2009/documents/dt/619/619330/619330fr.pdf).

Stessens, G. (2003), 'The EU–US agreements on extradition and on mutual assistance: how to bridge different approaches?', in G. de Kerchove and A. Weyembergh (eds), *Sécurité et justice: enjeu de la politique extérieure de l'Union européenne*, Bruxelles: éd. de l'Université de Bruxelles: 263–75.

Wechsler, H. (1952), 'The Challenge of a Model Penal Code', Harvard Law Review, p. 1097.

Wessel, R.A. (2000), 'The inside looking out: consistency and delimitation in EU external relations', *Common Market Law Review*, No. 37: 1135–71.

Wichsmann, N. (2007), 'The intersection between Justice and Home Affairs and the European Neighbourhood policy: taking stock of the logic, objectives and practices', Brussels: CEPS working document, October 2007.

11 Global governance

A challenge for common foreign and security policy and European security and defence policy

Barbara Delcourt and Eric Remacle

Summary

This chapter's main objective is to discuss some of the principles and ideas which are commonly evoked, in both academic and political circles, regarding the EU as an international actor and its specific participation in global governance. A substantial part of it is devoted more specifically to the European security and defence policy and to the strengthening of the EU's ability to intervene in crisis-stricken areas. Accordingly, both the unleashed potential born of the EU's ambitions on the international stage, as well as the difficulties that the EU has to face in the current state of the world system, are to be detailed.

Introduction

Since the official start of the European Political Cooperation (EPC) in 1970, global challenges have boosted the need for foreign policy coordination between member states of the European Communities. Issues such as energy supply, transformations of the international economic and monetary system, crises in the Middle East and Central America, and the impact of the cold war and arms race between the superpowers have all contributed to Western European powers' eagerness to increase political consultations and action on the world stage. However, the establishment of the political union itself, and its legalization under the name "common foreign and security policy" (CFSP), was acknowledged when the Maastricht Treaty established the European Union (EU) in 1991. Subsequent Treaty revisions were negotiated in Amsterdam (1997), Nice (2000) and Lisbon (2007) with an eye to reinforcing its efficiency and legitimacy as well as adding a military dimension to CFSP, named "common European security and defence policy" (CESDP, often shortened as ESDP).[1]

Since the 1990s, most EEC/EU member states have agreed to take further steps so as to give both a clear political dimension to the European project as well as fostering a more effective grip on international affairs. Although the new mechanisms and institutions falling under the second pillar, and dedicated to external actions, did not really create the conditions to develop a genuinely *common* policy, because they stuck to the same intergovernmental logic that underpinned the EPC, these

Table 11.1 Chronology of major Treaty reforms regarding CFSP and ESDP

Maastricht Treaty (1991)

CFSP (second pillar) replaces EPC with little change
Defence remains outside EU (WEU)
Inter-governmentalism (unanimity) is the rule; few new legal instruments (joint actions, common positions, complex budget procedure)
Low level of institutionalization (rotating Presidency – Council and Working Groups – Political Committee composed of Political Directors – Commission)

Amsterdam Treaty (1997)

CFSP remains as second pillar
Petersberg Tasks (crisis management) are quoted as EU tasks; WEU maintains power while receiving guidelines from the European Council
Inter-governmentalism remains, with more sophistication in legal instruments (common strategies) and procedures (constructive abstention is possible in case of unanimity voting, but the clause of the Luxembourg compromise is also possible in case of qualified majority voting (QMV) for joint actions and common positions) and clarification of budgetary procedures
Increased level of institutionalization (High Representative for CFSP, Policy Unit, Special Representatives)

Nice Treaty (2000)

CFSP is completed by (C)ESDP
Defence is incorporated into EU (WEU into the refrigerator)
Inter-governmentalism remains (primacy of unanimity, same rules for constructive abstention, and QMV as in the Amsterdam Treaty)
Increased level of institutionalization (permanent committees: PSC, EUMC + EUMS and transfer of several WEU assets/agencies)

Lisbon Treaty (2007)

End of pillars (but procedures remain *de facto* different) – the acronym CSDP replaces ESDP
List of Petersberg Tasks is extended
Solidarity clause is introduced
Self-defence clause is introduced (opt-out for neutral states)
Possibility of closer cooperation between member states for missions or multinational forces
Inter-governmentalism remains – notion of ícommon approachí
End of rotating Presidency for the European Council and for the Foreign Affairs Council
A President of the European Council is established who will represent the Union on the world stage (term of 2.5 years)
Concentration of institutions into the hands of a permanent High Representative of the Union for Foreign Affairs and Security Policy (terms of 2.5 years; gets power of initiative; sits both in Council and Vice-President of the Commission; chairs Foreign Affairs Council and all committees and agencies – including the new Armaments Agency, EDA)

Table 11.1 (continued)

Lisbon Treaty (2007)

Slight extension of the potential for QMV in CFSP: to be used when the proposal comes
from the High Representative
Creation of the European External Action Service under the High Representative
Military benchmarking led by the EDA and a core group of countries, named "permanent
structured cooperation"

innovations were nevertheless officially designed and further improved to enable
the EU to "project power" abroad and to tackle the perceived new threats and risks
emerging on the international stage, while promoting European interests and values.
These are the core arguments underpinning the EU's discourse, notwithstanding
the complementary notion that the Union could be a template for a more rational
global regulation and is thus predisposed to take a particular responsibility in global
governance. Similarly, the conviction that the EU has to play a leading role on the
international stage, in particular in the security area – because of its demographics
(almost 500 million people) and its political and economic weight (being the largest
trading power and disbursing 55 percent of the total development and humanitarian
aid funds) – is a common feature of the European discourse. The Union's capacity
to "project its power" beyond its own territory, to stabilize its borders and reshape
political and economic institutions in third countries, notably by demanding liberal
democracy and a market economy, lies at the core of the European Security Strategy
adopted by the EU in December 2003.[2] Furthermore, the need to shape the future
and to be more outward looking, instead of being a mere witness undergoing events,
has increasingly become a shared concern for Europeans.

The unfinished theoretical debate on CFSP/ESDP and global governance

Academic literature offers a vast array of analyses on the sources underpinning the
EU's external action (or inaction). In the name of clarity, this chapter will focus on
four main types of analyses.

A first group of scholars – mixing realists and liberal intergovernmentalists –
emphasize member states' central role in European foreign policy decisions. They
argue that such decisions result mainly from convergence of preferences between
member states, thus explaining the continued predominance of intergovernmental
procedures in CFSP and ESDP despite member states' increasing interest in speaking
with one voice in international affairs. This distinctive intergovernmental slant of the
CFSP and ESDP maintains a difference between the evolution of "low politics" and
"high politics" arenas of the EU's external action.

A second explanation is neo-institutionalist. It considers the efficiency of the
EU's external action as being mainly dependent on the ability of institutions to
go beyond national interests and shape a common vision and policy. Likewise,
failures of the EU come from weaknesses of the institutional apparatus, mainly

the absence of a strong supranational driving force. Successes are the result of institutional dynamics, especially of the new (intergovernmental) institutions set up after Amsterdam and centered on the position of the High Representative and its "Brussel-ized" bureaucracy. The institutional dynamics are seen as the source of a slow process of socialization and Europeanization of national structures and decisions, which ultimately leads to the transformation of domestic dynamics, including new perceptions of the national interest.

Those two theoretical visions mainly take into account internal (either domestic or institutional) factors and actors. They pay little attention to external constraints and therefore consider that, under favorable circumstances (either convergence of national preferences or institutional virtuous circle), CFSP and ESDP will contribute to global governance while not themselves being influenced by global issues or external actors. Such external variables are emphasized by a third of explanations which highlight international constraints and the fact that, for instance, the EU's behaviour as an international actor can also be conditioned by transatlantic relations. Cases such as the Middle Eastern and Yugoslav crises, or the fight against terrorism after September 2001, are usually quoted as good examples of US influence. Apart from the many detailed studies of this American factor, there have been until now few attempts to assess the influence of other global or systemic issues on the EU's external action. Furthermore, the emphasis on those external variables has to be related to domestic and institutional variables in order to offer a more comprehensive analytical toolbox.

During the 1990s, such a fourth theoretical approach was proposed by the "expectation–capability gap" school of thought; whereas the 2000s saw the rise of those concerned with the EU's "actorness". According to the expectation–capability gap school of thought, the EU's external (in)action comes from the dialectics between expectations (from domestic scenes and from external actors) and capabilities (defined by Christopher Hill as the ability to decide, to rely on resources and to maintain consistency between existing EU instruments)[3]. Though mixing explanatory and normative proposals, as well as being partly dedicated to the plea for EU military capabilities, implemented after the establishment of ESDP in 2000, this approach is not outdated since it offers the widest and most dynamic explanatory toolbox allowing for an articulation of internal and external variables of CFSP. Furthermore, it is compatible with the constructivist literature emphasizing identities and representations since they contribute to the shaping of expectations, as well as with the recent studies on legitimization which discuss the tensions between the internal and external performance of CFSP.

The EU and multilateralism: from principles to practices

A faithful pledge for multilateralism?

The EU's choice in favor of multilateralism is clearly stated in official documents and declarations delivered by its institutions.[4] According to the European Security Strategy, multilateralism is "the development of a stronger international society, well functioning international institutions and a rule-based international order".[5] This commitment is deemed to be anchored in the European political culture and on its own multilateral integration experience, whereas interdependence and globalization are supposed to further foster cooperation at the global level. Moreover this structural process would be needed for the kind of governance the EU is able to deliver. In this regard, the distinction made between "milieu goals" and "possession goals" could shed light on the peculiarities of the EU's external actions. Pursuing possession goals is a traditional way of doing international politics by defending national interests. Developing milieu goals aims instead at building an international environment in which different actors can interact peacefully through institutions without having to stick to predefined interests. Drawing on this distinction, Karen Smith concludes that while only the first of the five milieu goals, the encouragement of regional cooperation and integration, can be considered to be unique to the EU, the way in which it pursues the other four (international cooperation, strengthening the rule of law, responsibility for global environment and diffusion of equality, justice and tolerance) makes it different from other actors in the international system. The case made for the EU's being a *sui generis* international actor is even stronger when one considers the two principal foreign policy tools used by the EU. The first are legal agreements with actors, support for international agreements and conventions, institutionalized dialogue, the conditional promise of EU membership, and support to non-government organizations (NGOs). The second is the EU's reliance on persuasion and positive incentives rather than coercion, although non-violent coercion is used as well – especially in the (albeit inconsistent) application of negative conditionality.[6]

Most of the time the pledge for multilateralism is linked to the United Nations (UN), since it represents the highest level of political cooperation on the international stage. The intention to work hand-in-hand with the world organization has been realized in concrete steps. The EU has also stated that one of the main aims of its multilateral policy is to improve the level of coherence of its representation in the UN system. Since 1974, the European Economic Community (EEC) has been granted the status of observer within the UN that allows the Commission to participate in the General Assembly and the specialized commissions when they deal with topics like fisheries, agriculture and trade falling under its exclusive competences. In other cases, its role is to support the Presidency that is officially the voice of Europe or to push for more coordination between member states. From the 1990s onwards, and despite the fact that states are not always prone to delegate authority to the Commission or the Presidency, convergence in voting appears more apparent while annual meetings between EU and UN representatives testify to the existence of a closer relationship. A thorough examination of official documents and reports dealing with political and security matters will also show many commonalities between these organizations, regarding both the perceptions of new threats and risks and the best ways to manage them; as well as a generally increasing convergence between their strategic documents dealing with global governance issues. Both organizations have furthermore converged in shaping a common vision on merging security and development agendas.

A European foreign policy that promotes the consolidation and expansion of institutions that foster international cooperation can also be consistent with the overall strategic aims of the Union. In this case, the commitment to multilateralism is less an end in itself; it ultimately serves the material interests of the EU, which are to conduct foreign policy through peaceful means and to use its economic power to the best of its ability. In this perspective, the strengthening of the international multilateral system through the institutionalization of international relations and increased observance of international law will allow the EU to grow in significance as a global actor over the medium to long term. In so doing, the EU uses its political and economic power to change the structure of the international system (and build up the institutions of international society) in order to fashion one in which its own capabilities are favored.

The EU as normative power?

Besides promoting multilateralism, the EU is also portraying itself as a vehicle for the expansion of international law, and in particular the legal rules regarding fundamental human rights, as well as for the spreading of democracy and the rule of law across the globe. Because the EU's project rests on these liberal norms and principles, it would be normative by nature. Such a conclusion is drawn by Ian Manners, who has identified five core values (peace, liberty, democracy, rule of law and respect for human rights) and four subsidiary values (social solidarity, anti-discrimination, sustainable development and good governance) that enable us to speak about the *sui generis* nature of Europe.[7] The "normative power" concept encapsulates a prominent identity discourse which coalesces with the pledge towards multilateralism and cosmopolitan accounts of EU's foreign policy. Here again, the fact that the EU does not behave as do other powers should be underlined, in particular the fact that it does not rely on an "other-ing process" or the identification of an "enemy." The troubled history of the European continent itself and the return to isolated nation-states and nationalism are considered to be the real threats or enemies against which the EU is fighting by proposing cooperative and multilateral strategies.

According to the Preamble and Article 11 of the EU Treaty, universal norms enshrined in the UN Charter constitute the substance of the normative framework of the EU's external action, while reflexivity and inclusiveness, which are supposed to be the core features of the contractual relations developed with third countries, point to the quality of the process in regard to their elaboration and implementation. For instance, the policy of economic sanctions, which is indeed a powerful instrument in the hands of the EU, has been revised in order to take into consideration the negative effects of the sanctions bearing on powerless people. It tries to be more directly targeted at those who are in charge of state affairs and directly responsible for human rights violations or other major violations of international law. A further token of the EU's normative engagements is the principle of ownership, which is deemed to ensure a genuine participation of recipient countries in the definition of aid and development policies.

This normative power thesis has not convinced all scholars. Several critical analysts think that the achievements of the EU in the field of democracy and human rights are not so clear. Its allegedly post-modern diplomacy has not yet produced obvious positive outcomes for recipients. It might contribute mainly to a liberal peace order aimed at keeping control of the world economy and of turbulent areas in the periphery rather than answering to needs of local populations and to state reconstruction. Conditionality and sanctions are difficult to implement and the rule of law seems more and more dependent on political and strategic concerns. EU officials feel uneasy with the interpretation and implementation of provisions dealing with human rights and democracy as enshrined in some international agreements. Many scholars acknowledge that interest-driven concerns could explain the decisions taken and the poor record of EU policies in this field. Even when EU officials have a direct bearing on domestic politics, as in the international administration of Bosnia-Herzegovina, it seems that if the overall objectives point to the transformation of war-torn societies into liberal democracies and market economies, the means used are either at odds with democratic standards or with international law. The most radical critics will use the term 'empire' to describe the very nature of the imbalanced relations between some countries (particularly candidate countries and poorest states) and the EU.[8] In a way, this kind of analysis shows that the more Europe becomes powerful, the less it behaves on normative grounds or along established and fixed rules.

The revival of the notion of empire is also discussed from a post-modern perspective. The main writer of the European Security Strategy, the British senior diplomat Robert Cooper, formerly advisor to Prime Minister Blair, now Director in the EU Council Secretariat-General, authored a famous essay in favor of the establishment of a European "liberal imperialism" based on economic transformation by international economic organisations and by an EU neighbourhood policy (ENP) exporting stability, democracy, the market economy and good governance.[9] European discourses and documents do not refer to such an imperial turn. On the contrary, expressions like "partnership" and "ownership" seek to illustrate the will to apply the concept of shared sovereignty that underpinned the European integration process to the relationships with third countries. The EU presents itself as a facilitating partner for building a shared project rather than as a coercive external power.[10]

A less controversial position is taken by those who consider that Europe is certainly a normative power but not of the same nature as the one described by Ian Manners. They show that European standards in areas such as product-safety, environmental protection and corporate governance are more and more spreading over the globe. Based on data provided by a Commission's policy paper stating that "increasingly the world is looking to Europe and adopts the standards that are set here"[11] – something that helps European businesses in beating their rivals abroad "since it works at the advantage of those already geared up to meet these standards" – their analysis matches a more traditional vision of an international scene that would be characterized by multipolarism and competitive policies between major trade powers. Thus counterbalancing major powers, notably the USA, would be the real incentive of the EU foreign policy. Latin America, for example, is sometimes viewed as the scene for indirect EU–US competition; and more generally the relationship with the USA is considered as a litmus test for the extent to which the EU has become a key power. The mere fact that there are growing concerns in the USA about the

EU's ambition to be a pace-setter for worldwide business regulation – notably in the fields of genetically modified food, the chemical industry, and telecommunications – gives credibility to this thesis. With its 500 million consumers and its unified market, the EU will indeed be in a position to shape global norms and therefore to challenge the US's soft power. The EU is also active in influencing other important trading nations and other international organizations or jurisdictions, like the International Maritime Organization and the Geneva-based branch of the UN dedicated to economic cooperation. This development has led the US ambassador to the EU to lament the Europeans being "aggressive" about exporting an approach that favors their own companies. EU officials have not denied such ambitions, since they seem to be convinced that becoming the "regulatory capital of the world" is also good news for the values they are fighting for.

The more the EU's structural power improves, and its position within the international society is enhanced, the more it is tempting to resort to the concept of hegemony. To some extent, the EU has been able, through its regulatory push, to oblige the USA to accept principles of regulatory cooperation. According to Thomas Diez, the mere fact that the EU's foreign policy aims mostly at "changing the others"[12] would testify to the messianic character of its transformative power and would generate contradictions with the pluralist conception of the world that underpinned the Copenhagen Declaration on the European Identity (1973). Indeed, "normative power" is designed to "shape the conception of the normal" by a smooth diffusion of ideas and opinions whereas different forms of "*other-ing*" are taking place in order to legitimize more coercive or traditional actions.[13]

A power like the others?

Vogler and Bretherton have proposed the concept of "hybrid identity" when describing the two facets of the EU's identity[14]. On the one hand, the EU can be considered a value-based community, and be seen as inclusive insofar as it provides opportunity for non-members to join or gain privileged access to its markets. But on the other hand, the EU can also be exclusive because of some of its practices ranging from market protection (criticized often as being counter to the needs of developing countries) to immigration and asylum – a policy which is criticized for its securitization and contradictions with human rights principles. The Janus-faced EU foreign policy is particularly visible in agreements concluded with African, Caribbean and Pacific (ACP) countries or, more generally, in official development policy. While, in the post-September 11, 2001 context, there has been no massive reallocation of aid resources from the poorest states of Africa to more "strategic" countries in the front line of the war against terrorism, some increases in resources undoubtedly reflect European interests and security concerns. More and more agreements include new provisions dealing with illegal immigration, border management and security patrols in the Mediterranean, anti-terrorist clauses and readmission procedures which are not, to say the least, top priorities for the recipient countries. The major EU demand during the revision of the Cotonou Convention in 2005 was the introduction of anti-terrorist and anti-proliferation clauses in agreements with ACP countries.

The picture arising from some analyses casts a doubt on the normative power thesis while the development of the European military seems to create contradictions with the emphasis on "civilian power Europe." In some cases, EU foreign policy seems to lose its peculiarities; and its external actions can hardly be distinguished from other powers' policies. At the theoretical level, such statements often rely on a reflection on how strategic calculation invests the normative agenda. Far from going back to classical realist explanations and instrumental rationalism, Youngs, for example, offers an analytical framework in which security concerns and normative values inform each other.[15] In this logic, norms are not good or just ideas or merely woven in ethics; they can be based on material interests and are defined as practical collective expectations that are socially sanctioned. This kind of epistemological choice implies a more sociological than normative approach in order to understand the complex relationship between identity, values and interests. Through these lenses, it can be explained that the EU might faithfully abide by multilateralism and the UN Charter, but also act unilaterally by default or "necessity." Such an analytical framework also provides a compelling analysis of the human rights policies work by unveiling the strategies and interests that inspire those who are in charge of disbursing about 1 billion euros a year in this field. In some circumstances, as for instance the Palestinian conflict, the necessity to be recognized as a "player" instead of a "payer" has clearly led the EU to align itself with the US strategy in the region. It has consequently developed common actions that would not be inconsistent with US policy options. This constraint has been considered as the only way for the EU to be invited to the negotiation table. In this regard, it is worth remembering that the Israeli bombing campaign against Lebanon during summer 2006, which was supported by the USA and some EU members, was not condemned in a CFSP declaration. The subsequent deployment of national European troops within UNIFIL II (United Nations Interim Force in Lebanon) in Lebanon, as well as the recent endeavours of the EU geared at the reconstruction and stabilization of states – Iraq and Afghanistan – previously bombed by the USA and its allies, would so far be in line with the burden-sharing concerns that have been clearly articulated in transatlantic circles. The collective management of crises threatening the stability of world order is clearly a powerful engine explaining the lightning speed of development of the military dimension of the EU's foreign policy as well as an illustration of the "normalization" of the EU's political project.

The EU and crisis management: between power politics and global governance

The possibility of resorting to force is mostly seen as a condition for ensuring the efficiency of the EU foreign policy and completing the previous stages of the European construction, ultimately leading to the creation of a fully fledged external actor. Accordingly, the launch of ESDP in 2000 represented a new qualitative step for the EU's international actorness. It meant the creation of novel institutions and procedures,[16] the development of military capabilities which for the first time opened up the possibility of foreign missions and an initial conceptualization of the EU's security interests through the adoption in December 2003 of the European Security Strategy. According to some analysts, such militarization of the EU represents the end of the peculiarity of the EU as a civilian power; for others, it is compatible with the maintenance of certain specific identity, characterized by more readiness than traditional powers to be constrained by multilateralism and the rule of law.

The European Security Strategy and its critics

Javier Solana, the EU's High Representative for CFSP appointed in 1999, has proposed not to oppose military and civilian designs but to use the diversity of EU external means as the ground for building a holistic and multi-faceted approach to security in order to establish the identity of the EU on a new legitimacy distinct from previous civilian power discourse while not undermining it. The European Security Strategy (ESS), adopted by the European Council on December 12, 2003, perfectly illustrates this position. The strategy articulates a framework based upon a comprehensive approach to security which helped to reconcile the EU's positions after the divergences over the Iraq War. The EU and its member states are compelled to cooperate in security matters by promoting "effective multilateralism" and the rule of law, but also by building a strategy of "threat prevention," while keeping the use of force as a last resort. Some interpret this wording as the indication that the EU identity requires it to tackle security threats through "effective multilateralism." In other words, it implies acting by supporting the UN system, strengthening national responses through EU synergies, and addressing root causes such as poverty and weak governance through community instruments and regional dialogue.

As a matter fact, Javier Solana considered that such a holistic approach would cement the difference between Europe and America. He argued, with reference to a comprehensive notion of security, that active engagement is in Europe's security interests since these are affected by poor governance, insecurity, poverty and conflict far beyond its borders. Europe must therefore meet these challenges, which it is well placed to do with a range of diplomatic, development, economic, humanitarian and military instruments.[17] This peculiar approach points to what Solana described as the "new environment" where diffuse challenges must be addressed by the Union. These include poverty, energy dependence, climate change and weak governance as key security challenges for the Union because of their contribution to regional instability, such as in the Middle Eastern or Central African conflicts. The ESS, when mentioning "new threats" like the proliferation of weapons of mass destruction (WMD), terrorism and state failure always insists that the answer to such problems implies the use of a full range of instruments, a "comprehensive security toolbox," not only the use of force. Moreover, such a holistic approach is further promoted as it clearly states that the novelty of such threats lies in their combination; because of:

> these different elements together – terrorism committed to maximum violence, the availability of weapons of mass destruction and the failure of state systems – we could be confronted with a very radical threat ... In contrast to the massive visible threat in the cold war, none of the new threats is purely military; nor can

any be tackled by purely military means. Each requires a mixture of instruments. Proliferation may be contained through export controls and attacked through political, economic and other pressures while the underlying political causes are also tackled. Dealing with terrorism may require a mixture of intelligence, political, military and other means. In failed states, military instruments may be needed to restore order, humanitarian assistance to tackle the immediate crisis. Economic instruments serve reconstruction, and civilian crisis management helps restore civil government. The European Union is particularly well equipped to respond to such multi-faceted situations.[18]

According to its supporters, the second originality of the European approach is the emphasis on international cooperation and multilateralism: "no single country is able to tackle today's complex problems entirely on its own." The ESS therefore emphasizes the depth and primacy of the transatlantic link and collaboration, even with an unusual messianic discourse: "acting together, the European Union and the United States can be a formidable force for good in the world." It quotes as other strategic partners the other members of the G8 and the United Nations Security Council: Russia first, then Canada, China, Japan, and also India.[19] "Effective multilateralism" aims at three strategic objectives: extending the zone of security around Europe (enlargement and neighborhood policy); strengthening the international order; countering potential threats. Interestingly, when discussing multilateralism, Javier Solana not only quoted the UN system, but also the North Atlantic Treaty Organization (NATO) and transatlantic relations. When he referred to instruments for addressing security threats, he insisted on third-pillar instruments (see Chapter 10) like the European warrant and criminal cooperation, and on the diverse tools to be activated for implementing the new Strategy and Action Plan against the proliferation of weapons of mass destruction. The case of the negotiations surrounding the Iranian nuclear programs between the Iranian government and the representatives of the three major European states (France, Germany and the UK), in parallel with the pressure from International Atomic Energy Agency (IAEA), has been quoted as an example of the European methodology in this field.

The reference to effective multilateralism allows two interpretations. One is that multilateralism matters: therefore the EU sticks strongly to the multilateral frameworks at the universal level (United Nations, World Trade Organization), but also at the regional level (NATO and the ESDP–NATO relations are quoted among the key policy implications of the ESS, and OSCE, Council of Europe, MERCOSUR, ASEAN, African Union as other key regional organizations). The other interpretation is that effectiveness matters: multilateralism is nothing if there is no determination and readiness to use force for implementing its decisions. This implies, according to some analysts, developing a "robust" approach to so-called Petersberg Tasks[20] (the EU's military missions in the EU vocabulary) and a strategic culture, whereby "the institutional confidence and processes to manage and deploy military force as part of the accepted range of legitimate and effective policy instruments, together with general recognition of the EU's legitimacy as an international actor with (albeit limited) military capabilities."[21] Among the two emphases associated with effective multilateralism, the latter makes the EU very similar to the USA while the former contributes to shape Europe's identity in opposition to an oversimplified unilateral America. And again these two interpretations, as well as their different rationales, are part of the constructive ambiguity of the document. As such they are to be the substance of future divergences when discussing the scope of Petersberg Tasks and the EU's military capabilities. Interestingly, the ESS also maintains a balance between the call for increasing capabilities (via a rise of military expenditures) and the plea for their improvement (via pooling, rationalization, specialization and other qualitative approaches).

A last point takes in the peculiarity of the European approach to regionalism and its impact on security. Javier Solana considered that the Union's security interests come from its ability to build a security community: "The creation of the European Union has been central to this development. It has transformed the relations between our states, and the lives of our citizens. European countries are committed to dealing peacefully with disputes and cooperating through common institutions."[22] This regionalist dimension of the ESS is another way of defining multilateralism. It also implies developing the enlargement and neighborhood policies as key security instruments. Extending its own security community, stabilizing its environment and promoting deep regional integration on other continents are considered to be interrelated policies all dedicated to the Union's security interests in a way which is not only original but finally also inspired by its civilian power approach.[23]

As shown, the EU's discourse on its preferred holistic and comprehensive approach to security is obviously ambivalent. It might seem paradoxical that the paragraphs which shape an EU international identity and differentiate it from the USA are those referring to the global challenges and civilian means, in line with the tradition of "civilian power Europe" discourse inherited from the 1970s and 1980s; while the threat assessment in the hard security sphere is very similar to the American one (except for the removal of the term "pre-emption", considered as too American, as well as some slight change of the language regarding WMD). These changes and the new balance between the emphasis on challenges and threats are a potent mix when striving to reconcile member states' diversity of interests and security cultures. This confirms that the differences between Europe and America are not as important as both actors have themselves emphasized towards their own public opinions; but also that the internal European diversity obliges the European security discourse to combine civilian power and militarization approaches in order to reduce divergences and build internal and external legitimacy.

The ambivalence of civilian–military operations and about the use of force

Legitimacy-building was of course a key motivation for the adoption of the ESS. This document was intended to become an integrating conceptual framework for the EU's external action, insofar as it rested upon a comprehensive concept of security. After 2003, *mutatis mutandis*, the same is true for ESDP and the start of the EU's military and civilian missions. Indeed, the push for ESDP came from the willingness of key member states to jointly address crises of the magnitude of those unfolding in

Bosnia, Kosovo or Rwanda, by pooling military capabilities. However, ESDP has also served to label an important number of missions that do not involve soldiers but only civilian police, judges, customs officers or administrators. The Lisbon Treaty even strengthens the legal basis for civilian crisis management activities, since its Article 27 widens the list of Petersberg Tasks in order to integrate civilian activities for stabilization, disarmament or cooperation against terrorism. Furthermore, the Treaty provides for a solidarity clause which allows for using civilian and military means in case of natural or man-made catastrophes. This ambivalent civilian–military policy mix not only reflects the actual needs of UN-type of peacekeeping missions but also the need of the EU to fill its own niche and build success stories at the start of ESDP as well as to combine the different visions of its member states about ESDP.

The Petersberg Tasks were historically defined by the ministerial Council of the Western European Union[24] (WEU) during its meeting in Petersberg (Bonn) in June 1992. After its experience of naval contribution to the 1991 US-led war on Iraq, the WEU was trying to find a role after the adoption of the Agenda for Peace by the UN and the move by all regional organizations to propose their services to the UN for performing crisis management. In parallel, NATO and the CSCE (Conference on Security and Cooperation in Europe (Helsinki Summit)) took similar decisions and the three organizations had to find a division of labor when the UN asked for the support of regional organizations in the management of the Bosnian War. Since NATO had taken the responsibility of collective defence of Western Europe since the 1950s, the WEU tried to find a niche by developing West European military assets, earmarking multinational forces and defining its contribution to crisis management through Petersberg Tasks, stretching from rescue operations of European nationals in crisis situations to the use of combat forces for peacemaking and from the military escort of humanitarian conveys to the traditional interposition of peacekeepers. This list was purely military. Furthermore, though mentioning the UN as the mandatory organization for peacekeeping or peacemaking (or CSCE as regional organisation), the WEU never referred to the need to systematically obtain a mandate from the UN Security Council. West Europeans wanted to keep some free-riding option, anticipating the current ambivalence of effective multilateralism.

The EU was gradually absorbed into this discussion in order to manage the complex compromises between Atlanticist, Europeanist and neutral member states. Treaty reforms of the EU have illustrated this slow evolution.[25] The Maastricht Treaty of 1991 mentions only that CFSP includes all dimensions of security, envisages a common defence policy in the future, and evokes the possibility of a common defence policy (Article J.4). It therefore delegates these responsibilities to the WEU. The Amsterdam Treaty of 1997 (Article 17, TEU) integrates Petersberg Tasks into the CFSP and gives to the European Council a political guidance for mandating the WEU in their implementation while keeping the two organizations legally separate. The Nice Treaty of 2000 creates CESDP as the policy framework for performing Petersberg Tasks and establishes all necessary political–military institutions, while the WEU decided to freeze its own ministerial activities in order to let the EU take the lead.[26]

This progressive transfer of military responsibilities as well as the conduct of the Petersberg Tasks from the WEU to the EU is the result of changes in national preferences crystallized by the Bosnian and Kosovo wars: Germany's decision to break its constitutional prohibition and to send troops outside NATO territory; French cooperation with NATO on the ground; neutral countries' deep involvement in peacekeeping operations with other Europeans and NATO; and British interest to use defence as a means to return to the core of Europe and combine its European interests with the Anglo-American alliance through NATO. The turning point of this process of convergence of national preferences was the French–British Summit of Saint-Malo in December 1998, held on the eve of the Kosovo War. President Chirac and Prime Minister Blair agreed on the principle of an EU security and defence policy which would be compatible with NATO. Those principles were agreed upon by the other member states and implemented by the next summer and winter summit meetings of the European Council (Cologne, June 1999; Helsinki, December 1999). The Cologne European Council transferred most of the WEU assets to the EU; and the Helsinki European Council adopted a headline goal aimed at pooling military capabilities in order to be able to deploy 60,000 troops in crisis areas for one year under EU auspices. The new political–military institutions of the EU (Political and Security Committee, EU Military Committee, EU Military Staff) started work in March 2000. ESDP was concretely formed and set into law by the Nice Treaty, at the end of 2000.

In the meantime, the Yugoslav wars between 1992 and 1999 had tested and proved the capability of NATO to provide troops to the UN (Bosnia) and to conduct wars on its own, without UN mandate (Kosovo). Despite its military build-up, the WEU had only been able to perform modest, sub-military tasks (control of the embargo in the Adriatic and on the Danube, and de-mining operations in Croatia) because its own member states had preferred to use the frameworks of the UN and NATO. Furthermore, the EU itself had been able to act as a political mediator (co-presidency of the Peace Conference with the UN between 1992 and 1994, association to the work of the Contact Group after 1994, initiative of the Stability Pact in 1999) and as a contributor to important civilian tasks related to peacekeeping and peace-building (EU monitoring mission, surveillance of elections, funding of reconstruction, increasing responsibility of the international administration of Bosnia).

Consequently, the debate surrounding the Petersberg Tasks had tremendously changed when ESDP was established. NATO had proven its military predominance in crisis management (which was confirmed later in Afghanistan) and the EU was prompted to mix civilian and military tasks in order to legitimize its own role. The militarization of the EU started paradoxically with a civilian mission in January 2003, the replacement of the UN civilian police force by a EUPOL mission in Bosnia and Herzegovina.

The parallel reference to civilian and military dimensions of crisis management emerged from the ESDP's onset. Though the French President, Jacques Chirac, and his British counterpart, Tony Blair, had pushed for European military responsibility in their Saint-Malo compromise of 1998, the decisions taken in the Helsinki European Council one year after looked much more balanced. In the meantime, other member states, mainly the neutrals and Germany, but also the European Commission whose legitimacy resides mainly in civilian tasks, and which was facing the competitive emergence of the newly appointed High Representative for CFSP, pushed for the adoption of a catalogue of civilian tasks in crisis management. Therefore the Helsinki European Council not only agreed on the document regarding the military aspects of crisis management, but also on another one regarding the civilian aspects of crisis management. This two-track approach was promoted by the 1999 Finnish Presidency, and deepened under both the Portuguese Presidency of 2000, with the adoption of the Feira Document on civilian crisis management; and the Swedish Presidency in 2001, when the EU adopted the Gothenburg Platform for Conflict Prevention. This helped all member states to fill a niche within the EU's security policy, while simultaneously giving shape to a particular profile for the EU by emphasizing the originality of its approach, the distinctiveness of which resides in the specific combination of military and civilian crisis management instruments – especially in light of President G. W. Bush's emphasis on the use of force. Through its reference to a policy mix combining the military and civilian dimensions, the EU could at the same time build an internal consensus, involving both NGOs and the military; maintain an international profile distinct from that of the USA and even, to some extent, go on referring to its civilian power temperament despite the militarization of its agenda.

By 2008, the portfolio of Petersberg Tasks looked rather different from both the original expectations identified by the WEU in 1992, as well as the 1999 EU Helsinki headline goal. In 2008, fewer than 8,000 troops were deployed under EU flag (in Bosnia and Herzegovina and in Chad/Central African Republic). Previous operations were carried out either in the Balkans (FYRoM) or in the Democratic Republic of Congo (DRC). Major contingents of European troops deployed abroad are under the direct responsibility of the UN (Lebanon, Sierra Leone, Ivory Coast, DRC and even Cyprus, now part of EU territory), under NATO's command with a UN mandate (ISAF in Afghanistan, KFOR in Kosovo), under US-led "coalitions of the willing" without UN mandate (Iraq, "Enduring Freedom" in Afghanistan) or under bilateral defence agreements (some French and British deployments in Africa, the Middle East or Asia). This is the result not of a lack of capabilities but of an absence of interest among EU member states in using the EU framework for such deployments. Until now, the military dimension of ESDP has been used mainly for addressing two types of cases: either ensuring the stabilization of the Balkans in order to prepare for future enlargement to this part of Europe, or contributing to local and short-term peacemaking in Central Africa.

The rest of the ESDP's record during its first five years (2003–08) of operational existence consists of a more frequent and more geographically varied set of civilian missions, among which those deployed in: Aceh/Indonesia (AMM, cease-fire monitoring); Afghanistan (EUPOL); Bosnia and Herzegovina (EUPOL, civilian police); Darfur/Sudan (EU support to AMIS-II); the Democratic Republic of Congo (EUPOL, EUSEC, civilian police and support to security sector reform); Gaza/Palestine (EUBAM, COPPS, border control and police cooperation); Georgia (EUJUST Themis, training of judges, and border control mission); Guinea-Bissau (EUSEC); Iraq (EUJUST Lex, training of Iraqi legal experts in Europe); and Transnistria/Moldova (border control by the team of the EU Special Representative).

Last but not least, in 2008, the EU decided to deploy its largest civilian mission (2,200 persons: civilian police, judges, customs officers, administrators) in Kosovo under the heading EULEX Kosovo in order to replace the UNMIK grouping (in 2008 the UN mission was also still ongoing). By contrast with all previous missions, this one has no endorsement either by the state of deployment (Serbia) or by the UN Security Council (UNSC) since there is no agreement in the UNSC about the recognition of the independence of Kosovo. Those EU member states who do not recognize Kosovo have also decided to abstain from taking part in the mission, but did not block the decision of the EU Council to deploy it.

The latest case illustrates that the civilian dimension of crisis management is useful for building internal consensus and projecting power in the EU's neighborhood but that it also generates ambivalence regarding the consistency of the EU in its multilateralist stance. In the case of the Kosovo mission, the EU has clearly bypassed several principles of international law (territorial integrity of states, competence of the UNSC) and will face complex legal consequences (for example, when its mission contributes to the establishment of Kosovo's border controls or to the abolition of Yugoslav legislation or to the signing of international agreements by an independent Kosovo). This case will repeat the contradictions already existing in international administrations endorsed by the UN, like the administration of Bosnia and Herzegovina which is now under the almost complete responsibility of the Special Representative of the EU. This representative has important decision-making powers, oscillating between very intrusive and rather authoritarian attitudes and the need to promote ownership by local authorities and help them to establish sovereignty on their own territory. Controversies about consistency with rules of multilateralism and global governance also exist with regard to the Gaza deployment, which has become politically very delicate in light of the self-imposed limits to the EU's political support of the Palestinians, and even more following the EU's decision to boycott Hamas. In the Democratic Republic of Congo, several problems arose over the impartiality of EU troops in Kinshasa during the electoral process, the brutality of EUPOL, and the level of intrusion of EUSEC into internal affairs. The more the EU acts with transformational diplomacy, the more it will face dilemmas between the discourse of global governance and the raw realities of power politics. Major powers like the USA, Russia, France or Britain have resolved this dilemma to some extent by recognizing that their foreign policy is both interest- and value-driven, but for the EU it seems more complicated since its internal composite nature obliges it to keep a constructive ambiguity of catch-all concepts as a cornerstone of its internal and external legitimacy-building.

In fact, the evolution of the European discourse on the use of force is also full of ambiguities. At first glance, it seems quite obvious that it reveals a legalistic view based on clear normative features. The resort to force is indeed presented as a means of ensuring the implementation and efficiency of the rule of law. If law needs institutions to be implemented, coercion appears to be a condition for the operability of a legal system, be it internal or international. In the eighteenth century, Immanuel Kant expressed this conceptual link between law and coercion, surmising that only coercion could bring the inherent rights of a person into existence. In this regard, the public constraint – the state – is in charge of implementing the law. With the prospect of an emerging cosmopolitan state – that is to say a community of sovereign states bound by law – the legitimate constraint must rely on a cosmopolitan constitution and a coercive apparatus. But the more European governments have developed political ambitions at the international level (encompassing the development of a security and defence policy), the more they seem to have introduced elements of distortion in regard to this Kantian narrative. From the beginning, ESDP has been conceived as a means for Europe to become a major actor on the international stage and to face new threats with up-to-date armed forces. Since Helsinki, heads of state and government have consistently underlined the need for Europe to "play its full role on the international stage" and to be able to influence events outside its borders. Such concerns increasingly appear as an inherent objective of ESDP, whereas the reference to universal norms and values seems to be a strategy to attain this specific goal.

The notion of civilian power implies the use of civil (as opposed to military) means to support policy objectives. For many observers, the development of ESDP could even transform the EU into a civilian superpower. But the substance of the political project would not be affected by the use of the new instruments and means put at the disposal of the EU by the member states. Their opponents consider instead that the notion of civilian power in presence of military capabilities has become a contradiction in terms.

The EU is not simply facing such contradictions by default. It contributed more widely to forge those ambivalent concepts of crisis management within the UN, such as the "responsibility to protect," as a new guideline for interventions. Another discrepancy confronts the responsibility to protect principle and the current ESDP missions. Troop contributions by the EU itself remain under the 1999 ambitions as already mentioned. The obvious example is Darfur, where the UN lacks troops while the EU has launched operation EUFOR Chad/Central African Republic for protecting the border with Darfur. As summarized by Richard Youngs

> while ESDP missions have proliferated, the proclaimed security–development linkage does not appear significantly to have increased the EU's political will to undertake large scale, combat military interventions in conflict situations. The consensus on development insists that the EU 'cannot stand by' as conflict rages, in part because this undermines its development efforts. But in practice 'standing by' remains the European proclivity. If many critics feared that the commitment to coherence between security and development would be used as a banner under which a far-reaching militarization of EU foreign policy would occur, to date these concerns have not proven justified.[27]

Indeed, the risk of inflating normative discourses is to face increasing demands for moral and political accountability in their implementation.

EU contradictions between normative discourses about global governance and multilateralism on the one hand, and increasing resort to the practices of power politics on the other, are likely to increase in the foreseeable future in line with rising ambitions to shape the world and become a global actor. According to the Lisbon

Treaty, the ESDP might contribute to these trends. Besides the already quoted extension of the list of Petersberg Tasks and the "solidarity clause," the Treaty contains new paragraphs in its Article 27 that all contribute to give more robustness to the EU's military assets and actions:

- the creation of the European Defence Agency (EDA), which has started to function even before the signing of the Treaty
- the authorization of closer cooperation between member states to perform missions on behalf of the Union or to establish multinational forces, as had been done previously for the creation of Eurocorps, Eurofor, Euromarfor and other multinational forces; as well as for the decision concerning the earmarking of well-equipped rapid-reaction troops under the concept of EU battle groups
- the collective self-defence clause in case of armed aggression[28] and as counterpart the emphasis on the predominance of NATO for collective self-defence of its member states[29]
- the clause establishing the so-called "permanent structured cooperation" which will allow the most militarized states to create a core group leading efforts for joint military endeavours, military benchmarking and the definition of convergence criteria.

Those provisions would increase the military capabilities of the Union and procedures for pooling those capabilities. They would complement, deepen and widen previous efforts for developing multinational forces and battle groups, but also for relying on headquarters and command structures offered by member states, multinational forces or NATO pending the full development of the recently established EU civilian–military cell.[30] Last but not least, the Union is soon to adopt some sort of White Paper on Defence which will complement the ESS by more operational aims and means. The more the EU makes use of those means for acting in an assertive and robust way on the world stage, the more it will become a power like others and face tensions and contradictions with its multilateralist stance.

Enduring challenges of global governance

Side-effects of a stronger EU: bad news for multilateralism?

A more united Europe is not *per se* a guarantee of a more efficient functioning international organization. This kind of side-effect has already been identified in other fields. Some authors have noticed that the European Commission's concerns for visibility and autonomy in funding UN activities are a manifestation of the challenge to the UN posed by a stronger EU human rights policy. The UN is the forum in which universal human rights standards have been developed and enforced. Regionalist groupings can threaten this because they sometimes promote conflicting conceptions of human rights. Therefore, the more the EU represents an ideological and powerful bloc, the more other regional groups will demand recognition of their own conception of human rights. The contradictions between regional governance (for instance, within the new neighborhood policy) and global governance are crystallized most conspicuously when European actors privilege regional entities such as NATO over the UN, as was the case in Kosovo.

The challenge of coherence and the impact of the Lisbon Treaty

The EU is obviously an arena within which states sharing common interest can interact and work together wherever possible; but as it was acknowledged during the Convention which drafted the failed Constitutional Treaty (2002–03)

> ensuring coherence therefore matters greatly. But few international events produce the same reaction, or intensity of reaction, in every member state. Geographical situations and historical backgrounds differ, as do human and economic factors. National traditions of involvement in particular geographical areas, and the extent to which member states are willing to engage in such areas, vary considerably [...] All agree that where the Union can act together it should do so. When a member state considers that its vital interests are seriously affected, pressure from public opinion and its national parliament could require to take action [...] The establishment of the CFSP, with specific legal framework, instruments and procedures, represents the acknowledgment by member states that while their vital interest do not always coincide, they share a common interest in working together wherever possible.[31]

At the international level, it is not always obvious to identify the institution in charge of speaking for the EU. Even if efforts for coordinating European interests are made, and are moreover successful in terms of influence as a number of other countries add their voice to the European one, EU member states are not always inclined to delegate authority to the Presidency or the Commission. Besides, there is also a tendency to develop *ad hoc* diplomacy that is supposed to be more flexible and less bureaucratic. Larger member states, speaking in the name of Europe, sometimes prefer acting through *directoires* (the EU-3 dealing with Iran, the Contact Group for Kosovo) in order to overcome the ongoing difficulties associated with finding a common path within the EU. The international system does not seem designed to function along a regionalist model of governance and the time is not ripe for a unitary representation of the EU in international organizations. The example of the IMF is striking in this regard, as is the fact that EU members are not part of the same groups within the UN General Assembly.

The EU's ambition is, according to some national leaders, to be one of those powers within a multilateral but also multipolar system. The success of the EU is indeed to influence norms at the world level by making them compatible with its own interests and values. From this respect, interests and values, as well as civilian and military dimensions of power, are not opposed to each other but complementary. Therefore the question of coherence and consistency in external action is central. But this centrality does not lie so much in the traditionally addressed issue of input legitimacy, i.e., institutional legitimacy. It is more related to output legitimacy, consistency between discourse and practice. As detailed above, the increase of input coherence might even lead to more assertiveness and power politics behaviour and therefore to more tensions with partners and contradictions with universal norms and principles of multilateralism, hence leading to potentially more output incoherence.

From this respect, the record of the Lisbon Treaty is likely to increase input coherence but not necessarily output coherence. First of all, the dismantling of the pillar structure inherited from the Maastricht Treaty does not mean that the EU foreign policy is becoming a common policy. There are many elements of continuity between the old and the new regimes governing external actions. In particular, decision-making processes have not been harmonized so far between the different dimensions of external relations (trade, development), CFSP, ESDP and the external dimensions of the former third pillar. As far as global governance is concerned, member states are strongly invited to cooperate in international institutions or conferences but, inside the UN Security Council, France and Great Britain have retained a right to defend whatever they think appropriate with regard to their special responsibility for the maintenance of international peace and security. Second, the creation of the positions of President of the European Council and of High Representative, the latter mixing Commission's and Council's sources of legitimacy, is a clear answer to the problems of input but also output coherence. There will nevertheless remain tensions at a higher political level than today since the tension between the European Commission, the rotating Presidency and the High Representative is likely to be replaced, according to some comments, by a new bout of bureaucratic infighting between the President of the European Council, the President of the European Commission and the High Representative. Third, internal democratic accountability has not been reinforced so far since the European Parliament has not received more powers in external action and the conference of national and European parliaments (COSAC) is unlikely to play a more substantial role than the current WEU inter-parliamentary assembly. The creation of the hybrid position of High Representative might even increase problems of democratic accountability since the control of this hybrid function might generate legal uncertainties.

Furthermore, institutional innovations do not tell the whole story. As noted by many specialists, while power still rests upon national governments, EU foreign policy is more and more elaborated and implemented by civil servants permanently housed in Brussels. The "Brusselized process," understood as the existence of common cognitive maps (the mental representations of reality that shape an actor's understanding of their interests and guide their practices), along with "Europeanization," which refers to the progressive integration of the European dimension into national policies, are thus deemed to reinforce the convergence between the actors. This socialization process explains why, although foreign policy was established along intergovernmental lines, it has the potential to become far more institutionalized than the negotiators had intended or expected. To date, there is a strong intuition that socially constructed rationality based on a collective position prevails over instrumental rationality based on predetermined national interests. The success of the ESS, the drafting of a European White Paper on Defence, and the major reform of the Lisbon Treaty – which integrates external action by establishing the hybrid

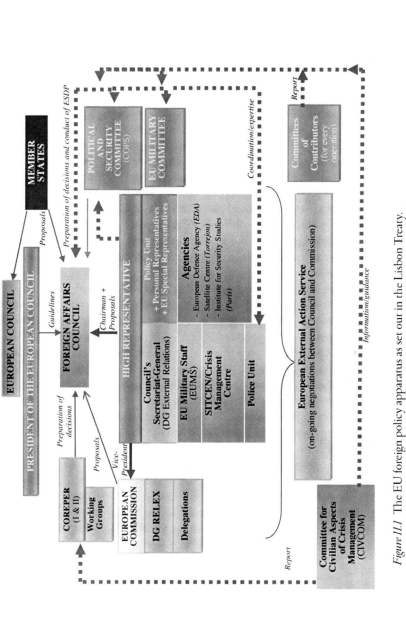

Figure 11.1 The EU foreign policy apparatus as set out in the Lisbon Treaty.

position of the High Representation and the permanent structured cooperation in ESDP – all confirm this analysis.

The new capability–expectation gap

These developments also confirm that issues of coherence are related to internal and external legitimacy. Whereas the need to enhance efficiency and coherence has been taken into account, the problem of legitimacy arising from the so-called "democratic deficit" still has not been seriously tackled. In this regard, the Lisbon Treaty falls short of any real improvement, and nourishes the thesis that a *raison d'état* spirit still largely prevails within European institutions. Moreover, intergovernmental cooperation can also come to be understood as the result of collusive delegation, i.e., an attempt by governments to loosen domestic constraints by shifting decision-making to international organizations. All these concerns suggest that the problem of legitimacy is not yet resolved.

Insofar as international legitimacy is concerned, the EU refers mainly to its ethical approach to international affairs, and to the performance of its external actions. A thorough analysis of European foreign policy nevertheless highlights the enduring damage control function of CFSP. In fact, this function was the cornerstone of the preceding EPC, which was mainly driven by a need to ensure convergence between the member states, and is still a key legitimizing function of CFSP and ESDP. At the time, it justified the reactive nature of EPC and also confirmed that power projection was not at the top of the European agenda. However, since the launching of CFSP, and even more with the development of ESDP, legitimacy through action has moved to the forefront. A performance-driven strategy as a legitimizing argument became predominant within EU discourse. EU diplomacy has increasingly appeared more outwardly directed. The ESS and Javier Solana's discourses have been of particular relevance, as for instance when the High Representative states that: "in order to offer a brighter prospect to mankind, the EU has to develop three strategic objectives: extending the zone of security around Europe, strengthening the international order and countering old and new threats."[32] Performance clearly points to the outputs of the European foreign policy; yet CFSP actions and positions and ESDP missions are still mainly the result of *ad hoc* arrangements reflecting temporary and shifting preferences of major member states. Imprecise and fluid arguments regarding the final destination or the strategic objectives of the European foreign policy give the impression that its essence is mainly procedural while the need to present a united Europe sometimes prevails over a more problem-solving orientation.

Conclusion

The challenges of global governance and multilateralism highlight the fact that the EU is now facing new global responsibilities. However, they also foster new contradictions between normative discourse and the practices associated with power politics. Its search for internal and external legitimacy has led the EU not only to build new capabilities, as suggested by Christopher Hill[33] and others, but also to raise new expectations. For this reason it remains pertinent to analyse the EU's external action and inaction as the result of a complex interaction between expectations and capabilities. Global governance will simply become a more important reference in the definition of legitimacy and expectations than it was at the start of CFSP. To some extent this mirrors where the EU lies in its move towards global actorness. The cycle associated with the EU's capability–expectation gap is not over; it is only just starting.

Notes

1 See Table 11.1 for the chronology of Treaty reforms and Figure 11.1 for a summary of institutions and decision-making processes.
2 European Council, *A Safer Europe in a Better World*, European Security Strategy, Brussels, December 12, 2003.
3 Hill, C. (1993), "The capability–expectation gap, or conceptualising Europe's international role," *Journal of Common Market Studies*, 31(3): p. 315.
4 Commission of the European Communities, Communication of the Commission to the Council and European Parliament, *The European Union and the United Nations: The Choice of Multilateralism*, COM (2003) 526 final, September 10; European Council, *A Safer Europe in a Better World*, European Security Strategy, Brussels, December 12, 2003.
5 *Ibid.*
6 K. E. Smith, "Still civilian power EU?," *European Foreign Policy Unit Working Paper 2005/1*, 3. Available online: http://www.arena.uio.no/cidel/WorkshopOsloSecurity/Smith.pdf〉 (accessed April 1, 2008).
7 I. Manners, "The European Union as a normative power: a response to Thomas Diez," *Millennium: Journal of International Studies*, Vol. 35, No. 1, 2006, 167–80.
8 H. Behr, "The European Union in the legacies of imperial rule? EU accession politics viewed from a historical comparative perspective," *European Journal of International Relations*, Vol. 13, No. 2, 2007, 239–62.
9 R. Cooper, *The Post-Modern State and the World Order*, London: Demos, 2000.
10 D. Chandler, *Empire in Denial*, London: Pluto Press, 2006.
11 *Financial Times*, February 18, 2007 and July 9, 2007.
12 Th. Diez, "Constructing the self and changing others: reconsidering 'normative power Europe'," *Millennium*, Vol. 33, No. 3, 2005, 613.
13 *Ibid.*, p. 628. He refers to the mechanisms of constructing the "self" and the "other", like the representation of the other as an existential threat, as an inferior, as violating universal principles, as different ...
14 This concept can be found in the *European Union as a Global Actor* 2nd ed. 2006, London: Routledge, p. 56.
15 R. Youngs, "Normative dynamics and strategic interests in the EU's external identity," *Journal of Common Market Studies*, Vol. 42, No. 2, 2004, 415–35.
16 Political and Security Committee, EU Military Committee, EU Military Staff, increased role for the High Representative, transfer of agencies from WEU to EU (see Figure 11.1).
17 J. Solana, *Speech on the State of the Union*, European Union Institute for Security Studies, Paris, 30 June 2003.
18 *Ibid.*
19 Since then, a strategic partnership has also been signed with Brazil, in 2007.

20   See Article 17 of the Treaty on European Union. The Petersberg Tasks cover humanitarian and rescue tasks, peacekeeping tasks, and tasks of combat forces in crisis management, including peacemaking.

21   P. Cornish and G. Edwards, "Beyond the EU/NATO dichotomy: the beginnings of a European strategic culture," *International Affairs*, Vol. 77, No. 3, July 2001, 587–603.

22   Solana, *Speech on the State of the Union, op. cit.*

23   M. Telò, *Europe: A Civilian Power? European Union, Global Governance, World Order*, New York: Palgrave, 2006.

24   WEU is a European defence and security organization established by the Treaty of Brussels of 1948 (signed by the UK, France, Belgium, Luxembourg and the Netherlands). The founding members have been further joined by Germany, Italy, Greece, Spain and Portugal.

25   See also chronology in Table 11.1.

26   The WEU, although not abolished nevertheless has very limited remaining functions (collective self-defence clause, armament cooperation, parliamentary assembly, association of European members of NATO) and might well become obsolete after the entry into force of the Lisbon Treaty.

27   R. Youngs, "Fusing security and development: just another Euro-platitude?," Brussels, Centre for European Policy Studies, CEPS Working Document 277, October 2007, 9.

28   Not to be confused with the "solidarity clause" which is a mechanism of assistance between member states when one is the victim of a terrorist attack or a natural or man-made disaster.

29   This explains why, in contrast to the Maastricht, Amsterdam and Nice treaties which each had one reference to compatibility between CFSP/ESDP and NATO's policy, the Lisbon Treaty refers twice to NATO: first to state this need for compatibility between the security policies of the two organizations, and second to remind that NATO is the framework for collective self-defence of its member states despite the EU's self-defence clause (this wording requested by Tony Blair corresponds to the spirit of Article IV of the WEU Treaty, which provides for non-duplication of NATO military structures by WEU).

30   The issue of operational headquarters and command structures was subject to controversies between Europeanists and Atlanticists in 2003. Jacques Chirac, Tony Blair and Gerhard Schroeder finally agreed on a compromise in Fall 2003, allowing for EU to rely either on national headquarters (French, German, British, Italian and Greek armed forces are *de facto* the only ones who have a fully fledged capacity in this field) or on NATO structures via SHAPE or on a modest EU "civilian–military cell."

31   European Convention, July 2002, CONV 161/02, Note Praesidium, 12–13.

32   J. Solana, "'Europe: security in the twenty-first century,'", *The Olof Palme Memorial Lecture*, Stockholm, June 20, 2001.

33   C. Hill (1993); C. Hill (1998), 'Closing the Capabilities–Expectations Gap' in John Peterson and Helene Sjursen (eds) *A Common Foreign Policy for Europe? Competing Visions of CFSP*, London: Routledge, pp. 18–38.

Bibliography

Bickerton, Ch. J. (2007), "The perils of performance: EU foreign policy and the problem of legitimization," *Perspectives: The Central European Review of International Affairs*, 28: 24–42.

Bono, G. (ed.) (2006), *The Impact of 9/11 on European Foreign and Security Policy*, Brussels: VUB Press.

Delcourt, B. (2006), "The normative underpinnings of the use of force: doctrinal foundations and ambiguities in the CFSP/ESDP discourse," *Baltic Yearbook of International Law*, 6: 155–81.

Diez, Th. (2005),"Constructing the self and changing others: reconsidering 'normative power Europe'," *Millennium*, 33 (3).

Hill, C. (1993), "The capability–expectation gap, or conceptualising Europe's international role," *Journal of Common Market Studies*, 31(3): 305–28.

Howorth, J. (2007), *Security and Defence Policy in the European Union*, Basingstoke and New York: Palgrave Macmillan.

Kissack, R. (2003), "Theoretical approaches to the study of the EU as an actor in the multilateral system," *FORNET Working Group I: Theories and Approaches to CFSP*, London School of Economics, 7–8 November.

Koening-Archibugi, M. (?), "International governance as a new *raison d'état*? The case of EU common and foreign policy," *European Journal of International Relations*, 10 (2): 147–88.

Laatikainen, K.V. and K. Smith (eds) (2006), *The European Union at the United Nations*, Basingstoke: Palgrave McMillan.

Manners, I. (2006), "The European Union as a normative power: a response to Thomas Diez," *Millennium: Journal of International Studies*, 35 (1): 167–80.

Peterson, J. and H. Sjursen (eds) (1998), *A Common Foreign Policy for Europe?*, London: Routledge.

Tonra, B. and Th. Christiansen (eds) (2004), *Rethinking European Union Foreign Policy*, Manchester: Manchester University Press.

Part III

Europe as a global actor

Horizontal issues

12 The EU's neighbourhood policies

Reimund Seidelmann

Summary

The European neighbourhood policy (ENP), which was officially established in 2004, aims at harmonising neighbourhood policies of member states, complementing national policies with an EU policy, and initiating a comprehensive strategy of good neighbourhood, notably towards the Mediterranean and Eastern Europe. Following traditional EU policy modes and patterns, ENP combines economic incentives with political cooperation aimed at peace-building, democracy-promotion, economic transformation and development in line with the EU's economic–political interests and normative standards. ENP aims to bridge the gap between membership and non-membership, and subscribes to the idea that the EU has a role to play not only in the far abroad but in the near abroad areas as well. ENP as a relatively recent EU policy has shown a number of structural shortcomings and raised dilemmas such as: the duality between the EU's and its member states' neighbourhood policies; the heterogeneity within the near abroad neighbourhood, for instance the differences between the Mediterranean and Eastern Europe; and the limits of the EU's will when building and implementing its role as a global, pan-European and common foreign and security policy actor.

The concept of neighbourhood

Although the concept of neighbourhood has been developed within the political–geographic approach long-dominated by geopolitics, it has in principle two dimensions. First, using a narrow definition, it can be understood as a horizontal relation within multilevel governance characterised by proximity – i.e., a neighbourhood between individuals, groups, local regions, nation-states and regions which are near to each other in terms of distance, have common borders, and show a high degree of interaction. Second, in a broader understanding, it can be conceived of both in global terms following such ideas as the 'global village', and as a vertical relation characterised by interrelations between actors on all levels – i.e., in the case of the EU, the neighbourhood with the North Atlantic Treaty Organization (NATO), nation-states (Council of Ministers), the European Union (European Commission, European Court, European Parliament), the regions (Council of Regions – CoR), and individuals, groups and cross-European actors.

The structures, patterns, modes and dynamics of such neighbourhoods can be explained with reference to a multi-causal approach, which characterises the European neighbourhood policy (ENP) as a multi-tier and multi-circle governance model, taking into specific account four different dimensions, as discussed below.

First, by referring to an understanding of a political process as being both the object and subject of history, neighbourhood relations result from historical experiences between the neighbours. Such historical ties are to be seen both in their objective relevance, and the subjective perception of objective relations within the policy-formation process of the neighbours. By introducing the notion of 'learning from history', neighbourhood experiences can cause long-lasting traumas as well as possibilities for new beginnings born from the lessons of history. The history of Franco-German relations illustrates such negative and positive learning cycles: the wars of 1870–71 and 1914–18 as well as the Treaty of Versailles exemplify negative, dissociative and military threat-dominated neighbourhood relations. The European integration process and the Franco-German friendship after 1945 illustrate how bad neighbourhoods can be turned into good neighbourhoods in conjunction with a constructive reform of the regional system. The history of East–West conflict illustrates the dynamic of confrontational neighbourhoods, where military and political threat perception and its explanation – such as the Soviet threat as the logical consequence of communism, and aggressive NATO as the logical consequence of late capitalism – served each bloc's consolidation and the legitimisation of their internal repression policies. Recent examples of the relevance of the historical factor in neighbourhood relations can be found in the Balkans, and in the relations between the independent Former Soviet Republics and Russia.

Second, with regard to the political process being shaped by ideas, norms and values, these are fundamental when addressing the concept of identity. Inter-regional and inter-state neighbourhood relations can be understood as the logical projection of the principle that individuals and groups within a nation-state and its regional and local communities should interact as good neighbours – i.e., treat each other as they would wish to be treated by others. For intra-state neighbourly relations one can refer to the 'social contract', which defines neighbourhood relations as being good – in the modern interpretation, civic – relations, when the use and threat of violence or force are excluded, and such norms as solidarity and equality are included. Whether such a good neighbourhood results from Rousseau's idea of the enlightened individual, or from Hobbes' idea of the need to prevent a 'neighbour' wolf against 'neighbour' wolf system, is of less relevance as long as such relations are based on a common identity, or a norm-value community, which promotes good neighbourly conduct. If one understands European integration as a regional social contract, good neighbourhood relations within the EU are one of the essential rationales for the success and attractiveness of EU integration, as well as its widening, deepening and identity-building. But while both the intra-state as well as the intra-EU social contracts are based on the principle of good neighbourhood, and are willing and able to ensure its application, inter-state neighbourhoods show a significantly reduced prevalence and intensity of order. Due both to the lack of an effective global social contract, and to the nature of the international system as a nation-state system based on the principle of sovereignty, the pursuit of two of the prerequisites of a good neighbourhood policy offers a particular challenge: marginalisation of the use of force, and fostering the concomitant respect for all actors' equal claim to existence. These are not a matter of the system's order, mechanisms and institutions but depend on the individual goodwill of the actors involved. Although conflict research has shown that democracies are more peaceful than non-democratic states, Kant's observation and demand that democratic nation-states, and supranational actors such as the EU, are *per se* 'civic' or 'civil' actors, are more normative in character than an objective generalised rule in an international system in which sovereignty allows not only the maximisation of a nation-state's interest against its neighbour, but also the use of military, economic and political force to pursue zero-sum game behaviour.

Third, in light of the political process as being shaped by interests, neighbourhood construction is conditioned by common and/or competitive economic, political and military interests. Here, the proximity factor has special relevance. Common borders and disputed trans-border claims can cause wars[1] as well as military alliances; proximity of neighbouring markets results in both more intensive competition as well as market penetration; and the close neighbourhood allows higher political transparency, accessibility and exploitation for domestic consumption. In the economic dimension, neighbourhood proximity creates a special comparative advantage – particularly in cases of complementary economic profiles and growth dynamics, which is often the case within Europe and was and is the case in the EEC/EC/EU widening process. Again, French–German relations illustrate such overall negative and positive effects of neighbourhood, i.e., competitive versus cooperative economic interests (Airbus Industries), military conflicts and territorial annexations versus joint cooperation (French–German Corps, Western European Union, joint armament ventures), and exploiting enemy-projections for improving domestic policy formation, acceptance and legitimacy versus political cooperation and alliance-building both for the better and joint pursuit of domestic and foreign/EU interests. And the fact that in Europe national borders often do not follow ethnic geography underlines both the positive opportunities as well as the potential conflicts for neighbours born from the difference between ethnic and national identities.

Fourth and finally, neighbourhood relations are shaped by power politics as well. Due to geographical proximity, neighbours are the easiest objective for both positive and negative power projection. The territorial definition of the modern state translates this into policies of annexation. This has led to equating the loss of territory with the loss of power, illustrated by the Treaty of Versailles after the end of World War One, or division improving the balance of power stability, illustrated by the division of Germany after World War Two. European integration in general and EU widening in particular illustrate the power calculation of good neighbourhood, membership and coalition-building. EU membership is not only based on the calculation that a loss of national power is overcompensated by influence in a significantly more powerful entity, but also on the idea that both intra-EU as well as trans-EU neighbourhood policies are efficient strategies for improving both relative power inside the EU as well as power projection towards one neighbourhood. EU history and the relation between geographic proximity and EU enlargement demonstrate such power calculations: united Germany's support for EU enlargement towards the East, new Greek–Turkish cooperation, Nordic assistance for the Baltic states, and other similar examples illustrate the advantages of such power tactics and strategies.

Defining and locating EU neighbourhood policy

Defining the ENP can start with a reference to its official definition, which is based on the fact that it deals with EU-neighbouring countries, that it defines neighbours predominantly by geographic proximity, and that it limits itself to the relation between the EU as supranational and the neighbours as nation-state actors. In addition and following the idea of the EU's foreign policy as based on the model of concentric circles (intra, near abroad, far abroad, global governance), ENP has to be regarded as a horizontal link between membership as the ultimate option for neighbouring countries and non-membership for the foreseeable future combined with cooperative relations and close ties.

Given the existing interests and power hierarchy in Europe and its near abroad, this means *de facto* a multiple asymmetric relation:

- on the one hand, the EU as a European supranational actor; and on the other hand, the neighbouring nation-states of which the broad majority is not affiliated or part of an equal supra- or even multinational actor
- on the one hand, the EU as an economic superpower; and on the other hand, the neighbouring nation-states not only with a much smaller power base but in general highly dependent on the EU economy
- on the one hand, the EU as an attractive model both for idealists as well as realists; and on the other, neighbouring nation-states with limited or declining acceptance and legitimacy
- on the one hand, the EU which could limit, drop or reverse the neighbourhood policy without critical consequences; and on the other, neighbouring states, which have neither an alternative to good-neighbourhood relations with the EU nor the ability to pursue their political, economic and security interests independently or alone – even if their societies perceived continued full autonomy as a viable and necessary political option.

This basic asymmetry can be found both in EU–Mediterranean[2] and EU–Eastern Europe relations. It is the EU – and not the countries of both regions – that sets the norms, objectives, patterns and modes for neighbourhood policies. The neighbouring countries can accept, influence and interact with such policies; but they cannot dominate, control or restructure these policies because of the asymmetry in general power, economic influence and political attractiveness.

Although neighbourhood policy is normally understood and executed as an object–subject relation – i.e., as a policy in which one actor, the EU, projects its norms, interests and power onto its neighbour – the good neighbourhood policy extends beyond mere technocratic and normatively dictated policies. Like all foreign relations, neighbourhood is the product of an interactive dynamic; it therefore depends not only on the object–actor but on its willingness and ability to adequately take the subject–actor's – i.e., the neighbour's – norms, interests and power design into account, to respect its identity, and avoid the zero-sum model in favour of a win–win model, in which sometimes the less powerful neighbour might have an even greater share of the common surplus. In this understanding, neighbourhood policy is a matter of mutual reciprocity within a bilateral or multiple-bilateral set of relationships.

Defining EU neighbourhood policy

Following such a general understanding of EU neighbourhood policy, its systematic definition can be based on a dual approach, which combines political geography with a classification of the quality of relations maintained with regard to the EU, and can be summarised as shown in Table 12.1.

Nonetheless, geographic proximity is not an absolute condition since it can be neutralised by improved communication, transport infrastructure and other

Table 12.1 Systematic classification of the EU's ENP

Political classification	Quasi-member	Candidate for membership	Association / privileged relations	Special relations
Geographical classification				
Northern region	Norway Iceland			
Inside the EU	Switzerland			
Southern Mediterranean			Morocco Tunisia Algeria	Libya
Eastern Mediterranean		Debated: Turkey Turkish Cyprus	Turkey Turkish Cyprus Israel Palestine	*Egypt* Optional: *Syria* Jordan Lebanon
Eastern region			Moldavia Ukraine	Optional: *Belarus*
South-Eastern region		Croatia	Bosnia-Herz. Serbia Macedonia Montenegro	Albania Kosovo
Caucasus				Armenia Azerbaijan Georgia

Note
In italic = officially listed as ENP-partner in 2008.

variables. The classification of political proximity either in the narrow sense of the Copenhagen Criteria or a broader sense of norms/identity, interests and power orientation can evolve over years from both sides. Neighbourhood relations are subject to political interpretation, definition and change – the cases of Turkey and Israel illustrate the scope and the broad margin for such interpretation–reinterpretation of neighbourhood.

However, such a definition of the scope of the neighbourhood policy would be incomplete without referring to two structurally and politically important complements to the above outlined scope.

First, both the USA and Russia[3] have to be understood as cases of complementary neighbourhood policy, whether this is part of the official terminology or not. The above-mentioned factors – history, norms, interests and power – together with the economic, political and military involvement of the USA within Europe, including the EU framing within NATO and the aspiration of the EU to become a stronger partner to the USA, all add up to a case for classifying US–EU relations as an additional case of neighbourhood, but one based on a completely different set of power asymmetries. Although the Russian case is differs again at nearly all levels, the EU–Russian relationship does fall under neighbourhood policies – not only because of common borders with the Eastern EU members and Russia, but because of the political understanding of causes and objectives for special neighbourhood relations.

Second, and despite all official terminology, EU and NATO present another type and case for a broader definition of neighbourhood policy. Despite all differences in profile, model, power base, and the like, EU–NATO relations can be understood as neighbourhood relations between two regional actors based on nearly complementary membership, common values, mutual interests and power relations. Whether one regards NATO as the necessarily helpful neighbour to the EU's ESDI (European Security and Defence Identity) and peace-keeping ambitions or as an eventual starting point for a new Two-Pillar Alliance between the USA and the EU is a matter of political evaluation and aspiration. *De facto*, and in particular *vis-à-vis* the EU's CFSP and its implied global ambitions, good neighbourhood policy between the EU and NATO is a political necessity for the EU's interests and power status.

Locating EU neighbourhood policy

Like other EU policies, the ENP is not autonomous but must be understood as a policy influenced by the general settings of the EU, the European integration process, and the political dynamics both in the greater European region as well as the global ones. When analysing and evaluating the ENP, four settings are deemed to be of specific relevance: the historical development, the will-building and will-implementation, the interrelation between governance and civil society, and the budgetary settings. These together not only define scope, dynamics, patterns and modes of neighbourhood policy but interact between each other and create a political environment for neighbourhood policies, including its improvement and its role for European integration in general, and the further development of the EU in particular.

However, such an understanding of the EU's neighbourhood policies has to be related to objective and subjective prioritising of the EU agenda, which limit its political relevance and weight. In objective terms, the EU needs a consistent, cohesive and comprehensive neighbourhood policy as an important component of both CFSP as well as future enlargements. In subjective terms, the EU has responded to such necessity by establishing a particular policy – i.e,. its neighbourhood policy. However, European integration in general, as well as the widening process and the global actor policies in particular, can and will survive even with a non-cohesive, erratic and ineffective neighbourhood policy. Thus, neighbourhood policy is in objective terms much less essential than – for example – the establishment of a coherent legal system through the Charter approach, or the successful management of further growth and political stability. This means that in terms of political priorities on the EU's agenda, neighbourhood policy ranks lower and is more open to be instrumentalised with an eye on package deals and bargaining compromises or even sacrificed for other policies.

The historical context

In terms of historical development of an explicit EU neighbourhood policy one can distinguish between three periods: a phase deprived of common neighbourhood policies, a period of gestation, and the current cycle of common neighbourhood policies.

The first period covers the years of the European Coal and Steel Community (ECSC), the European Economic Community (EEC) and the European Community (EC) – i.e., from the 1950s to the late 1980s. This period is characterised by non-explicit, multiple, uncoordinated and pragmatic neighbourhood policies of the member states and only limited, eclectic and highly reactive supplementary policies at the European level. This can be explained by two main factors: first, the integration process was and had to be of an inward-looking nature and, following the EDC (European Defence Community) failure, integration was reduced to an economic integration project; second, the East–West conflict in Europe and its global effects limited neighbourhood policies both in its dimensional and political–geographic terms. Neighbourhood, association and widening policies were of an intra-Western character – anything else was politically neither feasible nor acceptable. Even though the emerging Africa, Caribbean and Pacific (ACP) regime can be regarded as an implicit far-away neighbourhood, it cannot be counted as an explicit neighbourhood policy. Moreover, although the EC activities towards Israel and the Middle East in the early 1970s, the idea of a Mediterranean Conference for Security and Cooperation in Europe (CSCE) regime in the mid-1970s, and the early cooperation with the Maghreb countries all fall into the category of neighbourhood policy, they all miss the overall concept, sustainability and political will-building of an explicit common neighbourhood policy.

The second period covers the years marking the transformation of the EC into the EU during the Maastricht process – i.e., the end of the 1980s to the early 2000s. It is characterised by a new constellation of basic conditions for an EU neighbourhood policy. First, both economic quantitative and qualitative growth had resulted in a new absolute as well as relative power base, combined with the need to complement an inward-looking with an outward-looking integration project. Second, the dissolution of the East–West conflict had created fundamentally new political, economic and peace-in-security projection opportunities. Third, the Maastricht process had not only revitalised the integration identity, but had defined the EU as a political–economic security actor for both the near and the far abroad areas. In addition, the establishment of European Monetary Union (EMU) and common foreign and security policy (CFSP), the gradually growing involvement in pan-regional and global governance, and finally the initiated widening process had all made an explicit neighbourhood a political necessity. Within this field fall the Barcelona Process (beginning 1995), the association agreements with Eastern European countries, and the official start of EU–Soviet relations.

The third period starts with the official establishment of the EU neighbourhood policy in 2004. As a joint project of both the European Commission and the Council, the ENP avoided from the very onset the institutional–political competition between Commission and Council as witnessed in the case of ESDP. It developed in three directions: further conceptualisation, improving comprehensiveness *vis-à-vis* the neighbouring target countries and sub-regions, and establishing and streamlining existing and new supportive financial instruments towards EU's neighbours.

In sum, the pattern of the historical development of EU neighbourhood does not follow a ready-made design (*finalité*), which the relevant actors developed and applied according to the given and emerging opportunities, but came more as a reactive realisation of a political logic dictated by changing conditions and constellations, emerging interest opportunities and related cost–benefit rationalities. As one looks into the future of the ENP, its options entail on the one hand, the regression into pragmatic muddling-through, but on the other, the further gradual development of a pro-active understanding of neighbourhood policy, *vis-à-vis* both the neighbours as well as further widening, improving CSFP, and a consequent global actor approach.

The decision-making context

Decision-making with regard to EU neighbourhood policies faces not only actual but also structural problems – both in political will-building as in will-implementation. The most important of these problems are discussed below.

First, unlike the EU's monetary, agricultural and other fully integrated policies, the division of labour between the European Commission following an integrated model and the European Council following an intergovernmental model has not only separated the economic from the political and security dimension of neighbourhood policies, but has resulted in the well-known institutional competition on competences and power between the Commission's External Relations Director General – and its President – and the Council's CFSP responsibilities, including the political and security aspects of neighbourhood policies. Although both the design of the European Charter and its Treaty substitute (the Reform Treaty) plan to overcome this institutionalised competition and imbalance of power through

Table 12.2 Scope of actors and fields involved in the ENP

Dimension level	Political dimension	Economic dimension	Security dimension	Cultural dimension
Local level and local governments	Partnership of local communities (cities, etc.)	*Ad hoc* support in crises and long-term support for development	*Ad hoc* and systematic trans-border cooperation in crime prosecution	Exchange and cooperation in cultural, sports, youth, activities
Regional level	Cooperation within and beyond CoR, Euro regions, inter-regional cooperation and alliance-building	Trans-border cooperation in developing planning, coordination of infrastructure-building	Trans-border cooperation of migration, crime control, joint border management	Inter-regional cooperation in various cultural fields
National level	Traditional bilateralism, axis-building, friendship treaties	Transnational and cross-border economic planning, management, and bilateral economic partnerships	Bilateral cooperation in domestic security (crime, migration, asylum) and selected bilateral military cooperation and mutual support of armed forces and defence policies	Bilateral exchange and cooperation programmes in cultural and non-political issues
European level	EU's near and far abroad policies and bi-regionalism	EU's near and far abroad policies and bi-regionalism, such as EU–ACP relations	EU–NATO, EU–OSCE and other official and *de facto* cooperation schemes	Cultural activities of the EU through various programmes (e.g., PHARE, TEMPUS, ALPHA)
Global level	EU's CFSP, EU's involvement in the UN system	EU/EMU, IMF, World Bank EU and WTO.	EU's CFSP/ESDP and EU's Crisis Prevention Force activities, EU activities in peace-keeping	EU–UNESCO etc.

interlinking decision-making in both dimensions, it is still an open question whether and to what degree this will create a comprehensive grand strategy and allow for its cohesive implementation.

Second, again well known from national foreign policies, neighbourhood policy *per se* is both multilevel and multidimensional and spans a variety of actors and activities, as illustrated in Table 12.2.

Thus, decision-making with regard to the ENP demands a significant amount of coordination between actors on different levels, and across the different dimensions. And given the supranational character of the EU, the limited power of the EU *vis-à-vis* the actors on lower levels, and the complexity in the pursuit of interests in the different dimensions, the ENP faces a major problem of either effective cross-level and cross-dimensional interlocking or else duplication, competition and contradiction within a heterogeneous multitude of neighbourhood policies and activities.

Third, and once more well-known within nation-states' foreign policies, traditional governmentalism in managing and controlling foreign relations and a developed civil society, which considers itself as a complement to governmentalism, create both an opportunity as well as a challenge for neighbourhood policies within the EU. Relations between both range from mutual support (such as in pre- and post-governmental activities of actors like parties, trade unions, churches, media and so-called non-political organisations) to over-coordinated and uncoordinated parallelism and even to competitive and hostile confrontation. As the CSCE process and related activities on the various levels demonstrated, governmentalism and non-governmentalism or civic society activities can successfully reinforce each other – the case of the political transformation of Franco's Spain into a democratic Spain is an illustration. On the other side, peace-building in the former Yugoslavia illustrates that the resistance by parts or the whole community against governmentally introduced social and political change can severely delay, damage and even block policies designed to introduce democracy, security and peace between social groups including minorities and between newly established nation-states.

Fourth, the well-known problem of the EU's budgeting – i.e., securing the adequate financing of effective neighbourhood policies based on economic/financial direct and indirect benefits as part of the doctrine of civic/civil plus constructive engagement – is an issue. While the concept of the EU budget is based on the understanding of the EEC/EC – and therefore gives priority to agricultural politics and related measures – neither the available amount nor the composition of the EU's budget reflects or responds to the new understanding of the EU as a pro-active actor towards its near and far abroad partners as well as its new global responsibilities, which all demand significant budgetary means.

In such a multitude of complexities, a more narrowly defined problem of the ENP reflects the very nature of a supranational actor or the specific in-built competition and cooperation of nation-states and the European bodies. Already the EEC of the Six had to coordinate, balance and actively absorb intra-EEC and outer-EEC neighbourhood policies. Again, such various neighbourhood patterns have promoted the integration process as well as created problems for existing and future integration. The close cooperation or better good neighbourhood policy within the

Belgium-Netherlands-Luxemburg (BENELUX) group illustrates how neighbourhood policies can exert important positive influence both on intra- as well as outer-EEC, EC and EU policies. Improving Greek–Turkish bilateral neighbourhood policies will have a significant impact on the EU–Turkey neighbourhood and might assist in overcoming the division of Cyprus. Past problems in British–French relations contributed to the delay of British membership, and current difficulties in Polish–Russian relations affect the EU's policies towards Russia. In sum, ENP is a particular showcase for the possibilities and limitations of the supranational integration model pursued by the EU. Coordinating, harmonising and – if possible – integrating the twenty-five or twenty-seven or more geographically and politically diverse specific national neighbourhood policies and sometimes competing projections of political, economic and security interests into the neighbourhood and the near abroad is and will be a major challenge for the EU's aim of speaking 'with one voice' and presenting as a truly effective and influential actor.

The grand strategy context

As has been mentioned above, ENP is only one element each of the EU's CFSP and of the EU's ambition to become a relevant global actor. Following the old model of concentric circles and links to the dimensionality approach, Table 12.3 illustrates the components of a grand foreign relations strategy and the dimensions effectively involved.

Again, it has to be underlined that good neighbourhood policy results not only from norms and values and the projection of the civic society approach to the outside, but also from a cross-level and cross-dimensional optimisation based on cost–benefit risk rationality, which is implied by the notion of a good grand strategy. It should be remembered that the conceptualisation and implementation of a grand strategy for foreign behaviour is already difficult for the nation-state; for a supranational actor such as the EU – with its duality of nationalism and supra-nationalism, integrationist and inter-governmentalist tendencies, widening and deepening tendencies, and Europeanist and globalist ambitions – the development of such a good grand

Table 12.3 Components of the EU's grand foreign relations strategy

Dimensions EU CFSP policies	Political– diplomatic dimension	Economic dimension	Security dimension	Cultural dimension
EU widening policy	+++	+++	+++	+++
EU neighbourhood policy (near abroad)	+++	+++	+	+
EU far abroad policy	+++	+++	+	–
EU bi- and inter-regionalism	+++	+++	–	–
EU global governance policy	+++	++	+	–

strategy is a major challenge to the will and ability to coordinate, harmonise and communalise norms, interests and power. Thus, the notion of good neighbourhood policy carries not only a demand for good object–subject policies and good bilateral relations, but also a demand for good integration of this specific policy into a grand strategy for the EU.

Strategies, instruments and modes of ENP

Since its official establishment in 2004,[4] the ENP strategy has been conceptually widened and deepened on the one hand, and criticised both within and outside the EU on the other hand. The major steps in further developments of the strategic concepts are the strategy papers of 2006[5] and 2007.[6] While the early strategy papers developed objectives and the general architecture, the later ones added the ENP-Initiative (ENPI) as one of the major specific instruments for implementing policy, mainly through assistance programmes.

At present, ENP consists of a comprehensive concept of partnership with the EU's neighbours, a regionalised approach particular towards the East, the Balkans and the Mediterranean, and action plans for each neighbour country.[7] However, such actions plans, association treaties and special agreements mention and refer to the prospect of membership but do not provide specifics, conditions or promises which go beyond the existing EU treaties in general and the Copenhagen Criteria in particular. Following the 2004 enlargement of the EU, the state of formal and informal relations is as described in Table 12.4.

Basically, there are two debates about and within ENP. The first follows a technocratic rationality and focuses on the goals–means relation, asking whether the chosen ENPI-instrument is effective for the implementation of the objectives and how this instrument can be interrelated to other instruments and strategies.

The second debate, however, has a much stronger political character – i.e., an interest, power and competition dimension. It focuses on the regional/country priorities, both in terms of political attention as well as the distribution of financial assistance, political support and perspectives for closer association or even membership.

Behind such controversies lie not only a competitive race among EU neighbour countries to get better conditions, more advantages and more chances for eventual membership, but also the interests of EU member states in prioritising their neighbouring regions, their preferred neighbours, and their idea of the future of the EU's widening. Thus, Poland's and the Baltic states' initiatives *vis-à-vis* the further East – i.e., Belarus and Ukraine –, the South-Eastern member states' interests in consolidating the Balkans through the ENP, and Mediterranean countries' interests in improving ENP relations with North Africa reflect the differences between member states' individual neighbourhood policies as well as their views about the future of the EU's ENP. If one understands the EU's role as being to complement national policies with ENP, to harmonise governmental and non-governmental activities of the different levels, and eventually to inter-governmentalise or even integrate the specific neighbourhood policies of EU members, the EU faces a double and criss-cross competition in the further operationalisation and implementation of its ENP:

Table 12.4 State of relations entertained by the EU in its neighbourhood (2008)

Sub-region	ENP activities	Membership perspective	Problems
North Africa Morocco Algeria Tunisia Libya	Barcelona Process, Association, Special Support Programmes, Migration Control Initiatives	Not in the foreseeable future	Socio-economic development, political stability, migration
Middle East Egypt Syria Lebanon Jordan Israel Palestine	Middle-East Initiatives, Special Economic Support Programmes, Selective Peace-Stabilisation Actions, Selective Association Agreements	Not in the foreseeable future	Middle East conflict, economic performance, political stability and democratic rule
Eastern Europe Belarus Moldova Ukraine	Special Economic Support Programmes, Selective Association Agreements	Not in the foreseeable future	Economic performance, political stability and democratic rule
Balkans Bosnia-Herzegovina Serbia Kosovo Albania Macedonia	Stability Pact, Special Economic Support Programmes, Selective Association Agreements, Selective Peace-Keeping Actions	Possible if political–economic conditions are met	Balkans conflict follow-up problems, economic performance, political stability and democratic rule
Turkey Turkish Cyprus	Association Agreements	Disputed but possible if political conditions are met	Political developments, Cyprus reunification
Caucasus Armenia Azerbaijan Georgia	Special Economic Support Programmes	Not in the foreseeable future	Political stability and democratic rule, economic development

on the one side, the competition between its members about political and budgetary priorities and, on the other side, the competition between the neighbours to receive the best available privileges, economic advantages and financial assistance.

The economic–financial dimension

ENP is not only a political project but an economic one as well. It is based on – and reinforces – mostly asymmetric (both in terms of quality and quantity) trade and investment flows, which constitute direct or indirect dependencies of ENP countries

Table 12.5 Ratio of total exports to exports to EU (2007)

Algeria	*50.3 %*
Armenia	*47.6 %*
Azerbaijan	*68.0 %*
Belarus	*45.6 %*
Egypt	*42.7 %*
Georgia	*47.4 %*
Israel	27.7 %
Jordan	5.5 %
Lebanon	10.6 %
Libya	*76.3 %*
Moldova	*38.5 %*
Morocco	*62.8 %*
Syria	*32.3 %*
Tunisia	*73.5 %*
Ukraine	25.6 %

Source: S. Bendiek 2008.

Note
In italic = ratio over 30 %.

from the EU. Table 12.5 quantifies such asymmetries in the light of prevailing export ratios.

Following its traditional character and projecting power in a benevolent mode and its economic strength, the EU implements its ENP predominantly with economic-financial instruments in a strategy of economic incentives and financial assistance programmes for political cooperation plus a preparation for upgrading relations/associations. For that purpose, the EU refers to its existing and specific ENP assistance programmes, of which the most important are listed in Table 12.6.

Although such totals are relatively small in absolute numbers and in comparison to the assistance programmes of the major EU member countries, they must be related to the mostly small size, population and GNP of ENP countries. That means that these assistance programmes are highly relevant in relative terms, and that good neighbourhood relations towards the EU are not only necessary for continued and increasing trade and investment flows, but they pay in terms of direct financial assistance.

Problems and perspectives of ENP

In comparison with other policies of the EU, its ENP – officially established in 2004 – is a relatively new project. Nevertheless, its perspectives are not only a matter of political will-building and will-implementation, both as a specific policy and in the framework of CFSP. Instead, both in institutional as well as in implementation terms ENP depends on the role, place and relevance of CFSP in the European integration process, on the future of the EU's institutional reform and on the state of EU–NATO relations.

Table 12.6 Major EU financial assistance programmes related to the ENP

Programme	Earmarked funds for 2007–13 in euros
Assistance for future candidates/members	11.6
ENP and Partnership Programmes (ENPI)[1]	11.2
Governance Programme for reform-willing countries	0.35
EIB credits for potential candidate countries	8.7
EIB credits for ENP countries	12.4

Note
ENPI included former assistance programmes such as TACIS for the East and MEDA for the South.

But even in the case of positive developments in these three elements of conditionality for ENP, the latter faces a number of structural problems which restrain its effectiveness. The major ones are the following:

1   *the finalité (endpoint) problem*: Like many other components of CFSP – for example the EU's development aid policies – the *finalité* of ENP is still open. But whether ENP supplements, complements or even substitutes national neighbourhood policies is not only a conceptual problem but depends on whether, and if so how and to what degree, the duality between *integrationism* and *inter-governmentalism* will be solved and how the concept of multilevel governance, with its horizontal and vertical synergies, will be translated into a comprehensive and cohesive ENP concept. And even if the EU follows the current pragmatic approach and defines itself as only one actor in a network of actors of different types, different levels and different political nature, its role in such a network is still undefined. Whether the EU acts as a leader, or the leading actor, or as a coordinator to fill gaps is an open question.

2   *the norm versus interest problem*: As in traditional foreign policy, ENP faces the problem of combining a norm and order approach with the pursuit of its specific interests plus its power projection. In cases where norms, interests and power projection reinforce each other – as in many cases of classical enlargement policies – this problem does not occur. But in many cases involving Mediterranean, Balkan and Eastern countries, the EU's traditional projection of norms – e.g., democracy in general and the rule of law, adequate treatment of minorities, peaceful and non-provocative security and defence policies – collides with other EU interests – e.g., access to resources, control of migration, widening of military security areas. While traditional enlargement policies have demonstrated how norms, interests and power policies can reinforce each other, a number of ENP cases, where future membership is out of the question, force the EU – as well as the geographically directly concerned EU member states – into an either/or choice between norms or interest policy. Pragmatic, case-by-case solutions and the doctrine of constructive engagement may downplay the

problem but do not eliminate the well-known, fundamental issue of democratic and/or civic foreign policy.

3 *the cohesion and priority problem*: As has been outlined above, ENP has to be regarded in a variety of ways – first, as a component of CFSP in general and of security and stability projection in particular; second, as an instrument for controlling/preventing trans-border problems like migration, transnational crimes, pollution and environmental damage; third, as an instrument for widening trade and investment or creating an 'EEA plus' or an enhanced European free-trade area; and fourth, as a tool for preparing association and membership. The first aspect of the cohesion and priority problem is that these four components are each of a different political nature, demand different strategies, and need different instrumentations. While the political approach of ENP demands comprehensiveness, cohesion and priority-setting between these elements, the current reality is that ENP is more a cumulative policy than a coherent grand strategy with an effective interrelating of elements. The second aspect of this problem results from the fundamental difference of the neighbouring countries. Even if one limits ENP to the official ENP, which means excluding countries like Norway and Switzerland, the differences between North African, Eastern European and Balkan countries are so large and the perspectives of their political and socio-economic development so divergent, that a systematic or cohesive ENP approach with clear priorities is extremely difficult – even if EU member countries would agree on a common overall ENP strategy, which is not the case. And if one limits ENP to a pre-enlargement policy, it still has to be noted that the EU has no coherent concept or the necessary prioritising criteria about its future enlargement policies. Whether the EU gives priority to the East – and to which part of the East? –, to the South – and to which part of the Mediterranean?, or to the Balkans, and which countries should get privileged ENP relations because of which criteria, is another open conceptual and political problem. The Turkish case illustrates on the one hand the far-reaching disagreements about enlargement, and on the other hand, the non-cohesiveness of traditional pragmatism *vis-à-vis* enlargement.[8]

4 *the one-dimension problem or the malevolent neighbour problem*: Although the EU has tried and still tries to complement its economic integration process with CSFP, the catalogue of instruments for the projection of the EU's norms, interest or power even to its near neighbourhood – i.e., political-diplomatic, economic, military and socio-cultural instruments – is unbalanced. Both because of political will and ability, the EU is predominantly both an economic and a traditional benevolent power. Its peacekeeping and peace-making abilities are still in their infancy – again, both because of restrained political will and budgetary-military ability. In the case of a malevolent neighbour – with malevolent understood in terms either of de-democratisation or of the regional projection of military threats – the EU is not fully equipped to curb such behaviour with preventive deterrence. It does not have the military or the peace-and-democracy policing capacity to solve such problems but rather has to refer to NATO to step in. The case of the war on Kosovo illustrates such a general shortcoming.

5 *the budget problem*: Although the cumulative assistance programmes directly and indirectly related to ENP are impressive in range, substance and relative importance for the EU's neighbours, they are insufficient *vis-à-vis* the problems of the neighbour countries and – with a yearly amount of 3–4 billion euros – they are too small to secure the fullest good neighbourhood policies from problem countries towards the EU and to accelerate modernisation, transformation and the build-up of good governance policies in the EU's neighbourhood or to solve problems like migration, crime, unemployment, and further deterioration of the environment. In addition, such budgetary limitations restrict the EU's capacity to act as a benevolent coordinator of national and sub-national neighbourhood policies through co-financing or seed money. Again, this is not a specific problem of ENP but the reflection of the budgetary problem of CFSP and the EU in general.[9]

6 *the performance problem: De facto*, ENP replaces the old Barcelona Process[10] as well as the past cumulative membership efforts *vis-à-vis* the Central Eastern and South-Eastern European countries, which have both been criticised because of a lack of political cohesiveness, effectiveness and will to prioritise the issues of these sub-regions. It is not clear whether and if so to what degree the new ENP overcomes the problems of the old neighbourhood policies, creating a political–economic balance between power and norm projection in all sub-regions targeted by ENP: North Africa, the Middle East, the Balkans, Eastern Europe, Turkey, Caucasus and the special problem, Russia.

ENP between membership, association and partnership

As has been mentioned above, the EU's idea of ENP is to bridge the gap between membership and non-membership by a variety of special agreements, support programmes and association agreements, mostly addressing economic-financial issues and, in the case of North Africa, the migration issue. The challenges, feasibility and range of such a strategy can be illustrated by three examples: the former Yugoslavia, Turkey and Russia.

In terms of history, socio-economic relations and culture, Yugoslavia has been traditionally close to EEC/EC/EU Europe, despite the political character of the Tito regime. But while this political-economic plus geographic proximity to the widening EC/EU, plus the end of the East–West conflict, opened perspectives for closer relations and even membership, the break-up of the Yugoslavian state, the militarisation of the old conflicts in former Yugoslavia, and the brutal way in which the new states reorganised their society and foreign policy not only postponed all ideas of Yugoslavia's becoming part of Europe but also made Yugoslavia a major multiple political challenge for the new EU.

First, the combination of civil and interstate war created a challenge for the EU's ideas of peaceful neighbourhood in general, and peaceful and cooperative secession in particular, to which the EU was not prepared, willing or able to adequately respond. As a result, the USA revitalised its security-building role in Europe and established the Dayton Solution, and the EU understood its political–military failure as a problem to be avoided in the future.

Second, the Yugoslavian developments demonstrated the severe political and military shortcomings of CFSP, both in terms of political will-building as well as of will-implementation. Again, these developments initiated a selective learning process in CFSP, which contributed to political improvements as well as the later establishment of the European Crisis Intervention Force.

Third – and while defining and redefining the former Yugoslavia as an integral part of the new Europe – these developments served as a testing ground for strategies to re-establish security in peace, democratic norms and rules, and restart economic growth in a highly volatile sub-region.

The EU's answer to such challenges was a consecutive mix of strategies based primarily on economic means supplemented by peacekeeping operations first dominated by NATO and later dominated by the EU. This mix aimed at fostering both good neighbourhood within the sub-regions – i.e., ending military activities, overcoming the effects of the war and the related ethnic policies, and re-establishing peace and cooperation between and within the new states – and good neighbourhood relations with the EU in general and its Austrian, Italian, Hungarian and Greek members in particular. To realise such a double strategy of good neighbourhood, the EU combined different strategies:

- offering membership to those new states which were willing and able to meet the Copenhagen Criteria and also to subscribe to the good neighbourhood doctrine
- introducing the Stability Pact (1999–2008) as an economic and financially very attractive means of re-establishing good neighbourhood between the EU and the new states as well as between the new states themselves – i.e., introducing sub-regional cooperation and peaceful conflict solution
- combining a policy of economic-financial incentives with both a policy of sanctions and military and peacekeeping activities to ensure the implementation of EU standards, norms and interests

In sum, the double good neighbourhood policy carried the option for selective and highly conditional EU membership. And given the economic and political attractiveness of even remote EU membership, this linkage between good neighbourhood and membership can be regarded as a major factor for the successful political-economic transformation, the new minority policies in the new states, and their willingness to improve sub-regional relations based on peace in security. The success of this strategic mix and conditional gradualism is listed in Table 12.7.

Despite the developments in the former Yugoslavia, all of these new states have a conditional but calculable option for future membership, while the case of Turkey illustrates the ambivalence of the EU and its member states in terms of linking association and good neighbourhood policies with membership options. EU–Turkey relations, which sometimes overlap, reinforce or conflict with Turkey's policies within NATO, rely on the one hand on decades of association agreements (since 1964), on Turkey's participation in ENP and on membership negotiations since 2005; and on the other hand on a significant Turkish minority in Germany

Table 12.7 The ENP's successful use of its strategic mix and conditioned gradualism

Country	EU membership	EU association agreement (as of 2008)
Slovenia	EU membership, plus membership in ECU since 2007	
Croatia	Negotiations about membership since 2005	SAA since 2005
Macedonia	Membership candidate since 2005	SAA since 2004
Albania	Future membership possible	SAA since 2006
Serbia	Future membership possible	SAA under negotiation
Montenegro	Future membership possible	SAA under negotiation
Bosnia-Herzegovina	Future membership possible	SAA under negotiation
Kosovo	Future membership possible	Future SAA possible

and other EU countries, plus significant trade and economic cooperation between Turkey and the EU. Although both association as well as ENP towards Turkey are undisputed, EU membership for Turkey – an option projected for around 2015 – is under discussion. Supporters of Turkish membership underline its economic performance, its geo-strategic relevance, and its political change according to European demands and norms. Critics of Turkish membership refer to deficits in democratic rule and European political standards *vis-à-vis* minorities such as the Kurdish community, the support for the division of Cyprus, and the general non-European character of the Turkish society and state. Thus, Turkey faces the possibility of either unsuccessful or further postponed membership negotiations, or an EU policy which substitutes membership for ENP-plus association. Again, it has to be noted in reference to the abovementioned asymmetry that it is the EU which ultimately decides about membership or non-membership – as in the case of the former Yugoslavian states, Turkey is more object than subject of ENP despite ENP's 'soft-power' and 'cooperative partnership' approach.

While Turkey is an open case for the use of ENP as a preparatory strategy for membership, the outcome of which finally depends on Turkey's future performance, its perception within the EU and its member states, and the general development of the EU's grand geopolitical concept, EU–Russian relations illustrate that ENP can even exclude all membership options. Neither the EU nor Russia seeks Russian membership in the EU, but what is sought is rather a combination of selected association agreements, a privileged economic relationship, plus special cooperation in the field of energy and resources (Energy Charter) and a general political – and in some cases peacekeeping – strategic partnership. Underlining good neighbourhood policy results from factors such as:

- historical conflict and cooperation experiences between Russia/USSR/Russia with Europe in general and EU member states such as Germany, Poland and Finland in particular, plus the experiences with *détente* and post-*détente* policy towards the USSR/Russia

- common complementary economic interests in trade – and energy in particular – investments and the financial market
- selected common interest in cases of peacekeeping in the Balkans and other areas and cases
- the EU's role as a global actor and a potential strategic partner for Russia.

From the view of the EU, Russian membership has to be excluded because of the size and the quantity of political-economic problems faced by Russia, which would be a major burden for the EU in the case of membership, and the problems in democratic rule and European norms, as well as the general problem of overextending the EU. From the Russian view, EU membership seems unthinkable because of its political conditioning, its economic effects for Russia's underdeveloped industrial and service sector, and its political restraints *vis-à-vis* Russia's identity, sovereignty and interests. The combination of good neighbourhood policy, special economic relations – particularly in the field of energy and resources – and strategic partnership, however, furthers both EU and Russian interests in an optimal way without restraining Russia's domestic development and foreign policy too much.

In sum, these three cases illustrate on the one hand the flexibility of ENP and its interrelation with other components or strategies within a broader CFSP: ENP can exclude and include membership and can keep the membership open as both a bargaining chip and an instrument to impose change in the neighbouring states' policies. On the other hand, this flexibility can lead to a cumulative and non-cohesive pragmatism, which ignores the necessity of a coherent grand strategy for the EU as a constructive global actor. Nevertheless, all three cases underline the very nature of ENP: that it is only one element of CFSP and only one aspect of the EU's aim of becoming a truly pan-European and global actor. Therefore ENP must always be interrelated to the other components of CFSP in a multi-tier, multi-level governance and a cohesive grand concept of a true common policy.

Conclusion

In spite of all its limitations, contradictions and unsolved dilemmas, the new ENP constitutes a major opportunity for progress, good integration and beneficial foreign relations policies for the EU in general, notably with regard to three specific aspects in particular. First, it translates the historical experience of good neighbourhood born from the intra-EU integration process – and the control and resolution of the East–West conflict – to the outside, i.e., the relations between the EU and its neighbours. Second, it combines the relation between civil society and civic foreign policy to the outside with its legitimate interests towards EU's neighbourhood and it does this in accord with a benevolent partnership. Third, it projects its traditional intra-EU-focused idea of a democratic community, of economic growth in peace and stability, not only to a greater Europe but to its neighbouring eastern and southern regions. Thus, the ENP has to be regarded as a new European project, which interrelates historical experience, good governance as the combination of good internal, neighbourhood and regional governance, and shared legitimate interests for peaceful well-being in Europe and beyond. Like European integration and peace-building, such a re-invention of good neighbourhood policy is not only important for the EU and its near abroad, but it also exemplifies that the idea of good neighbourhood can be translated from political wish to reality. Immanuel Kant would have welcomed such a project.

Notes

1 Systematic analysis of military conflicts shows that wars between neighbours account for the biggest percentages of traditional high-intensity warfare.
2 The idea to establish a Mediterranean Union promoted during the French Presidency of 2008 has to be considered as a revitalisation and widening of the Barcelona Process and promises a more concrete and consistent EU-Mediterranean policy.
3 Peace-making and mediation initiatives of the EU and supported by bilateral policies of EU memer states are important elements of ENP towards Russia, which was illustrated in the military conflict between Georgia and Russia in 2008, where the EU – despite political differences between the member states – initiated major conflict management and conflict solution efforts.
4 European Commission, *European Neighbourhood Policy: Strategy Paper*, Brussels, 12 May 2004, COM (2004) 373 final. It has to be underlined that ENP was a joint project of the European Commission, the Commissioner External Relations and the Council's High Representative.
5 *Communication from the Commission to the Council and the European Parliament on Strengthening the European Neighbourhood Policy*, Brussels, COM (2006) 726 final.
6 Regulation (EC) No. 1638/2006 of the European Parliament and the Council of 24 October 2006 laying down general provisions establishing a European Neighbourhood and Partnership Instrument.
7 In the end of 2007, such Action Plans existed for twelve out of the fourteen ENP countries.
8 The conflicts in the Caucasus and in particular the military conflict between Russia and Georgia in 2008 underlined not only the geo-political problem of ENP or ENP-plus but illustrated in addition the many problems of norm and power projection into a region relatively far in geography as well as political will and ability to follow EU's norms and modes in conflict solution policies.
9 For the conceptualisation as well as the implementation of ENP or a future ENP-plus the international financial crisis of 2008 has highlighted the sever problems of EU's budgetary power – or better its limits. Even with the support from the European Central Bank or the European Monetary Union the EU does not have the necessary financial-monetary means – such as the U.S. – to provide quick and effective solutions to financial crisis either of nation-states or regions.
10 It has to be seen whether the initiative of the French Presidency in 2008 to establish a Mediterranean Union will lead to a revitalisation of the Barcelona process and the creation of a specific Mediterranean substructure within a reorganised ENP. Like in the case of Eastern Europe, the Mediterranean region could be defined as a particular regional priority of EU's ENP.

Bibliography

Attina, Fulvio and Rosa Rossi (eds) (2004), *European Neighbourhood Policy: Political, Economic and Social Issues*, Catania, 2004.

Gloser, Guenter (2007), 'Europaeische Nachbarschaftspolitik nach der deutschen EU-Ratspraesidentschaft – Bilanz und Ausblick', *Integration* No. 04, 493–8.

Kirchner, Emil and James Sperling (2008), *EU Security Governance*, Manchester: Manchester University Press.

Lippert, Barbara (2008), 'Die EU-Nachbarschaftspolitik: viele Vorbehalte – einige Forschschritte – unsichere Perspektiven', Paper Friedrich-Ebert-Stiftung, Berlin, March.

Council of the European Union (2007), *Strengthening the European Neighbourhood Policy – Presidency Progress Report*, 10874/07, Brussels, 15 June.

Seidelmann, Reimund (ed.) (2002), *EU, NATO and the Relationship Between Transformation and External Behavior in Post-Socialist Eastern Europe The Cases of the Slovak Republic, Bulgaria, Romania and Ukraine*, Baden-Baden: Nomos Publishing House.

Telo, Mario (ed.) (2005), *European Union and New Regionalism: Regional Actors and Global Governance in a Post-hegemonic Era*, Aldershot: Ashgate.

Websites

Sources/documents: http://ec.europa.eu/world/enp/index_en.htm

Collection of acadenuc analysis etc: http://ec.europa.eu/world.enp/academic_en.htm

13 The EU and its far-abroad

Interregional relations with other continents

Sebastián Santander and Frederik Ponjaert

Summary

Since the end of the cold war, interregional dynamics have become a fixture both of the global multilayered multilateral system, as well as of the EU's efforts to strengthen said international system. Such interregional arrangements are deeply rooted in the new regional associations which emerged at the end of the 1980s. Since the collapse of the bipolar world order, various regional dynamics have flourished across the globe. This new wave of regionalism included a broad variety of forms and scopes of regional cooperation, nonetheless it has allowed a growing number of regional entities – among which first and foremost the EU – to develop multifaceted region-to-region relations. These complex multi-issued interregional arrangements have grown exponentially as they have come to meet functional and structural needs of their constituent members. Among the various roles such interregional initiatives can assume, one can distinguish between: power-balancing efforts, agenda-setting and cost-cutting concerns, protection against unwanted external pressures, institutionalizing political dialogue and consultation, and reflexive region strengthening. All of these functions can be called upon in varying degrees according to the specific context and history of any given arrangement. A detailed study of two of the EU's core region-to-region relationships – the EU–Latin America and the EU–East Asia interregional arrangements – clearly illustrates the systemic foundations, the historical path-dependencies and the contextual factors, both endogenous and exogenous, which have come to shape these different yet comparable interregional dynamics.

Introduction

In the early 1990s, international relations underwent a renaissance and saw a major proliferation of regionalism, i.e., cooperation among neighboring states. The strengthening of these relations led to the development of novel forms of foreign relations, notably those of an interregional nature. Interregionalism implies that two regions interact as regions. This chapter explores the phenomenon of interregionalism on the basis of both historical and topical perspective, without neglecting to analyze its theoretical and empirical dimensions. Particular attention will be paid to the role played by the EU in the development of interregionalism and its implications for global governance. A series of core questions will structure this analysis: To what end do regional groups develop interregional relations? What is the relationship between interregionalism and the global political economy? How have interregionalism and multilateralism come to interact? Which roles have regionalism and interregionalism come to take on within global governance efforts? These various questions will be addressed throughout this chapter, thus teasing out the specific contribution such interregional arrangements have come to make within an ever more interdependent global/international society.

Specific interregional dynamics will be understood as being equally the reflection of a given constellation of endogenous and exogenous factors, as well as the result of general systemic changes within the international system and the corollary strategic innovations they engender. An analysis of various interregional relations will therefore allow us to isolate the root causes and institutional mechanisms that have persuaded a growing number of actors to engage in such external arrangements. Moreover, the juxtaposition of the two major institutionalized interregional relations developed by the EU will also offer us a clearer view of the strategy the EU has developed towards its far abroad. Interregionalism is consequently seen as both a symptom of the new multilateral interdependent system in which the EU must act; as well as an identifiable long-term flexible strategy developed by the EU towards its potential partners on other continents, and adapted incrementally as its engagement with said partners has increased.

This chapter is divided into three sections. First, it looks at the global context in which new regionalism, interregionalism and the EU operate. This initial section will offer further details on the overall nature of regionalism and interregionalism within the post-cold war period and their mounting impact on global governance. Whereas the aforementioned section is more theoretical, the second and third sections offer detailed case studies of two key interregional relationships entertained by the EU. Sections two and three will thus comprehensively tackle the emergence of the EU–Latin America and the EU–East Asia interregional dealings.

EU, new regionalism and the development of interregionalism in global politics

Since the late 1980s, a new wave of regional integration has developed in different parts of the world. This new generation of regional agreements can only be understood in the light of a profound transformation of the world system, the end of the bi-polar cold war. This critical juncture was typified by: an acceleration of global competition, the state's weakened control over its national economy, the recurrent difficulties of the multilateral trade order and the ensuing lack of satisfactory global structures. All of these post-cold war evolutions have encouraged the development of regional structures. This resurgence of regionalism fostered a great variety of regional cooperation schemes, which is why some prefer to speak of a wave of "new regionalisms" (Marchand, Boas and Shaw 1999). Finally, in contrast to the old regional projects that appeared during the cold war period, the new regionalism is not the result of a top-down process. In other words, it has not been imposed by a global hegemonic power.

However, these new regional projects share common features. They are all molded both by their respective component states as well as by the increasing role played by new actors on the international stage (non-states actors, international organizations, transnational corporations). Moreover, by covering a large range of issues (economic, trade, environment, political, security), new regionalism has emerged as a multidimensional phenomenon. New regionalism is further discernible because of its increasingly prevalent external impact. Indeed, some of these regional schemes have reached a level of development enabling them to play a distinctive role on the global stage. As more regional groups have adopted varying legal statuses in international law, this has given them the means to develop relations with third countries or regions. This is particularly true of the EU which, to strengthen its international influence and thus contribute to shaping the international global order, deepened its institutional architecture through the *Single European Act* (1986); developed new instruments to consolidate its external action (notably within the fields of low politics); and allowed for broader relations with both third countries/ regions and multilateral bodies. Such novel regional groupings formed in line with the new regional associations – first and foremost among which, the EU – have shown a preference for group-to-group relations. Accordingly, interregionalism has become an important feature of the new regionalist wave.

Finally, the post-cold war regionalist wave is characterized by the fact that it is taking shape in a time of accelerated globalization, in which the nation-state has been profoundly restructured. The world's states and their respective economies have become increasingly open to the outside world, thus making them more interdependent, while exposing them to more economic competition and rendering their national economic policies less effective and more dependent on the independent strategies developed by various transnational corporations. This trend has been further facilitated by the development of new information technologies, which structurally favor deregulation. It is against this background that the development of regional structures would become more important and beneficial in the eyes of the states themselves. Accordingly, regional repositioning of states, since the late 1980s, contributed to the rise of new regionalism. Yet such new regionalism and globalization are not mutually exclusive trends. Regional processes are clearly outward-oriented phenomena compatible with and receptive to the rapidly evolving global economy.

Akin to new regionalism, the current trend of interregionalism is not a phenomenon in contradiction with globalization and economic multilateralism. Interregionalism evolves within, and is constrained by, the global political economy. Certain observers, such as Bhagwati (Bhagwati 1993), consistently present regional economic arrangements as a theoretical distraction from, and even threat to, global multilateralism. However, practical experience has in fact shown that regional and interregional arrangements fostered within the context of globalization and the post-cold war system are intrinsically linked to the development and maintenance of a broader global multilateral context. They do not therefore constitute stumbling blocks but building blocks towards an open world economy. Indeed, regional and interregional agendas include mutual trade-liberalization programs in keeping with the rules and disciplines of the multilateral economic institutions, such as detailed by the World Trade Organization (WTO). Moreover, the trade programs of the former are even more ambitious than those negotiated at the multilateral level. So, regionalism and group-to-group associations act as a supplementary catalyst for multilaterally negotiated global trade liberalization.

Both regionalism and interregionalism have become characteristic elements of the post-cold war multi-level global governance structure. Current interregionalism is a corollary of the wave of new regionalist agreements. However, as illustrated by the case studies, interregionalism can also contribute to the consolidation of regionalism. A two-way relationship therefore exists between regionalism and interregionalism (Santander 2008).

Akin to regional initiatives, the nature of the new wave of interregionalism, developed since the early 1990s, is different from the one associated with the interregional relations developed during the cold war. Interregionalist initiatives which took place during the bipolar system were associated with "old" regionalism. These were the fruit of the isolated actions of the European Community (EC). The Community directly supported regional integration efforts in Africa, Latin America and Asia during the 1970s and 1980s. The European strategy at the time was based on regular and institutionalized political dialogue, a strengthening of development and cooperation policies, and the buttressing of other regional institutions.

That being said, "old" interregionalism was both sporadic and markedly constrained by the bipolar international context. With the end of the cold war, the increase of economic interdependency, the emergence of new regionalism and the deepening of European integration, the EU found itself in a favorable position capable of developing a series of new interregional agreements which were much more ambitious than in the past, for instance the group-to-group association which it negotiated with regional groups in Latin America (see below). The EU also seized this window of opportunity to forge new region-to-region ties, previously non-existent, such as the post-cold war dialogue with East Asia. As a result and as previously detailed, the interregional agenda was broadened to include mutual trade-liberalization programs in keeping with the rules of global international economic institutions. Henceforth, interregional trade agreements were to be WTO-plus agreements. This implied that additional topics were also handled at the interregional level, including environmental, social and regional integration policies. Interregionalism has become a multidimensional phenomenon.

In order to better understand these international developments, we will focus on two different yet telling case studies: the EU–Latin America and the EU–East Asia interregional dynamics.

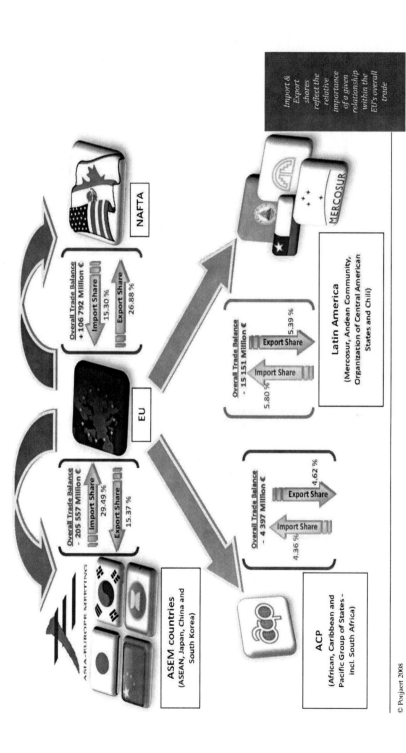

Import & Export shares reflect the relative importance of a given relationship within the EU's overall trade

NAFTA

Overall Trade Balance
+ 106 792 Million €
Import Share 15.30 %
Export Share 26.88 %

EU

Overall Trade Balance
- 205 557 Million €
Import Share 29.49 %
Export Share 15.37 %

ASEM countries
(ASEAN, Japan, China and South Korea)

ASIA-EUROPE MEETING

MERCOSUR

Latin America
(Mercosur, Andean Community, Organization of Central American States and Chili)

Overall Trade Balance
- 15 151 Million €
Export Share 5.39 %
Import Share 5.80 %

Overall Trade Balance
- 4 397 Million €
Export Share 4.62 %
Import Share 4.36 %

ACP
(African, Caribbean and Pacific Group of States - incl. South Africa)

© Poujaert 2008

Figure 13.1 Weight and constellation of the EU's major trade flows with its far-abroad (2006).

Table 13.1 Historical overview of exogenous changes affecting the internal dynamics of existing interregional dynamics

Historical Phases of Regionalism	Systemic Reality	Main Critical Junctures	Impact on Inter-Regional Arrangements	Exogenous Drivers of Inter-Regionalism	Some Examples
US lead Regionalism (1950-70)	Cold War / De-colonization *Bi-polarity*	Bretton Woods (1944) / IMF; GATT	Hegemon-centric	Neo-realist geo-strategy & Hegemonic Structures	- **NATO** - **OECD** - **ASEAN-US**
Neo-Regionalism I 1st Regionalism Wave / Accelerated at the end of the Cold War	Eroding Hegemony / End of Bipolarity / Accelerated Globalization Liberalization	Washington Consensus ('89) / Collapse of the USSR ('91) / Balkan Crisis (1991-2001)	Multi-directional, Indiscriminate and Generalized	Historical links with former colonies / Globalization / Commercial Competition / Domino knock-on Effect from other initiatives	- **APEC** - **EU-ACP** (Lomé Convention) - **EU-Mercosur** - **ASEM** (1st sum.) - **OSCE**
Neo-Regionalism II 2nd Regionalism Wave / New Economic and Political Challenges	Critic of the Bretton Woods System / Drive for Regional Governance *Emerging Multi-leveled Multilateralism*	WTO Challenged in Seattle ('99) / Asian Crisis ('97-8) / Lisbon Agenda (2000- 2010) / Chang Mai Initiative (2000) / Argentinean Crisis (2001)	Challenged and Re-evaluated	Need to Address decreasing legitimacy and efficiency of the liberal Global Governance system	- **EU Strategic Partnerships** (1st Wave) - **FTAA** - **ASEM** (summits 2-5) - **Barcelona Process**
21st Century	New Threats / Changing Balance of Power / Crisis of Established Int. Gov. mechanisms	9/11 2001 Terrorist Attacks / New US security Strategy (2002) / Rise of the BRICs / UN by-passed in Iraqi Crisis (2003) / Stagnation of Doha Round (2005-) / EU Constitutional Crisis (2005-07)	Strategic response to growing Need for International Order and Regulation	Geo-strategic considerations articulated through bilateral imperatives and contacts	- **EU Strategic Partnerships** (2nd Wave) - **Shanghai Cooperation Organization** (SCO) - ASEM (6th sum.) - **EU-African Union (AU)**

EU—Latin American interregionalism[1]

The cold war and the emergency of the EU strategy toward Latin America

In their current form, relations between the EC/EU and Latin America date back to the 1980s. This period was characterized by the beginning of the end of the cold war, and the gradual revival of European regional integration. The armed Central American conflicts[2] and the difficulties facing the processes of regional integration in this area and in the Andes led to a more coherent structuring of relations between the two sides of the Atlantic. Until then, the Community's strategy towards the

Latin American sub-Continent had seemed confused. Above all, until the end of the 1980s the strategy was lacking in political clout and was conditioned by the cold war's bipolar system. But the conflicts that broke out in Central America allowed the EC to play a major political role as an international intermediary, just when European Political Cooperation (EPC)[3] was being developed, i.e., in the early 1980s.

There are two main reasons for this European commitment. The first stems from the fear within the Community and the member states that the events in Latin America would result in a confrontation between the USA and the USSR, which would have had serious repercussions for Western Europe. The role played by the German Presidency of the EC during 1983 was influential in determining the European commitment to a peaceful resolution of conflicts in Central America. The second had to do with the intermediary position occupied by the Iberian countries – especially Spain – between Latin America and the Community, even before these countries had joined the latter.[4] The foreign policy of the Spanish Socialist-led government of Felipe González had twin, interrelated priorities: European integration and strengthened relations with Latin America. Spain would seek to play a leading intermediary role in the peaceful resolution of the Central American conflicts while completing its accession to the EC, which came into force in 1986. Once full membership was secured, the Spanish government pushed for the EC and member states to show a greater commitment towards the Central American isthmus.

The stance defended by the Iberian authorities in this international policy issue was similar to that favored by the Community. However, the European approach *vis-à-vis* these conflicts was very different from that favored by the USA. Both sides of the Atlantic differed in opinion with regard to the interpretation of these conflicts and the way to respond to them. While the Reagan Administration (1981–89) read the Central American wars through the lens of the East–West confrontation, the EC searched for the causes within the North–South divide. Seeing the hand of Moscow and Havana in these conflicts, and viewing them as the result of communist influence, Washington called for armed intervention. Conversely the Europeans, who had clearly identified the critical economic and social situation in which the debt crisis had plunged Latin America, saw the roots of the conflicts in poverty and the extreme inequalities within Central American societies. To the great displeasure of the USA, the EC and its member states called for a peaceful and negotiated solution to the conflicts as set out in the Stuttgart Declaration adopted by the European Council of June 1983, thanks to the pro-active role played by the German Foreign Minister, Hans-Dietrich Genscher. The diplomatic initiative of the Community and its member states not only ran counter to US policy, but it also legitimized the Latin American peace plans of the Contadora Group (Colombia, Mexico, Panama and Venezuela), which were contrary to the objectives of US foreign policy. One of the causes for European support for this group was that it favored an approach encompassing the whole Central American region, whereas the Reagan administration was proposing a peace plan for Nicaragua alone. Inspired by its own integration model, the Community gradually realized that "[...] subjects of a political nature, such as the prevention of conflicts and the war on drugs, could be tackled in a more appropriate way by increasing the efforts made at the regional level."[5]

In September 1984, the foreign affairs delegations of the EC, Spain and Portugal met with both their Central American colleagues from the Central American Common Market (CACM) – Costa Rica, Guatemala, Honduras, Nicaragua and Salvador – as well as the Latin American mediators coalesced within the Contadora Group. This meeting, the first in a long series, gave rise to the institutionalization of an interregional political dialogue, better known as the San José Process. The Community had agreed beforehand on a series of values and principles that it would seek to promote in Central America – such as the rejection of authoritarianism, the institution of democracy, the protection of human rights and the promotion of regionalism. These have continued to bear the principled substrata of the ongoing EU–Latin American interregional dialogue.

The San José Dialogue would become an opportunity for the Community to build up its profile as a benevolent international actor focused on the legality of international law, the use of diplomacy, negotiation and cooperation, distinct from national approaches founded on unilateral action by nation-states and the use of force. Overall it sought to be seen as encouraging a development-oriented approach rather than a security-fixated one (Crawley 2006). Moreover, the European authorities were particularly interested in reviving the Central American integration process. Taking stock of its own experience, the EC saw regionalism as the best way for Central American nations to develop and consolidate cooperation, thus ensuring stability and development. The EC signed an interregional cooperation agreement with the CACM. It then assisted the Central American regional integration process with European know-how in order to help regional development, boost the process of regional economic integration and develop intraregional trade. This agreement would also enable the Community to promote its own regional integration model and enhance its international legitimacy. One of the main consequences of the EC's involvement in Central America was the inauguration of new institutionalized relations with Latin American sub-regional groupings, which would expand dramatically following the end of the cold war.

The EU strategy towards Latin America in times of accelerated globalization

While the erosion of the bipolar system during the 1980s had resulted in stronger links between Europe and Latin America, the fall of the Berlin Wall led to a new consolidation of the relationship. This was reinforced when the Soviet bloc's disappearance removed the stifling context underpinned by the superpowers' rivalry. And so there came to be an opening of unprecedented opportunities to reinforce ties between the two sides of the Atlantic. The 1990s would become a fertile time for interregional relations between Europe and Latin America. The relationship between the two regions has substantially evolved over the past fifteen years. The EU has established regular meetings between the heads of state and government of the EU, Latin America and the Caribbean; thus opening the way for the Rio Process. The first summit held in Rio de Janeiro in June 1999 had as its main aim "to strengthen the political, economic and cultural understanding between the two regions in order to encourage the development of a strategic partnership, establishing a set of priorities for future joint action in the political and economic fields." In so doing, the EU is gradually pursuing its strategy of *rapprochement* with Latin America and the Caribbean, a sub-Continent that, for decades, has been subject to what could only be described as the discretionary domination of the USA. The EU is now a relatively important economic and political partner for Latin America; it is the leading donor in the region, first foreign investor, and second most important trade partner after the USA.

How do the countries of Latin America perceive this *rapprochement*? In fact, they have greeted with enthusiasm the structuring of a Community strategy for their sub-Continent, precisely because they view it as the emergence of a new international player capable of rebalancing their relations with the USA. This strategic thinking is a constant in Latin America. Latin American authorities have constantly sought an external counterweight to offset the dominant power of the time.

As early as the nineteenth century and the start of the twentieth, many Latin American states had relations with European powers, especially Great Britain, as well as with the USA; the aim was to achieve a better balance within their foreign relations. After World War Two, the situation changed. The countries of Latin America sought an external counterweight to the hegemonic power of the USA. Weakened by the war, Europe could no longer offer this counterweight, so during the cold war it was the Soviet power which provided the most important international alternative. But with the gradual consolidation of the European regional project and the *détente* that occurred in the second half of the 1980s, the Community began to be considered by the Latin American authorities as an actor that should not be ignored in their international strategic planning. Indeed, the Community and its member states were viewed in the sub-Continent as actors on the international stage capable of presenting a "third way" between the two cold war superpowers. Once Soviet power had been sidelined, the EC appeared to be, in the eyes of Latin Americans, not so much an alternative as a balancing pole in the new relation that began to be established with the USA following the speech on the Enterprise for the Americas Initiative (EAI) given by President George Bush (senior) in June 1990.

It is clear that the Americas began to acknowledge the prestige of US power, thanks to the US "victory" over the USSR, as well as that country's intellectual, moral and economic leadership. They also feared an emerging "fortress Europe." But in spite of all this, the EC/EU was seen by the Latin American authorities – in the same way as the regional integration "model" – as the only real way of increasing their negotiating power with Washington by realistically counterbalancing the influence of the USA in the sub-Continent. Moreover, in the context of globalization and structural reforms undertaken to revive the Latin American economies, the EC/EU was seen as a potential partner for diversifying these countries' opportunities and their sources of supplies, technologies and capital. For both the Latin American states and the new regional groups, the EC/EU emerged as an ideal counterweight within the overall equilibrium of their foreign relations, especially because the EU had been a staunch supporter of the different Latin America regional schemes.

Integration is fundamental to understanding Europe–Latin America relations.

Regionalism has become an important feature of the current foreign policy of the European and Latin American states. While the EU has deepened its institutional architecture and strengthened its international influence without precedent, Latin America has reinvigorated regional structures. A trade area between Argentina, Brazil, Paraguay and Uruguay (MERCOSUR) was created in 1991, the Central American Integration Project and the Andean Community (CAN) were re-launched respectively in 1991 and 1997. The Europeans as well as the Latin Americans consider regionalism both as a way to reinforce their influence at the international stage while preparing their respective economies to compete on the global stage. The revival of the regional processes in Europe and Latin America created a common interest in outward-looking regionalism and interregional relations. Since the Treaty of Maastricht, the EU has adopted a new type of cooperation agreement in order to develop relations with third parties. These agreements have enabled the EU to negotiate region-to-region associations with other regional groups.

These "new" interregional relations developed by the EU with Latin America since the early 1990s are much more ambitious than the "old" interregional agreements signed during the cold war era. Former interregionalism was based solely on a political dialogue and on European cooperation policy (technical, economic, trade and/or assistance). Today, the interregional agreements promoted by the EU not only rest on the political and aid pillars, but they now also include mutual trade-liberalization programs in keeping with the rules and disciplines of the WTO. These new programs are even more ambitious than those at the global multilateral level; yet, conversely the necessary compatibility required between WTO regulations and any other kind of free-trade agreement has meant that there is less and less room within the interregional agreements for traditional development cooperation policies, such as the Generalized System of Preferences (GSP) granted unilaterally by the EC/EU to regional areas made up of developing countries such as the CAN or the CACM.

With regard to the political dialogue promoted by the EU within the new interregional schemes, it is now distinguished by its democratic principles clause – introducing a democratic conditionality – which could be interpreted as an increasing politicization of interregional economic cooperation. Furthermore, the institutionalization of a regular political dialogue strives to favor interregional consultation and coordination among the partners' positions on the multilateral question touched upon within the international global bodies.

As far as the policy-cooperation pillar is concerned, it foresees cooperation in fields such as the war on drugs and its consequences, culture, information and communication, as well as training in regional integration. In the policy-cooperation pillar, European support for the strengthening of regional integration projects has become increasingly important. The EU has given technical, financial, institutional and diplomatic support to Latin American regionalism in order to prepare it in view of further negotiations of interregional projects. By providing such support, the EU plays a role as an "external federator" for new regional experiences through its interregionalist projects.

Today, the EU is negotiating interregional association agreements with three different Latin American regional schemes: with MERCOSUR, with CAN and with Central America. The mid-term goal of these interregional negotiations is to conclude region-to-region agreements covering political dialogue, policy cooperation and trade.

Besides its region-to-region initiatives, the EU is also pursuing bilateral relations in the form of "strategic partnership" with major powers in the developing world (particularly China, India and Brazil), yet the impact of these policies on interregionalism needs to be qualified. With regard to Latin America, the EU is particularly aware of the need to adapt its interregional strategy in light of the evolving political and economic situation on the sub-Continent. For instance, the EU adjusted its position as a majority of the countries in Latin America came to lean towards the left of the political spectrum. Yet, one of the most fundamental changes in the EU's post-cold war Latin American strategy is the Europeans' growing willingness to develop a closer relationship with Brazil. The latter is considered an emerging economic power of particular interest, since it has developed "serious macroeconomic policies" which favor external investments, and has entertained "healthy" relationships with both the USA and the EU. The EU has since July 2007 developed a new "strategic partnership" with Brazil. The latter constitutes a political dialogue between the EU and Brazil about regional and international political and economic issues. However, this new partnership implies the end neither of the EU–MERCOSUR relations nor of the negotiations of an interregional free-trade agreement (Santander 2007). In fact, the EU is legally bound to conclude an association agreement with the South American regional bloc, since the mandate the Council gave the Commission in June 1999 only empowers the European executive to negotiate an interregional agreement.

The EU considers closer bilateral relations with Brazil as a means to further foster interregional trade negotiations. In other words, it hopes to facilitate the conclusion of an association agreement with MERCOSUR. So, in spite of closer relations with Brazil, the EU is still committed to interregionalism in South America and does not seek to conclude a free-trade agreement with Brazil. In order to underline its commitment to South American regionalism, the EU decided in December 2007 to allocate 50 million euro to the support of the further development of the common institutions (Parliament, Court of Justice and Secretariat) and strategies of MERCOSUR. Furthermore, the EU has proposed to reinvigorate interregional trade negotiations, scheduled for May 2008. So, the EU willfully deems EU–Brazilian relations to be a further incentive fueling the EU–MERCOSUR process and not necessarily a hindrance.

EU–East Asian interregionalism

The Euro–East Asian process formalized within the Asia–Europe Meeting (ASEM) offers a second distinct yet complementary example of region-to-region dialogue initiated by the EU. Both its distinctive features as well as its commonalities with the EU's interregional policies towards other regions, such as the previously described EU–Latin America initiatives, allow us to better distinguish the structural and the region-specific elements within interregional contribution to global governance championed by the EU. As such, the historical process of ASEM's evolution bears witness both to the common trends underlying all interregional dynamics, as well as to the specific challenges facing Europe and its East Asian partners as they seek to cooperate in a growing number of fields. Moreover, since its inception in 1996, ASEM has come to illustrate both some of the key facets of the structural significance of such interregional initiatives, as well as the key challenges they are currently facing.

The Commission first produced an overall Asia strategy paper in 1994 under the title *Towards a New Asia Strategy*.[6] This initiative would eventually give way to the ASEM process proper. The first Asia–Europe Summit was held in March 1996 in Bangkok and brought together for the first time the heads of state and government of ten Asian countries (Brunei, China, Indonesia, Japan, South Korea, Malaysia, the Philippines, Singapore, Thailand and Vietnam) and those of the fifteen member states of the EU, as well as the President of the European Commission. The summit established an ongoing process, based on summit-level meetings every two years, regular ministerial meetings (Foreign, Economic and Finance), and more frequent meetings at the senior official and working level. As such, the region-to-region dialogue between Europe and East Asia has thus been ongoing for over a decade and has produced a multitude of formal, semi-formal and informal initiatives which have come to shape the least prevalent, and therefore often overlooked, third side of the global triangle (US–EU–East Asia) connecting the global economy's major centers of production and consumption.

Founding ambitions: from brittleness to an optimistic founding moment

Contrary to other interregional dynamics, the EU would come to launch and/or deepen at the end of the cold war, the dialogue with the East Asian region could not rest upon existing region-to-region structures. East Asia at the end of the cold war was still a deeply divided Continent with only embryonic region-wide dialogue and but one existing sub-regional institutional arrangement, ASEAN. Moreover, the Continent remained entangled in various remnant conflicts born from, or sustained throughout, the cold war (e.g., the divided Korean Peninsula, various territorial disputes, differing historical perspectives). These simmering potential flash points had mired any previous attempts at regional dialogue in deep mutual mistrust.

Throughout the cold war, the European relationship with East Asia had continued to be largely uncoordinated, since most interregional political dialogue remained reactive, nearly exclusively steered at the national level and quite often simply aimed at maintaining historically established long-term relationships. The near absence of an interregional dimension within the contacts entertained between Europe and East Asia can be ascribed to, among other factors, the inexistence on the European side of strong internal vectors of "Europeanization," such as the activism of the Iberian countries with regards to Latin America. Moreover, historically the Asia–Europe relationship had been engaged on a particular path since the European colonial powers were forcefully evicted from Asia by the 1950s; whereas, for example, Europe had left Africa around the same time more or less on its own terms while retaining the colonial ties through the Cotonou Agreement. Consequently, a mere drive for "policy and cost rationalization" – which drove the EU's interregional approach in its development policy aimed at the Africa, Caribbean and the Pacific (ACP) countries – would prove insufficient to jump-start any meaningful institutional interregional relationship.

This minimalist and passive stance between Europe and East Asia came under increasing stress as the bipolar world order on which it rested came to an abrupt end. As the international system entered a period of flux, both Europe and East Asia felt the need to respond to a heightened call for new vectors of necessary international public goods. An increasingly more pro-active contribution to global governance needs was expected on their part as the free-riding possibilities offered by the tense but stable bipolar context receded. Moreover, parallel to these increased calls for more burden-sharing, certain key actors both in Europe and East Asia felt a growing need to seek new forms of cooperation through which to increase their profile on the international stage. Countries on both sides, such as France and Singapore, which were traditionally concerned with *balancing* the various powers within the international system, notably by hedging their policy options, rapidly came to the conclusion that the weakest link within the "global triangle" needed to be strengthened. Thus, both Paris and Singapore championed the establishment of a new multidimensional dialogue (Gilson 2002) between Europe and East Asia. Initial reservations were to be found on both sides as certain players, such as Japan and the UK, remained uncertain how such an initiative would impact on two key exogenous factors: the USA and existing global multilateral arrangements. However, once sufficient guarantees were provided that such an initiative would neither challenge broader global multilateral arrangements such as the WTO, nor endanger the fundamental security role played by the USA in both regions, all countries involved rallied enthusiastically behind the idea.

Consequently, from a geostrategic point of view, the establishment of ASEM does not entail any major realignment on the part of its members. The belated establishment of an EU–East Asian multidimensional dialogue should more appropriately be seen as the correction of an unsustainable political vacuum which the bipolar straightjacket of the cold war had artificially maintained. Nevertheless, the creation of ASEM did bring with it some major policy innovations as it proved to be the first sustainable and flexible institutional arrangement set up to promote far-reaching cooperation both within East Asia as well as at the interregional level (Gilson 2002). Although the overly optimistic tone of the closing statements at the first ASEM meeting in Bangkok, which called for the creation of a new common European and East Asian vision, has over time proved naive, ASEM 1 was nevertheless a historic event born from unique opportunities offered by the weaking constraints of the cold war. It marked the establishment of the first broad, multi-faceted Euro–Asian dialogue among equals. As such, from an institutional and practical point of view, ASEM would bring together for the first time an impressive group of leaders which until then did not have any specific venue in which to foster cooperation and dialogue in light of the changing dynamics of global governance.

The dust settles: from disappointments to stable and sustainable cooperation

From the onset, ASEM's evolution has mainly been determined by exogenous factors. At first, still surfing on the wave of the Asian economic boom, ASEM could count on the active cooperation of all its members as they sought to engage in a new form of "multidimensional dialogue" aimed at strengthening the weakest link within the dominating international economic triangle (US–EU–East Asia). However in 1998, the second ASEM meeting in London opened under a cloud of general pessimism and disinterest born from Asia's deep financial crisis (Yeo Lay Hwee 2003). Given the limited aid the EU had offered East Asia in the aftermath of the crisis, Asian leaders questioned the relevance of the fundamental proactive *balancing* principles on which ASEM had supposedly been build.

During the following years, and in spite of a growing willingness on the part of several Asian partners to negotiate, European interest remained lukewarm and ASEM's agenda continued to be dominated by contingent externalities; for example, the third ASEM Summit in Seoul was dominated by the host country's "Sunshine Policy" towards its Northern neighbor, and the emerging willingness of certain European actors – most notably France – to see the EU take a clearer stance on issues related to the Korean Peninsula. ASEM 4 in Copenhagen was overshadowed by the aftermath of September 11, 2001. As a result, recent evolutions have been characterized by an increasing prevalence within ASEM of functional and technical cooperation which, once launched, can be driven and steered by bureaucratic coordination; whereas the strategic political dialogue has partially shifted back to the bilateral (interregional) level, most notably following the increased importance of such strategic partnerships as the EU–Japan, EU–China and EU–India relationships.

The political frustrations and often mitigated results born from the interregional dialogue between Europe and East Asia became a growing source of concern and criticism throughout the second half of the 1990s. The at times vocal dissatisfaction within the process was mainly the result of misaligned expectations, the ill-understood extent of the interdependencies connecting both regions, and differing levels and areas of commitment. As Europe and East Asia engaged for the first time in sustained multifaceted political consultation, diverging strategies and realities became more apparent.

The East Asian partners were increasingly frustrated by the cumbersome and fragmented European decision process which, in their eyes, stood in the way of necessary and decisive action at key junctures, such as during the 1997–98 East Asian financial crisis. European players were aggravated by East Asian unwillingness to deepen the ASEM's institutional framework so as to fully harness the beneficial windfall from institutionalized international cooperation, namely increased predictability, reduced long-term costs, and the creation of a more level playing field for all actors involved. These diverging agendas were firmly rooted in deeply held convictions and different historic experiences. On the one hand, the often recently decolonized and economically resurgent East Asian nation states remain passionately attached to their national sovereignty, which they see as the best guarantee for

Table 13.2 The diverging themes broached at the various ASEM Summits over the years

ASEM SUMMIT	European Interests	East Asian Interests
ASEM 1 1996 Bangkok	1. Profit from the East Asian Economic miracle through enhanced market access 2. UN Reform	1. Preventing a 'fortress Europe' through enhanced market access 2. UN Reform & Balancing the US
ASEM 2 1998 London	1. Limiting the fallout from the East Asian Financial Crisis 2. Value Debate on 'Democracy' and 'Human Rights'	1. Managing the fallout from the East Asian financial Crisis
ASEM 3 2000 Seoul	1. Institutional Formats of cooperation 2. Values Debate 3. Regulatory Harmonization 4. Korean Peninsula	1. Korean Peninsula 2. Informal Formats of Cooperation 3. Economic Management
ASEM 4 2002 Copenhagen	1. Anti-terrorism 2. Multilateralism 3. Values Debate 4. Economic Cooperation 5. Institutional Cooperation Formats	1. Economic Management 2. Anti-terrorism 3. Multilateralism
ASEM 5 2004 Hanoi	1. Anti-terrorism 2. Economic Cooperation 3. Values Debate	1. Anti-terrorism 2. Market opportunities born from EU enlargement 3. ASEAN Enlargement and its implications for ASEM (e.g. Myanmar question)
ASEM 6 2006 Helsinki	1. Non-Proliferation 2. Deepening of institutional cooperation 3. Values Debate	1. Economic Cooperation 2. Non-Proliferation
ASEM 7 2007 Beijing	1. Sustainable development and the Future of Climate Policy beyond the end of the Kyoto protocol 2. Addressing the International financial Crisis (notably through the IMF) 3. Building consensus for the European drive to strengthen global economic regulation and its underlying institutional arrangements	1. Sustainable development linked to overall development (i.e. millennium development goals) 2. Worries regarding extreme fluctuations of food and commodities prices 3. Avoid an unfettered spread of the financial crisis into East Asia and guard against protectionist backlash in the West.

stability, security and development; and on the other, deeply integrated European states have endorsed institutionalized pooled sovereignty as the key to sustainable development and effective cooperation.

These fundamental diverging strategic options have obviously hindered the emergence of a new and transformational strategic outlook shared by both East Asia and Europe, as had been called for at the end of the first ASEM Summit. Nonetheless, after the outbursts of enthusiasm witnessed at the first ASEM Summit, and the deep pessimism of the second summit, the mood surrounding the whole ASEM process became more muted but also more nuanced and pragmatic. A certain political pragmatism encouraged all parties to revise their stances. The European partners increasingly considered lighter forms of institutionalization, thus seeking to meet East Asian calls for informal and open cooperative dynamics.

Alongside this new-found willingness to compromise, changing contextual elements – such as the enlargement of both the EU and ASEAN or the emergence of new prevailing transnational challenges (e.g., international terrorism, transnational crime, global warming) and a mounting sense of interdependency, as both regions have increasingly became each other's primary trading and investment partner – have opened up new areas of functional cooperation which have further deepened the ASEM relationship. This incremental, bottom-up-driven deepening and stabilization of ASEM has rested mainly upon two positive developments: a growing mutual understanding born from ongoing exchanges allowing the different actors to more realistically align their political positions, and the increasing involvement of the various bureaucracies – both during the preliminary phases as well as at the policy implementation stage – which greatly strengthened the efficiency of the ASEM process as a whole. The interregional relationship developed between Europe and East Asia within the ASEM process crystallizes the continuity as well as the technical and bureaucratic underpinnings that any relevant international arrangement must possess so as to make a noteworthy contribution to global governance. The EU–East Asian interregional relationship has thus proven itself a mature, sustainable venture, which is deeply rooted within the emerging interdependent world order.

Maturity: ASEM's structural significance within the multilateral world order

As a mature international arrangement, the Euro–East Asian dialogue has become a persistent and routine contribution to the various EU initiatives aimed at building up a multilevel, multilateral system compatible with its own preferences and constraints. As such, ASEM's agenda and formal arrangement clearly reflect the EU's strategy of comprehensive effective multilateralism. ASEM's workings are consistently organized along a comprehensive agenda encompassing three so-called pillars: Political Dialogue, Security and the Economy, and Education and Culture. All of the pillars have seen various new initiatives launched and have thus all three deepened and expanded in scope. Such a broad and evolving agenda ensures that the interregional dynamic at play remains open and reactive to new developments or changes within the broader political strategies. As such, ASEM has proven to be particularly efficient at fostering and channeling political dialogue in a growing number of fields as new challenges have emerged over time. This broad scope is also reflected in ASEM's complex structure, which rests upon bureaucratic coordination and necessary leadership provided by the executive branches of its members.

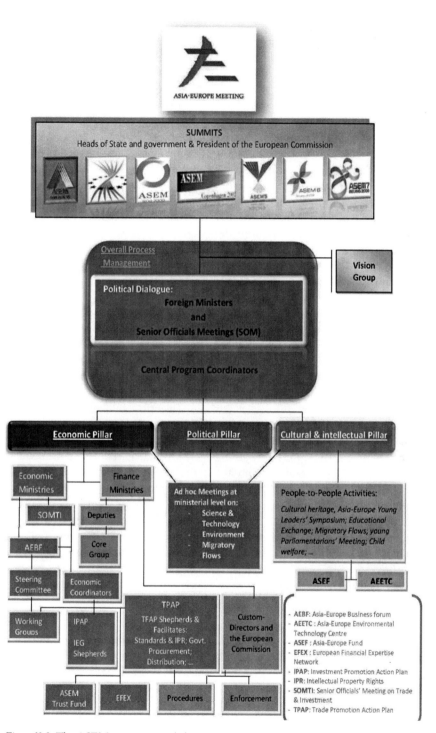

Figure 13.2 The ASEM organizational chart.

In view of the often contextual and even reactive nature of the leadership provided within ASEM, it remains unclear how this specific interregional relationship will be mobilized in the future. Nonetheless, certain structural characteristics can be identified. First and foremost, the "regionalist" discourse has increased markedly over the years, and region-building has become a shared objective. Although the exact contours of such regions remain open for discussion, and the preferred vehicles of regionalization differ substantially between Europe and East Asia, both regions see their interregional involvement as a means to concomitantly strengthen their own regional cooperation. Thus, interregional cooperation is seen to have a positive spill-over effect on the various attempts within Europe and East Asia to set up regional vectors of cooperation. Both the concluding remarks of the 2004 and 2006 summits dwelled upon the need for further regional cooperation, and called for the development, alongside an effective EU, of an East Asian Community. This structural effect or "feedback effect" aimed at buttressing underlying regional dynamics has become one of the main functions of interregional initiatives such as ASEM (Gilson 2002). They thus contribute to the integration of strengthened regional entities within the broader context of the multilateral global governance system.

Beyond this fundamental structural role, mature interregional dynamics such as ASEM are above all a functional exercise. Such interregional efforts are essentially multi-issue-bound international arrangements. To varying degrees, and depending upon a given interregional arrangement's formal arrangement as well as the objectives initially defined by the founding constituents, the possible functions of interregionalism are: strategic dialogue and balancing (Rüland 1996); policy rationalization and agenda-setting (Aggarwal 2001), reflexive regional identity-building (Gilson 2002) or reducing unwanted exogenous pressures. Each of these functions can be advanced within a single sector or a plurality of sectors within the broader scope of foreign policy challenges, according to the arrangement's formal objectives and means. The history of ASEM has shown an initial focus on strategic dialogue and balancing as well as the desire to reduce unwanted exogenous pressures; both of these have incrementally been supplanted by the interregional dialogues contribution towards policy rationalization, agenda-setting and especially reflexive regional identity-building. ASEM performs an intermediary function, as do other interregional dynamics, contributing to the effective and legitimate development of a multi-leveled, multilateral global governance system by fostering increased trust and understanding through political consultation, and more effective policy implementation through bureaucratic coordination and the dissemination of best practices.

Key questions and debates facing ASEM and the Euro–East Asian dialogue

The preferred level of institutionalization

In 2006, in light of the relative stability and routine that the ASEM process had achieved over the course of its first decade of existence, its members thought it appropriate at the sixth ASEM Summit, held in Helsinki, to evaluate the interregional arrangement's

Condensed Summary of the ASEM Process' Key Characteristics

→ *Informal*
It is an open forum for policy makers and officials to discuss any political, economic and social issues of common interest. In this way it aims to *complement* work carried out in bilateral and multilateral for a within the international system, such as the United Nations (UN) and World Trade Organization (WTO).

→ *Multidimensional*
It covers the full spectrum of relations between the two regions, devoting equal weight to the three pillars its mandate comprises: Political Dialogue, Security & Economy and Education & Culture.

→ An equal partnership
Strives to establish a dialogue and cooperation based on respect and mutual benefit.

→ Driven by meetings at a *high level* (heads of state or government, ministers and senior officials)
The biennial ASEM Summits, featuring Heads of State or Government, give the overall political impetus to the ASEM process. Foreign Ministers and their senior officials have an overall coordinating role and are assisted by Coordinators. There are also ministerial and working-level meetings and activities on a wide range of political, economic and cultural subjects.

→ Increasing Weight of Bureaucratic and Expert coordination
Foreign Ministers and their senior officials have an overall coordinating role and are assisted by Coordinators. There are also ministerial and working-level meetings and activities on a wide range of political, economic and cultural subjects.

→ Also focused on People-to-people contacts
ASEM partners have established the Asia-Europe Foundation (ASEF) in 1997 to promote mutual understanding and cooperation of the peoples of Asia and Europe through cultural, intellectual and people-to-people exchange programs.

Figure 13.3 ASEM's key traits summarized.

progress and its future prospects. The Helsinki Declaration on the Future of ASEM[7] was adopted in the hope of avoiding potential future marginalization, either due to an overburdened agenda or through ineffectual or irrelevant policy choices. This prospective document's aims were to:

> identify the key areas where ASEM should focus its work in the second decade. These include strengthening multilateralism and addressing global threats, globalisation and competitiveness, sustainable development and intercultural and interfaith dialogue. The Declaration also proposes, in its Annex on ASEM Working Methods and Institutional Mechanisms, improvements to ASEM's institutional mechanisms, while stressing its informal nature.[8]

As such, this document recognized the need to strengthen ASEM's institutional instruments for dialogue and cooperation, so as to effectively accompany the deepening and widening of the process. The suggested compromise between the identified needs and the reaffirmed principle of "informality" was the creation of an ASEM Virtual Secretariat, aimed at fostering more interaction among partners and expanding stocktaking and information-sharing. For the Europeans, more used to formal and legalistic vectors of cooperation, this was a novel form of institutionalization. As the main venue of the ongoing dialogue and tensions between the differing modes of regional cooperation developing in Europe and East Asia within the broader new regionalist paradigm, the EU–East Asian interregional process has advanced novel modes of institutionalized cooperation and arrangement-building. Such flexible venues of cooperation focus on trend-setting, agenda-fixing and the coordination of policy implementation. Nonetheless, the question remains whether such lax structures suffice to provide for the primary functions of any international institution: long-term cost savings, heightened mutual trust through increased predictability, and a partially equalized playing field through commonly accepted rules.

Uncertainties surrounding the future relationship with the USA

In light of renewed debates on the role and place of the USA within the international system – fuelled both by the recurring unilateralist stance of Washington, and the emergence of powerful new regional actors – one can identify a reawakened interest among certain constituent actors in the *balancing* and *isolating* ambitions originally hinted at as ASEM was founded. Therefore, the overarching and fundamental question of both regions' future relationship with Washington will undeniably have a determining impact on ASEM's future developments. Various recent disagreements and advances within the EU–East Asia broader relationship can be explained in light of Washington's position. The USA emerges at times as the key driver or as a restraining external factor. For example, the overall disagreement on the implications of lifting the "arms ban" imposed on China by the EU following the Tiananmen incidents led to acrimonious disagreement within the interregional relationship, which came to directly involve the USA as a divisive factor. By contrast, the absence of American leadership in the field of climate control has opened up a window of opportunity for the EU and its East Asian partners to play a novel and significant role. As such, ASEM's future developments can once again be identified not so much as a vehicle for strategic (re-)alignment, but as a clear reflection of broader exogenous factors, and most notably the nature of the preferred relationship *vis-à-vis* Washington.

The uncertainties surrounding global systemic factors

The stalling of the Doha round within the WTO created an increasing vacuum within global economic governance and highlighted the existing rigidities within the global system. This has led various actors to engage in alternative dynamics, such as preferential trade agreements, in the hope of providing the necessary international public goods within an ever more interdependent world. This phenomenon has been particularly manifest in East Asia and has brought with it questions relating to the sustainability and equity of such ill-coordinated and often politically motivated strategies. Within this broader context, interregional initiatives – which clearly rest upon the concomitant existence of stable regional dynamics and a secure global multilateral framework – have to face a particular challenge as both their regional foundations as well as their natural multilateral environment are affected. However, as meso-level intermediary arrangements, interregional initiatives are uniquely equipped to favor compatible choices at the various levels of cooperation (bilateral, regional and multilateral). It is in this area that the contribution made by interregional arrangements to norm diffusion and homogenization can come to play a key role. The ongoing efforts within ASEM to clarify such regulatory norms as sanitary and phytosanitary guarantees, intellectual property rights or the principles behind rules of origin have helped to make sure that the various levels within the multilayered international system remain compatible. Moreover, the compelling combination within ASEM of both the increasingly dominant regulatory power – the EU – and the world economy's major centers of production – the resurgent East Asian economies – make this specific interregional arrangement a potent vehicle for disseminating any regulation at a global level.

Pressures due to endogenous tensions at the interregional level

As the relationship between East Asia and Europe has deepened and gained in significance over the last decade, the number and importance of policy tools developed to cultivate it have increased exponentially. When considering the relationship between East Asia and Europe, beyond the strictly bi-regional relationship developed within the context of ASEM, one should also take into account the pre-existing and deeply rooted bilateral relations between the various states. At the EU level, the Europeans have also concluded three major strategic partnerships directly affecting their relationship with East Asia. These political initiatives, steered by the European Council of Ministers in cooperation with the Commission, rest upon jointly agreed action plans and institutionalize what are perceived by Brussels as key bilateral interregional relationships. The first to be concluded was the EU–Japan partnership, followed by similar ones with China and India. These distinct foreign policy tools, although all concerned with strengthening the EU–East Asia interregional relationship, often have diverging hierarchies among their shared aspirations. Since these various policy tools are championed by different actors – with bilateral relationships remaining the privilege of nation-states, the ASEM process is championed by the European Commission whereas the strategic partnerships, as a component of the Union's common foreign and security policy (CFSP), fall under the auspices of the European Council – the risks born from misunderstandings, instances of incoherence and ineffective resource allocation are substantial. Such multilayered and multi-actor-driven cooperation requires streamlined institutions and effective coordination, both *ex ante* and *ex post* of a given political decision. This remains a key challenge within the complex tapestry of interregional contacts currently connecting Europe and East Asia. The risks of reduced actorship are particularly acute in the case of the EU's complex, multileveled external relations. Indeed the increasingly complex decision and implementation mechanisms involved in the EU's interregional initiatives might affect both their efficiency as well as their legitimacy. Possible risks include: reducing its faculty to make autonomous, clear and coherent decisions as different centers of decision vie for control; weakening its capacity to mobilize sustained and adequate means of implementation as policy fragmentation induces increasing strains; and decreasing both external as well as self-recognition of its achievements because of their complexity. As the interregional relationship matures, and bilateral interregional partnerships increase in importance due to the growing weight of the individual countries – Japan, China and India – so the need for the EU to provide clear unequivocal political guidance and strong policy coordination will become ever more important. This calls for a clear, functional division of labor between the different policy vectors – one that is more often than not already clearly enshrined in the legal basis of the various mechanisms of the EU's external action but which is at times misread by its external partners. Furthermore, such functional clarity must be doubled with clear political decisions on the relative opportunity of various policy options; this in turn calls for an increasingly coherent and cohesive decision-making process within the EU.

Pressures due to endogenous stress at the domestic and/or regional level

The accession of Burma/Myanmar to ASEAN brought a key problem to the fore: the existing tension between the principle of non-intervention held dear in East Asia, and the increasing impact that interdependent and institutionally linked states are having on one another. In light of the EU's continued boycott of the Burmese/ Myanmari junta due to their appalling human rights record, their entry into ASEAN, and therefore into ASEM, posed an existential question: How should the two incompatible political stances dividing the different sovereign entities within ASEM be squared? In a spirit of pragmatism, a face-saving and largely symbolic arrangement was found, depriving Burma/Myanmar of any presidencies within ASEM and limiting its role to the *minimum minimorum* possible. Nevertheless, such challenges rooted within the internal political dynamics of the member states will remain an open question as long as the artificial political pretence of a hermetic separation between the internal order and external order of the sovereign state is maintained. Interregional initiatives such as ASEM offer a privileged forum for all involved to seek new acceptable settlements between the necessities of an interdependent international order and the minimal guarantees rightly associated with a given sovereign domestic order. Thus, the emergence of the Burma/Myanmar question within ASEM has fuelled a parallel debate within both partner regions on the acceptable negative impact that domestic factors may have on necessary international public goods providers. This question touches upon one of the more sensitive yet recurring bones of contention within the EU–East Asia dialogue: the value debate. As illustrated in previous chapters, the promotion of democratic values remains a core concern of the EU's external action, yet as stated, this has met with staunch opposition from its East Asian partners more concerned with preserving their national sovereignty. Nonetheless, as the costs of incompatible values and arrangements have increased, thus spawning a variety of practical policy problems, a growing willingness has emerged to go beyond a stifling opposition between Western and Asian values.

Conclusion

In conclusion, interregional arrangements appear as a long-term contribution to global governance, most notably through the development of the EU's external action. This varied *ensemble* of external policy initiatives is the structural outcome of deeper, more systemic developments. Nonetheless, their specific results are directly proportional to the relative international impact of their underlying regional dynamics. Interregional initiatives are international arrangements which can meet certain challenges facing global governance. However, the potential contained within these initiatives is determined by the policies developed by its constituent actors, as well as by overriding exogenous factors. Indeed, contrary to states and certain regional organizations, interregional initiatives are not autonomous actors. These are issue-bound, macro-level arrangements which are aimed at meeting the increasing need, as perceived at the national and regional levels, for international efficiency and legitimacy.

The example in both case studies of fluctuating yet constant impact on the international stage empirically confirms that interregional arrangements are both a clear marker of the multilevel, multilateral international world order envisioned by the EU's strategic outlook, as well as a recurring and useful external policy tool for the regional and national actors involved. As an active proponent of such multilateral global governance logics, the EU has consistently sought to promote such interregional dynamics. Accordingly, interregional initiatives such as ASEM, or the varied dialogues between the EU and Latin America, are seen as stable intermediary levels between a converging global multilateral order and diverging dynamics of regional cooperation. As such, the interregional relationships built up by the EU emerge as multi-issued, functional arrangements aimed in varying degrees at: strategic dialogue and balancing, policy rationalization and agenda-setting, reflexive regional identity-building or reducing unwanted exogenous pressures.

Interregional arrangements are a relevant policy strategy *vis-à-vis* the EU's far abroad. Such interregional arrangements play a part when striving to meet the current challenges within the international system:

1 First, *the collapse of the bipolar order* had major consequences for the balance of power and profoundly altered the outlook and calculations of all relevant international actors. In turn, adjustments took place in their external relations choices. Thus, as older external policy practices and certainties waned, new arrangements such as interregional relationships multiplied, filling particular policy "vacuums." These were then emulated from one region to another, along the lines of a "domino effect."

2 Second, under the pressures of accelerating *globalization*, interregionalism emerged among others as a new means of addressing the reshuffled relationship between foreign policy and foreign economic policy. As international interdependency has increased, these two must increasingly be considered in tandem and interregional arrangements offer a privileged venue for raising and addressing such transversal questions within the broader context set by global multilateral frameworks, and in particular the WTO.

3 Third, *increasing challenges to the Westphalian state's sovereignty* and its principles of non-interference have pushed states to develop new means of collaborative international management respectful of a given state's internal affairs. Interregional arrangements comply with that requirement. They seek to meet

major shared challenges but their agenda remains subsumed to the internal imperatives of constituent members, be they national or regional.

The adoption by a growing number of actors beyond the EU of interregional arrangements as a component of their external action further confirms that these region-bridging institutions are widely seen as a useful element within an actor's external policy toolkit. They offer their constituents identifiable prospects for fostering change and promoting certain preferred solutions, as well as desirable checks on unwanted policy options.

Notes

1 For further detail, see also the article by Sebastián Santander and Philippe De Lombaerde (2007), "EU–Latin America–Caribbean interregionalism and effective multilateralism," [available at http://www.reseau-amerique-latine.fr/ceisal-bruxelles/INT/INT-3-Santander-DeLombaerde.pdf].
2 The Central American Crisis began in the late 1970s when major civil wars erupted in Central America, and especially in Guatemala, El Salvador, Honduras and Nicaragua. These armed conflicts resulted in the region's becoming one of the world's foreign policy hot spots in the 1980s. The USA, which feared the spread of communism in Latin America and the reinforcement of Soviet power in the region, supported counter-revolutionary forces (the Contras).
3 The EPC was institutionalized in 1986 with the signature of the *Single European Act*.
4 For the first time, in 1989, Spain assumed the Presidency of the EC; while Portugal assumed it for the first time in 1992.
5 European Commission (1995), *European Community Support for Regional Economic Integration Efforts Among Developing Countries*, COM (95) 219 final, June 16, Brussels, 2.
6 European Commission (1994), *Towards a New Asia Strategy*, Communication from the commission to the Council, COM (94) 314 final, June 13, Brussels.
7 See ASEM (2006), *Helsinki Declaration on the Future of ASEM*, Helsinki, September 10–11.
8 European Commission Website, see http://ec.europa.eu/external_relations/asem/asem_summits/asem6/index.htm

Bibliography

Aggarwal, V. (2001), *Winning in Asia European Style: Market and Nonmarket Strategies for Success*, London: Palgrave Macmillan.
Bhagwati, J. (1993), "Regionalism and multilateralism, an overview," in J. de Melo and A. Panagariya (eds), *New Dimensions in Regional Integration*, London: Cambridge University Press: 22–46.
Crawley, A. (2006), "Europe–Latin America (EU–LAC) relations: toward interregional coalition building?," in H. Hänggi, R. Roloff and J. Rüland (eds), *Interregionalism and International Relations*, London: Routledge, 167–81.
Gilson, J. (2002), *Asia Meets Europe*, Cheltenham, London: Edward Elgar.
Marchand, M., M. Boas and T. Shaw (1999), "The political economy of new regionalisms," *Third World Quarterly*, 20, 5: 897–910.

Ponjaert, F. (2008), "Cross-regional dynamics: their specific role and contribution to global governance efforts within the international system," in R. Seidelmann and A. Vasilache (eds), *European Union and Asia: A Dialogue on Regionalism and Interregional Cooperation*, Baden-Baden: Nomos, 177–96.

Rüland, J. (1996), "The Asia–Europe Meeting (ASEM): towards a new Euro–Asian relationship," in *Rostocker Informationen zu Politik und Verwaltung*, No. 5, Rostock: Rostock University Press.

Santander, S. (2008), *Le régionalism sud-américaine, l'Union européene et les Etats-Unis*, Brussels: Editions de l'Université de Bruxelles.

Santander, S. (2007), "Le nouveau 'partenariat stratégique' avec le Brésil: point d'inflexion dans la stratégie latino-américaine de l'UE?," *Europa & America Latina*, 2: 57–73.

Söderbaum, F. and L. Van Langenhove (eds), *The EU as a Global Player: The Politics of Interregionalism*, London: Routledge.

Telò, M. (2007), *European Union and New Regionalism*, London: Ashgate.

Yeo Lay Hwee (2003), *Asia and Europe: The Development and Different Dimensions of ASEM*, London: Routledge.

14 Europe in the world

Imperial legacies

Pieter Lagrou

Summary

Europe and its relationship with the wider world do not constitute two distinct objects of study and even less two distinct stages of an incremental development, with a first phase characterised by European integration and a second stage of Europe engaging with the world around it. European integration was born from the rapid transformation of the relationship of European nations with the wider world. In other words, Europe was born from the defeat of empires. To a large extent, European nations transferred their imperial projects to the European project: an evolutionary framework of ever closer integration, bent on institutionalisation and harmonisation. European nation states have never been able to afford a policy of isolation. Unlike the USA, the frontier of their nation-building project has always been an external one. However, the gradual deepening of the cooperation and the geographical enlargement of the Union has left European public opinions disoriented and unwilling to support the costs of a policy of global hegemony. It is therefore unlikely that Europe will simply take the place of a declining American superpower. Rather, the challenges ahead are of the same order as those of the recent past: transforming neighbourhood policies into internal policies and drawing Europe's periphery into the dynamic of integration. Turkey, the successor states of the Soviet Union and North Africa constitute the new horizons of the European project. A multiplication of initiatives of regional cooperation as the basic unit of global cooperation seems more compatible with Europe's historical trajectory than the new hubris of world hegemony.

Introduction

At the start of the twenty-first century, the EU appears as a novel actor on the world stage. The last decade of the twentieth century saw the end of the cold war. This implied the end of the division of Europe between two superpowers, allowed for the unification of the Continent and the first hesitant efforts at a common external policy. It also left standing only one contender for world hegemony: the USA. The course of events during the first decade of the twenty-first century, however, created an increasing perception of failure of the only remaining superpower. Indeed, whereas the power of the USA had appeared unrivalled in the 1990s, ten years later its military might seemed utterly counterproductive when judged by its strategic and political results in Iraq and Afghanistan. The structural deficit in government spending, trade balance and household consumption increasingly eroded the hegemonic position of the dollar on the world financial markets in the same years. The neo-conservative credo of free-trade, unilateralism and the export of democracy at the point of the gun had created a global consensus against it. What many had still seen as the American dream in the early 1990s, especially in formerly communist countries, had turned into an American nightmare. The coincidence of these two central geopolitical transformations in the course of twenty years – the unification of Europe and the decline of the USA – naturally raised expectations for a new role for a new type of European power.

Europe's virginity in world affairs is very relative, of course, and the weight of historical legacies on contemporary perceptions is hefty. Either this legacy is phrased in prudently euphoric terms of renaissance, whereby a Europe estranged from itself and its manifest destiny during the long aftermath of World War Two retakes possession of its historical role and returns to its rightful place under the sun, like a phoenix resurrecting itself from the ashes of war and defeat. Or, echoing a central and at times obsessive historical debate of the last few decades, both within the profession and in society at large, on colonial and post-colonial legacies, it elicits mistrust and hostility with those anticipating a return to a centuries-old history of European imperialism and violence. Yet, pride and guilt are each moral categories of limited conceptual value. It seems therefore more rewarding in this chapter to explore two different lines of historical argument that continue to occupy a central place in contemporary public discourse on Europe's engagement with the wider world: the narratives of decline of empire and the question of European agency in recent history.

Decline of empire

The rise and fall of empires – even if some have preferred the yet more tainted vocabulary of civilisations – is one of the most popular narrative plots in world history and a central obsession for many historians, scholars of 'geopolitics' and international relations, commentators of current affairs, prophets of doom and gloom and politicians in search of grand and alarming arguments. To stick to the former: Montesquieu and Edward Gibbon, Oswald Spengler and Arnold Toynbee, Henry Luce, Paul Kennedy, Immanuel Wallerstein, Niall Ferguson and Charles Maier clearly illustrate that intellectual engagement with the issue spans more than three centuries, incessantly revisited from different angles: military and economic supremacy, cultural and political influence, civilisational cycles and many more.[1]

The rise and fall of the great empires

The rise and decline of the Roman or British empires, for instance, elicit different interpretations, but by and large their geography and chronology are rather straightforward. 'European expansion' is an object with far more problematic contours, involving a history of 'discoveries', maritime expansion, European emigration and

United Kingdom
France
Spain
Portugal
Netherlands
German Empire
Ottoman Empire
Belgium
Russian Empire
Japan
Italy

Figure 14.1 Colonial empires in 1914.

settlement, slave trade, religious conversion, political oppression, colonial violence, racism, decolonisation, to name only a few. To take the question of chronological delimitation, one could quite cogently argue that 1492 and 1960 constitute its most obvious outer limits. The year 1492 was that of Christopher Columbus's first voyage to an island not far from the mainland of the American continent, and also the one in which the Spanish *Reconquista* was completed, thus accomplishing simultaneously two major transformations of the Spanish kingdom: eliminating religious diversity in Spain itself, by the killing, expulsion and conversion of Muslims and Jews, while vastly expanding the reach of the kingdom's political and economic power over indigenous populations in other parts of the world and thus radically diversifying the king's subjects. By 1960, it was clear that the era of European colonial empires was over, with only marginal remnants left standing (the Portuguese colonies and some limited Pacific, Caribbean and South American 'overseas territories' in French, British or Dutch possession).

Yet 1492 hardly signalled the end of Muslim presence in Europe, since Spain's policy affected only the southwestern tip of the Continent. At most, it shifted the Ottoman crescent counter-clockwise around the Mediterranean and deep into the Balkans and Central Europe – a progression halted in 1683 only forty kilometres from the gates of Vienna. The Ottoman presence in Europe lasted until 1912, precisely when European imperial expansion reached its zenith, and just before the start of its descent into the inferno of World War One. At the same time, if 1492 signalled the start of European conquest of the Americas, then 1776, the declaration of independence of the USA, or 1825, the end of Spanish and Portuguese colonial rule on the continent, are more appropriate closing dates than 1960. When the European colonial expansion in the Americas was over (with the exception of Canada, Cuba and Puerto Rico), colonial expansion in Africa largely still had to begin, with the carve-up of that continent only being completed at the Berlin Conference in 1885.

More fundamentally, however, the notion of 'European expansion' is largely anachronistic, with the central dynamic of the process being the rivalry and confrontation of European empires against each other, rather than a confrontation of Europe with the rest of the world. In the rivalry that opposed the Spanish to the Dutch, and next the French to the British, control of overseas territories was a means of overpowering their European rivals. Depending on the angle of the analysis, the rising and declining curves and cycles of power will differ. Taking economic hegemony as the central criterion, for instance, Immanuel Wallerstein identifies three instances and three hegemons: the United Provinces of the Netherlands from 1625 to 1672, Great Britain from 1815 to 1873 and the USA from 1945 to 1967 – a chronology that does not necessarily coincide with those of military might, political power or cultural influence (Wallerstein 1974–89). Rather than looking at the actors and epochs of hegemony, we will therefore focus on structures and institutions of hegemony.

The nationalist master tale

A quite different, but implicitly probably even more influential narrative plot, offering a global and teleological interpretation of contemporary history, is that of the decline of empire and the inexorable rise of the nation-state. It is a tale of emancipation from foreign oppression, of the fulfilment of omnipresent immanent dreams of nationhood, self-determination and democracy, of being admitted into the egalitarian school of independent nations. The privilege of independence, self-determination and democracy spread out in concentric circles from the two moments of revelation of the collective destiny of humanity: 1776 in Philadelphia and 1789 in Paris. As we already mentioned, for the Americas, the process was completed by 1825. For most of the rest of the world, it is still in full swing, in Europe no less than in Asia and Africa, as the vast majority of early twenty-first-century conflicts seem to suggest. The year 1918 saw the end of three Continental empires – the Habsburg Empire, the Tsarist Empire and the Ottoman Empire – and allowed dozens of nations to free themselves from the imperial yoke, from the Baltic to the Gulf of Yemen. The same year also anticipated colonial retreat, as former German colonies in Africa were attributed to European tutors under a League of Nations mandate, to accompany these nations to political adulthood, i.e., eventual independence. The dissolution of the European colonial empires dramatically accelerated between 1945 and 1962, thereby vindicating the global validity of the evolutionary process towards the universality of the nation-state.

Still, quite surprisingly in view of the human tragedies that scarred the twentieth century, the happy master tale of nationalism survived almost unscathed, nearly until its end. The epic history of freedom-fighters and oppressed nations finally acquiring independence from imperial villains continued, in Athens and Brussels in 1830, in Riga and Warsaw in 1918, in Islamabad and Tel Aviv in 1948, in Kinshasa and Nairobi in 1960, in Hanoi in 1975, in Riga again in 1991, in Pristina in 2008, all providing unlimited fuel for the nationalist hopes of Tamil Tigers, Basque militants, Ingush guerrillas, Flemish separatists and an in-principle open list of future hopefuls. After all, twentieth-century history had shown that it was easier to change the demography of a country than the mindset of its nationalists – Greeks and Turks got a green light from the international community in Lausanne in 1923 for their mutual if brutal solution of the minority 'problem', Adolf Hitler succeeded in solving the 'problem' of Jewish minorities through conquest and genocide and that of German minorities through defeat and expulsion.

It is only by the late 1990s that a more critical understanding of this master tale became audible in academic circles. In the bloody dissolution of Yugoslavia and the Rwandan genocide, the murderous brutality of nationalism resurfaced. As Michael Mann observed, in both cases, the discourse of ethnic cleansing developed in a context of democratisation, i.e., in a transition to a multi-party system under international pressure (Mann 2005). Slobodan Milosevic and Juvenal Habyarimana were both heirs to a one-party system, who decided to cling to power by substituting the modernising ideology of shared progress of the former regime with a discourse of ethnic hatred. Not only did nationalism appear uglier, but empire on the rebound appeared a lesser evil to some. Sarajevo definitely seemed a more civilised place to live in under Ottoman and Habsburg rule than under Serb artillery. Lvov, Thessalonica, Vilnius, Jerusalem or Baghdad all seemed happier places in their imperial epochs than under nationalist rule. As Charles Maier put it bluntly: nations are good at

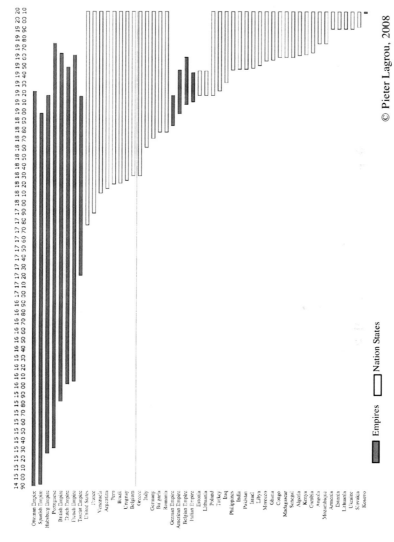

Figure 14.2 Empires and nation-states.

© Pieter Lagrou, 2008

equality; empires are good at tolerance (Maier 2006). Such an affirmation finds a more fertile soil in the at times nostalgic debates on the merits and shortcomings of the Austro–Hungarian or Ottoman Empires and their succession states[2] than in a discussion of French rule in Algeria, British rule in Kenya or American rule in the Philippines, of course. But it might still be rewarding to reflect on the commonly accepted opposition between empire and nation-state in order to understand the historically intricate links between Europe and the surrounding world.

Sovereignty, equality and symmetry

Very schematically, the difference between empire and nation-state originates in the concept of sovereignty. In a nation-state, the people are sovereign, which implies a perfectly symmetrical relationship between any given individual citizen and the state, and thus equality within a homogenous constituency. In an empire, the issue of sovereignty is more complex, since sovereignty rests either with the head of state or with the geographical centre of the empire, who exercise the sovereignty over their subjects and/or colonies. Not only is the status of the centre and its inhabitants different from the status of inhabitants of the periphery, but the relationship between the centre and any part of the empire, and within each part, the legal status of different constituent groups of the population, is asymmetrical.

For instance, the Algerian departments, the Moroccan protectorate and Western French Africa had a very different formal status in the French colonial empire and different metropolitan ministries – the Ministry of the Interior, Foreign Affairs and the Colonies – administered them, respectively. European residents of the Algerian departments, many of them Italian and Spanish immigrants rather than French settlers, resided under the same jurisdictions as French citizens right from the time of conquest in 1830 and they obtained full citizenship in 1889. Jewish residents obtained full citizenship with the *décret Crémieux* in 1870, while the Muslim population continued to be ruled under the *code de l'indigénat* until 1962, even though the latter had been formally revoked in 1946. Residents of Saint-Louis du Sénégal and Gorée enjoyed full citizenship from 1833 – a right that residents of neighbouring municipalities never acquired as long as French rule lasted. Similarly, in the Austro–Hungarian empire, under the compromise of 1867, the legal status of the German and Magyar elites were formally equal, but within the constituent regions, cultural and political rights differed. In Galicia, Polish, Ukrainian, Yiddish and German speakers did not enjoy the same level of legal protection and political participation, nor did Catholics, Orthodox Jews and Protestants. Neither were the status of the Czech lands in the Cisleithan part of the empire and the Croat lands in the Hungarian part symmetrical. Cohabitation of Germans and Czechs in the Sudeten and of Croats and Italians in Dalmatia could only complicate the picture further.

Clearly, the way the issue of sovereignty translates into administrative structures creates radically different social realities. In Ottoman Thessalonica and in colonial Oran, litigation between a spouse and her husband, or between heirs, was settled before different courts, applying different legal traditions, depending on whether the plaintiffs were Jews or Muslims, for instance. But what in one case sometimes figures as a model of tolerance and as a precursor of a multicultural society, appears as a paramount expression of racist contempt and republican double-standards in the other. Quite rightly so, it seems. First of all, racism was an essential element of the colonial ideology. Discrimination in the Ottoman empire between Muslims and those belonging to minority *millets* was very real, but confessional differentiation was much more permeable and open to social promotion than the fixed categories of racial belonging instigated by colonial powers. Second, of course there were double-standards at work where a modern nation-state ruled over peripheral populations to whom it denied citizenship, a manifest inconsistency of its political rationale inapplicable to the pre-modern political systems of the Ottoman or Tsarist empires. Which comes to a vindication, after all, of the nationalist master tale? One last observation therefore, in defence of empire, and to guard ourselves from anachronism and anathema.

Evolutionary utopias

The European discourse of empire in the nineteenth and twentieth centuries was always cast in an evolutionary perspective. Evolutionary thinking is of course only a different formulation of the concept of racial and civilisational superiority. It was the *white man's burden* to elevate the uncivilised populations under their custody to higher cultural, social and political standards. This was an explicitly infantilising discourse of European grown-ups and non-European toddlers. The evolutionary ideology was also consistently evasive on timing and never committed itself to a concrete agenda for its educational project. Adulthood was a remote and hypothetical perspective in an empire entirely committed to expansion and consolidation. It seems a bitter irony that the French Third Republic (1870–1940) vastly expanded and intensified the colonial projects of Napoleon III's Second Empire (1852–70). The ideology of the *République coloniale* thus appears as a manifest *contradictio in terminis* (Bancel 2003). The contradiction is more apparent than real, however.

The central aim of the Third Republic was to consolidate the *acquis révolutionnaire* (revolutionary principles), at home and abroad. From the start, the revolutionary project had been at the same time both national and universal. The conquering republican spirit fixed itself accordingly both internal and external frontiers. The internal frontier was to turn, in Eugen Weber's expression, peasants into Frenchmen.[3] Three central institutions of the Third Republic were instrumental in the pursuit of this goal: military conscription, obligatory and free primary education and universal male suffrage. The three were inseparable. Military service implied a form of political participation. The nation in arms paid a 'blood tax' to the state and could thus hold the state accountable for its acts. Conscription implied a new form of legitimacy, replacing the previous legitimation of voting rights for taxpayers only that had applied in most European countries until World War One. Since the primary task of a parliament was to vote the budget, it seemed only fair that only those who paid taxes had a voice in the debate on how tax money was spent. If taxation as a criterion limited participation in politics to the bourgeoisie, the 'blood tax' limited it to all adult males. However, voting rights were also dependent on basic educational attainments: in order to participate in the suffrage, voters had to be able to read and write and to understand the *lingua franca* of the state, whence the indispensable connection between universal suffrage and universal primary education. The existence of a constituency of equal, informed and consenting citizens was not the prerequisite for the existence of a modern nation-state, but the central goal pursued by these states. In Eric Hobsbawm's words, the state creates the nation and not vice-versa (Hobsbawm 1990).

The developmental scheme of the nation-state was explicitly based on a centre–periphery scheme. The Third Republic's consolidation worked in concentric circles from the educated classes to the peasants and workers and from Paris to the provinces. Lifting Provencals, Alsatians, Bretons and Corsicans out of rural backwardness, clericalism, illiteracy and vernacular languages constituted the internal frontier of the republican project.

The empire was no more than a logical extension of this project to its outer frontiers. Active service at the front during World War One thus naturally entailed claims for political emancipation from Senegalese marksmen and Moroccan troops. And, quite logically, political participation was subordinated to the progress – or absence of progress – in the development of the colonial education system. Such a system would show itself no less capable of transforming colonial subjects into citizens of the empire than was its metropolitan equivalent at the centre of the empire. Similarly, in Victorian England, the heart of darkness was not just located in the African colonies. Proletarians and aboriginals were the object of parallel civilisational projects, lifting them out of abject poverty, misery, ignorance and sin. Theorists of social and racial degeneration, hygienist and eugenist modernisers, missionaries and social utopians waged their noble battles on internal, no less than external frontiers. Welsh and Scots, Irish, Indians, Boers and Zulu were all located on a continuum of the graduated scale of the civilisational process and could hope to be admitted to modernity according to differentiated timetables.

This, of course, is not to plead the sincerity of the colonial ideology, but merely to show the coherence of the modernising political agenda of European nation-states in the nineteenth century and throughout more than half of the twentieth century, in the centres of empire as well as in their outer reaches. The manifest contradiction between political democracy in the centre and authoritarian and discriminating rule in the periphery would find its eventual solution in a gradual emancipation in a distant future. This is not to say that the evolutionary discourse was generally shared. Many colonial administrators, European settlers and imperial theorisers were convinced of the immutable racial inferiority of colonial subjects. Many, incidentally, did not think any higher of democracy in the centre than of its prospects in the far outposts. But the innate connection between the ideology, the aims and instruments of nation-building and empire-building are indispensable to an understanding of how the imperial order proved to be such a durable mental and political construction in Europe's engagement with the wider world.

European agency

By 1945, the same rivalry between European powers that had motivated the imperial hegemony of Europe over much of the other continents had destroyed the Continent.

Europe had destroyed itself, and was saved from itself by the Soviet Union (USSR) and by the USA. Both powers henceforth had the destiny of the Continent in their hands, in a role inversely proportional to their wartime contribution. The USSR, which had done the lion's share of the fighting against Nazi Germany, merely recovered the sphere of influence along its western border which it had lost at Brest-Litovsk in March 1918. The USA found itself in charge of the reconstruction of Japan and most of Germany and extended its influence and military presence to all but the eastern rim of the European continent. How did European political leaders envisage the future? What was their capacity to project their country into alternative and ambitious plans on a global scale?

One of the most improbable, even if most widespread, narratives of Europe's painful awakening in 1945 is one of catharsis and conversion. In the midst of rubble and ashes, Europeans finally understood the ruinous nature of nationalism and imperialism and wholeheartedly embraced the idea of European brotherhood. It has been convincingly demonstrated for many years that national – and nationalist – reconstruction was the absolute priority in postwar Europe, both in economic policies and identity policies (Milward 1992). But what about empire? As the painful, humiliating and bloody history of Europe's colonial retreat between 1945 and 1975 (the victory of the Frelimo guerrillas in Mozambique over Portugal) shows, foresight was certainly not on the European side.

From the Union Française to the Union Européenne

Take Charles de Gaulle, one of the most visionary politicians of the twentieth century. In his appeal of 18 June 1940 he rejected Marshal Pétain's defeatism essentially by contrasting the latter's narrow, France-centred view to his own vast imperial perspective. 'Because France is not alone! She is not alone! She has a vast empire behind her [...] This war is not limited to the unfortunate territory of our country. This war is not decided by the battle of France. This war is a world war.' This was a visionary statement indeed, and one that saved France from the humiliation of being seated at the side of the vanquished at the table of postwar settlements in 1945. By that time, however, it seemed to have exceeded its use-by date. In 1940, Brazzaville became the capital of the Free French Empire, profoundly shaking up its mental geography. In February 1944, de Gaulle organised a conference in the same town on the future of French Africa, with representatives of all French territories, all of whom happened to be white. The general proclaimed his ambition to engage the empire on 'the road to new times' but categorically rejected the perspective of autonomy for the French possessions. On 8 May 1945, the official end of the war in Europe, the Algerian independence struggle started, with the explosion of the Setif insurrection. By February 1946, de Gaulle had withdrawn from politics, after failing to impose a constitutional project for a presidential republic. In 1958, he would return as a saviour of the nation and, in the eyes of many, as the saviour of French Algeria. In fact, he would be obliged to use the new powers conferred to the president under the constitution of the Fifth Republic to impose the final retreat from the Algerian quagmire.

The constitution of the Fourth Republic, adopted on 27 October 1946, is a crucial turning point in French history. After the collapse of the Third Republic, the longest lasting French constitutional regime since the Revolution, the adoption of a new constitution was supposed to respond to the new era opened up by the defeat of fascism. Its preamble read: 'On the dawn of the victory of the free nations over the regimes that have tried to enslave and degrade the human person, the French people proclaim once more that every human being, without distinction of race, religion or belief, owns inalienable and sacred rights.'[4] The new constitution was far more progressive than its predecessor, affirming the social rights of the welfare state and full employment and stipulating the obligation for the state to nationalise private enterprise fulfilling a public service or exercising a monopoly. The constitution formally forbade the undertaking of 'any war of conquest' and assured 'never to use its forces against the freedom of any people'.

The constitution replaced the empire by a *Union Française* (French Union), presented in the preamble under an almost canonical formulation of the evolutionist theory of imperial rule:

> France forms with the overseas people a Union founded on the equality of rights and duties, without distinction of race or religion. The French Union is composed of nations and of people who mutualise or coordinate their resources and their efforts to develop their respective civilisations, to increase their well-being and assure their security. Faithful to its traditional mission, France intends to lead the people which it has taken in charge to the freedom to administer themselves and to manage democratically their own affairs; discarding any system of colonisation based on arbitrariness, she guarantees to all equal access to public office and the individual or collective exercise of the rights and liberties proclaimed or confirmed hereunder.[5]

The constitution of 1946 was not born from a rear-guard conservative reflex. It was an ambitious projection into a new future. And the future constellation into which France projected itself was most explicitly the empire, even if it was called henceforth 'French Union'. The project of this Union was defeated on the plains of Dien Bien Phu, in the hills of Madagascar and the streets of Algiers. This in spite of the mobilisation of millions of French conscripts, uninterruptedly engaged in counter-insurgency warfare for almost twenty years, costing tens of thousands of French lives, hundreds of thousands of colonial civilians' and combatants' lives and deeply disrupting colonial and post-colonial societies. In 1958, de Gaulle could once more claim foresight in his rejection of the 1946 constitution, which has led to a succession of weak governments and endemic political instability. Yet in the constitution of the Fifth Republic, the French Union was succeeded by a project for a new *Communauté Française* (French Community), a particularly short-lived proposition, utterly inadequate for the profound and rapid transformation which France faced in its relationship with its colonies, rejected as it was by Guinea the very same year, Mali and Madagascar the next year, followed in 1960 and 1961 by all other former French African territories.

The Vietnamese, the Madagascans and the Algerian nationalists rejected the French Union, and were willing to die for this conviction in vast numbers, not because they had a fundamentally different political agenda, but because they did not buy the evasive imperial timetable or the concrete terms of the imperial project of modernisation and homogenisation. Building up a central administration, developing the economy, a national education system, conscription, universal suffrage, imposing a *lingua franca*: the political agenda was largely the same, but it would be carried out by different elites and instantly. Contrary to their imperial creed, reaffirmed solemnly in the French constitution of 1946, colonial powers did not know better than their colonised populations what was good for them. Agency, in the 1945–75 period, was definitely on the side of the colonised. European powers underwent the course of history: in Delhi in 1947, when India gained independence from Great Britain; in Suez in 1956, when France and the UK were forced to a humiliating retreat facing the Egyptian leader Nasser in their conflict over the rights to the canal linking the Mediterranean to the Indian Ocean; and in Kinshasa in 1960, when Congo obtained its independence from Belgium. More strikingly still, however, European nations did not know what was good for themselves, either.

The Dutch paradox

One looks in vain for solemn affirmations of unshakable confidence in the European future of any European nation in the immediate postwar years. None can be found in the previously quoted French constitution of 1946. It will come as no surprise that 'Europe' as a political project did not figure prominently in the Speeches from the Throne of George VI and Elizabeth II in the 1940s and 1950s. King Baudouin of Belgium, who rose to the throne in catastrophic circumstances in 1951, would devote the first decade of his reign in the first instance to the Congo colony and appeared only modestly interested in European projects like the European Coal and Steel Community (ECSC), founded the same year. More ironically still, when Queen Juliana of the Netherlands rose to the throne in 1948, her grand visions for her future reign overwhelmingly concerned the Indonesian empire – which vanished only one year later – rather than *rapprochement* with the kingdom's European neighbours. The Netherlands lost its empire in 1949, after an intense but comparatively short conflict when compared with the protracted decomposition of the other colonial empires. As such, the Netherlands figures as a European precursor, and the impact on the Dutch imperial centre was closely observed all over Europe. In the 1950s, in debates in France in particular, the Dutch turnaround came to be known as the Dutch Paradox.

Since the seventeenth century, the Netherlands had considered itself to be only tangentially a European nation. Through the hazards of geography, it shared a border with Germany and Belgium, but the nation had consistently turned its back to the Continent and its political turmoil, while busily overseeing its own maritime empire. The Netherlands itself had no known natural resources (before the discovery of natural gas in the 1950s) and its industrialisation was slow compared to that of its Eastern and Southern neighbours. Its wealth was based on trade, which was inseparable from empire. The nation was a harbour for the Continent, but also a haven of tolerance and stability, unaffected by religious strife, political polarisation and revolutionary upheaval. Apart from the short Napoleonic interlude, its history was one of peace, stability and non-involvement in European conflicts. Whence the astounding outrage of Queen Wilhelmina in May 1940, denouncing the German aggression as 'unprecedented in history'. Fundamentally, for Wilhelmina, the violation of the territory and sovereignty of other European nations in the course of recent history – notably World War One, during which the Dutch kingdom had thrived under a neutral status – was incommensurable with that of the Netherlands, because of the latter's insular, exceptional and exemplary status as a nation which never meddled in European affairs since the focus of its geopolitical interests was located 11,000 kilometres away, in the southern hemisphere.

The loss of the colony, subsequent to a second outrage – the Japanese occupation of Indonesia – was thus a disaster of unimaginable magnitude. '"Indië" verloren, Rampspoed geboren' (Indonesia is lost, a catastrophe is born) summarised the moods of the times. By the mid-1950s, however, it was increasingly clear that the loss of the colony had been an unmitigated windfall, creating the conditions for the Dutch economic miracle. The Dutch economy geared itself towards the reconstruction of Germany, the engine of European economic growth, and diversified into future-oriented sectors like chemicals and consumer electronics. Its multinationals, like Philips and Heineken, and the two Anglo-Dutch giants, Royal Dutch Shell and Unilever, revealed themselves as pioneers of neo-colonialism thriving in a post-imperial world.

European business and colonial nostalgia

By the mid-1950s, this Dutch miracle inspired alternative thinking in French business circles, splitting economic elites between a colonial rear-guard and pro-European neophytes (Marseille 1984). The Fourth Republic had become bogged down in a myriad of costly colonial wars ever since its creation. The empire proved to be an unwieldy and costly structure, requiring a huge colonial administration, investments in infrastructure, financial transfers and incontrollable expenses for policing and counter-insurgency. It ever less appeared as a future-oriented project. The booming European economy and, particularly, the explosive growth of intra-European trade offered far more challenging perspectives for French business and industry, at a far lesser expense. Similarly, the British Tory Party was increasingly divided on international politics between the colonial lobby, unshakable in its imperial creed, and a younger generation of pro-European, pro-business politicians, comparing with envy and desolation British stagnation to the Continental economic miracle.

The rift between pro-European and pro-colonial *milieux* divided not only business elites and the political right wing; the left was not homogenously anti-imperialist and even less homogeneously pro-European. For some in the British Labour Party in particular, the Empire and the Commonwealth, taken in their evolutionary and emancipatory dynamic, were a much more enticing and challenging project for an alternative political order – resolutely internationalist, cosmopolitan, multiracial and culturally diverse – than the conservative, clerical, staunchly anti-communist and conformist European Community (EC) emerging in Rome in 1957 (Darwin 1991). The official picture of the signing of the Treaty, with dozens of middle-aged greying men in boring grey suits summarised their aversion remarkably well. The EC was the very symbol of the failure of postwar hopes for participatory democracy, social emancipation and international solidarity. As described above, empire was also a utopian project invested with hopes and longings for a bright future of international solidarity and emancipation. This investment also transpired in the support of the French left wing for the empire, with the partial exception only of the Communist Party, stauncher in denouncing torture and military violence of their government than in reneging the utopian thought behind the *République Coloniale* (Colonial Republic), which was part and parcel of its very own ideological traditions.

The Suez debacle in 1956 showed that the option of a European defensive colonial cartel was a hopeless strategy. Imperial nostalgics could not really count on the solidarity of weakened colonial powers. By 1956, it was clear to most that hard choices had to be made between Europe and empire, two henceforth incompatible strategic, political and economic options. It is therefore no hazard of history that the Treaty of Rome was signed just one year later, between two losers of colonial wars, France and the Netherlands, and two losers of World War Two, Germany and Italy – in all, four powers bereft of alternative geopolitical strategies due to their historic defeats. Only Great Britain indulged in imperial nostalgia and refrained from drawing drastic conclusions from its military and economic decline. The fact that Britain never wholly abandoned the empire, the Commonwealth and the sterling zone explains its belated entry into the EEC in 1973 and its aloofness towards the common currency and later the euro.

Other losers

It is a retrospective illusion and a consequence of rigid periodisation to situate the rude awakening of the Netherlands and France and that of Italy and Germany as developments worlds apart on the timeline of history. After all, only six years separate the Italian capitulation in 1943 from the Dutch retreat from Indonesia in 1949 and hardly fifteen years separate the total defeat of the German *Reich* from that of the French empire. Unlike Franco in Spain, Mussolini did not content himself with consolidating fascist power at home. By the time he had achieved just that, in the early 1930s, he fixed new ambitious frontiers for Italy: first, in 1935, belatedly acquiring its own colonial empire and next, from 1938, entering into a European fascist alliance, convinced that the fascist experiment could not survive in autarchy and reclusion. Adolf Hitler was similarly obsessed with Germany's *Sitz im Welt* (place in the world). In *Mein Kampf* (My Struggle), he radically criticised the Wilhelminian second *Reich* for having launched Germany into colonial adventures on faraway African shores, while betraying fellow German *Blutbrüder* (bloodbrothers) in Europe as fragile minorities outside the German borders. The imperial project of the third *Reich* was the creation of a continental empire in Europe, based on political and military hegemony, economic integration into a *Grossraum Europa*, colonisation and settlement on the Eastern frontiers – Germany's Wild East. Clearly, no major European nation could afford splendid isolation, for a mere matter of size and scale, of economic and political rivalry and longing for *Lebensraum* (living space).

Italian fascism and German Nazism in their immoderate expansionism were tragic accidents of history, but the project of inserting their nations into a wider geopolitical framework was much more ancient and it ran to some extent parallel to the centuries-old imperial projects of the historic colonial powers. With only between half a decade and a decade and a half of delay, each one was left without an alternative strategy. They were thus bound to join hands in desperation, as they increasingly did in the course of the 1950s, even though this meant granting unmerited pre-eminence to France and making Germany pay for part of France's post-colonial woes, as it would accept to do under the precursors of the Lomé Agreements with the former colonies. Portugal in 1975 would be the last case in kind. Salazarism and Portuguese imperialism were symbiotically linked. Defeat in the colonial wars in Angola and Mozambique entailed a regime crisis, a democratic revolution and the end of European isolation. Once more only could imperial defeat catapult a former colonial power into Europe, opening the way for the 1986 enlargement.

In short, in the 1940s and 1950s, for their crucial contribution to the process of European integration, more credit should be given to the leader of the Indonesian nationalists, Sukarno, than to Queen Juliana or her Prime Ministers, Willem Drees and Louis Beel; more to the Vietnamese guerrilla leader Ho Chi Minh than to the French Prime Ministers, René Pleven, Guy Mollet or Georges Bidault; in the 1970s, more to the Mozambique liberation movement Frelimo than to the anti-Salazar opposition in Portugal itself. In 1946, the French saw their future in the framework of the French Union; they ended up with European Union in 1992. Similarly, since the nineteenth century the UK had projected itself into the Commonwealth for its economic development, military security and the survival of the cultural values of a long imperial tradition, but ended up in 1973 relying on the Common Market to a far greater extent. More importantly still, what occurred in the course of the 1950s and 1960s was a genuine transfer from empire to Europe. Europe became what empire had always been: an evolutionary project (as the Treaty of Rome formulated: 'Determined to lay the foundations of an ever closer union among the peoples of Europe; Resolved to ensure the economic and social progress'), a heavily institutionalised process, inscribed in a long-term projection of homogenisation, convergence and, ultimately, an extension of state-building at a superior geographical level. The increasingly disappointed and disavowed hopes of France's 1946 constitution and of so many other failed projects for a new postwar international and imperial order were manifestly reinvested into a new project, or, at least, a spare solution. Europe and its relation to the wider world are one single issue, since Europe is born from its relationship with the wider world – failed relationships, essentially.

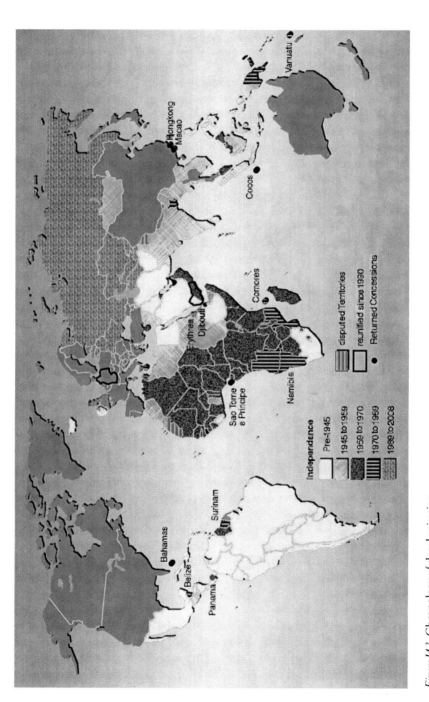

Figure 14.3 Chronology of decolonisation.

The Americanisation of Europe?

The Copernican revolution of postwar geopolitics proposed here above – that the history of the centre was written in the periphery – might come as a surprise. In any more traditional presentation, agency is indeed what Europe lost, after 1945, but it is also what the USA inherited. As we have tried to show, there is at least one inappropriate opposition generated by standard histories of international relations: that of cynical European imperialism versus American naive utopianism. There was much utopia behind the European imperial projects, and the twentieth century has abundantly shown how ruthless, violent and ultimately counterproductive utopias can be. There is another more appropriate contrast suggested by the development above. Small European nations, which in some sorts they all are, could not afford to be without an international strategy and they have accordingly constantly been obsessed with inserting their nation into larger geographical and sophisticated political architectures. Projection beyond the national frontiers has been a major endeavour in contemporary history and an object of considerable physical, political and identity investment. The USA is a nation on the scale of a continent. For most of its history, the frontier of the American national project has been an internal one. For European nations, isolationism has never been a luxury they could afford; for the USA, it has always been an option – in 1776, in 1918, in 1945 and again, maybe, at the start of the twenty-first century.

At least twice in its history, the USA has been in a position to mould a new international order. Woodrow Wilson's world vision in Versailles in 1918 translated into the League of Nations, and Franklin Delano Roosevelt's vision translated into the United Nations Organisation, created only weeks after his death in San Francisco in 1945. Both institutions offered a light and non-constringent structure (compared to empire, for instance, or to the EU), based on an illusion of multilateralism and egalitarianism among independent nations. Both also suffered from the non-committal nature of the American engagement, assorted with an undisguised hegemonic ambition. American hegemony never amounted to empire. The USA was not ready to institutionalise its relationship with its periphery in binding legal or constitutional arrangements, or to invest in the administrative and infrastructural attributes of empire. The American sphere of influence was just that, not an extension of the American state-building project, as had been the case of colonial empires first and of European integration next. Possibly, 1989 offered a third occasion for the USA to mould a new international order. The least one can say is that Republican and Democratic Presidents alike endeavoured coherently to avoid giving a new lease of life and a new role to the UN in the construction of such an order.

In any case, coming back to 1945, it follows from the above that the process of European integration went way beyond what the American hegemon had in mind with the conditional clauses of Marshall Aid. The ECSC was not simply an intergovernmental negotiation on tariffs and quota under multilateral trade agreements, nor even a free-trade zone, but rather a supranational extension of national policies of far-going state intervention in the economy and central planning in the allocation of primary resources and raw materials. Pretending that, from the start,

European integration has been first and foremost an American policy is therefore utterly unconvincing. Economists argue that the economic impact of Marshall Plan aid was marginal compared to the real engine of growth, the explosion of internal European trade. In so far as this is true, the Marshall Plan was partly a failure from the American perspective, since it was mainly designed to perpetuate and strengthen transatlantic trade, and, particularly, to finance American exports to Europe. In total numbers, these exports grew, but in relative numbers, they were very rapidly dwarfed by a trade dynamic beyond American control (Milward 1992). Agency in the origins of European economic integration was on the European side, not the American side.

The first two postwar decades were witness not to the Americanisation of Europe, but to the development of an alternative European model. Inspired as it was by the failure of the European order of the interwar period, it consisted of three central elements. First of all, it included a European New Deal, through an explosion of state intervention in the economy, central planning for full employment, social negotiation and the elaboration of an unparalleled welfare state. Second, it featured a domestication of parliamentary democracy. The uncontrolled and uncontrollable enfranchised masses of the 1920s and 1930s were integrated into new political parties through trade union affiliation, conservative or reformist ideological mobilisation and partisan distribution of the benefits of the welfare state. The political extremes were ostracised – the extreme right through de-Nazification or the purge of wartime collaboration, the extreme left through the cold war. Fundamental political projects of economic and administrative modernisation were delegated to top-level bureaucrats rather than to elected officials and government ministers. Third, this vast expansion of the role of state administrations in public life was made possible through intense intergovernmental cooperation on a European level.

The nation-state took root deeper and in a more vastly increased number of domains than had previously been possible, creating prosperity, social cohesion and political consent, if not conservatism, with European electorates. Military defeat had freed European nations from their imperial dreams and finally offered them new geographical horizons in their immediate vicinity. The evolutionary agenda of nation-building finally found a harmonious framework for its implementation, through an ever closer union, on an ever larger number of policies and with and ever greater number of participants. From the start, European integration was strongly committal, legally binding, prodigiously bent on institutionalisation, on costly, unwieldy bureaucracy and on profusely producing harmonisation, homogenisation and convergence.

The process that started earnestly with the Treaty of Rome vastly surpassed even the most visionary or exalted hopes of its signatories. They most probably would have been horrified by the prospect of a Union of twenty-seven member states. Still, the ever receding horizons of the unification process – progressively including the British Isles, Scandinavia, the Iberian Peninsula and, by 2007, large swathes of what used to be the Tsarist, Habsburg and Ottoman empires – constitute an unparalleled geopolitical process, not by its geographical extension, but by the depth and constringent nature of the Union.

Conclusion

An international world order based on the formal repudiation of empire and the axiomatic proclamation of the equality of independent nation-states is not a convincing road map for the future. The emergence of institutionalised forms of regional cooperation, of which the EU is the most accomplished example so far, calls to go beyond the opposition of two mutually exclusive models of political organisation that dominated the nineteenth and twentieth centuries, namely empire and nation-state. The EU clearly has some attributes of both, particularly its capacity to create homogeneity within and emulation without. The rapid promotion – in a historical perspective – from association to full membership in the enlargement process shows that, in the case of the EU, evolutionary thinking was not only rhetoric. The Union does seem to dispose of the transformative power to impact its periphery to the point of recognising its equal status. The question is how far it will be able to carry this dynamic. Like the equilibrium of the cyclist, it seems to depend on the speed of its progress. The geographic horizon of the European project continues to recede. Ignoring the immediate surroundings of the Union is once more a luxury Europe cannot afford. The status of Turkey, the prospects of the Western successor states of the USSR, including Russia, and the nature of the relationship with North and West African countries are all pressing issues in which the future not just of these countries but of the Union itself is at stake. In the 1990s, the question was whether Europe could afford to allow the formerly communist countries to linger in a political no-man's land and whether it could let the Balkans founder into civil war and anarchy. The question was even, to some, whether Eastern Europe and the Balkans would draw Western Europe into chaos, crisis and instability, or vice-versa; whether the EU had the capacity to stabilise its immediate vicinity. The choice for enlargement was imperative. The results are unquestionably positive. And the EU remained a symmetrical structure, where inevitable tensions and differences between centre and periphery were not formalised in different statuses in the institutional architecture. The current temptation is to abandon this scheme of enlargement, whereby association ultimately leads to membership, and to set up unegalitarian and asymmetric relationships with the immediate periphery. The imperial temptation risks to imperil the whole architecture of the Union, since empire, however lofty its evolutionary utopias, breeds anger, envy and violence.

Thus, is the only logical horizon of the EU to become the Union *tout court*, once its concentric circles have covered the whole planet? Such a claim is evidently absurd and dangerous. The rest of the world has not been passively waiting until European expansion reaches them. The EU is only the most institutionally advanced experiment in regional integration. Similar initiatives are in full swing in Asia, Latin America, Africa and even North America. European public opinions are exhausted by enlargement and deeply distrustful of hegemony. It is utterly unlikely that they would be more willing to bear the costs of global dominance in the future than is the American public opinion of today. The increasing failure of American hegemony has caught Europe by surprise, since it has no alternative project for a new world order, nor the political will or capacity to enforce it. It stands to gain precious little from new imperial rivalries that would oppose it to the USA or North Asia. There does not seem to be a genuine alternative to the multiplication of dynamics of regional integration, none of which are necessarily mutually incompatible or inherently engaged on a collision course. The twenty-first century will neither be a century of empire, nor one of nation-state. Or at least, let's hope so.

Notes

1 Charles-Louis Montesquieu (1689–1755), the most influential thinker of the Lumières, published in 1734 his *Considérations sur les causes de la grandeur des Romains et de leur décadence*, which allowed him to formulate his ideal of a modern state. Edward Gibbon (1737–94) published in 1776 *The Decline and the Fall of the Roman Empire*, one of the most influential contributions ever to the history of Ancient Rome. Oswald Spengler (1880–1936) published in 1918 his *Decline of the West*, capturing the spirit of cultural pessimism prevalent in Europe at that time. Arnold Toynbee (1889–1975) published his twelve-volume *A Study of History* entirely organised on the scheme of cyclical growth and decline of civilisations between 1934 and 1961. The American journalist Henry Luce (1898–1967) coined the expression 'the American century' in an article in the popular magazine *Life* in 1941, calling upon the USA to abandon its isolationism and save the world from itself. More recently, several major authors have revisited the theme of the decline of empire: Immanuel Wallerstein, *The Modern World System*, 3 vols (1974–89); Paul Kennedy, *The Rise and Fall of the Great Powers: Economic Change and Military Conflict, 1500–2000* (1987); Niall Ferguson, *Empire: The Rise and Fall of the British World Order and the Lessons for Global Power* (2003); Charles Maier, *Among Empires: American Ascendancy and Its Predecessors* (2006).

2 See, for instance, François Fejtö, *Requiem pour un Empire défunt: histoire de la destruction de l'Autriche–Hongrie*, Paris: Lieu Commun (1988); Istvan Deàk, *Beyond Nationalism: A Social and Political History of the Habsburg Officer Corps, 1848–1918* (1990), Oxford: Oxford University Press.

3 Eugen Weber, *Peasants into Frenchmen: The Modernisation of Rural France, 1870–1914* (1979), London: Chatto & Windus.

4 'Au lendemain de la victoire remportée par les peuples libres sur les régimes qui ont tenté d'asservir et de dégrader la personne humaine, le peuple français proclame à nouveau que tout être humain, sans distinction de race, de religion ni de croyance, possède des droits inaliénables et sacrés. Il réaffirme solennellement les droits et libertés de l'homme et du citoyen consacrés par la Déclaration des droits de 1789 et les principes fondamentaux reconnus par les lois de la République.'

5 'La France forme avec les peuples d'outre-mer une Union fondée sur l'égalité des droits et des devoirs, sans distinction de race ni de religion. L'Union française est composée de nations et de peuples qui mettent en commun ou coordonnent leurs ressources et leurs efforts pour développer leurs civilisations respectives, accroître leur bien-être et assurer leur sécurité. Fidèle à sa mission traditionnelle, la France entend conduire les peuples dont elle a pris la charge à la liberté de s'administrer eux-mêmes et de gérer démocratiquement leurs propres affaires; écartant tout système de colonisation fondé sur l'arbitraire, elle garantit à tous l'égal accès aux fonctions publiques et l'exercice individuel ou collectif des droits et libertés proclamés ou confirmés ci-dessus.'

Bibliography

Bancel, Nicolas (ed.) (2003), *La République coloniale: essai sur une utopie*, Paris: Albin Michel.

Bitsch, Marie-Thérèse and Gérard Bossuat (eds) (2005), *L'Europe Unie et l'Afrique. De l'idée d'Eurafrique à la Convention de Lomé I*, Bruxelles: Bruylant.

Darwin, John (1991), *The End of the British Empire: The Historical Debate*, London: Blackwell.

Hobsbawm, Eric (1990), *Nations and Nationalism since 1780: Programme, Myth, Reality*, Cambridge: Cambridge University Press.

Maier, Charles (2006), *Among Empires: American Ascendancy and Its Predecessors*, Cambridge, Mass: Harvard University Press.

Mann, Michael (2005), *The Dark Side of Democracy: Explaining Ethnic Cleansing*, Cambridge: Cambridge University Press.

Marseille, Jacques (1984), *Empire colonial et capitalisme français: histoire d'un divorce*, Paris: Hachette.

Milward, Allan (1992), *The European Rescue of the Nation State*, London: Routledge.

Wallerstein, Immanuel (1974–89), *The Modern World System*, 3 vols, New York: Academic Press.

15 European integration and the cosmopolitan way

Jean-Marc Ferry

Summary

In what direction is European integration headed? This chapter defends the Kantian conception of a cosmopolitan union[1] structured around three levels of law: internal, international and transnational. This conception entails a new sense of political identity, based on a reflexive view of national traditions and of history itself. This new European spirit is most notable in the EU's foreign relations, and particularly in the ideology that dominates the EU's neighborhood policy. Comparison of the respective strategic cultures of the USA and the EU further illustrates the evolving European identity.

Introduction

An understanding of the EU's construction is subject to two conflicting interpretations: either it is perceived negatively, as an adaptive accompaniment to globalization; or it is understood positively, as a political adjustment designed to counterbalance the global economy.

According to the first interpretation, the EU's function would be to adopt and transmit the norms of global governance and its mission would be to make its member states manage the consequences of externally imposed decisions. This perspective is clearly suspicious of neoliberal collusion between European construction and capitalist globalization. The second interpretation stipulates that the EU's primary task would (or should) be to socially domesticate the global markets, to balance American power in major international organizations such as the World Trade Organization (WTO), to promote European options in matters of fair development, international peace, environmental protection, global energy policy and humanitarian aid.

The first interpretation is no more realistic than the second, merely more pessimistic. In addition to having an equally plausible future perspective, the second interpretation poses a political mobilisation challenge. Consider the path opened by the second interpretation: European construction as an active response to globalization and as a political adjustment to global economic constraints. The question that arises is: under what conditions would such an adjustment be possible and what would be its systematic implications? From a political theory perspective, the answer is simply *co-sovereignty*. This notion of co-sovereignty goes against the imaginary construct of political modernity, based on the values of unity, indivisibility and inalienability – the heritage of medieval theology and the Christian doctrine of the individual. Possibly the most profound resistance to European integration, the most deeply rooted in the cultural subconscious, is based on an attachment to this theological heritage to which political modernity owes its essential criteria.

In the modern era, however, this theological legacy has only served to create a structure of competing national principles on the European continent. Through the same historical movement, modern politics has developed transversal elements that underpin the notion of European identity. These elements include civility, legality and public space whose respective diffusion in the sixteenth, seventeenth and eighteenth centuries created modern Europe; and it was based on these civil accomplishments of *historical Europe* that construction of *political Europe* could be undertaken in the twentieth century. It is in this very tension between the civil unity of Europe and the cultural plurality of its nations that its universalism is found.

This is, in other words, the *cosmopolitan idea*. Moreover, it is today in the EU that this philosophical idea is beginning to be fulfilled, as a response to the challenge of political adjustment to economic globalization. For every legally constituted entity that claims to form a community of citizens, be it national or meta-national (like the EU), functional integration can only be successfully completed where it is matched by political integration of its constituents. *Functional integration* designates the expected organizational coherence of measures arranged to effectively regulate the global system through discrete sub-systems. *Political integration* refers to the experiential aspect in which individuals feel that they belong to the same community of solidarity.

What is a 'cosmopolitan union'?

Cosmopolitan unity is a complex political entity based on the specification of three levels of relations governed by public law.

- The *internal* level of *state law* organizes the relations of citizens within each member state. These legal relations correspond to the different types of individual fundamental rights (i.e., civil, civic or political, social, moral or cultural). It is the first level of relations of public law.
- The *external* level of *law of peoples* is understood as the rights of states in their reciprocal relations, but also as the rights of peoples without a corresponding state, and even as the rights of minorities in their relations with their own state. Within the EU, this level of law is much more developed than in general international law.
- The cosmopolitan aim of a non-state or post-state integration implies, however, a third level of law, after the internal level of state law and the international (external) level of the law of peoples: it is the *transnational* level of *cosmopolitan law* in the strictest sense. It is a right that relates to the individual citizens of the world, or for the time being of the EU. The cosmopolitan right dissociates citizenship from nationality without necessarily doing away with nationality, as long as the transnational element is legally founded on a principle of *conditional* universal

hospitality – i.e., that no hostile intentions exist towards the hospitable country. However, European integration implements cosmopolitan law that goes beyond the minimalist concept proposed by Kant.

The constitutional originality of the EU is that it undertakes political implementation of the third level, which has only ever existed as a philosophical idea until now. But the second level of relations of public law also warrants further explanation. The values previously related only to fundamental individual rights – i.e., the values of integrity, participation, solidarity and identity, respectively attached to civil rights, political rights, social rights and moral rights (understood as including cultural rights) – are presently being transposed onto the level of relations between the peoples of the EU – i.e., to the second level of relations of public law.

Concerning the value of integrity, transposition to the level of the law of peoples is not an innovation of the European construction. A partial transposition has already been accomplished in international law generally, with the principles of non-interference and territorial integrity.

As for the value of participation, linked to political or civic rights, transposition to the level of general international law has as yet reached only a weak early stage: it is the right of self-determination of peoples, to which must be added the status of legal member for each state-based people that participates in the United nations (UN). In the EU, however, transposing the political right of participation to the second level, that of the law of peoples, is noted on the negative side by the right to withdraw or secede from the EU, explicitly foreseen by the constitutional Treaty, and on the positive side by the formal right of equality between member states in determining common policies, which translates practically as the notions of co-sovereignty and co-responsibility.

Above all, the value of solidarity, which relates to the principle of social rights, has not undergone any systematic transposition to the level of general international law. However, this is not the case in the community law of the EU. Redistributive mechanisms are in place at the second level of EU public law between the member states of the EU, including structural funds and regional adjustment policies that engender solidarity among the member states.

Finally, the 'European law of peoples' is an exemplary formalization of the value of identity, attached to moral rights (e.g., copyright royalties) and cultural rights. In the same way that individual citizens of democratic nations have had the right to develop and express their personal identity – including their cultural rights –so have the nations and peoples of the EU (including the non-state-based peoples like the Roma and traveling peoples generally) been expressly recognized by the EU as collective identities, with a singularity of language, culture, memory and history. This recognition reveals the incipient cosmopolitan aspect of fundamental rights, the rights of individuals (human rights) like those of peoples (right of peoples). The universal principle is the repeated recognition of distinctive identities.

This remarkable enrichment of the second level of the legal structure must be completed by a transnational complement. This is the level of cosmopolitan law in the strictest sense. Only in the EU has cosmopolitan law begun to be implemented;

elsewhere it remains simply a philosophical idea. In the EU, cosmopolitan law is positively demonstrated by the transversal rights granted to European citizens as such; four types of opportunities exist, with the first two corresponding to transnational rights and the last two corresponding to meta-national rights:

- the right to free movement and free residence for nationals in all extra-national territory within the EU
- the right to participate and vote in the state of residence
- the ability of European citizens to exercise their rights before an EU tribunal, if necessary against their own state (i.e., the post-national right to appeal)
- the ability of European citizens outside the EU to seek refuge and assistance from the Consulate or Embassy of any EU member state (i.e., the post-national right to protection).

These are the characteristics of the EU *as a cosmopolitan union*. Based on the type of integration proposed, it is an original political entity. From this point of view, the prospect opened to European integration, the Kantian orientation (Kant 1795), must be conceptually distinguished from the integration prospects represented by the *federal state* and the *federation of states*. The European federal state corresponds to the notion of a *supranationalist orientation*, whereas the *federalist orientation* conceptually characterizes the federation of states (which the EU is, *de facto*). If the nationalist options are disregarded, three paths are available to the future of European integration, within the institutional perspective: the supranational way, the federal way, and the cosmopolitan way.

Supra-nationalism, federalism, cosmopolitanism

The supranational way

The supranational way seeks to unscrupulously eliminate national sovereignties in favor of a supranational sovereignty of the European federal state. This state-centric orientation runs up against the objection of *ad hoc* institutionalism (Mairet 1996), devoid of any conceptual power or realism. It appears philosophically weak and politically dangerous.

It is philosophically weak because, in substance, this orientation is merely the reproduction of the nation-state constitutional model at the supranational level. This was the temptation of the founding fathers of European integration: a *supranational federal state* which, in principle, is strictly dependent on "methodological nationalism," in the words of Ulrich Beck. Ironically, it is the proponents of the European federal state who are the most hostile towards maintaining the nation-states within the EU. Their institutional dream or fantasy is the United States of Europe, which construes the EU as a sort of European nation whose constitution relegates the member states to the status of mere federated states.

By comparing this model of a supranational federal state to the more highly developed Kantian model of cosmopolitan union, it is evident that the supranationalist orientation of the United States of Europe only addresses the first level of legal relations: that of internal state law designed, in principle, to regulate the civil and social relations between nationals but not between nations, while political relations between these nationals and their state are organized *by the principle of subordination*. The articulation of three levels of legal relations is replaced by a conventional construction organized around a *single* level that is *globalized*.

Moreover, such a construction is politically dangerous because it would considerably aggravate the existing problem of EU *non-governability* and its inherent risks, including simultaneous authoritarianism and impotence. The construction of a European federal state would be fraught with a governance crisis leading to a disconnect of EU (or simply, European) authorities from public opinion and national civil societies. The European project would thus lose all democratic legitimacy.

The federal way

The way of a federation of nation-states is presented as an intermediary orientation between a federal state and a confederation (Beaud 1998). Systematically, within the Kantian framework that specifies three levels of law, the construction of a federation of states corresponds not to the articulation of a first level, like the European federal state, but to the second level: the organization of interstate relations according to the law of peoples (which is, in fact, the right of states in their reciprocal relations). From this point of view, the European republic would consist not of a community of citizens as the European federal state, but of intensified interactions and relations between the member states. The political aim is thus a *second degree* (or second level) *democratization*. The European model can even be viewed as an instructive experiment for the future of international relations in general.

For several reasons, notably because of its mixed political nature which capitalizes on the balance between supranational and intergovernmental mechanisms, this formula is the most often supported by legal theoreticians interested in the European question (Weiler 2004). This mixed political nature translates as a mixed legal model, somewhere between international law and internal state law, and suggests the delicate alternative between an organization governed by treaties and a constitutional organization; hence the idea of a constitutional pact or treaty (Chopin 2006). This further fosters a mixed procedural model in terms of constitution-building, which oscillates between diplomatic negotiation and democratic deliberation. A further structural uncertainty relates to the methods of ratification and revision for constitutional treaties: unanimity or majority voting? A qualified majority of states, or of the total population, or a combination of both? The federal formula accommodates this mixed nature. It preserves the identity of member nations, but remains undecided on their sovereignty. Although the federal construction is theoretically organized around a regime of co-sovereignty, it provides little insight as to the ways and means to go about a political integration that would be capable of guaranteeing the transition from an *international* organization to a *transnational* union without veering towards the form of a *supranational* state. This is the general ambiguity of the federalists (Dumont 2003).[2]

In order to lessen this equivocacy, the expression "multinational federation" has been proposed to highlight "the difference with the federal state, which is generally mono-national" (Dumont 2003); but this is exactly the difficulty of conceptualizing the EU – a difficulty which is not simply conceptual. Accentuating the multinational aspect dissipates the misunderstandings implied by invoking the term "United States of Europe" (Habermas 2006).[3] However, an important difference between the multinational federation and the cosmopolitan union is the member states' right to secede. This commitment is only necessary within the cosmopolitan framework. This difference precisely concerns what can be called the negative sovereignty of member states. This fact alone – that within the cosmopolitan framework, the member states retain the right to withdraw from the Union – changes the nature of the constraint placed upon them, if need be, to subject them to common compliance: states can, in the latter instance, refuse to submit to the authority of the EU, so their *legal submission* to common compliance is not assimilated as *political submission*, which would clearly constitute a partial breach of the supranational state model. This decisive difference, which testifies to the authentic *post-state* originality of the cosmopolitan framework, is coupled with the fact that the fundamental rights on which the cosmopolitan union is based are not strictly limited to individual rights, or human rights, but also extend to the fundamental rights of peoples, while in addition a *third level of relations according to public law* is implicated, after the internal and international levels: the *transnational* level of cosmopolitan law in the strictest sense. The concept of a federation of states does not, in and of itself, provide any glimmer of this dimension.

The cosmopolitan way

The cosmopolitan way is thus understood – in the Kantian sense of legal cosmopolitanism with a tri-level structure: internal (state law), international (law of peoples) and transnational (cosmopolitan law). Like the federation of states, the cosmopolitan union internally allows for state sovereignties as well as differences based on national identities. It is important to understand that the cosmopolitan orientation is not in opposition to the federalist way; it is rather a lengthening and deepening of the federalist framework, in terms of a *transnational democratization, distinct from an inter-state collectivization*. Thus the cosmopolitan way takes the federation of states as a point of departure. However, the federation of states is inscribed in the perspective of a horizontal non-state democratic integration, which is based on a framework of variable geometry in the broadest sense: the map of the EU is physically altered according to a given perspective defining differential integration – whether it be according to *functional sectors* (e.g., the Eurozone for monetary union), or *groups of partners* (potentially the member states in an area of reinforced cooperation) or the *areas of EU competence*, from exclusive competences (customs union, common commercial policy, monetary policy in the Eurozone) to supportive competences that infringe on matters principally reserved for the member states (such as social policy, education, health) and including shared competences (internal market, agricultural policy, security, justice) and the coordination competences of economic policies.

In contrast to the supranational orientation, the cosmopolitan way does not envisage a European federal state.[4] However, it is distinguished from the federal schema in that the stabilization of associated states is not the ultimate goal, but the means to a "multilateral democratic integration" which ultimately gives way to a transnational organization (Cheneval 2005). This is the conceptually precise interpretation of the direction of European integration. It prescribes a *post-state* formula for *transnational* political integration that is already foreseen in policies such as the free movement of persons and freedom of residence throughout the EU, the diplomatic protection and consular guarantee of any member state to citizens outside the EU, the structural policies in favor of regions risking economic failure, as well as measures designed to promote cultural, university and scientific exchanges based on transversal programs. These measures are part of a strategy that aims to promote reciprocal overtures of political cultures and historical memories among the nations. The cosmopolitan vision offers a conceptualization that is receptive to paradigmatic changes that affect citizenship, notably the general phenomenon of *deterritorialization* of political identities. For example, the multiplication of cultural diasporas develops trans-state forms of national solidarity, creating a bond between members of a national community that is no longer based on spatial criteria; so much so that the nation is presented as an extra-territorial or ultra-state reality (Dufoix 2006). Nations do not disappear; but what tends to dissolve is the former corollary linkage between nation and territory.[5] This promotes, in the imaginary political realm, progressive integration of new differentiations: between nationality and citizenship, between state and constitution and between nation and people. Thus previously insubstantial ideas such as *post-state constitution* and *multinational people* begin to be plausible, as well as the groupings without which it would be quite difficult to conceptualize Europe.

History and identity in a reflective perspective

With regard to a constitution for Europe, it is relevant to distinguish between a people and a nation. The distinction between people and nation is of heuristic interest to the European project because it suggests that a *differentiation process* is underway, so the idea of a European people can be discussed while simultaneously affirming the federation's *multinational* character; the idea of a *multinational people* has become accepted. Indeed the modern republican tradition, from Bodin to Hegel, held that a people can only be *politically* constituted. Giorgio Agamben highlighted the political meaning of the word "people", noting that this meaning was unduly usurped by the word "nation." In order to establish a post-nationalist integration, it is essential to initiate the recognition of self in the other. The self-reflective relation that Europeans have with their own history and identity enables their democratic integration beyond the limits of their state, i.e., the expansion of civic solidarity on a continental scale. This extension is inseparable from a self-critical historical conscience that tends to stigmatize events that have impeded the process of reciprocal recognition and led to mistrust. Concerning the EU, as much in the relations among its member states as those with the rest of the world, this reconstructive logic is quite significant; the authenticity of recognition of federating political principles is tested by it. For example, there seems to be an inherent link between the internalization of the values of a democratic state by Turkey and the official recognition of the Armenian massacre.

Furthermore, the reflexive perspective that the *politics of memory* instills in the past does not itself merit the virulent stigmatization that it suffers in France, across party lines. Beneath the guise of honest self-esteem lies French chauvinism opposed to the fact that Europe and the European nations are committed to a reflective perspective of history, which allows for mutual understanding between national memories, and consequently initiates a reconstructive process authenticated by public recognition of violence that was perpetrated in the past and the accumulation of resentments that compromise the future. This new perspective on history, the self-critical relationship of Europe to its own history, is the quintessential means for eliminating the past debts of international relations; and Europe thus begins its new history in which the relations between nations, previously dominated by mortal struggles for recognition – a dialogue imperfectly relieved by that of crime and punishment[6] – are now committed to a process that promotes reconciliation.

By definition, the cosmopolitan way is an original legal structure that is well suited to accomplish the necessary organization and domestication of transnational power, without violating the multi-level expectations of recognition, solidarity, co-responsibility and collective autonomy that are necessary to political integration. Of course the democratic vitalization of Europe, that is the effective promotion of a European public space, remains to be completed. But in so far as the EU's basic structures correspond to the criteria of cosmopolitan law, non-contradictory conciliation between the preservation (i.e., expansion) of national identities that make up the EU and the adaptation of political power to independent transnational levels, without the subordination of member states to a sovereign supranational power, becomes feasible. This principle of "free federalism" (Kant) on which cosmopolitan construction is based was almost actualized in the 2004 constitutional Treaty: if authority is granted to the EU as such, the member states that compose it retain their sovereignty, on the condition that they commit to the reciprocal conciliation of their public policies. Regular and organized cooperation between states, not their subordination to a superior power, is in fact the basic principle of such a union.

It is important to understand that the European project is a risky enterprise that aims to successfully complete the political integration of the Continent according to non-traditional paths. To understand this originality one must refer to such cosmopolitan ideas, more so than to the federalist idea. The legal concept of a federation of states is by no means irrelevant. Conversely, it describes fairly accurately the state of affairs achieved by the treaties, whereas the cosmopolitan idea remains to be clarified. It is true that the EU is *de facto* a multinational federation, in terms of *what is there*; but in order to understand what is happening behind what is there – in order to understand the process that is underway, rather than merely to map its progress – the idea of a cosmopolitan union is more appropriate than that of a federation of states, because it presents the perspective of a horizontal, transnational integration, a perspective that is no less pertinent than the current state to the reality of integration. In the same manner, the notion of a constitutional pact is more exact than that of a constitution, as it describes a text that legally regulates the organization of EU public powers, their interrelations and their relations with the member states. But the term "constitutional pact" does not do justice to the symbolic element that is introduced with the inscription of a declaration of fundamental rights and constitutional values; in this case, it is clearly the establishment of an authentic *European social contract*. Such is the symbolism that the *idea* of constitution is more convenient than that of constitutional treaty or pact, which only seems to consider the states as its logical subjects, when in fact it is the peoples that *as united peoples* are the beneficiaries of the contract. Rather than resort to neologisms to describe new realities, philosophy prefers to use classic terms, even if forced to accept that some terms take on new meanings.

Thus it must be admitted that the notion of a constitution is not strictly tied to the nation-state, as many legal scholars would wish. In fact, the idea of a constitution predates the reality of the modern nation-state: it was used to designate the manner of organizing cities in Ancient Greece from 400 BC, as well as in Christian Antiquity to describe the ordinances governing monastic communities, such as the Saint-Benoît Rule, which were veritably small constitutions. Why then can the idea of a *post-state* constitution not also become relevant, in the procedural perspective of differentiating between *state* and *constitution*? One of the main tasks of political philosophy is to propose heuristic models to understand the dynamics of underlying structures. It is in this perspective that significant differentiations are hypothesized: differentiation between *nationality* and *citizenship*, between *nation* and *people*, between *state* and *constitution*. Rather than clinging to the categories prescribed by doctrine, will legan scholars examine whether their legal concepts are neither too strict; nor lacking in their capacity to grasp transnational developments (e.g., freedom of movement and residence) and post-national developments (e.g., the ability of EU citizens to exercise appeals against their own nation states)? These amount to legal trends that are conceptually inscribed in the domain of legal cosmopolitanism, the domain of the third level (beyond the internal level of political rights and the international level of peoples' rights), whose existence orthodox legal scholars quite simply do not recognize. Political scholars could encourage this recognition among jurists by simply outlining the vast empirical evidence that supports the transition from classic international law to cosmopolitan law.

In this regard, the debate over whether the EU can be considered a laboratory for global governance is an update to the more classic perspective of a European republic which would be the precursor of a global cosmopolitan union. This was an unrealistic vision in the time of Kant, but today other humanities than European humanity and other worlds than the democratic world have become important actors in the international realm. This fact justifies that the reflection on Europe has become part of a larger field of enquiry, and the importance accorded to the EU's external action and the unique style of relations the EU undertakes with its periphery marks an orientation that proposes a multiregional vision of global order. This is accompanied by a new concept of power, which surpasses the objections of idealism and is already in effect in the reality of international relations. Today it is realism itself which requires breaking with the conventional reductive conception of military power. The end of the bipolar world left an opening for a new form of power, and the recognized failure of the logic that underpinned intervention in Iraq invites a renewed reflection on political power resources in international relations.

Which European power?

It is clear that the EU's external policy, like that of the USA, is fundamentally realist, primarily dictated by geopolitical and economic interests; in light of the deplorable catastrophes presently generated by politics that are driven by intense conviction, this is a generally reassuring fact. In normal international relations, neither Europe nor the USA – the two primary democratic entities in the world – is more angelic than the other, and neither has anything to envy in terms of pragmatism. The EU and the USA both wish to develop democracy throughout the world, however, the two engage different strategies in pursuit of this goal. It is not simply a matter of the difference between American messianics and European passivism, or between American democratic imperialism and European legal cosmopolitanism. The primary difference is between the American strategy of *legitimation based on content* or results and the European strategy of *legitimation based on method* or procedure.

The USA acted in Iraq as though what mattered was the end of a dictatorship and creation of a democracy: *legitimation based on content*. The fact that the desired result has not come about – that the intervention in Iraq is now an avowed failure by almost any criteria – has certainly intensified but in no way fundamentally modified the fact that peoples do not easily forgive the procedural fault of not respecting their right to autonomy, their right and responsibility to resolve their own problems internally. A peoples' right to autonomy must be respected, so that the very physical existence of minority populations is not endangered; if a third-party "liberator" power, such as the USA in Iraq, appropriates the right of intervention in the name of duty – i.e., an armed *coup d'état* – it violates the "liberated" peoples' political self-esteem, thus exposing itself to eternal resentment. Hubert Védrine, the former French Foreign Minister, firmly holds in his critique of American foreign policy: democratization, notably in regard to Iraq, "can not be an externally imposed conversion; it is a long and complex internal process; impossible to impose by armed force in heterogeneous countries lacking a democratic base."[7]

In comparison to the American strategy of external democratization and legitimization, the European strategy is as yet only skeletal, but does not espouse the substantialist (i.e., fundamentalist) policy of results even to the detriment of methods, or ends justifying means. This is the remarkable character of European identity. It is clear that Europe's profound political principles are different from those of the USA, as exemplified by the practices of the EU itself and its accompanying political culture. There exists a new European mindset and thus there is much to learn from the alleged "young Europe." Unlike Americans, Europeans – i.e., those who are bonded by the *acquis communautaire* (fundamental principles of the Community) and the established new public culture – are almost too inclined to consider that in order to democratize the rest of the world, one must obstinately promote methods of dialogue, coordination, cooperation and discussion designed to establish partial consensus or compromise. In doing so, the democratic culture of compromise, understood as a culture of cooperation and civilized confrontation under the law, is surreptitiously installed. European politics holds that cooperative procedures are the true vehicles to deepening interactions in international relations and achieving transnational democratization. Diplomatic interaction cultivates civility, legality – to a lesser extent public space – and democratic virtues in general, including patience, understanding of compromise, the search for harmony, and a modicum of loyalty and openness to criticism. This is the strategy of cosmopolitan and procedural democratization that Europe seems to strongly prefer to the hegemonic and neo-imperial formula of eliminating tyrants and *nation-building* according to "good governance."

It is still important to consider in what context and under what conditional constraints the EU has achieved actual success on this multilateral, cooperative path in the spirit of soft power. It is most notably in the context of enlarging the EU itself: in relations with its candidate countries and under the conditions of maximum political pressure on the EU's part. Thus, the political promise of world peace is fundamentally that of European peace. But does the same go with regard to other partners who, like those involved in the Barcelona Process – on the south and east coasts of the Mediterranean, and notably in the Middle East – have no apparent prospect of direct inclusion in the EU, but only of sustained development or reconstruction aid, and at most regular cooperation through a privileged partnership?

In this instance, success is variable. Without going so far as to call the Barcelona Process a failure, the methodology – although it is no less realistic than the inter-ventionist American method – only seems to encounter sensibilities open to democracy among a restrained circle of cosmopolitan elites – journalists, writers, professors and opposition leaders – who consider the recent integrative and clerical evolution of secular national authorities as a regression. The small cosmopolitan elite of the Muslim Middle East potentially views the 'post-modern' passage (in the Robert Cooper sense) to political identity freed from nationalism itself as progress. But in the contemporary context – in light of which Samuel Huntington's clash of civilizations theory must be admitted as relevant – where charismatic power indefinitely dismisses any mode of rational, legal legitimacy, it is possible that Europe's Kantian way will not effect democratization at the level of relations between peoples, let alone federate these peoples in a South Mediterranean Union or open them to the democratic preconditions of privileged partnership with the EU. At least, such goals will not be reached until the peoples themselves – assuming their states do not regress to religious politics but achieve secular autonomy – have undergone trials similar to those that Europe suffered throughout the short twentieth century (1914–89), and until the struggle for mutual recognition among peoples in the peripheral regions has given way to common recognition of ethical and politico-legal principles.

In any case, the EU must immediately present itself as a *global player*, a unitary and coherent world actor, distinct from the state model. What relevance, or what future does the European model of non-conventional power have on the international stage? According to Nicole Gnesotto, the European model is essentially better suited to addressing the challenges of globalization than is the American model, because "the entire history of European construction for the last sixty years is a slow learning process on the sharing and relativity of power." Without ignoring the current EU crisis, Gnesotto defines what makes Europe a model for the future: "To share in order to lead together: this revolution that the Prince Salina had to accept to maintain the power of his house in *The Leopard* [novel by Giuseppe di Lampedusa], the West must sooner or later integrate on a global scale." (Gnesotto 2007)

This is a very different diagnosis than that which merely elaborates the European post-national crisis. The question of coherence in European foreign policy is indubitably inseparable from the decisions made according to Europe's internal constitution. For example, the advent of Community pillars, particularly the common foreign and security policy (CFSP) and the European security and defense policy (ESDP), is an important step. The original character of EU external action is revealed particularly in the European neighborhood policy (ENP), which combines such elements as engagement with partners who favor EU values, intensified commercial relations, eventual participation in the internal market, cooperation on energy, transport, research and innovation, deepening political dialogue and regional cooperation. The matter at hand is to create such a partnership with the EU periphery – i.e., the Caucasus and the Mediterranean Basin. Europe utilizes conditionality to promote economic integration and political interaction to impress EU values. The faster that the partner is willing to undertake the required measures, the faster the EU will develop cooperation.

The EU thus tends to conceive and promote itself internationally as a prosperous and neighborly political entity, based on a declaration of values.[8] The EU has the economic assets of a superpower, with 12,000 billion euros of domestic product (in 2006), 500 million inhabitants, the second strongest currency reserve in the world, and the first rank in terms of humanitarian and development aid. Moreover, in political terms, the EU is more in line with what Mario Telò has called a "civilian power" (Telò 2007) that, prior to the 2007 Baker Report on the disastrous Iraq War, already understood that *hard power* is not the appropriate means though which to export democracy. As the administrative functions of the state come up against new risks that are no longer limited to national borders (Beck 1992), not to mention the basic fiscal pressures of global movements, it seems that the only choice for Europe is to promote active cooperation with other regions of the world in the spirit of *soft power* and positive conditionality. Then, internally, Europe will need to organize flexible coordination of national policies around the cardinal principles of civility joined with legality, an open public space of negotiation, deliberation and political decision. As for the sovereign state's exercising authority over a fixed territory in the name of a given people, it has been surpassed by the real scale of political decision, and the imaginary unitary self-governing people has been surpassed by the emergence of new actors, such as non-government organizations (NGOs), that make decisions not according to parliamentary debate, but in terms of international cooperation that is an intermediary form between deliberation and negotiation – again, this is only an expansion of the political decision-making field. More worrying is the emergence of what Ulrich Beck calls "meta-power": apart from the meta-power of civil institutions that have created a network of interstate connections that circumvent the nation state, there is the meta-power of the economy, a "winged power" (without territorial anchorage) that develops in isolation from democratic institutions, and exercises a "trans-legal domination" whose legitimacy is based solely on rational economics criteria (Beck 2005). Since capitalism is freed from external checks on legitimacy, legitimacy itself is becoming separated from the state, so that, to address this political crisis, the nation states – according to Beck – must determine their own transformation by converting to cosmopolitan states.

Nonetheless, this does not imply the "strong" postulate of a supranational *state*. The term "empire," proposed by Ulrich Beck and Edgar Grande[9] in order avoid the connotations of "methodological nationalism," offers an ambiguous alternative to the notion of state. This term carries more baggage than it is worth, however, and so the more serious term "union" seems more appropriate. *Union* appears particularly useful when associated to the idea of *procedural cosmopolitanism* propounded by Francis Cheneval. It is certainly the cooperative orientation of interstate and transnational collaboration on which the EU progressively bases its constitutional nature, despite a few instructive setbacks. The opposition between supranationalists and intergovernmentalists thus loses political interest, with the question becoming instead whether to maintain the open method of coordination created by the 2004 European Council Summit in Lisbon, whose transnational orientation already surpasses this opposition, or to create deliberative structures at all levels of desirable participation, in order to strengthen a transnational conscience of civic solidarity. Although an understanding of the limits of the managerial approach to European governance is being reached, today's Europe is still not being constructed in opposition to its nations. European politics, for what it is worth, is achieved with and through its member nations. The philosophical spirit of European politics does not break with that of European history. Moreover, the cosmopolitan idea is a fundament of modern political philosophy; it is its hidden nature and its normative cornerstone.[10]

Conclusion

The cosmopolitan union entails a basic structure that is not a federal state, or a simple association, league or confederation. Europe is being integrated not on the basis of the subordination of member states to a superior power, for example a supranational state, but on the practice of permanent cooperation between states and coordination of their public policies. There is, of course, the difficult procedural task of creating agreement between numerous partners on each occasion. Shortcuts are tempting, which is why there is pressure to generalize majority voting; but this would by no means do away with consensual practices. On the contrary: within reasonable limits, the already advanced transition from unanimity to majority voting would induce a transition in consensus-seeking practices from negotiation to deliberation, corresponding with a change in orientation from a diplomatic logic to a democratic logic. This is perhaps a necessary, though by no means sufficient (because leader cooperation does not equal citizen participation), condition for the creation of durable legitimacy born of effective, reciprocally contracted public policies. This is the original framework of *cosmopolitan integration*. Contrary to the simplified framework, the dynamic is *not* transition from an international organization ruled by treaties to a supranational state headed by a constitution. The right to free movement and residence, and the right to transnational civic participation correspond to a horizontal strategy – both directly, as they favor transnational intermingling which will create both a symbolic decompartmentalization and a cosmopolitan mentality; and indirectly, as transitional citizens, or European cosmopolitans, will thus be able to influence their national fiscal and social systems, which will benefit from the offered advantages. This is the idea of *competitive federalism*, of which the negative consequences are already being felt, as the least fiscally, socially and environmentally demanding states benefit the most.[11] For now, it is businesses that benefit over states and individuals; this may propose a dark future for the EU.[12] Furthermore, states and individuals have a common interest in this scenario: states have to control their fiscal competitiveness and individuals want an improved quality of life. If the citizens and their states form a political alliance against economic powers, it will push for positive integration bound to fiscal and social harmonization as well as deepening internal democracy within each member state.

In the meantime, the existing negative integration process can easily create suspicion that European construction is a technocratic and inauthentic enterprise, which attempts to halo itself in humanitarian values – human rights, freedoms and soft power – as though using political innocence to mask ill-reconciled history.[13] This perception incites the defense of history and identity – in the name of heritage, debt and affiliation – against Europe and its supposed post-political compulsion. Those who hope to thus ruffle the sensibilities of nationalists, or simply loyal citizens, present the EU's official position as denial of European identity, in some manner tied to masochism and self-loathing.[14] This interpretation neglects the emergence of a civil conscience that prefers the constitutional guarantee of liberal order to the sovereign affirmation of the national cause – which entails a shift from state to constitution, i.e., a progressive decoupling of constitution from state (Brunkhorst 2004). In reaction to this post-nationalist orientation, the revival of nationalism is based on reductionist convictions: reduction of the EU's *political* identity to *historical* or cultural European identity. Confusion is created between the effective order that has historically defined Europe and the normative order that is required to define the EU.[15] Moreover, the EU *should* create a strictly political identity based on democratic practices including republicanism, but which also permits the latter to free itself from prior political attachments and to engender transnational civil solidarity.[16]

It is important to note that the EU will not, without dilution, be able to directly introduce its cultural heritage into its normative order. European identity claims a rich cultural heritage – Greek metaphysics, Roman law, Germanic freedom, Christianity, humanism, rationalism; it is nonetheless unnecessary for political Europe, in defining its particular identity, to claim exclusivity of these traditions. If no one can be considered naturally European, then in contrast anyone can become so.[17] The heritage of Europe is not a principle on which the Union should be closed. Rather, it is a resource of values and principles whose normative prospects transcend their origins to cast meaning in all contexts to which they are relevant. Before becoming a substantial concept, identity is a relative concept: what counts is not of what one is made, but what one makes of what one is. Should Europe withdraw into its own particularities, or, even at risk of transforming itself, offer its civilizing message to the world?

Notes

1 Immanuel Kant (1795), "Zum ewigen Frieden" [Towards perpetual peace], in W. Weischedel, *Gesammelte Werke [Collected Works]*, Frankfurt-am-Main: Suhrkamp, 1977.

2 See also Olivier Beaud, *La Puissance de l'État* [The Power of the State], Paris: Presses Universitaires de France, 1994, 488: "The process of European construction underway leads to a loss of sovereignty and the substantial constitutional modification of each state."

3 Habermas in fact attacks the "Euro-skeptic objection", namely that "there could never be a United States of Europe because the necessary basis for such a construction of a European people is lacking" (see Jürgen Habermas, "Constructing political Europe" (Reception speech for the Land de Rhénanie of Nord-Westphalie Prize in Petersberg), *Le Monde*, December 27, 2006).

4 For a pluralist discussion of this orientation, see the thematic volume of the *Revue suisse de science politique*, dedicated to "The idea of a European state," Vol. 4, Winter 1998 (edited by Mark Hunyadi and Jean-Marc Ferry). For a militant defense of the European state, see Bernard Guetta, "L'Europe: une ambition, déjà une réalité" [Europe: an ambition, already reality], in Korine Amacher and Nicolas Levrat (eds), *Jusqu'où ira l'Europe?* [Where Is Europe Heading?], Université de Genève, Louvain-la-Neuve: Bruylant-Academia, 2005, 73–6.

5 See Giorgio Agamben, *Au-delà des droits de l'homme* [Beyond Human Rights], Paris: Payot-Rivages, 1995 (cited by Jean Picq et Yves Cusset, *Philosophies politiques pour notre temps. Un parcours européen* [Political Philosophies for Our Era. A European Course], Paris: Odile Jacob, 2005.

6 Because of an uncontested supranational authority, legal sanctions on the international level for crimes against humanity retain certain aspects of victor's vengeance, according to public opinion.

7 See Hubert Védrine, debate with Elie Barnavi (former ambassador of Israel in France), *Le Figaro*, Saturday 16 – Sunday 17 September, 2006.

8 The EU, according to Section I of the Project, "is founded on the values of respect for human dignity, freedom, democracy, equality, the rule of law and respect for human rights, including the rights of persons belonging to minorities. These values are common to the Member States in a society in which pluralism, non-discrimination, tolerance, justice, solidarity and equality between women and men prevail."

9 See Ulrich Beck and Edgar Grande, *Pour un empire européen* [For a European Empire], translated by Aurélie Duthoo, Paris: Flammarion, 2007.

10 See Francis Cheneval, *La Cité des Peuples: Mémoires de cosmopolitismes* [The City of Peoples: Memories of Cosmopolitanism], Paris, Cerf, collection Humanités, 2005.

11 In contrast, Paul Thibaud advances the idea of "equitable competition" in "De l'échec au projet" [From failure to project], *Le Débat*, No. 140, May–August 2006, Paris: Gallimard, 17–29.

12 This is the worrisome prophesy expressed by Jean-Luc Gréau ("Les contradictions de l'empire" [The contradictions of empire], No. 123, January–February 2003, *Le Débat*, Paris: Gallimard, 32–47.

13 For an intelligent rebuttal to this Euro-skeptic charge, see Paul Magnette, "Le sens de l'Europe" [The sense of Europe], *Le Débat*, No. 140, May–August 2006, Paris: Gallimard, 30–5.

14 See Marcel Gauchet, *La Condition politique* [The Political Condition], Paris, Gallimard, 2005, in particular, "La nouvelle Europe" [The new Europe]; also Pierre Manent, *La Raison des nations* [The Reason of Nations], Paris: Gallimard, 2006.

15 In contrast, see Justine Lacroix, *L'Europe en procès*, Paris: Cerf, collection Humanités, 2004; see also, on Joseph H. H. Weiler, *L'Europe chrétienne? Une excursion*, Janie Pélabay, "Lorsque la clarification des sources se fait politiquement constitutive," in *Raison publique*, No. 8, Paris: Presses de l'Université Paris-Sorbonne, 2008.

16 For further detail, see Jürgen Habermas, *Sur l'Europe* [On Europe], translation by Christian Bouchindhomme, Paris: Bayard, 2006.

17 For further detail, see Rémi Brague, *La Voie romaine* [The Roman Way], Paris: Criterion, 1992–93.

Bibliography

Beaud, Olivier (1998), "Fédéralisme et souveraineté. Éléments pour une théorie constitutionnelle de la fédération" [Federalism and sovereignty: elements for a constitutional theory], *Revue du droit public*, 83–122.

Beck, Ulrich (1992), *Risk Society Towards a New Modernity*, translation by Mark Ritter, London: Sage Publications.

Beck, Ulrich (2005), *Power in the Global Age: A New Global Political Economy*, translation by Kathleen Cross, London: Flammarion.

Brunkhorst, Hauke (2004), "Verfassung ohne Staat?" [Constitution without state?], *Leviathan*, 30th year, No. 4, 530–43.

Cheneval, Francis (2005), "Legitimation der multilateralen demokratischen Integration" [Legitimation of multilateral democratic integration], in Francis Cheneval (dir.), *Legitimationsgrundlagen der Europäischen Union*, No. 27, Hamburg and London: Lit. Verlag.

Cheneval, Francis (2007), "Multilateral democracy: the 'original position' and the principles", Paper presented at the annual meeting of the American Political Science Association, August 30, Hyatt Regency Chicago and the Sheraton Chicago Hotel and Towers, Chicago, IL.

Chopin, Thierry (2006), "Convention, constitution et fédéralisme: Europe/États-Unis, l'utilité d'une étude comparée" [Convention, constitution and federalism : Europe/United States, the utility of comparative study], in Mokhtar Ben Barka, Jean-Marie Ruiz (eds), *États-Unis/Europe. Des modèles en miroir*, Villeneuve d'Ascq: Presses Universitaires du Septentrion, 35–68.

Dufoix, Stéphane (2006), "Nations extra-territoriales et nations ultra-étatiques: de nouvelles formes historiques de la nation" [Extra-territorial and ultra-state nations: nations' new historical forms], *Controverses*, No. 3, October, 115–34.

Dumont, Hugues (2003), "La question de l'État européen du point de vue d'un constitutionnaliste" [The question of the European state from a constitutionalist perspective], *Droit et société*, No. 53.

Ferry, Jean-Marc (2006), "The new European question: the problem of post-national integration," in Alain Dieckhoff and Christophe Jaffrelot (eds), *Revisiting Nationalism, Theories and Processes*, London: Hurst & Company,. 222–38.

Gnesotto, Nicole (2007), "La sécurité dans un monde post-occidental" [Security in a post-Western world], *Esprit*, May, 74.

Mairet, Gérard (1996), "Sur la critique cosmopolitique du droit politique" [On the cosmopolitan critique of public law], in Gérard Duprat, *L'Union européenne: Droit, politique, démocratie*, Paris: Presses Universitaires de France.

Telò, Mario (2005), *Europe: A Civilian Power? European Union, Global Governance and World Order*, Basingstoke: Palgrave.

Weiler, Joseph H.H. (2004), "Federalism without constitutionalism: Europe's *Sonderweg*," in Kalypso Nicolaïdis and Robert Howse (eds), *The Federal Vision: Legitimacy and Levels of Governance in the US and the EU*, 2nd edition. Oxford: Oxford University Press, 2004, 151–76.

Index

Entries in bold represent text in tables or figures.

LaVergne, TN USA
11 December 2009
166702LV00001B/2/P